ROUTLEDGE LIBRARY EDITIONS:
PRISON AND PRISONERS

Volume 11

# PRISONERS AND THEIR FAMILIES

# PRISONERS AND THEIR FAMILIES

## PAULINE MORRIS

Routledge
Taylor & Francis Group

LONDON AND NEW YORK

First published in 1965 by George Allen & Unwin Ltd

This edition first published in 2024
by Routledge
4 Park Square, Milton Park, Abingdon, Oxon OX14 4RN

and by Routledge
605 Third Avenue, New York, NY 10158

*Routledge is an imprint of the Taylor & Francis Group, an informa business*

*British Library Cataloguing in Publication Data*
A catalogue record for this book is available from the British Library

ISBN: 978-1-032-55549-2 (Set)
ISBN: 978-1-032-56270-4 (Volume 11) (hbk)
ISBN: 978-1-032-56275-9 (Volume 11) (pbk)
ISBN: 978-1-003-43476-4 (Volume 11) (ebk)

DOI: 10.4324/9781003434764

**Publisher's Note**
The publisher has gone to great lengths to ensure the quality of this reprint but points out that some imperfections in the original copies may be apparent.

**Disclaimer**
The publisher has made every effort to trace copyright holders and would welcome correspondence from those they have been unable to trace.

# PRISONERS
# AND THEIR FAMILIES

PAULINE MORRIS
*for*
P.E.P.

*London*

GEORGE ALLEN & UNWIN LTD
RUSKIN HOUSE   MUSEUM STREET

PRINTED IN GREAT BRITAIN
*in* 10-*point Times Roman type*
BY UNWIN BROTHERS LTD
WOKING AND LONDON

## ACKNOWLEDGEMENTS

This report is based on the results of an enquiry which was made possible by a grant from a Trust Fund the Directors of which prefer that it should remain anonymous.

The report was written by Mrs Pauline Morris. She joins PEP in thanking the members of the Steering Committee who gave valuable support and advice, as well as many colleagues working in related fields. Footnotes in the text indicate where individual contributions are used in this book, but particular thanks are due to the following people whose work made the project possible:

|  |  |
|---|---|
| Mrs Elizabeth Cooper | *Research Assistant* |
| Mrs Eileen Staples | *Secretary* |
| Mrs J. Bickerstaffe | *Clerical Assistant* |

|  |  |
|---|---|
| Miss Suzanne Davies | |
| Miss Ann Hurley | |
| Miss Diane Parker | *Interviewers* |
| Mrs Jeannine Sadler | |

|  |  |
|---|---|
| Miss Marilyn Bowman | |
| Mr Alistair Davie | |
| Miss Joyce Miles | *Coders* |
| Miss Mary Wilkie | |
| Mr Killian Zumpe | |

|  |  |
|---|---|
| Mr Z. Ali | |
| Mr A. John | *Statistical* |
| Mr M. Must | *Assistants* |
| Mr A. Treacher | |

Finally Mrs Morris wishes to express her especial gratitude to her husband whose active help, as well as constant support and advice, was of inestimable value.

# Foreword to 2023 Reissue
## *Prisoners and their Families*

It is almost 60 years since anthropologist and criminologist, Pauline Morris, first published her groundbreaking study exploring the complex interactions between men in prison and their wives and families in the community. Before this research little attention had been paid either to the families themselves or to the impact on prisoners of the strengths and weaknesses of relationships fractured by incarceration.

The study used a combination of a structured, quantitative, epidemiologically based, study of a nationally representative sample of almost 800 men in 17 custodial establishments, stratified by the class of prison, together with extensive interviews with their wives or common law girlfriends. These were used to explore the impact of social, psychological and economic factors affecting the families over time. A second part of the enquiry set out to identify 100 men and their families for intensive, longitudinal study to put flesh on the bones of the numbers.

The methodology deployed was both descriptive and analytic and sought to test a number of hypotheses, based on a set of typologies into which each family could be placed, as the basis for understanding the significance of the crisis represented by imprisonment. Five hypotheses were to be tested:

- Family relationships following upon conviction and imprisonment will follow a pattern set by family relationships which existed before imprisonment.
- Wives with kinship networks will seek additional support from them during the husband's imprisonment.

- Utilisation of the statutory and voluntary social services will be greater amongst the families of first offenders.
- The wives of prisoners with children of school age will seek employment; by contrast, those with children under school age will not be employed, nor will those where there are children in both groups.
- The adjustment of the family to imprisonment will vary with the type of offence, and with the extent of previous criminal experience.

Although I was only ten years old when my mother published Prisoners and their Families, I had already been exposed to the nature of the work that both she and my father, fellow criminologist Terence Morris, were so immersed in and it was not unusual for me to be involved in their prison visits at the weekend as an outing for me. Reading Prisoners today is to be immediately aware of the passion and humanity that was brought to bear on what was until then a much-neglected area of life and social policy. The desperate beat of poverty proclaims itself in the personal interviews along with the remarkable but objective empathy of a researcher whose own background was so very different from that of her subjects.

The findings of the studies give vivid insights into the experiences of a very specific subset of the population at a particular point in time. Although some of the language and cultural attitudes now seem dated, for example with regard to domestic violence where quite a few of the wives said they missed their husbands 'knocking them about', other aspects including the roles of alcohol, infidelity, perceived oppression by in-laws, and debts from gambling, hire purchase, and the sheer grind of the struggle to put food on the table, are as relevant today as they were in 1965. Mental health issues loomed large, then as now. At the time of the studies only a small proportion of the prisoner sample were of a minority ethnic background, and mainly Irish; it would be different today.

In drawing together her conclusions, Pauline Morris points to the decline of the family as a productive unit, the increasing individualisation of society and the increased emphasis on the balance of interpersonal relationships within the family in dealing with crises, not least the specific crisis of imprisonment.

She argues that whilst various welfare services, both statutory and voluntary, had become more important, at that time virtually nothing systematic was known about either the extent or the kind of help given to such families; in particular, she drew attention to the material, psychological, and social hardships endured by wives and the stresses created on relationships by incarceration far from home with frequent moves of prisoners between the prison estate.

One finding of particular poignancy, given the recent chaos in the Probation Service, was the important contribution made to families by probation officers reaching out to provide family support. These specific points are wrapped up in her main findings of the importance of financial provision for families to prevent their slide into extreme poverty and the need for improved social casework to provide support in family separation, together with improved facilities for ongoing contact between prisoners and their families, including home visits towards the end of sentences where this is prudent.

The re-publication of Prisoners and their Families is timely, given the continuing crisis in our penal system and the lack of consensus about the purpose of imprisonment. It is also an opportunity to remind students and academics of the heyday of research in this area in the 1960s and Pauline Morris's other contributions that include Put Away, which explored the scandal of the incarceration of patients with learning disabilities and was influential in bringing about the programme of de-institutionalisation begun by Richard Crossman in the Labour government, and Pentonville, which explored life inside Pentonville women's prison which was a joint work of Pauline and Terence Morris.

As a child of these two giants of criminology, it is only in retrospect that I can see how the childhood influences have impacted on my own career as a public health consultant and Director of Public Health. There is considerable overlap between the worlds of criminology and public health, both in the methods used to describe and understand the conditions and challenges of some of the most disadvantaged, and the policies and interventions needed to tackle entrenched social and medical inequalities.

Catherine B. Morris
(now Montague-Ashton)
April 2023

# FOREWORD AND
# RECOMMENDATIONS

This study, as far as is known, is the first attempt in this country to look at the problems of the families of prisoners on a national scale. It was spread over three years and based upon a representative sample of prisoners and their dependants. The experience of imprisonment does not occur in isolation for a man with a family, and the prison wall can never be a complete barrier to the emotional currents which flow between a man and his wife and children. Too often in prison work, the family is thought of as some external appendage, remote and irrelevant to the processes of treatment and training, rather than as a continuous influence upon the man in custody. For the family, the sense of isolation from the prison world is often greater than the isolation of the prisoner from the world outside. He has newspapers, radio and often television to keep him in touch; wives and children see little of the prison world save what is glimpsed during brief visits.

The importance of the family in pre-sentence investigations has already been recognized by the Streatfeild Committee: our survey reinforces these findings and illustrates the need to bear in mind the man's relationships with his wife and children throughout the sentence and after discharge.

The survey has been both descriptive and analytic. We have attempted to portray objectively the conditions of life for a wide range of families of men in prison, first offenders, recidivists, and civil prisoners. The catalogue of their problems is considerable, and not all can be directly attributed to imprisonment, but there seems little doubt that many are aggravated by it. Some are undoubtedly intractable, and of the sort that would resist the most competent social work; others are capable of solution by relatively straightforward administrative action.

The primary object of this research has been to elicit facts upon which penologists and administrators might base future policies, and the main findings of the survey are to be found in the summaries which form the substance of Chapter XIII. There are, however, three principal issues upon which we have specific recommendations to make: (1) the financial provisions for prisoners' families, (2) the improvement of social casework in prisons, and (3) the improvement of facilities for contact between the prisoner and his family.

(1) There is little doubt that the majority of prisoners' families, by being wholly dependent upon the National Assistance Board, are living in conditions of considerable poverty. The Board ensures that these families do not starve, and that they normally have a roof over

their heads, but beyond the bare necessities of life there is little provision. There is a great need for assistance in respect of clothing, which in the case of children is an acute problem, and the replacement of household goods. Too many families are advised to turn to the WVS for second-hand clothing, too many children have to endure the stigma of free school meals which stridently proclaim their poverty. In a society distinguished for its affluence and dramatically rising standards of living for manual workers, the poverty of the prisoner's family and similar under-privileged groups is starkly silhouetted, but for prisoners' families it is aggravated by a sense of shame (not always admitted), as well as of anxiety. We are not suggesting that the financial position of *prisoners'* families dependent on national assistance is worse than that of others wholly dependent on the State; furthermore many such families have acute social problems which money admittedly will not solve, but which the lack of money will nevertheless aggravate. The improvement of national assistance rates, and the rationalization of discretionary grants would do much to alleviate hardship and improve the conditions of family life. It may be argued that poverty is part of the punishment these families deserve; we take the view that there can be no justification for imposing poverty on the family simply because the husband is in prison.

(2) The prison welfare service, despite improvements on the provisions existing until recently, is still inadequate for the task. Apart from the overworking of welfare officers, we question the nature of the service. The separation of social work done with the prisoner from that carried out with his family is both unreal and likely to lead to difficulties. It ought to be possible for the prison welfare officer to maintain close contact with the prisoner's family— but he can do so only if the family and the prison are in the same area—and to assist in the treatment of family problems as a whole. It should be possible for wives to visit the prison and spend time together with their husband and the welfare officer, and for wives to participate in group discussions. At present we see the provisions of the welfare service as tending to reinforce the barriers separating the prisoner from his family. The families themselves for the most part feel isolated, and wives are consumed with anxiety born of ignorance of what is happening.

Criticisms of the prison welfare service may appear churlish in the light of the burdens of existing welfare officers, but without more adequate provision their work must often remain sterile and bureaucratic.

(3) Currently there is little, other than that which occurs fortuitously, to ensure that a prisoner serves his sentence in a place where he can be visited by his family without the necessity of a long

journey. Local prisons are only local in the sense that men sent there have committed their offence in that particular area. In order to relieve overcrowding, as well as in the interests of training, prisoners may be transferred to institutions miles from home, which are often at the same time located in inaccessible country places. Women on national assistance rarely have cars at their disposal to reach these isolated spots, and women with small children cannot reasonably be expected to wait hours for some country bus at the end of a complicated and expensive cross-country rail journey. If family contact is to be maintained the system of transfers must be radically modified, and prisons must be organized on a regional basis.

Prison visiting conditions themselves are in need of improvement to allow husbands and wives to maintain proper contact; such visits should, for the sake of the family, be an inalienable right. Their number should be increased and there should be an extension of home leave arrangements to a larger number of prisoners.

The families of prisoners, like those of mental patients, suffer disabilities which stem from situations which they themselves have not, for the most part, brought about. Their condition of less eligibility for social support ought to be a moral affront to an affluent civilized society. But more than that, every stress suffered by such families weakens the family and increases the likelihood of other family members, especially the children, becoming social casualties, thus adding not only to the charge upon the community but to the sum of human unhappiness.

# CONTENTS

*Chapter I*

# INTRODUCTION

THE ORIGINS OF THE ENQUIRY

In recent years a great deal of attention has been focused on the delinquent inside an institution: his background, his treatment and his rehabilitation; but so far as we know there has been no systematic attempt in this country to study the families of men experiencing separation as a result of imprisonment.

Earlier work carried out by the writer amongst the recidivist populations of two maximum security prisons indicated that a high proportion of men appeared to have severe family problems. Their relationship with their wives seemed frequently to be very unstable; often they were separated either permanently or intermittently, and cohabiting with another woman (or women) by whom they may have had a number of children. Sometimes it was the wives themselves that appeared to be unfaithful and producing illegitimate children. In his report for 1961 the General Secretary of the Central After-Care Association refers to the increasing demand for help with domestic problems during imprisonment.

Current thinking about the family[1] tends to polarize between those who feel that it is in the process of disintegration and decay, and those who consider that the demands placed upon it in contemporary society are so great that its ability to withstand these additional stresses is indicative of its very great durability. Both groups are agreed upon the importance of the basic family unit in a society as at present constituted, and that the function of the family in industrial society has changed greatly over the past hundred years.

Perhaps the most important change has been the decline in importance of the family as a productive unit and its metamorphosis into a consumption unit. This has produced an increasing degree of individualization, and placed additional emphasis on the balance of interpersonal relationships within the family. These have now become more delicately poised than at any other period, and not only are individual relationships within the family regarded as important, but

[1] For a discussion of attitudes to the contemporary family see Fletcher, R., *The Family and Marriage*, Penguin Special (1962).

equally important are the relationships between individual family members and outsiders. The net extends wider, since a third dimension includes the articulation of the family unit as a whole with the wider community of which it forms part.

Great stress has also been laid on the process of 'role stripping'— the removal from the family of what were previously family-centred roles, and which are now gradually being replaced by the formal institutions of the State: education, child welfare, social medicine and the welfare provisions 'from birth to the grave'. But at the same time the pressure towards material success is increasing, since this is the outward symbol of status, and failure to achieve success is looked down upon from quite early years. If a husband fails in his economic role as the chief family bread-winner, he is also likely to have problems in all his other social roles. If he is removed from home and placed in an institution,[1] the effect on the lives of all the other members of the nuclear family might be assumed to be quite severe. This is, however, purely speculative, and it would seem important to establish whether this *is* the case, and, if so, the degree and manner in which different types of family are affected.

Looking at the problem from the point of view of the wider community, it seems likely that various welfare services, both statutory and voluntary, will be called into operation if the bread-winner is removed from the family, yet virtually nothing systematic is known about either the extent or the kind of help at present given to such families. Over the past few years there has been a great deal of discussion regarding the after-care of men discharged from prison, but relatively little attention has been paid to their families. It seems likely, however, that in order successfully to plan for a man's training and rehabilitation it is important to consider him as a member of a family unit (assuming he has one in being) and to recognize that it is to this unit that he is likely to be returned on discharge. This being so, the relationships existing in the family, and the effect of the man's imprisonment on them, are likely to be important factors in the success or otherwise of his prison training[2] and his rehabilita-

[1] Morris, P., 'Some disturbances of family functioning associated with psychiatric illness', *British Journal of Medical Psychology*, 1958. It was noticeable that in the case of a small sample of mental hospital patients, the family was prepared to tolerate a great deal of deviant behaviour, but it was not until the husband or son failed in his economic role that he could be defined as 'ill', or that abnormality was really recognized.

[2] See Fenton, N., *Treatment in Prison: How the family can help*. Printed by Vocational Training Offset Printing Class, California State Prison—Soledad, California. Also *Report of H.O. Advisory Council on Preventive Detention*. HMSO, February 1963. This report refers to the loss of contact with families experienced by preventive detainees, and the need to maintain such relationships whilst in prison. The Report comments on the failure of after-care for long-term prisoners who lose contact with their families.

tion on discharge.[1] Selsky[2] points out that Probation Officers often play an important part in pre-sentence investigation (a situation which will undoubtedly increase in this country now that this recommendation of the Streatfeild Committee[3] has been accepted) and that much weight is given to family relationships and cultural factors. Yet, Selsky continues, the family is almost forgotten whilst the man is in prison. If treatment following commitment is to be viewed in a total sense, it must be concerned with important factors in his life, most significantly his family.

### OBJECTIVES OF THE STUDY

With these issues in mind, this study aimed to do five things:—

1. To discover the extent of social deviance[4] amongst a sample of married men in the prison population of England and Wales.
2. To study the economic, social and psychological problems and needs of the families of a sample of men currently serving a sentence of imprisonment.
3. To evaluate the social service arrangements currently available for dealing with such problems, and to review the policy towards prisoners and their families, both inside and outside prison.
4. To assess the families in terms of their adjustment to separation, and to see to what extent such adjustment is related to a number of factors in the environment. Such information might then prove useful in predicting how different types of family will adjust to the enforced separation associated with imprisonment.
5. To set up a typology of family situations into which each family could be placed.

### THEORETICAL FRAMEWORK OF THE RESEARCH

Most major studies of families under various kinds of stress and crisis have been carried out in the United States, but it is felt that they have considerable relevance for this country and in particular the

---

[1] Zemans, E., and Cavan, R., 'Marital Relationships of Prisoners'. *Journal of Criminal Law, Criminology and Police Science.* Vol. 49, 1 May/June, 1958. The authors refer to the need for rehabilitating the family prior to the release of the prisoner.

[2] Selsky, C., 'Post-Commitment Family Counselling'. *Federal Probation,* September 1962.

[3] Report of the Inter-Departmental Committee on the Business of the Criminal Courts. December 1960. HM'SO., Cmd. 1289.

[4] For a discussion and definition of this term see p. 21.

work of Hill[1] and Koos[2] has provided a very useful theoretical background against which this study could be carried out. So far as is known only one study exists[3] which is specifically concerned with the effect of enforced separation due to *imprisonment*. This work aims 'to discover factors which would be fruitful in predicting how families adjust to involuntary separation resulting in imprisonment, and to determine the significance of a family's perception of involuntary separation as a crisis and as a factor relating to adjustment to separation'. The author worked alone, and the number of families involved was necessarily limited; nevertheless he made full use of scales of adjustment and participation which had been well tested for reliability, and the leads provided by his research have made a very valuable contribution to the present study.

Hill[4] defines family crises as 'situations which create a sense of sharpened activity, or which block the usual patterns of action and call for new ones'. He goes on to suggest that there are three variables at work: (*a*) the situation or event itself, (*b*) the resources of the family, its role structure, flexibility and previous history of crises, and (*c*) the definition the family makes of the event, whether or not they use it as a threat to their status and objectives.

This crisis situation and the adjustment to it can be observed (1) as affecting the individual, (2) as affecting the pair (in our case the husband/wife), and (3) as affecting the whole family and its relationship with its neighbours.

The process of family adjustment is discussed by Hill in terms of 'role conception', the socially prescribed parts (roles) each member plays in a family's life. 'Good adjustment to separation involves closing of ranks, shifting of responsibilities and activities of the husband to other members, continuing the necessary family routines, maintaining husband/wife and father/child relationships by correspondence and visits, utilizing the resources of friends, relatives and neighbours and carrying on plans for reunion.'

Rapoport[5] used this concept of role performance as a framework for studying the families of mental patients in treatment and rehabilitation. He and his collaborators found that role performance could not be satisfactorily explained in terms of the individual's norms, and they developed the theory that an understanding of role performance

[1] Hill, Reuben, *Families Under Stress*, New York, Harper Bros., 1949.

[2] Koos, Earl L., *Families in Trouble*, Morningside Heights: New York, Kings Crown Press, 1950.

[3] Blackwell, James E., 'The effects of involuntary separation on selected families of men committed to prison from Spokane County, Washington'. Ph.D. thesis presented 1959 State College of Washington (unpublished).

[4] Hill, *op. cit.*

[5] Rapoport, R. N., with Rapoport, R. and Rosow, I., *Community as Doctor*, London, Tavistock Publications, 1960.

could only be arrived at if one looked at the 'fit' between the patients' own needs and those of others with whom they had relationships.[1] Role performance of the individual, they suggested, was determined hypothetically by three factors:

(i) The 'fit' between the individual's personality and the personality of the other person in the role relationship.
(ii) The 'fit' between the norms of the two individuals.
(iii) The 'emotional toning' of the relationship.

In the context of the present study it would seem reasonable to accept that imprisonment *is* a crisis as defined by Hill, but we would suggest that the impact on a particular family will vary greatly both according to whether the crisis is recurrent or unique, and according to the quality of family adjustment existing before imprisonment; satisfactory marital adjustment prior to imprisonment may not necesssarily result in good adjustment to separation. It is necessary to point out here that, when considering whether the crisis situation is recurrent or unique, crisis is taken to include all eventualities which would bring them within Hill's definition, and does not relate specifically to imprisonment. Thus all forms of traumatic separation, the addition of new family members, severe improvidence, infidelity, etc. *may* result in a crisis situation, and it seems likely that families who have had experiences of this kind before will respond differently to the separation caused by imprisonment from those for whom this is a unique crisis.

It might also be worth while at this stage to distinguish between family disorganization and social deviance. Many writers use the term 'family disorganization' to cover almost any form of unsatisfactory marital or home situation, but this seems as imprecise as the label 'psychopath' when applied to an individual whose disturbed behaviour does not fit any other more precise diagnostic label. Elliott and Merril[2] define family disorganization as including 'any weakness, maladjustment or dissolution of the ties binding members of this group together . . . not only the tensions between husband and wife, but those arising between parents and children and those between siblings . . .'. Other writers include as suffering from disorganization those families who neglect their children, contain a criminal or alcoholic member, are improvident, etc. We would suggest that these families are not *necessarily* disorganized, since this term implies a complete breakdown in family functioning, a failure in problem solving or in communication. This is very rare. It is much more

[1] Rapoport, R., and Rosow, I., 'An Approach to Family Relations and Role Performance'. *Human Relations*. 10. 209, 1957.
[2] Elliott and Merril, *Social Disorganization*, New York, Harper Bros., 1961, (4th edition).

common to find families functioning at a pathological level. They are social deviants in so far as they do not conform to the norms of their own group, but their deviant behaviour may in fact represent their way of solving problems. When tensions within the family become intolerable, for example, they may act out in such a way as to involve the community in social action which relieves the pressures. Our definition of social deviance is closely related to Jaffe's definition of family anomie,[1] which he distinguishes clearly from family disorganization.

Admittedly there remains some doubt about automatically accepting the view that imprisonment itself produces a crisis, since it is of course possible that it is failure to adjust to the imprisonment (or to the separation) which creates the situation of crisis. Those who accept that situations such as imprisonment constitute a crisis have, after further investigation, classified crises into three groups:[2]

(*a*)  those where dismemberment only occurs
(*b*)  those where demoralization only occurs
(*c*)  those where both dismemberment *and* demoralization occur.

They have usually placed imprisonment in the last category, but if an essential component of a crisis situation is the family's *perception* of the situation as one of crisis, it is conceivable that the crisis for them may relate only to one or other, i.e. dismemberment *or* demoralization. As an example of what is meant, it is possible that a family might actively, or even passively, support the husband's criminality, but suffer directly as a result of his physical absence. If they lived in an area in which anti-social behaviour was also tolerated, there might well be no crisis of demoralization. Conversely, a family which is used to the physical absence of the husband might accept the separation with no difficulty, but might find itself very demoralized by the stigma attached either to the offence or to the fact of imprisonment.

One of the major difficulties is to distinguish in what ways, if at all, the social implications of imprisonment affect the family situation. Even evidence of shame and guilt cannot definitely be said to relate only to criminality, since similar feelings may well surround separation due to mental hospital treatment. It is doubtful whether the present study can throw much light on this point, though it is

---

[1] Jaffe, L., 'Delinquency proneness and Family Anomie', *Journal of Criminal Law, Criminology and Police Science*, Vol. 54, June 2, 1963.

[2] See Koos, Hill, *op. cit.*

Ed. Becker and Hill, *Handling Family Strains and Shocks*, Boston, D. C. Heath & Co., 1943.

Waller, *The Family: A Dynamic Interpretation*, University of N. Carolina Press, 1951.

Cavan and Rank, *The Family and the Depression*, Chicago, 1938.

hoped that, in the discussion of the data, some indications will be given which would enable further research to be carried out on this aspect of the separation.

Again, even if one distinguishes between the effects of separation generally, and those resulting directly from the imprisonment, it seems desirable to make a further distinction between the effect of *imprisonment* and the effect of *criminality*. It is perhaps amongst the children, rather than the wives of offenders that one might expect to find the impact of the father's imprisonment and/or criminality to be the greatest, as distinct from the impact of separation. For example, it seems possible that children will be less directly affected by changes in material conditions—housing, finance, welfare facilities, etc.— which in fact may be of over-riding importance to the wife, whereas they may be more affected by the attitudes of other children or even school-teachers. One might also find more of the attitude 'if my father does it, it's O.K. for me', which is not likely to be paralleled by the wife. Unfortunately a study of this kind does not lend itself to a proper investigation of the children. Work carried out by other researchers to establish the proportion of delinquents coming from homes with parents who themselves have delinquent records seems to produce wide differences in their findings.[1]

HYPOTHESES

It is proposed to explore a number of hypotheses in this study; they resemble in many respects those tested by Hill[2] and Blackwell,[3] but are not directly comparable:

1. Family relationships following upon conviction and imprisonment will follow a pattern set by family relationships which existed before imprisonment.
2. Wives with wide kinship networks will seek additional support from them during the husband's imprisonment.
3. Utilization of the statutory and voluntary social services will be

[1] See: Reckless, W., *The Crime Problem*, New York, 1950. Glueck, S. and E., *Criminal Careers in Retrospect*, New York, 1943. *Unravelling Juvenile Delinquency*, New York, 1950. These authors report a very high correlation between juvenile delinquency and paternal criminality, but McCord and others (*Journal of Abnormal Psychology*, May 1962) are of the opinion that it is the absence of a generally stable home environment rather than specific absence of the father which is related to childhood delinquency. Gibbens, T. C., *Psychiatric Studies of Borstal Lads*, Oxford University Press, 1963, reports 17·4 per cent of his boys as having a criminal parent. West, D. J., *The Habitual Prisoner*, Institute of Criminology, Cambridge, 1963, reports a figure of 4 per cent.
[2] *Op. cit.*  [3] *Op. cit.*

greater and more systematic amongst the families of habitual offenders than amongst those of first offenders.

4. The wives of prisoners with children of school age will seek employment; by contrast those with children under school age will not be employed, nor will those where there are children in both groups.

5. The adjustment of the family to imprisonment will vary with the type of offence, and with the extent of previous criminal experience.

One of the objectives of the research[1] was to set up a typology of family situations into which each family could be placed, and it is suggested that the distribution of recurrent/unique crises will vary according to these types:

(a) Families already separated before imprisonment.

(b) Families where good relationships existed before imprisonment, but where the present crisis resulted in there being little or no likelihood of the marriage being resumed on discharge.

(c) Families where relationships were severely strained before imprisonment. Prison brings further material or psychological strain and the marriage breaks up during the sentence with little likelihood of resuming on discharge. Alternatively if relationships were severely strained before imprisonment the latter may bring psychological relief and create the 'opportunity' to break up.

(d) Families where relationships were strained before imprisonment and the separation is a severe crisis, but the family are likely to remain together because there seems no alternative (such families may be tied by either financial or emotional dependency[2]).

(e) Families where relationships were strained before imprisonment, and prison brings additional material difficulties, but psychological relief. Contact between the parties is maintained during the separation and the marriage is likely to be resumed as before. Alternatively there is little change in the strained relationships that existed before imprisonment, contact is maintained, and the marriage is likely to be resumed as before.

(f) Families where relationships were strained before imprisonment, and the experience, or the fact that the offence is now an acknowledged fact, brings the partners together and the marriage is strengthened.

(g) Families where relationships were good before imprisonment,

[1] See p. 19 *supra*.
[2] See Eisenstein, V. (Ed.), *Neurotic Interaction in Marriage*, London, Tavistock, 1957.

but deteriorate as problems become intensified during the separation; nevertheless the marriage will be resumed.

(*h*) Families where good relationships before imprisonment remain unimpaired, or where the relationship contains a certain amount of conflict which is tolerated before and during imprisonment, and where the marriage will be resumed with a similar degree of toleration.

## Chapter II

# THE DESIGN OF THE ENQUIRY

OTHER INTERESTED ORGANIZATIONS

In the initial stages of the research, we endeavoured to make contact with as many individuals and organizations as possible who, it was thought, would be in a position to contribute useful information regarding prisoners' families. We are grateful to all these organizations for their help and advice.[1] In some cases discussions were held with the research staff; in others reports were submitted, including many from organizations not listed in the footnote below but whose evidence to the Advisory Council on the Treatment of Offenders then undertaking a study of Prison After-Care was found to contain useful comments.

Where possible we sought to know how families were referred to agencies and what were the presenting problems. In particular we were anxious to single out factors which distinguished the families of prisoners from other families with whom the organizations had contact. Reference to the report of the Advisory Council and the comments of these organizations will appear later in the text, when the subject of social welfare is discussed. Unfortunately we found that most organizations had only very limited experience of prisoners' families, but the National Council of Social Service were sufficiently interested in our project to undertake a special enquiry amongst the secretaries of their Citizens' Advice Bureaux.[2]

Discussions also took place with research workers carrying out work in related fields, in particular Dr John Martin of the Cambridge Institute of Criminology,[3] and Dr Charlotte Banks[4] of the Department of Child Psychology at University College, London. Although their work proved to be somewhat different in orientation from ours, we found it useful to continue the discussions at various stages of the research, and we are grateful for their comments and advice.

[1] National Council of Social Service, Family Welfare Association, Family Service Units, National Society for the Prevention of Cruelty to Children, Church Army, Soldiers, Sailors and Airmen's Family Association, Church of England Temperance Society, Council for Child Welfare, Guinness Housing Trust, Peabody Donation Fund, Sheriffs' Fund, Consumers' Advisory Council.

[2] See Appendix E.

[3] Carrying out an enquiry into the Social Consequences of Conviction.

[4] Carrying out an enquiry into recidivism amongst young offenders.

Before the setting up of this research project, the Home Office Research Unit had requested that a small-scale study of civil debtors be carried out in Brixton Prison. This report, made by the principal psychologist Mr de Berker, assisted by Miss Raeburn, was made available to us in the initial stages of the research, and will be referred to later in the text when discussing civil prisoners.[1]

Visits were paid to three county courts in different parts of the country and the problems of civil debtors were discussed with county court judges and members of their staff.

### THE POPULATION TO BE STUDIED

In considering the problems involved in separation and how they were dealt with by families, it seemed likely that there might be considerable differences between those in prison for the first time and those who had served one or more sentences in an adult penal institution.

The penal system classifies men into a number of classes: 'stars' (who are normally serving their first term of imprisonment), 'ordinaries' (who have been to prison at least once), corrective trainees (men with previous convictions whom the courts consider will respond to special training), and preventive detainees (usually men having served many terms of imprisonment whom the courts consider should be deprived of their liberty for a long period). For purposes of this research, 'ordinaries', corrective trainees and preventive detainees were all included as one category under the label 'recidivists'. Civil prisoners constitute a further class of prisoner, but it should be noted that in this research we were concerned exclusively with those civils serving a sentence for non-payment of debt, or for arrears of maintenance.

In order to keep within the limits of the resources available to the research it was thought that approximately 800 prisoners and their families would constitute the maximum number which could be interviewed.

Members of the Trust Fund sponsoring the research had expressed a particular interest in the problems of hire purchase, and it was decided therefore to include in the sample a high proportion of civil prisoners on the assumption (erroneous as it turned out) that it would be amongst this group that the problems of hire purchase would predominate. Thus it was decided to select a sample of the married male prison population, to include 200 civil prisoners, 300 stars, and 300 recidivists. In the case of stars, as suggested above, the group was intended to include primarily first offenders, but as will be apparent from subsequent discussion of the data, many stars are by

[1] See Chapter IX, pp. 244 ff.

no means first offenders, nor necessarily serving their first term of imprisonment. Prison Governors are in some circumstances empowered to regrade suitable 'ordinaries', who then become known as 'Governor's Stars', though the use of this regulation varies widely from one establishment to another.

Although the population to be studied comprised both prisoners *and* their families, it was decided that selection should be based on the prisoners in institutions, since this provided the most convenient means of obtaining a sample of wives. Furthermore it was considered essential to obtain permission from the husband before visiting his family. The population studied was limited in the following ways: we were concerned only with married men over the age of twenty-one, with at least three months of their sentence still to serve at the date of the interview and who had been both convicted and sentenced.

A small pilot study was undertaken which resulted in further refinements: although only married men were to be included (whether separated from their wives or not), since a number of men appeared to be cohabiting with women to whom they were not legally married, the definition of 'marriage' was extended to include any man who admitted to living with a woman for three months or longer before his arrest. Thus a man might be separated from his legal wife, but living with another woman, in which case the present 'wife' was the person normally interviewed. In some cases, however, a man would refuse to allow us to see his common-law wife, but would give permission for us to make contact with his separated wife.

The decision to include only men with at least three months of their sentence still to serve was made in order to ensure that enough time would be available for interviewers to visit their families before the men themselves were discharged. This arrangement was not possible in the case of civil prisoners, since the maximum sentence for such prisoners is six weeks.

Details of the sampling and scaling techniques are set out in Appendix A of this report, and for simplification we record here only the fact that men were selected from seventeen prisons, stratified by class of prison (central, regional, or local), by type (open or closed), and by geographical region.

At the actual time of selecting the men it was found that in almost all cases the number of civil prisoners was insufficient to meet the requirements of the original sample design, since it was considered essential that they had a minimum of seven days to serve in order to allow time to visit their families before discharge. Many civils were in fact given sentences of less than seven days, and others 'paid out'[1]

---

[1] Men in prison for non-payment of debt may be released as soon as the money owing is paid. The amount due is reduced *pro-rata* according to the length of sentence already served.

a few days after reception; the total thus seen amounted to 177 instead of the 200 originally hoped for. A figure of 10 per cent was added to the number of stars and recidivists in the sample in order to allow for wastage, making a total of 330 men in each of these two categories. This number when combined with the 177 civils makes a total of 837 men selected for interview.

INTENSIVE STUDY

In addition to the extensive survey we have been discussing, it was decided to make a detailed study of the families of 100 prisoners living in the London area. The objects of this part of the enquiry were twofold:

(a) to trace the impact of social, psychological and economic factors affecting the family *over time*, since we did not expect the various patterns of family adjustment to remain stationary over the months. It was also hoped that some more detailed knowledge of the conditions prevailing in particular families before the husband's imprisonment would enable us to assess the extent and relevance of any subsequent changes.

(b) to illustrate, by the presentation of case material, the statistical data obtained from the extensive study.

In order to meet the requirements of (a) above, it was necessary to interview both the prisoners and their families within as short a time as possible after conviction. It was thought that ideally five or six visits at three-monthly intervals[1] would provide adequate information and would at the same time be both acceptable to the families and within the resources of the research. Since it was hoped that the last interview would be with both spouses, soon after the husband's discharge, it was decided that only men serving sentences of between fifteen and eighteen months should be included in this sample. Assuming that they gained full remission, such men would normally be released after serving approximately one year. After two months it became apparent that it would take a very long time to obtain enough men serving the specified length of sentence, so that it was decided to widen the terms of selection to include men serving sentences of between fifteen months and two years. Since the maximum sentence for civil prisoners of the type in which we were interested is six weeks, such offenders were automatically excluded from this sample, and the hundred men were divided equally between stars and recidivists.

[1] This was a purely subjective view held by the writer on the basis of research interviewing among the families of mental patients.

CONTROL GROUP

In the initial stages of planning the research a considerable amount of discussion centred round the desirability and practicability of using a control group for comparative purposes. It was finally decided to select a group of families in which the husband was under social stigma as a result of conflict with the law, but had been placed on probation and where there was no question of separation. It was intended that the nature of the offence be such that it seemed likely that, had he received a sentence of imprisonment, it would have been for approximately eighteen months to two years.

The necessary arrangements were made with the Home Office and contact was made with the probation officers at County of London Sessions and the Central Criminal Court through whom it was intended to work. Unfortunately, despite the willingness of the Probation Service to co-operate, these plans had to be abandoned. The main reasons for this decision were as follows:

(a) Probation records varied very considerably, and it would have been essential for us to interview many of the families ourselves, additional work for which we had no time.

(b) Attendance in court[1] by one of the research workers during the hearing of twenty-seven cases, where probation reports were asked for and orders made, suggested that it would be quite unrealistic to predict whether a man might, judging by the nature of the offence, have got a sentence of between eighteen months and two years had he not been placed on probation. Probation officers were therefore obliged to select cases for us merely on the basis of a man's marital status, and this was a severe limitation since it seemed that the majority of those placed on probation at that court and at that particular time were unmarried.

(c) Probation officers carry a very heavy case-load, and it seemed unfair to increase the burden of their work by asking them to obtain additional information for our research purposes *and* to spend a considerable amount of time discussing cases with us. It had been hoped that the information we required would be automatically covered in the course of their normal work, but this was not necessarily the case, and varied considerably from one officer to another.

In view of these facts, and since it was a comparative group of doubtful validity in the first place, this part of the research was abandoned.

[1] County of London Sessions.

## SELECTING THE PRISONERS[1]

*Extensive sample*

Each prison was visited in turn, and according to the number of men to be interviewed in any one category, names were selected from the nominal register, starting with the man who had been longest in the prison. As names appear strictly in order of entry into the prison, it was hoped that the distribution according to length of sentence would be representative of the prison population as a whole. This object was not in fact achieved in view of the decision to exclude men serving sentences of under three months: this matter will be discussed more fully in Chapter III (pp. 55 ff).

Since no information was available on the nominal register regarding the marital status of the men, it was then necessary to consult their individual records. If the man selected was found to be unmarried, the next name on the register was substituted and so on, until the required number had been obtained.

We found that 42·9 per cent of all recidivists were married, and either living with, or separated from, their wives (including those who admitted to cohabiting for a period of three months or more).[2] In the case of stars the figure was 57 per cent. Table I (see p. 32) shows how many records it was necessary to examine at individual prisons in order to obtain the required sample. It should be clearly understood that we have no way of knowing whether these figures are representative of the marital status of the prison population as a whole, since no official statistics are available.

Apart from being extremely time-consuming, this method of selection had certain other disadvantages. Prison records are not always accurate, and any changes in the marital situation occurring during the course of imprisonment are unlikely to be recorded. Thus we subsequently found men who were entered as 'married', who had in fact been divorced on this or even a previous sentence, and so did not fall within our terms of reference. One macabre story concerns the selection of a man recorded as 'married' who, when asked at the beginning of the interview whether we could contact his wife replied politely: 'I'm afraid you can't Ma'am, she was murdered when I was doing my last sentence'. On two subsequent occasions we found ourselves interviewing men who were in prison for themselves murdering their own wives.

It is also extremely likely that a number of men described as

---

[1] We are grateful to the Governors and staffs of all the establishments concerned. The facilities which they made available, and their kindness generally, were of the greatest possible help to us.

[2] It must be remembered that these figures do not include men with less than three months of their sentence still to run.

*Prisoners and Their Families*

'single' were, in fact, cohabiting and would have come within our terms of reference. Only where a single man admitted on entering prison that he had a common-law wife could he be included in the sample.

TABLE I

| Establishment | Number of married men required for interview | | Number of records checked to achieve this goal | |
|---|---|---|---|---|
| | Stars | Recidivists | - Stars | Recidivists |
| Parkhurst | — | 32 | — | 136 |
| Strangeways | 6 | 24 | 11 | 48 |
| Armley | 5 | 27 | 7 | 56 |
| The Verne | 33 | 15 | 56 | 35 |
| Cardiff | 3 | 18 | 5 | 36 |
| Thorp Arch | 43 | 8 | 54 | 18 |
| Winchester | 8 | 26 | 19 | 53 |
| Sudbury | 49 | 4 | 64 | 8 |
| Preston | 42 | 17 | 79 | 37 |
| Brixton/Wandsworth | 13 | 8 | 28 | 14 |
| Wakefield | 33 | 4 | 85 | 12 |
| Pentonville | — | 60 | — | 126 |
| Walton | 11 | 39 | 27 | 92 |
| Leyhill | 51 | 1 | 90 | 1 |
| Durham | 8 | 26 | 18 | 49 |
| Lincoln | 14 | 21 | 20 | 47 |
| Drake Hall | 11 | — | 15 | — |
| Total: | 330 | 330 | 578 | 768 |

*Note:* Information regarding the marital status of civil prisoners is not included in this table as it was necessary to check the records of *all* such men coming into the prison during the time we were there in order to get a sufficient number. Most of those coming in were sent to prison for non-payment of maintenance and so by definition had a 'wife'. Most of the debtors were also married, but no exact check was kept of the number of files consulted.

It had been thought initially that it might be easiest to obtain information regarding the marital status of prisoners from the prison welfare officers' records. Accordingly the General Secretary of the National Association of Discharged Prisoners' Aid Societies wrote to all the welfare officers concerned, asking them to co-operate with the research, and we are most grateful for all the help they afforded us. In a few instances it was in fact possible to obtain the information in this way, but unfortunately, because of the particular way the welfare records were kept, it was necessary for us to supply the man's discharge date. To do this proved as lengthy a procedure as checking his marital status, and whereas the latter only increased our own work, giving the welfare officers the earliest date of release also gave them additional work.

A list was then compiled of those men whom we wished to interview, and this was given to a member of the prison staff who subsequently arranged for them to be seen. For reasons which have been indicated earlier it was not possible to include enough civil prisoners at the time of our arrival, and for this category it was usually necessary to include all receptions of civil prisoners during the week spent at each prison.

## Intensive Sample

The procedure described above was somewhat modified in the selection of men for the intensive sample. We requested that an assistant governor at each of the three London prisons should advise us each time a married man living in the London area came into the prison with a sentence of between fifteen months and two years, and we then interviewed him as soon as possible after conviction. This arrangement had one disadvantage in so far as it put the onus of supplying us with names on to the prison authorities instead of selecting them ourselves. We believe that in this way one or two suitable people were missed, but we think we achieved as nearly as possible a sample of consecutive receptions into these three prisons comprising fifty stars and fifty recidivists meeting our particular requirements. To do so, however, took much longer than we had anticipated, and our original intention of taking receptions at only two prisons had to be modified in order to complete our sample selection within a reasonable time.

### INTERVIEWING THE PRISONERS

Senior officials at the prison were fully informed about the nature of the research. Some members of the discipline staff concerned with collecting prisoners for interview, or helping to find records, were interested in the project and provided helpful information about inmates well known to them. It was found advisable for officers *not* to tell prisoners the purpose for which they were being interviewed, since this eliminated any chance of distortion before we saw them. Naturally after the first morning the news spread round the prison like wild-fire, but there was very little mis-representation and any that existed was outweighed by the fact that women are rarely seen in men's prisons, and an interview with one tends to relieve the monotony of the daily routine. Prisoners are quite used to being 'called-up' to see a variety of people during the day, and are rarely told why they are wanted, so that this did not strike them as unusual. Furthermore the presence of a woman in a men's prison tends always to be associated with 'welfare', so that it was assumed that we represented some kind of welfare organization.

B

Our original intention in interviewing the men in prison was to obtain their permission to contact their wives. This remained the primary object of the interview, but in addition we attempted to obtain information regarding the man's family background, his offence and sentence and to learn something of what he thought was happening at home during his absence.

Of the 837 prisoners called for interview, twelve declined to be seen, saying that they preferred not to discuss their personal and domestic

TABLE II. *Reasons for refusing permission to contact wife*

| Reason for refusing | Stars | Recidivists | Civils | Total |
|---|---|---|---|---|
| Divorced or Divorce pending | 1 | 5 | 7 | 13 |
| Separated and husband feared visit would be interpreted as attempt at reconciliation | 2 | 4 | 1 | 7 |
| Too upsetting for wife, including because a common-law wife | 3 | 7 | 6 | 16 |
| Prefer not to discuss personal affairs (husband interviewed nevertheless) | 1 | 4 | 2 | 7 |
| Wife gone off during imprisonment | – | 5 | – | 5 |
| Simple refusals | 4 | 5 | 3 | 12 |
| Refusal unless wife contacts research | 1 | 3 | – | 4 |
| Other | 1 | – | 1 | 2 |
| Total refusing: | 13 | 33 | 20 | 66 |
| Percentage refusing of total selected: | 3·9 | 10·0 | 11·3 | 7·9 |

affairs. In three further instances the interviews were incomplete, since the men concerned seemed too emotionally disturbed to continue. Nevertheless sufficient information was obtained from two such cases to include them in the total which therefore stands at 824.

All interviews were in private, no member of the prison staff being present. Conditions for interviewing and for getting men to the interviews varied widely in different establishments, particularly as between open and closed prisons.

In the intensive sample interviews were carried out under similar conditions; no men in this sample refused to be interviewed.

Interviews were carried out on a structured questionnaire and took on an average twenty minutes each. Prison is, in more than one way, a closed community, and it proved helpful that, as a result of previous research work in prisons,[1] the interviewer was nearly always known to one or more of the inmates in each establishment as well as to some of the staff. Interviewing in prison creates rather special problems, in particular for the staff, and it is essential to fit in with the requirements of the prison routine, however inconvenient to oneself.

As mentioned above, twelve men declined to be interviewed: in the case of a further fifty-four we were not able to write to their wives, either because their whereabouts were unknown, or because the wife was living outside the confines of the research (i.e. outside England and Wales). There remained a further sixty-six who preferred us not to contact their wives for the reasons set out in Table II on page 34.

MAKING CONTACT WITH THE WIVES

Immediately after permission had been given by the prisoner to write to his wife, a letter was sent,[2] explaining the purpose of the research, and asking for permission to visit her. A post-card and a stamped addressed envelope (to preserve confidentiality through the post) were also included, and the wife was asked to indicate the most convenient time to call. Letters were actually sent to 672 wives; in thirty-three cases the men were serving such short sentences that we called without sending a letter.

The following table shows the response to these letters:

TABLE III

|  |  | % |
|---|---|---|
| Wives accepting by card | 374 | 55·7 |
| Wives refusing by card | 31 | 4·6 |
| No reply | 267 | 39·8 |
| Total | 672 | 100·0 |

Where the wife did not reply at all (267 cases) the interviewer called at the house at least twice; in thirteen instances an interview was refused and in seventy-three instances we were unable to trace the wife. Where no card was sent (thirty-three cases) interviews were obtained in each instance. Table IV (page 36) shows the numbers of interviews and non-contacts broken down by class of offender.

Thus the final number of interviews obtained with wives was 588, of which twelve were incomplete, an overall 'success' rate of 70 per cent (including the men who declined interview and the incomplete

[1] Morris, T. and P., *Pentonville: A sociological study of a maximum security prison*, Routledge & Kegan Paul, 1963.
[2] A copy of these letters appears in the Appendix C.

interviews with wives); 7·9 per cent of the non-contacts were caused
by refusal of the prisoner to permit an interview with his wife; the
remaining 21·9 per cent of non-contacts were the result either of
failure to contact the wife, or her refusal.

TABLE IV

| Type of Prisoner | Wives interviewed | Non-contacts* | Total | Wives interviewed % of total |
|---|---|---|---|---|
| Stars | 260 | 70 (22) | 330 | 78·7 |
| Recidivists | 217 | 113 (54) | 330 | 65·7 |
| Civils | 111 | 66 (46) | 177 | 62·7 |
| Total | 588 | 249 | 837 | 70·3 |

* The figure in brackets shows the number of non-contacts who were separated
from their husbands before imprisonment.

When cards were received from the wives, interviewers were supplied with a list of names and addresses, and instructed to call as
soon as possible, bearing in mind any special requests expressed by
the wives regarding appointments. They were also given the names
and addresses of wives who had not replied at all, and asked to make
at least two calls before considering the family a non-contact. It was
interesting to find that many wives said they had not bothered to
return the card, assuming it would be some elderly busybody who
wanted to call, but on seeing a young, attractive girl on the doorstep,
they felt relieved and so were prepared to be interviewed. On one
occasion, the interviewer called co-incidentally a few minutes after
the wife had seen the present writer on television. She explained that
she had not intended to be interviewed but felt that this was a sign
that she should see us, and so she agreed to the interview!

It was often extremely difficult to trace these wives; many of them
moved home frequently and left no forwarding address. Others were
stated to be unknown at the address when the interviewer called.
This part of the work proved extremely laborious and required
exceptional tenacity on the part of the interviewers. The work extended over a period of approximately six months; the interviewers
were based on London and covered the entire country from Cumber-
land to Lands End. They returned home at weekends and were given
an itinerary for the following week by a clerical assistant who was
responsible for allocating work according to the cards returned
from wives. Detailed planning was, however, impossible, since it was
uncertain whether or not a wife would be available when the interviewer called. Interviewers were, therefore, faced with considerable
problems of an organizational kind, planning their own itinerary

within a given area, finding hotels, arranging to call back where necessary, as well as carrying out interviews which were frequently long and exhausting.

### THE QUESTIONNAIRE[1]

This was a closely structured and mainly pre-coded questionnaire based upon the results of the pilot study which had been carried out by means of completely unstructured, free-ranging interviews. Since many of the questions were not relevant to wives who were already separated from their husbands prior to imprisonment, two separate schedules were used according to the marital situation at the time of arrest. The schedule for families living together, which comprised the bulk of our interviewees, contained 120 questions, of which eleven were open-ended. In addition to ringing the appropriate code, wherever possible interviewers also recorded verbatim the remarks made by the wives.

The questionnaire was designed to cover a number of general areas: family composition, finance, welfare, marital history, criminality, social contacts, and future plans. In addition interviewers were asked to report on home conditions and to give an assessment of family functioning and relationships.

### THE INTERVIEWS[2]

The interviewers were given very precise written instructions about the way the interviews should be conducted,[3] in order to achieve as great a degree of uniformity as possible. In addition, two days were spent discussing the work, and each interviewer was accompanied by a supervisor on her first two visits. Although it was intended that interviews should last about one-and-a-half hours, in very many cases this period was greatly exceeded, the wives often expressing a great need to 'talk to someone', particularly someone outside the family, who they felt would listen without making moral judgements. In almost all instances interviewers were very warmly welcomed, and where there was any initial suspicion or hostility, this was soon overcome. The relative youth of the interviewers (they ranged from twenty-one to thirty-five years of age) was felt to be a great advantage, since in most cases the wives were themselves very young and they expressed the feeling that a certain understanding existed between them. Despite frequent reminders that we were not a welfare organization, there is no doubt that the word 'research' was, in the majority of cases, meaningless, and interviewers were seen to represent

[1] Copies of this are available on request.
[2] For a discussion of interviewing with the intensive sample see Chapter VII.
[3] Copies of these instructions are available on request.

'welfare' of some kind. Nevertheless there were relatively few requests for direct material help, but a good deal of gratitude was expressed at our willingness to listen. Many hoped that the interviewer would be able to give news of their husband and were very disappointed that this was not the case.

It had been our original intention not to tell interviewers the nature of the man's offence so that they would start each interview knowing virtually nothing of the family. This decision was fairly soon reversed, however, when interviewers found themselves in embarrassing situations, for example in the case of sex offences, particularly incest, where the child concerned was in the room during the interview; or murder, where the man had killed his own child and a straightforward request for details of children could cause some distress. We also decided to tell interviewers when the woman they were visiting was a common-law wife and the man was living apart from his legal wife; this too avoided some rather difficult situations.

The number of people present at the interviews varied greatly; where wives lived with their parents, one or other was often present for part, if not all, of the time. Where wives lived alone, friends were frequently there, or dropped in during the interview. Children were usually present for at least part of the time and during particularly long interviews where the interviewer was offered a meal, most of the family was seen at some stage. This situation had both advantages and disadvantages, but we feel that the former outweighed the latter, in so far as interviewers were able to make a better assessment both of the reliability of the information given, and of family relationships. They saw how children were handled, or the amount of pressure that might be put upon a wife by her parents, or the degree of acceptance by friends and neighbours. As against this it must be recognized that on some occasions information given about family relationships was unreliable, since it reflected what the wife knew her relatives wanted her to say. As will be mentioned later, we were not able to verify much of the information obtained, so that we draw attention to this situation merely in order to indicate that future researchers might possibly wish to control this aspect of the interviews more rigidly.[1]

### CHECKING THE DATA

#### The Prisoners

After each prison interview, the man's record was made available, and from this information regarding background social data, previous convictions, etc. could be checked. Other information which

[1] For a discussion of different responses according to whether the interview is private or with other respondents present see Taietz, 'Conflicting Group Norms and the Third Person in the Interview', *Amer. J. Sociol.*, LXVIII, No. 1, July 1962.

proved useful in shedding light on a man's personality and family relations was sometimes recorded, as were assessments made by governors, chaplains, psychologists, and others. Such material was, however, very often highly subjective and there were no systematic records of this kind; it nevertheless provided a useful comparison with the research interviewer's comments. In the case of men serving sentences of a year or more, the amount of information was usually sufficient to give a very helpful picture; unfortunately there was no information whatever recorded in the case of civil prisoners, and very little in the case of men serving only short sentences.

Before leaving each prison contact was made with the prison welfare officers.[1] It was hoped that we should have an opportunity to discuss individual cases with them, but unfortunately there was not sufficient time available. We therefore asked them to complete a short questionnaire[2] in order to obtain information regarding the amount of contact they had had with the men in our sample, the type of problem such men presented, and the extent to which they had been able to help the men. These questionnaires were completed after we had left the prisons, and despite the willingness of the welfare officers to help, the data were not as complete as we had hoped and in 100 cases no information was available. This situation arose for a number of reasons:

(a) Prison welfare officers were already over-burdened with their normal duties and any additional work had to be carried out under pressure.

(b) Lack of personal contact with the interviewer probably limited the extent to which they felt personally involved in contributing to the research.

(c) The training and specific interests of welfare officers varied greatly so that whilst some were able to give a great deal of information, others had only a limited knowledge of these particular men.

(d) If a prisoner was transferred to another prison after our interview with him, but before the questionnaire was completed by the welfare officer, his notes went with him and no information was available.

(e) In some prisons a great deal of welfare work is done by people other than the welfare officer, e.g. by governors, assistant governors, and chaplains. In most cases this information is not available on the prison welfare records, and it was therefore

---

[1] We are very grateful for the help and co-operation afforded us. In some long-term establishments there was at that time no prison welfare officer, and in these cases we contacted the Head Office of the Central After-Care Association whose representative called at each prison at monthly intervals.

[2] Copies available on request.

not included by the welfare officer when he completed our questionnaire.

It should be made clear that in certain prisons, where the research worker was able to establish particularly good relations with the welfare officer, the quality of information was generally much higher, and we consider the failure to obtain relevant information to be largely a failure on our part to spend enough time on this aspect of the research.

## The Families

Contact was made early in the research with the Headquarters of the National Assistance Board in order to ascertain whether they would be prepared to give us information about the amount of help they gave to families. In view of the Board's insistence that they should preserve the confidentiality of their relationship with clients, they were prepared to give such information only if we first obtained written permission from each wife. This was felt to be an unsatisfactory procedure, on the grounds that it put the interviewers in the invidious position of implying that we did not necessarily believe the information wives had given. A compromise solution was arrived at, whereby the Board agreed to confirm or refute the information we obtained, without going into any details.[1]

### ANALYSIS OF MATERIAL

It had been our original intention to include the civil prisoners as part of the general survey and to make comparisons between the three groups of offenders, stars, recidivists and civils.

After the material had been collected, it became apparent that to include the civils in this way would, in fact, distort the material quite considerably, principally because many of them were in prison for such a short time as to make their replies (and in particular those of their families) much less meaningful than in the case of men serving longer sentences. For example we found that the problems presented by civil prisoners and their families were in the main not concerned with imprisonment or separation, since often they were apart for only a few days. Furthermore, since the civil prisoners represent such a small proportion of the total prison population, it was decided to exclude them from the general study, and to treat them as a separate category; a section of the report will therefore be devoted exclusively to this sub-sample (see Chapter IX).

[1] We are most grateful to those members of the NAB staff who co-operated in this way.

DATA PROCESSING

Most of the questions on the schedule used in the extensive sample were precoded; the open-ended questions were subsequently coded by a team of three, every tenth schedule being checked by a second person. Constant discussion took place between members of the coding team, and all queries were referred to the writer, who in turn checked every fifth schedule.

These data were then transferred to punched cards, and after sorting and tabulating, a careful analysis of the information was made, frequency distributions obtained on all counts and tables constructed in order to provide a descriptive picture of the prisoners and their families. In addition, comparisons were made between replies to similar questions on husbands' and wives' schedules. The information obtained in this way forms the basis of Chapters III, IV, V, VI, and VIII of this report.

Rating scales were then devised from the wives' schedules in an attempt to measure the families' adjustment to separation. A team of four coders was employed and every tenth schedule was coded independently by two coders.[1]

STATISTICAL PRESENTATION OF THE RESULTS[2]

Since the sample design employed had different sampling fractions for the three categories of prisoner, it has been necessary to use weights in presenting the results for combinations of the categories. As the civil prisoners are never combined with the other prisoners to give an overall picture, they present no difficulty. The sampling fraction for stars was, however, twice that of the recidivists; therefore, if a picture for stars and recidivists together is to be presented, the recidivists have to be given double weight. *The procedure of using a weighting factor of 2 for recidivists has been used in every table where stars and recidivists are combined.* For this reason the *actual* number of star and recidivist prisoners is given separately in each table, but the overall total is left blank.

In every case where comparisons have been made between groups of prisoners, tests of significance have been performed; the results of the tests are placed in brackets in the text. The symbols $\chi^2$, $t$, $F$ refer to the chi-square, standard normal, and variance-ratio ($F$) distributions respectively: the letters d.f. refer to the degrees of freedom of the

[1] Instructions to coders and details of rating scales are available for perusal by other researchers if required.
[2] We are very much indebted to Mr G. Kalton of the London School of Economics who acted as adviser on all statistical matters and whose students carried out all the necessary statistical tests.

distribution. The significance of the result is shown by $P < 0.01$ (significant at the 1 per cent level), $P < 0.05$ (significant at the 5 per cent but not the 1 per cent level), and N.S. (not significant at the 5 per cent level).

A description of the methods used in the statistical analysis is given in Appendix B.

## Chapter III

# THE PRISONERS

As indicated in the preceding chapter, it was decided for purposes of analysis to exclude the civil prisoners from the general study and to treat them as a separate category. Thus we are only concerned here with a description of the stars and recidivists in the sample. Furthermore, it has been decided to include in this chapter a description of *all* the prisoners interviewed who belonged to these two groups of offenders, and not merely the 'paired' couples (i.e. those whose wives we subsequently interviewed). This decision has been made in order to obtain as nearly as possible a profile of the married prison population. A subsequent chapter will deal with discrepancies between the information obtained from the husbands and that obtained from the wives of the 'paired' couples.

Whilst it is unfortunate, it must be remembered that any comparisons with official criminal statistics must be interpreted cautiously since such figures as are available relate to the prison population as a whole, and *not* to the married sector of it.[1] Furthermore official statistics relating to the total population include men with less than three months to serve. We consider, however, that it is justifiable to assume that our findings are representative of the married prison population in the sociological, economic, and psychological fields which we are investigating.

The emphasis in this research has primarily been on the *families* of offenders and whilst we have tried to include as much information of a factual kind as possible about the husbands, and to realize that even though they are in prison they are an important part of the family unit, our resources did not permit a really adequate study of these men.

Interviewing in prison has a great many limitations, amongst the most important being the unsatisfactory physical conditions under which most interviews take place. Frequently the research worker was given an enormous board room, with vast table and countless chairs;

[1] Published in the Annual Reports of the Home Office Prison Department (formerly the Reports of the Commissioners of Prisons for England and Wales). Although data on marital status and occupation are collected on each prisoner's reception, no attempt has been made to collate them for publication.

or a classroom with rows of desks and a blackboard; sometimes a cell; and even on one occasion the medical examination room, complete with the necessary apparatus.[1] Such conditions are scarcely conducive to creating a relaxed atmosphere in which to discuss one's family affairs.

To interview in prison requires a good deal of background knowledge about both prisons and prisoners. Workers who have the requisite specialist knowledge, and who are conversant with the problems of interviewing in an institutional setting, are rarely found amongst the ranks of the unemployed, and since we could offer only short-term employment, attempts to find suitable interviewers were unsuccessful. This meant that almost all the interviewing of prisoners was done by the writer and under very great pressure, since it was important that the family interviewers be supplied with enough addresses to keep them fully occupied, allowing for non-contacts, and making long journeys worth while. Furthermore, there are very definite limits on the amount of time each day when men are available for interview, so that it is necessary to see a large number of men in a relatively small space of time. This is important from the point of view of the staff, since it is extremely difficult for officers to be spared from their duties in order to fetch prisoners for interview and ensure that they return to work or to their cells. Whilst we do not wish to digress further on the subject we feel that some knowledge of the setting in which the answers to our questions were given will help the reader in understanding why, particularly by comparison with those chapters relating to the wives, our information is sketchy and somewhat 'depersonalized'.

### BACKGROUND FACTORS

It is generally known that most offenders in prison are drawn from the younger age groups. This fact appears to be confirmed even if the unmarried men are ignored, and Table I indicates that almost 40 per cent of our sample were under the age of thirty. Nevertheless there is a noticeable difference between the two groups, indicating that the married population tends to be somewhat older than the average for the prison population as a whole.

Data on ethnic status were collected in view of the fact that the post-war pattern of immigration into the UK has resulted in the recruitment of an admittedly small but not insignificant number of

---

[1] We should like to make it clear that we are in no way criticizing the Governors and staff of the various establishments. They went out of their way to be helpful with regard to accommodation as with all other matters. The overcrowding in prisons makes the provision of suitable interviewing facilities quite impossible, however desirable.

foreign-born persons to the criminal population. Although stereo-types of the foreign-born criminal, particularly those who are coloured, are now quite firmly established in the minds of certain sections of the public, well-founded information about such offenders is extremely sparse, and for that reason we decided to collect such information as was available. However only 1·6 per cent of men

TABLE I.   *Age distribution of sample of married prisoner population*
(*Percentages*)

| Age | Stars | Recidivists | Total | Prison population†of England andWales 1961 |
|---|---|---|---|---|
| 21–29 | 44·7 | 36·7 | 39·4 | 50·1 |
| 30–39 | 26·8 | 38·9 | 34·9 | 27·5 |
| 40–49 | 17·9 | 16·9 | 17·2 | 14·0 |
| 50 and over | 9·7 | 7·0 | 8·0 | 8·3 |
| No information | 0·6 | – | 0·2 | – |
| Total* | 100·0 | 100·0 | 100·0 | 100·0 |
| Number of prisoners | 328 | 325 | – | – |

* Throughout this report numbers do not always add to totals because of rounding errors.

† Report of the Commissioners of Prisons for the year 1961, HMSO, Cmd. 1798. It must be borne in mind that these figures represent *receptions* into prison, not daily average population. Furthermore they include all types of offenders (including civils) and all lengths of sentence.

interviewed were coloured; two of the stars were Asian and spoke so little English that the validity of their replies is somewhat doubtful. In particular they could not understand why anyone should be interested in their nuclear family, since their wives lived in India with the children and were, in addition, illiterate. The somewhat ephemeral relationships with the vast network of kindred which they seemed to have in this country were obviously of greater significance to them, but any true understanding of the situation required a far longer interview than we were able to give, in order to make the matter clear to both parties concerned.

A total of 6·8 per cent of those interviewed were born outside the UK, the largest single category (2·3 per cent of the total) being those born in the Irish Republic. In view of research carried out by McClintock[1] and others we had expected this figure to be considerably higher, and it is also surprising to find that whereas the number of

[1] McClintock and Gibson, *Robbery in London*, London, Macmillan, 1961.

foreign-born coming from all other countries is roughly the same whether they be stars or recidivists, in the case of the Irish-born twice as many were stars.

One explanation of our findings may be that the majority of those in prison who were born in the Republic are unmarried (or claim to be so). Moreover the age of marriage for males in Ireland is higher than in this country, as is the proportion of the male population remaining unmarried.[1] Certainly according to the nominal register which was used in order to select our sample, most of those with Irish-sounding names were described as 'single' on their prison record.

Almost all those born outside the UK came to this country when they were between the ages of thirteen and twenty-five.

Men were asked what job they were doing *at the time of committing the offence*. As will be seen from Table II below a very high proportion (36·5 per cent) were unemployed. From the job description as given by the man, certain classifications were used in the analysis; these do not correspond with those of the Registrar General, since it was thought likely that the majority of our sample would fall into the category of unskilled or semi-skilled, and greater refinement was thought to be unnecessary. Semi-skilled includes any job requiring a skill which could be rapidly acquired, e.g. a garage mechanic who was not a tradesman, bus conductor, etc. The category 'self-employed, small scale', largely covers street traders, self-employed painters and decorators, bookmakers, window cleaners, etc. 'Self-employed, large scale' normally includes only those employing more than twenty employees; however, there were in the research a few men about whom we had some doubts on this score. If they insisted, on being pressed, that they had in fact this number of employees, they were included in the category of large-scale. Equally, there were two instances where the man was obviously in business in a big way (financially and socially) and yet had fewer employees; these were also included under the heading large-scale. It is interesting to note that 1·7 per cent described themselves as professional or habitual criminals[2] and expected to earn their living in this way. This number is, however, undoubtedly an under-estimate, and many of those who claimed to be 'self-employed small scale' could more accurately be described as habitual (if not very 'professional') criminals.

As had been expected 31·3 per cent were employed in unskilled or semi-skilled jobs. If to this is added the 12·6 per cent of small-scale

---

[1] See Glass, D. V., *Population Trends and Patterns*, London, HMSO, 1955.

[2] A *professional* criminal can be defined as one whose livelihood and/or major source of income stems directly from crime. An *habitual* criminal is one who persistently indulges in crime whether or not it constitutes his largest or primary source of income.

self-employed the figure becomes 43·9 per cent. Only approximately
9 per cent could be described as white collar workers.

TABLE II.  *Type of work at time of committing offence*

(*Percentages*)

| | Stars | Recidivists | Total |
|---|---|---|---|
| Unemployed | 22·2 | 43·5 | 36·5 |
| Unskilled manual | 14·9 | 18·7 | 17·5 |
| Semi-skilled manual | 14·9 | 13·2 | 13·8 |
| Skilled manual | 12·7 | 4·9 | 7·6 |
| Clerical/supervisory | 6·7 | 1·5 | 3·3 |
| Managerial | 3·6 | 1·8 | 2·5 |
| Professional | 2·1 | 0·3 | 0·9 |
| Self-employed (small scale) | 13·7 | 11·9 | 12·6 |
| Self-employed (large scale) | 3·3 | 0·9 | 1·7 |
| Professional or habitual criminal | 0·9 | 2·1 | 1·7 |
| Armed Forces/Merchant Navy | 3·9 | 0·6 | 1·7 |
| No information | 0·6 | – | 0·2 |
| Total | 100·0 | 100·0 | 100·0 |
| Number of prisoners | 328 | 325 | – |

Those men who were unemployed at the time of committing the
offence were asked for how long they had been out of work. 20
per cent had been unemployed for less than one month, 55 per cent
for between one month and one year, the remainder for longer.
Comparisons between stars and recidivists showed little difference
except in relation to those who had never had regular work. The
proportion of unemployed stars who had never had regular work
was significantly less than the proportion of unemployed recidivists
in this category ($\chi^2 = 6·07$; 1 d.f. $P < 0·05$).

In the case of the recidivists in particular, the period of unemployment was often limited by the short time they spent out of prison
before the present sentence.

In interpreting figures for unemployment it is important to bear in
mind that short-term unemployment is a normal phenomenon in
certain industries, particularly the building trades in which so many
of the prison population are engaged as unskilled or semi-skilled
labourers. Bearing in mind the proportion of the sample who fell
into these categories, it would be unwise to draw any inferences
about the man's character or habits solely from the fact that he had
been unemployed for a period of less than one month. Nevertheless it
seems probable that unemployment for *any* period is likely to

increase, rather than diminish, the propensity to be involved in crime. Furthermore it will be noted in subsequent chapters that irregularity of work is an important contributory factor to marital conflict, and a combination of unsatisfactory social relationships *and* unemployment is conducive to criminal behaviour.[1]

TABLE III.   *Reasons for unemployment*
(*Percentages of those unemployed*)

|  | Stars | Recidivists | Total |
|---|---|---|---|
| No work available (including no *suitable* work) | 16·4 | 12·7 | 13·4 |
| Ill-health (physical or mental) | 19·2 | 22·5 | 21·8 |
| Professional or habitual criminal | 12·3 | 34·5 | 30·0 |
| Work problem | 34·2 | 33·1 | 33·3 |
| Other | 30·1 | 19·0 | 21·3 |
| Number of unemployed prisoners | 73 | 142 | – |

*Note:* totals do not add up to 100 per cent because some men gave more than one reason for unemployment.

The use of the term 'work problem' requires some explanation. This assessment was made by the interviewer and was based on the general attitude of the respondent towards work. There were a considerable number of men who said they could not find work, but who, in answer to probing, made it clear that if they *were* offered a job, they soon contrived to lose it or to leave it. It was sometimes difficult to distinguish between this group of men and the professional criminals, but the latter term was confined to those who freely admitted to living off crime, however unsuccessfully, and who made it clear that they never worked and had no intention of doing so in the foreseeable future.

Many of those with a work problem could be described in more pejorative terms as 'workshy', and indeed may well have created an unfavourable impression on the judges and magistrates who sentenced them, on account of their poor work record and their attitudes to work. From a clinical point of view they could be regarded as presenting the kinds of symptoms of personality disorder that are increasingly recognized by the Ministry of Labour and the National Assistance Board. Maxwell-Jones and his colleagues at the Social Rehabilitation Unit at Belmont Hospital[2] found that referrals of

---

[1] For a discussion of the bad work record of recidivists see West, D. J., *The Habitual Criminal*, Inst. of Crim., Cambridge, Macmillan, 1963. For a discussion of unemployment and crime see also Mannheim, *Social Aspects of Crime in England between the Wars*, London, Allen & Unwin, 1940.

[2] Now the Henderson Hospital.

'unemployable' men from the Ministry of Labour exhibited psychiatric symptoms and responded to treatment in an encouraging number of cases.[1] In other words a proportion of these men could be regarded as genuinely handicapped, in much the same way as if they had lost a limb. Less obviously workshy, but nevertheless presenting a severe work problem, were those of the 'accident prone' type who were physically disabled in consequence. Yet others developed psychosomatic symptoms which often appeared to be associated with a strong unconscious desire to avoid work, but which at the same time were recognized by society, and by their families in particular, as deserving of sympathy.[2]

On the other hand some of the men in this group, apart from professional criminals, had deliberately chosen worklessness as a desirable social condition. The distinction between petty criminality and vagrancy—or systematic worklessness—is often arbitrary, and in the view of a writer like O'Connor[3] vagrancy can arise from conscious choice and need not be a psychiatric symptom.

The fact remains nevertheless that such men are a concrete social problem in contemporary society, in that their existence demands the attention of our social services and the expenditure of public money. It is not inconceivable that some may have deliberately chosen to avoid work either because the margin between their potential earnings and social welfare benefits is small, or because they do not wish to support their estranged wives out of their own efforts.[4]

The category 'other' in Table III includes those who claimed that they got the sack when their criminal past was found out,[5] those whose business failed, and those who took time off for such reasons as their wives' ill-health.

All men were asked about any serious illness they had had and this matter will be referred to again in a later section of the report. However, at this stage we are including a list of the illnesses from which those men suffered who claimed that ill-health prevented them from being employed before their present sentence.

We did not have access to the prison medical records of the offenders, but where information relating to health matters was recorded on the general record, the relevant facts were included on the questionnaire.

[1] See Jones, *et al.*, *Social Psychiatry*, London, Tavistock, 1952.
[2] For a discussion of the 'sick role' see Talcott Parsons, *Social System*, Glencoe, 1951.
[3] *Britain in the Sixties: Vagrancy*, Penguin Books, 1963. An interesting comparison is to be found in Nels Andersen's *The Hobo*, Chicago, 1927.
[4] This will be discussed again in the chapter on civil prisoners.
[5] For a discussion of this issue see Martin, J. P., *Offenders as Employees*, London, Macmillan, 1962.

Table IV suggests that a very high proportion of illnesses reported were either psychiatric, or might be regarded as psychosomatic, as for example in the case of duodenal ulcers. The other large category, of chest complaints, reflects the fact that diseases of the respiratory system, and in particular bronchitis, have a disproportionate incidence amongst urban working-class populations.[1]

TABLE IV. *Nature of illness causing unemployment*

*(Percentage of those citing illness as cause of unemployment)*

|  | Stars | Recidivists | Total |
|---|---|---|---|
| Skin complaint | – | 3·1 | 2·5 |
| Hernia | – | 6·3 | 5·1 |
| Nervous breakdown | 14·3 | 6·3 | 7·7 |
| Neurotic/highly strung* | 14·3 | 3·1 | 5·1 |
| Concussion | – | 6·3 | 5·1 |
| Chest ailment | 14·3 | 12·6 | 12·8 |
| Epilepsy | – | 3·1 | 2·5 |
| Migraine/giddiness | – | 3·1 | 2·5 |
| T.B. | – | 6·3 | 5·1 |
| Loss of limb/sight | – | 3·1 | 2·5 |
| Deafness | 7·1 | 3·1 | 3·8 |
| Duodenal Ulcer | – | 15·5 | 12·8 |
| Kidney complaint | 7·1 | – | 1·3 |
| Other* | 42·9 | 28·1 | 30·8 |
| Number of prisoners | 14 | 32 | – |

* 'Other' almost always indicated 'nerves'. If a man stated that he suffered from 'nerves' the interviewer probed and if the man had received psychiatric treatment, either as in- or out-patient, it was included as 'highly strung'. If no treatment had been given it was entered under 'other'. The terms 'nerves' or 'nervous' as used throughout the report have a psychological connotation and bear no neurological implications.

It is worth noting here that a great many more men suffered from these same illnesses but were not unemployed as a result of them. In many instances the interviewer felt that 'work problem' would have been a more precise reason for unemployment, the illness being often used as a convenient scapegoat.

Men were asked how many jobs they had had in the twelve months before coming into prison on the current sentence. The information obtained does not give a very accurate picture of the situation, since some men who had only had one or two jobs had not, in fact, been out of prison for as long as twelve months; indeed a number had

[1] See Susser and Watson, *Sociology and Medicine*, 1962, also Registrar General's analysis of principal causes of death.

only been out a few days or weeks. However it is interesting to note that as many as 11·9 per cent had not worked at all during the year preceding their sentence.

Some of the comments made earlier on the interpretation of unemployment in the light of occupational conditions also apply to job turnover. Occupational security through continuous employment is very largely a white collar phenomenon; individual interviews indicate that a very considerable number of prisoners are for the

TABLE V. *Number of jobs in twelve months preceding sentence*

*(Percentages)*

| Number of jobs | Stars | Recidivists | Total |
|---|---|---|---|
| None | 5·5 | 15·0 | 11·9 |
| 1 | 57·8 | 40·4 | 46·4 |
| 2 | 22·8 | 22·9 | 23·0 |
| 3 | 5·8 | 7·9 | 7·3 |
| 4 | 1·8 | 3·9 | 3·3 |
| 5 | 1·2 | 1·5 | 1·4 |
| 6 | 0·9 | 0·9 | 0·9 |
| 7 | – | 0·3 | 0·2 |
| 8 | – | 0·3 | 0·2 |
| 9 or more | 0·9 | 0·3 | 0·5 |
| Don't know* | 3·0 | 5·8 | 4·9 |
| Total | 100·0 | 100·0 | 100·0 |
| Number of prisoners | 328 | 325 | – |

* 'Don't know' usually meant that men had had so many that they could not recall the number (or were reluctant to be specific).

most part reluctant to submit to a regular work routine and show a marked inability to remain in any job for long. This is particularly true amongst the recidivist population.[1] [The mean number of jobs for stars was 1·62 during the preceding year: for recidivists the mean was 1·86. The difference between these means is significant at the 5 per cent level.]

Data were obtained regarding the length of time men had remained in their last employment. It is difficult to assess how meaningful the information is, since many men could not have remained longer in their jobs as they had only been out of prison for a short time. However two factors emerged clearly: in the first place stars remained in their jobs markedly longer than recidivists ($\chi^2$ for trend for those with work = 19·40 1 d.f. $P < 0·01$) and secondly there

[1] See West, D. J., *op. cit.*

was a relationship between length of time in the last employment and the status of the occupation. This latter finding underlines the point that relative occupational instability can be accounted for by socio-economic status.

Men were asked to say roughly how much they earned each week before coming into prison, excluding their income from the proceeds of crime.[1] Some found it very difficult to give this information, since their normal work included a fair amount of 'shady' business. Though it is probably likely that men showed a tendency to exaggerate the

TABLE VI.   *Amount of earnings*

(*Percentages*)

|  | Stars | Recidivists | Total |
|---|---|---|---|
| Unemployed* | 23·1 | 46·0 | 38·4 |
| Under £7 | 1·5 | 1·2 | 1·3 |
| £7–9 | 9·7 | 6·4 | 7·6 |
| £10–14 | 29·1 | 26·7 | 27·6 |
| £15–25 | 28·3 | 13·2 | 18·3 |
| Over £25 | 7·9 | 6·1 | 6·7 |
| Total | 100·0 | 100·0 | 100·0 |
| Number of prisoners | 328 | 325 | – |

\* The figures for unemployed are slightly discrepant with those given in Table II above. It is likely that some men had jobs but were away owing to sickness and received only National Health Insurance so that their earnings are not included here.

amount of their earnings, it seems from Table VI that when they *do* work they earn good money. In a few cases men were reluctant to disclose their true earnings in case we supplied information to the tax authorities!

In view of the fact that so many claimed to be earning well, the data were further broken down to show type of work by earnings, since it was thought that if men claimed to be earning high wages in what are known to be poorly paid jobs, the information they gave was likely to be unreliable.

In fact there did not appear to be any particular abnormalities in the pattern of earnings. Among the unskilled workers, only 18 per

[1] It is not always recognized that the proceeds of crime are never equal to the value of the goods stolen. 'Fences' are notorious for the hard bargains they drive and goods which may be 'flogged off' in pubs and street markets—like watches, radios, cigarettes—must inevitably be sold at a heavy discount. Even the theft of cash is not automatically free of depreciation, for when notes are stolen (the numbers of which may be known to the police) they may have to be exchanged at a discount.

cent claimed to be earning over £15 per week. Moving upwards on the occupational scale the pattern of earnings followed an expected trend. Among small-scale self-employed men earnings ranged widely, and it is probably amongst this group that information is least reliable. As can be seen from Table VI above, 45·9 per cent of men in the total sample were earning between £10–£25 and 27·6 per cent of them between £10–£14 per week. The average weekly earnings of male manual workers in April 1963 (skilled, semi-skilled and un-skilled) were £16 3s 1d[1] which suggests that offenders are not ab-normally high earners. On the other hand, it is important to bear in mind that no less than 38·4 per cent of the sample were not working at all before imprisonment, and whilst some were undoubtedly getting money from crime, the majority were probably living exclusively from welfare benefits.

### THE PRISONER AND HIS CRIMINALITY

Men were asked to give details of their previous convictions and these were checked against their prison record. If any discrepancies occurred they were usually very minor and the information set out below is correct so far as the records show.

TABLE VII.  *Previous convictions (juvenile and adult)*

(*Percentages*)

| Number of convictions | Stars | Recidivists | Total |
|---|---|---|---|
| None | 35·0 | 0·6 | 12·1 |
| 1 | 17·3 | 2·8 | 7·7 |
| 2 | 12·2 | 2·8 | 5·9 |
| 3 or more | 35·3 | 93·8 | 74·1 |
| Total | 100·0 | 100·0 | 100·0 |
| Number of prisoners | 328 | 325 | – |

From this table it will be seen that 64·8 per cent of the stars have had at least one previous conviction.[2] However from the point of view of this research, it is probably more relevant to look at the previous *prison experience* of our population. Here the data show that 18·6 per cent of stars and 99·4 per cent of recidivists had been in prison before. On the other hand, 50 per cent of the recidivists had no

[1] *Statistics on Incomes, Prices, Employment and Production:* Ministry of Labour London. HMSO, September 1963,
[2] Under the First Offenders Act 1958 magistrates cannot send genuine first offenders aged 21 and over to prison unless no other methods of disposal are suitable.

experience of juvenile institutions, i.e. Approved School, Borstal, or Detention Centre.[1]

The fact that so many stars have been in prison before necessarily raises a problem in relation to the value of any distinctions between the two groups on all the other tables. Further refinement of the data shows that 13 per cent of recidivists had served only one previous prison sentence, so that there is a slight overlap between the two groups. This contamination, by making the two groups more alike, would therefore minimize any apparent differences, and any which *do* occur can be assumed to be real differences which would be even greater if only genuine first offenders were considered.

Having established the character of the population in terms of previous criminal experience, we may now consider the types of crime for which men were serving their current sentence. For purposes of this research the normal breakdown of offences used to compile the criminal statistics was not used. It was thought that eight basic categories would be meaningful in any discussion of family relationships and adjustment:

(*a*) Murder/manslaughter.
(*b*) Violence against the person.
(*c*) Sexual offences.
(*d*) Offences against property with violence (i.e. breaking and entering as well as robbery).
(*e*) Offences against property without violence.
(*f*) Fraud, embezzlement, and similar 'paper crimes'.
(*g*) Larceny bailee.
(*h*) Other.

A further two categories (debt and wife maintenance) were included, but will be dealt with in a later chapter since they relate to civil offences. Category (*g*) was included in view of our particular interest in problems of hire purchase, though as will be seen from Table VIII the number of men imprisoned on this charge is extremely small. Category (*h*) 'other' includes minor motoring offences, breach of probation, possession of hemp, etc.

The following analysis relates to offences and not to men, since a high proportion of men were charged with more than one offence, i.e. housebreaking *and* larceny.

This distribution of offences is not representative of the prison

[1] See Taylor, R. S., 'Observations on Some Characteristics of Men Sentenced to Preventive Detention', *British Journal of Criminology*, July 1960. Vol. 1, No. 1; also Hammond & Chayen, *Persistent Criminals*, in a study of Preventive Detainees (London, HMSO, 1963) found that 24·6 per cent of P.D.'s and 31·5 per cent of men given other sentences were first convicted at the age of 21 or over.

population as a whole since the sample excluded men with a sentence of less than four[1] months, thereby excluding such offences as drunkenness, vagrancy and loitering with intent. On the other hand, it may be representative of the married population, since the above offences are more likely to be committed by homeless men, who, if they were ever married, have long since lost touch with their families.

TABLE VIII. *Type of offence*
(*Percentage of offences*)

| Type of offence | Stars | Recidivists | Total |
|---|---|---|---|
| Murder/manslaughter | 3·2 | 0·5 | 1·4 |
| Violence against person | 5·0 | 5·5 | 5·4 |
| Sexual offences | 11·9 | 4·1 | 6·7 |
| Offences against property with violence | 25·8 | 34·3 | 31·4 |
| Offences against property without violence | 27·1 | 34·3 | 31·9 |
| Fraud, embezzlement, etc. | 15·7 | 11·7 | 13·1 |
| Larceny bailee | 1·0 | 0·7 | 0·8 |
| Other | 10·0 | 9·0 | 9·3 |
| Total | 100·0 | 100·0 | 100·0 |
| Number of offences | 437 | 435 | – |

TABLE IX(*a*). *Length of sentence*
(*Percentages*)

| | Stars | Recidivists | Total |
|---|---|---|---|
| 1 month under 3 months* | 0·3 | 0·3 | 0·3 |
| 3 months under 6 months | 3·0 | 0·3 | 1·2 |
| 6 months under 12 months | 9·1 | 11·3 | 10·6 |
| 12 months under 18 months | 19·8 | 13·8 | 15·8 |
| 18 months under 3 years | 33·5 | 28·5 | 30·3 |
| 3 years under 4 years | 17·0 | 21·1 | 19·8 |
| 4 years under 7 years | 10·9 | 13·5 | 12·7 |
| 7 years and over | 6·1 | 10·7 | 9·2 |
| Total | 100·0 | 100·0 | 100·0 |
| Number of prisoners | 328 | 325 | – |

* Strictly speaking these men should not have been included in our sample. An error was made in selecting them, but having begun the interview and obtained permission to visit their wives, it was thought unwise to change our plans.

[1] With remission such men would serve only three months and therefore would not fall within the limits of our sample.

As stated above, we cannot expect these figures to be closely comparable with the figures for the total prison population, but in order to obtain some idea of the extent to which they are paralleled, figures were obtained from the Prison Department of the Home Office giving the length of sentence of males over twenty-one in the daily average population in 1962.

TABLE IX(*b*). *Length of sentence of daily average population for all prisoners with sentences of three months or more**

|  | Percentages |
|---|---|
| 3 months under 6 months | 8·0 |
| 6 months under 12 months | 17·7 |
| 12 months under 18 months | 16·5 |
| 18 months under 3 years | 27·0 |
| 3 years | 11·2 ⎫ |
| Over 3 years under 4 years | 6·7 ⎬ 30·8 |
| 4 years under 5 years | 6·1 ⎪ |
| 5 years and over | 6·8 ⎭ |
|  | 100·0 |

| | |
|---|---|
| Daily average population of prisoners with sentences of 3 months or more | 16,273 |
| Proportion of all prisoners with sentences of less than 3 months | 5·3% |

* Source: Home Office private communication, April 1963.


TABLE X. *Length of separation from wife at time of interview*
(*Percentages*)

|  | Stars | Recidivists | Total |
|---|---|---|---|
| Under 1 month | 6·7 | 6·4 | 6·5 |
| 1 month under 3 months | 12·8 | 14·1 | 13·7 |
| 3 months under 6 months | 16·7 | 12·5 | 14·0 |
| 6 months under 1 year | 21·9 | 13·2 | 16·1 |
| 1 year under 18 months | 15·5 | 12·5 | 13·6 |
| 18 months under 3 years | 9·1 | 11·0 | 10·4 |
| 3 years and over | 3·6 | 4·0 | 3·9 |
| Separated prior to imprisonment | 13·4 | 25·7 | 21·7 |
| Total | 100·0 | 100·0 | 100·0 |
| Number of prisoners | 328 | 325 | – |

It will be readily apparent that our sample contains an undue proportion of men serving long sentences:[1] 41·9 per cent of men have sentences of three years and over, compared with only 30·8 per cent in the total prison population. [By stratifying our sample into stars and recidivists *only*—and by not incorporating other stratification factors, or the two stages of sampling—the difference is highly significant [$t = 5·44, P < 0·01$].]

Equally important, from the point of view of our research, with the length of sentence is the period men had been separated from their wives (including time spent on remand or in custody) when we interviewed them. This information is set out in Table X.

PRISONER'S PICTURE OF HIS FAMILY

Men were asked about their marital situation at the time of coming into prison. The questionnaire design did not originally include a category of 'fluid', but we found that some situations were so unclear or complicated that it was impossible to disentangle the mesh of inter-relationships in the familial field.[2]

If living together and being legally married is taken as an index of stable marital relationships, the data in Table XI confirm our experience in the selection of prisoners, namely that star prisoners tend

TABLE XI.　*Marital status at time of coming into prison*

*(Percentages)*

|  | Stars | Recidivists | Total |
|---|---|---|---|
| Legally married living with wife | 78·8 | 60·9 | 67·1 |
| Unmarried but living together | 1·8 | 2·4 | 2·2 |
| Legally separated living alone | 5·8 | 7·3 | 6·9 |
| Legally separated living with someone | 4·0 | 2·4 | 3·0 |
| Not legally separated, living alone | 7·3 | 19·2 | 15·3 |
| Not legally separated living with someone | 1·5 | 4·3 | 3·4 |
| Marital situation 'fluid' | 0·6 | 2·8 | 2·0 |
| Total | 100·0 | 100·0 | 100·0 |
| Number of prisoners | 328 | 325 | – |

[1] Although very short-term sentence men were excluded from the study on account of the difficulties involved in interviewing, there is a case to be argued for a study of the families of such men. We do not believe that our short-term prisoners, who were exclusively civil prisoners, are representative of this group.

[2] West, D. J., *op. cit.* Of 32 per cent of intermittent recidivists living with their wives, at least 12 per cent were 'on very uncertain terms and likely before long to become separated or divorced'.

to have more stable marital relationships [comparing the proportions of stars and recidivists legally married and living with wife $\chi^2 = 24 \cdot 5$, 1 d.f. $P < 0 \cdot 01$] (see Chapter II, p. 31). Disregarding the differences between stars and recidivists, it can be seen from the table that less than a third of the prisoners had experienced a breakdown of marriage in the form of separation at the time of imprisonment. But for several reasons this figure is misleading as an index of marital stability: some marriages broke up after the man had gone to prison, though not necessarily for that reason.[1] Nor can one assume that because partners live together and are legally married, the marriage is necessarily successful and harmonious. On the contrary some marriages which are characterized by perpetual discord are of the type that will only be broken by death or some other disaster.

Those men who said they were definitely not living with their wives were asked to give the reason for the break-up of their marriage. The answers appear to be extremely biassed, as will be seen to be equally true when we discuss the same question answered by the wives. The two main reasons given by recidivists were their wife's promiscuity and/or desertion and their own criminality—stars referred more often to mutual incompatibility, though they too often mentioned their wife's desertion. Both groups complained bitterly of in-law trouble, in particular interference and dominance by the wife's parents.

We were interested to know how the prisoner considered he got on with his wife and a number of alternatives were presented to him and he was asked to select one of them. These are set out in Table XII below.

TABLE XII. *How prisoner gets on with wife*

*(Percentages)*

|  | Stars | Recidivists | Total |
|---|---|---|---|
| Very well indeed | 16·1 | 8·6 | 11·1 |
| Very well | 40·0 | 34·9 | 36·7 |
| Fair/average | 14·3 | 13·8 | 14·0 |
| Good in old days, not so good now | 2·7 | 5·5 | 4·6 |
| Not so well | 3·3 | 1·2 | 1·9 |
| Not at all well | 1·5 | 2·2 | 1·9 |
| Ups and downs | 4·0 | 5·5 | 5·0 |
| Separated prior to imprisonment | 17·9 | 27·8 | 24·6 |
| Total | 100·0 | 100·0 | 100·0 |
| Number of prisoners | 328 | 325 | – |

[1] The number falling into this category is in fact very small as will be discussed in a subsequent chapter.

The number of men who claim to get on well with their wives seems remarkably high, and, as will be seen when discussing family relationships in a subsequent chapter, it is likely to be a question of 'wishful thinking' in many instances. There is a great tendency for men in prison to view the world outside, and their family relationships in particular, through very rose-coloured spectacles. However, it should also be remembered that the figure of those having very good relationships with their wives includes all those who are living with women to whom they are not married, and it is plausible that these 'illicit' unions are happier than those which preceded them, at least in the initial stages.

The great majority of men said they lived with their wives before marriage, but no systematic record was made of this information.

TABLE XIII. *How long living with wife\* at time of imprisonment*
(*Percentages*)

|  | Stars | Recidivists | Total |
|---|---|---|---|
| Under 1 year | 4·3 | 4·6 | 4·5 |
| 1 year under 3 years | 9·1 | 8·6 | 8·8 |
| 3 years under 5 years | 11·9 | 10·4 | 10·9 |
| 5 years under 9 years | 21·3 | 24·2 | 23·4 |
| 9 years and over | 38·6 | 21·1 | 27·0 |
| Not applicable (separated) | 14·6 | 30·6 | 25·5 |
| Total | 100·0 | 100·0 | 100·0 |
| Number of prisoners | 328 | 325 | – |

\* This table includes legal and common-law marriages.

They were simply asked how long they had lived with their wives and the answers relate to the person with whom they were living at the time of the arrest, not to the wife from whom they were separated.

It is interesting to note that such a high proportion have been living with their wives for more than five years, bearing in mind the youthfulness of the population (see Table I). 'Living with' must in some cases however be interpreted rather generally, as in marriages in which the partners tend to be emotionally volatile, there may well have been a number of 'comings and goings' when wife or husband storms out, only to return a day or so later.

Those men who were separated from their wives, either legally or otherwise, were asked for how long they had been separated, excluding the period of the present sentence. It is interesting to note that the majority (59·4 per cent) had been separated for over three years, though there was a slight tendency for stars to have been separated for somewhat shorter periods than recidivists.

*Prisoners and Their Families*

We also asked the men for how long they had known their wives before marriage. The majority of couples knew each other for over a year and 50 per cent for two years or more. It is worth mentioning that if these figures are broken down further into separated and non-separated families, those who are separated are in no way significantly different from the others in this particular respect.

One explanation of the fact that they knew each other so long before marriage is that so many lived with their wives before marriage. Most of these men said their wives were pregnant at the time of marriage, and it may well be that, having lived with the girl and got her pregnant, the pressure was strong to marry her; whether the marriage would be successful or happy then became of secondary importance.[1]

In the hope of getting men to talk in a general way about their families, we asked them to describe themselves and their wives. This proved exceedingly difficult for them and most declined to comment at first, saying that they had never thought about it. When pressed, they tended to describe their wives in somewhat prosaic terms; good wife and mother, hard working, etc. Describing themselves proved

TABLE XIV(*a*).   *Prisoners' opinion of themselves*
(*Percentages*)

|  | Stars | Recidivists | Total |
|---|---|---|---|
| Good husband | 3·0 | 0·6 | 1·4 |
| Good father | 4·0 | 0·9 | 1·9 |
| Good worker | 13·7 | 9·2 | 10·7 |
| Generally favourable comments | 39·2 | 28·8 | 32·4 |
| Bad husband | 0·6 | 1·8 | 1·4 |
| Bad father | – | 0·3 | 0·2 |
| Other women | 1·5 | 0·9 | 1·1 |
| Drink/gambling/lazy, etc. | 6·4 | 11·6 | 9·9 |
| Too easily led | 2·0 | 3·7 | 3·3 |
| Generally unfavourable comments | 34·0 | 42·2 | 39·7 |
| Don't know | 4·0 | 3·1 | 3·4 |
| Other* | 19·5 | 19·3 | 19·4 |
| Number of prisoners | 328 | 325 | – |

Totals do not add up to 100 per cent as most men gave two or three answers to this question.

* This category included: 'erratic', 'moody', 'take it easy', 'a rum bugger', 'a bit of a mug', etc.

[1] Paradoxically although many of the neighbourhoods from which such families as these originate are characterized by a high degree of promiscuity, the sanctions against *illegitimacy* are often strong. The results are often to be seen in the form of 'shotgun' marriages.

even more difficult, and it is interesting to note that a great many gave unfavourable views about themselves. The general picture is shown in Tables XIV (*a*) and (*b*), but it is doubtful whether these replies can be afforded much significance. Particularly in relation to themselves, prisoners required a good deal of probing and their negative views may, in the case of men in prison for the first time, have been a genuine expression of their feelings of 'badness'. Where recidivists were concerned, however, we feel it was possibly a deliberate expression of candour which it was thought would please the interviewer. Certainly most of the men did not appear very serious in their self-condemnation and were often proud of their misdemeanours.

TABLE XIV(*b*).   *Prisoners' opinion of their wives*

(*Percentages*)

|  | Stars | Recidivists | Total |
|---|---|---|---|
| Good wife | 21·0 | 17·1 | 18·5 |
| Good mother | 23·1 | 21·7 | 22·3 |
| Generally favourable comments | 67·2 | 60·6 | 63·0 |
| Bad wife | 1·5 | 0·3 | 0.7 |
| Bad mother | 0·3 | 0·3 | 0·3 |
| Other men | 1·5 | 3·4 | 2·8 |
| Too dependent on her relatives | 1·2 | 4·0 | 3·1 |
| Generally unfavourable comments | 8·5 | 18·4 | 15·1 |
| Other* | 23·2 | 11·9 | 15·4 |
| Don't know | 3·0 | 0·9 | 1·6 |
| Number of prisoners | 328 | 325 | – |

* In this question 'other' included: 'moody', 'more intelligent than me', 'a gossip', 'prudish about sex', etc. In general they were remarks which, when probed, indicated general incompatibility of personality rather than complaints about, or praise for, specific behaviour.

As might be expected, the number of negative comments was far higher amongst those who were separated from their wives. Subsequent analysis of the marital relationships of these families suggests that the number of positive statements is unduly high, and there is cause to think that they represent either what the man hopes for in his wife, or alternatively what he thought we expected as an answer.

We sought to know whether their wives were living in their own homes (whether buying or rented) or whether they lived with relatives, or in furnished accommodation, etc. (See Table XV, p. 62.)

The high proportion of wives who were living with their families of origin appears to confirm the material obtained by Young[1] and

[1] Young, M. and Willmott, P., *Family and Kinship in East London*, London, Routledge, 1957.

others regarding the wife's dependence on maternal kin. Other factors which confirm this will appear in those chapters relating specifically to the wives. We did not, however, ask the husbands why their wives were living with their mothers, nor did we ask if this were

TABLE XV.   *Type of accommodation*
(*Percentages*)

|  | Stars | Recidivists | Total |
|---|---|---|---|
| Residential job | 1·2 | 1·2 | 1·2 |
| Hospital (general or mental) | 1·2 | 0·3 | 0·6 |
| Own house (rented or buying) | 62·3 | 49·6 | 54·1 |
| Wife's relatives | 21·3 | 24·2 | 23·3 |
| Husband's relatives | 3·0 | 1·8 | 2·2 |
| Furnished rooms | 2·7 | 4·6 | 4·0 |
| Unfurnished rooms | 0·6 | 2·2 | 1·6 |
| Hostel | – | 1·2 | 0·8 |
| Friends | 1·5 | 3·1 | 2·6 |
| Other | 3·0 | 3·4 | 3·3 |
| Don't know | 2·7 | 8·0 | 6·2 |
| Total | 100·0 | 100·0 | 100·0 |
| Number of prisoners | 328 | 325 | – |

TABLE XVI.   *Number of children by present marriage*
(*Percentages*)

|  | Stars | Recidivists | Total |
|---|---|---|---|
| None | 15·2 | 22·6 | 20·2 |
| 1 | 23·7 | 23·6 | 23·7 |
| 2 | 27·0 | 26·3 | 26·4 |
| 3 | 17·6 | 11·3 | 13·5 |
| 4 | 8·8 | 6·1 | 7·0 |
| 5 | 3·3 | 4·6 | 4·2 |
| 6 | 1·5 | 2·8 | 2·4 |
| 7–9 | 2·4 | 2·4 | 2·5 |
| Total | 100·0 | 100·0 | 100·0 |
| Number of prisoners | 328 | 325 | – |

subsequent to, or before, his imprisonment. These questions were asked of the wives and the data will be discussed in the following Chapter.

The category 'other' most frequently represented a 'tied' house from which the wife was under notice to leave (i.e. police or coal board), or a caravan, usually kept in a relative's garden. Occasionally it meant that the wife was living with another man, though more often such cases came under the heading 'Don't know': the men merely assumed that their wives were somewhere with the other man.

Men were asked how many children they had by their present marriage.

Since only a few men had been living with their wives for less than a year (see Table XIII), the number of childless marriages seems surprisingly high.

About 15 per cent of the men had been legally married previously and were now remarried, and since so many in our sample were separated from their wives, we asked them for the total number of

TABLE XVII. *Total number of dependants*
(*Percentages*)

|  | Stars | Recidivists | Total |
|---|---|---|---|
| None | 1·2 | 14·0 | 10·0 |
| 1 | 18·0 | 16·2 | 16·9 |
| 2 | 24·6 | 18·1 | 20·3 |
| 3 | 23·1 | 21·7 | 22·3 |
| 4 | 19·5 | 12·5 | 14·9 |
| 5 | 8·2 | 6·1 | 6·9 |
| 6 | 2·4 | 4·9 | 4·1 |
| 7 or more | 2·4 | 5·5 | 4·5 |
| No information | 0·3 | 0·3 | 0·3 |
| Total | 100·0 | 100·0 | 100·0 |
| Number of prisoners | 328 | 325 | – |

people dependent on them. We included all previous wives and children for whom a maintenance order was in existence (including illegitimate children, and irrespective of whether men paid it or not), all children of the present union for whom they were financially responsible and any illegitimate children or step-children for whom they were responsible. No one claimed to have any elderly parents or other relatives dependent on them.

It was thought that the reliability and accuracy of many of the data collected from the prisoners would depend upon the amount of contact they maintained with their wives whilst in prison. After the first two months of their sentence, men are entitled to one visit per month.[1] In some cases, where the amount of travelling involved is very great, permission is granted by the Governor to save up and have two visits in one. In practice there appear to be considerable differences between establishments over such matters, though it can

[1] Special visits may be allowed under certain exceptional circumstances.

be said that in general arrangements for visits are far more flexible in open prisons than in closed. A man may be sent to a closed prison as far, or further, from home than any open one, and if this is the case he is usually penalized twice over, by the more rigid system and by distance. Since a wife can visit only when she receives an order from her husband, we asked men if their wives in fact came each time a visiting order was sent, irrespective of how often this was.

TABLE XVIII. *Frequency of visiting by wives*
(*Percentages*)

|  | Stars | Recidivists | Total |
|---|---|---|---|
| Only sometimes | 18·6 | 13·8 | 15·4 |
| Every time | 63·2 | 49·3 | 54·2 |
| No visiting order sent | 18·0 | 36·4 | 30·4 |
| Total | 100·0 | 100·0 | 100·0 |
| Number of prisoners | 328 | 325 | – |

Those who said they did not send visiting orders were by no means confined solely to men who were separated from their wives, although the majority of them fell into that category. Some knew their wives could not visit because of distance and/or expense, and therefore did not bother to send an order, but it may be wondered why there is relatively so little visiting amongst men who claim to get on so well with their wives. A fuller discussion of this matter will appear later in those chapters describing the wives. Men who did not get visits were asked why this was so. Most mentioned more than one reason; the two most frequently given were distance and/or expense, and the fact that their wives did not want to visit on account of poor marital relations. Some wives were said to be prevented by ill-health and a few had no one with whom to leave the children.

It seemed to us likely that wives might experience much difficulty in adjusting *financially* to their husband's absence, and we sought to know to what extent husbands were aware of how their wives managed in this respect. (See Table XIX, p. 65.)

The number of those living with relatives is lower than appears in Table XV; this arises because in some cases, although the wife is actually living with relatives, she contributes fully in terms of rent and keep, so that the husband considers she does not benefit financially from the arrangement. It is possible that this is a somewhat arbitrary view on the part of the husband. 'Other' usually meant that the wife was living with another man. 'Savings' and 'Private Income' seemed often to be euphemisms for 'proceeds of crime'.

It will be noted that only very few men mention help received from welfare agencies, whether statutory or voluntary. This is thought to be because husbands are not normally involved in this aspect of family life—even outside prison. 'I think a welfare lady called', or 'I think she's going down the welfare', are as explicit as they can get; this does not, of course, apply to national assistance or national health insurance.

That only 60·6 per cent should be in receipt of national assistance seems a surprisingly low figure. The number of wives at work corresponds very closely to the national figure: in mid-1961, 35·5 per cent

TABLE XIX.  *How wives manage financially*

*(Percentages)*

|  | Stars | Recidivists | Total |
|---|---|---|---|
| At work (part- or full-time) | 42·0 | 29·9 | 34·2 |
| National Assistance | 61·7 | 59·7 | 60·6 |
| Living with relations | 21·0 | 20·2 | 20·6 |
| Receiving material help from relations | 39·5 | 32·4 | 35·0 |
| Family Allowance | 41·9 | 39·8 | 40·6 |
| Material help from welfare agencies (statutory and voluntary) | 6·7 | 8·6 | 8·0 |
| Lodgers | 2·1 | 2·6 | 2·4 |
| Rent reduction | 1·8 | 0·9 | 1·2 |
| Pension | 1·5 | 1·5 | 1·5 |
| Private income | 0·9 | 1·5 | 1·3 |
| Savings | 14·3 | 6·1 | 8·9 |
| Other | 9·4 | 10·7 | 10·3 |
| Don't know | 3·0 | 10·1 | 7·8 |
| Number of prisoners | 328 | 325 | – |

Totals do not add up to 100 per cent since most wives had more than one source of income.

of married women were at work in the country as a whole,[1] while our figure is 34·2 per cent.

If the husbands were correct in assessing their relationships with their wives, then it was to be expected that few would admit to the existence of conflict within the marriage before coming into prison. Nevertheless it was decided to ask the men about it (see Table XX p. 66). 32·5 per cent of stars and 18·7 per cent of recidivists claimed to have no serious conflict in their marriage; the difference between these proportions is highly significant ($\chi^2 = 16\cdot4$; 1 d.f.; $P < 0\cdot01$). This is not perhaps surprising, particularly amongst recidivists, since

[1] Information obtained from population statistics division of the Registrar General's Office and the Annual Abstract of Statistics.

C

a life of crime, punctuated by imprisonment and economic disruption, is likely to alienate even the most tolerant wife. Approximately 34 per cent of those interviewed said that conflict existed in three or more areas of life.

In the great majority of cases 'other' referred to the wife's objection to her husband going out every night with his 'mates' and/or with another woman. If other women were involved, jealousy was also usually mentioned as a reason for conflict. Significantly more recidivists than stars $[\chi^2 = 24\cdot8; 1$ d.f. $P < 0\cdot01]$ referred to in-laws as a

TABLE XX. *Areas of conflict before imprisonment*
(*Percentages*)

|  | Stars | Recidivists | Total |
|---|---|---|---|
| Finance (disagreements re spending) | 8·8 | 11·0 | 10·3 |
| Finance (shortage of money) | 8·2 | 11·0 | 10·1 |
| In-laws (disagreements *with*) | 15·8 | 22·3 | 20·2 |
| In-laws (disagreements *over*) | 14·0 | 26·3 | 22·3 |
| Work | 14·6 | 22·0 | 19·6 |
| Health | 7·6 | 10·1 | 9·3 |
| Drink | 17·0 | 20·2 | 19·2 |
| Gambling | 5·2 | 5·5 | 5·4 |
| Child-rearing | 9·7 | 8·9 | 9·2 |
| Sex | 14·6 | 7·7 | 10·0 |
| Jealousy | 27·7 | 30·0 | 29·3 |
| Other | 31·0 | 41·6 | 38·3 |
| Number of prisoners | 328 | 325 | – |

Totals do not add up to 100 per cent since many gave more than one answer.

frequent source of friction, the husband mainly objecting to the 'interference' of his wife's parents. Men said their wives blamed them for going out so much, but they in turn blamed their wives for spending so much time with their mothers. This may, of course, be no more than a reflection of a conflict pattern which stems from the structure of working-class life. Young and Willmott,[1] although they do not stress it as a potential source of conflict, certainly report a pattern of separation in leisure activities between men and women; so too do Dennis *et al.* [*Coal is our Life*], Kerr [*The People of Ship Street*], and Bott [*Family and Social Network*]. The inference to be drawn from these writers is that the situation is institutionalized, and therefore to a degree acceptable; nevertheless, the changing position of women may be accentuating the element of conflict which is almost latent in the traditional pattern. Furthermore, it seems to us that

[1] *Op. cit.*

separation of leisure activities tends only to be acceptable if the husband performs his role as breadwinner adequately. A great many men in our sample fail to fulfil this role, as well as showing indications of irresponsibility in most social situations. The fact that they spend their time and money outside the home is bitterly resented by the wives who are then emotionally, as well as physically, deprived.[1]

Since such a large number of men do not work (or do so only irregularly) (see Table II), it is not surprising that this subject was a major source of conflict. In some instances the friction centred round the wife's work, though this was not very frequent.

Drink constitutes an important area of tension, and ties in with 'other'. It is often drink plus the annoyance at being left alone that the wife objects to, rather than drink by itself. However as will be seen later in discussing the wives, drink appears to result in a good deal of assault, particularly of a sexual kind, and the wives are, not surprisingly, frightened by this. Drink is often felt by wives to be a *cause* of crime, and for this reason too is a serious source of conflict; it is probably true to say that drink is an important factor in the reinforcement of criminality, rather than an immediate precipitant.[2]

Despite these figures, however, the interviewer was surprised at the degree of tolerance which, if these statements were true, existed within the marriage. Men would tell long stories of gambling, other women, and general irresponsibility which would lead one to expect conflict but which, according to the husband, his wife accepted and tolerated.

### PRISONER'S PICTURE OF HIS INDEBTEDNESS

Without hire purchase it is difficult to see how the majority of families in this country could manage to set up home,[3] and this seemed likely to be even more the case with our sample, in view of their often erratic work record. Men experienced some difficulty in differentiating between hire purchase and 'clubs' of various kinds when asked whether they had anything on HP at the time of arrest. 'Other' usually covers clothing (although other items mentioned were books, cameras, watches, and an electric razor in one case) and our information may inadvertently include clothing club or mail order purchases (see Table XXI p. 68).

[1] This will be enlarged upon in Chapter IV.

[2] See West, D. J., *op. cit.* Excessive drinking amounted to a serious problem in the lives of 20 per cent of preventive detainees and 40 per cent of recidivists. The majority appeared to be periodic drinkers of the 'symptomatic' type who resorted to the bottle as a means of relieving tension.

[3] Although second-hand furniture can often be bought cheaply, amongst working-class families to buy furniture other than new would generally be regarded as degrading.

According to Table XI over 22 per cent of men in the sample claimed to be living alone, and it is understandable that such men might have nothing on HP. However, as indicated in Table XXI (below) the number of men who said they had nothing on HP was, in fact, 45 per cent; this figure appears very high and it seems likely either that they were not sufficiently interested to give the matter any thought when replying, or alternatively (and most likely) that it is the wives who make all the arrangements—requiring only their husband's signature as guarantor on the agreement—and the husband keeps little or no check on whether goods are paid for or not; thus he was not in a position to say what items were still outstanding. This view was reinforced when men who admitted to being in arrears with their

TABLE XXI.   *Type of goods on HP at time of arrest*
*(Percentages)*

|  | Stars | Recidivists | Total |
|---|---|---|---|
| Furniture/furnishings | 33·1 | 25·4 | 28·1 |
| TV/radio | 17·3 | 16·8 | 17·1 |
| Domestic appliances | 24·3 | 15·0 | 18·2 |
| Car/motor cycle | 19·5 | 12·9 | 15·1 |
| Other | 13·4 | 9·8 | 11·0 |
| Nothing | 38·6 | 48·3 | 45·3 |
| Number of prisoners | 328 | 325 | – |

Totals do not add up to 100 per cent since some men had goods of more than one category on HP.

payments were asked how much was owed. Many had only the vaguest idea of how much was involved and the information collected was probably not very reliable. 21·9 per cent of stars and 20·5 per cent of recidivists admitted to being in arrears at that time; a third of them said they owed sums of less than £10, and 70 per cent said it was less than £50. Those who owed sums of over £100 were usually men who made their living from cheating HP firms, though only very few were in prison for this particular offence (see Table VIII).

A more detailed discussion of hire purchase will appear in a subsequent chapter devoted entirely to that topic, and we only wish to emphasize at this stage that HP arrears were not considered important by the majority of our sample. The attitude adopted was 'if you can't pay this week pay another', particularly in the case of cars, which are of great importance to many of these men as a status symbol.

Whilst only some 21 per cent of men said they had HP arrears, twice as many (42·6 per cent) owed money for other purposes, i.e. rent, fines, money owed to relatives or friends, bills outstanding, etc. Furthermore the amounts involved are often very high, particularly bearing in mind the relatively unstable earning pattern of the sample. Although the proportion of stars and recidivists owing money for purposes other than HP is not significantly different [$\chi^2 = 0\cdot5$; 1 d.f.; N.S.] the *amount* of debt for stars is greater than that for recidivists [$X^2$ for trend $= 10\cdot1$; 1 d.f.; $P < 0\cdot01$]. This is in part due to the fact that many first offenders commit their offence because their business fails and the debts are a consequence of this. So far as recidivists are concerned, debts are usually unpaid fines for past offences, or loans from relatives or friends. Table XXII sets out the reasons for both debt and HP arrears.

TABLE XXII.   *Reasons for debt and HP arrears*

(*Percentages of those in debt*)

|  | Stars | Recidivists | Total |
|---|---|---|---|
| No work available | 6·1 | 6·5 | 6·4 |
| Unemployed (not wanting work) | 3·5 | 5·5 | 4·8 |
| Ill-health | 8·1 | 7·1 | 7·5 |
| Drink | 3·0 | 6·0 | 5·0 |
| Gambling | 2·5 | 3·3 | 3·0 |
| Pressure from HP salesmen | 2·0 | 0·5 | 1·1 |
| Wife's improvidence | 6·6 | 6·5 | 6·5 |
| Husband's improvidence | 15·7 | 17·5 | 16·9 |
| Other | 52·2 | 46·6 | 48·6 |
| Total | 100·0 | 100·0 | 100·0 |
| Number of prisoners in debt | 197 | 182 | – |
| Number of prisoners | 328 | 325 | – |

Apart from 'business failure', 'other' includes: 'they just accumulate', and similar statements; wife maintenance which they refuse to pay 'on principle'; a loan that could not be repaid because they came into prison; or, in a considerable number of cases, the man prefers crime but cannot make a regular income from it so spends a good deal of time in debt. Although drink and gambling are not mentioned very often as individual items, they are often covered by the category 'husband's improvidence', which includes drink, women, gambling and generally 'living it up'.

### THE PRISONER AND PRISON WELFARE

A fuller discussion of this problem will appear in Chapter X when discussing the whole range of welfare services available for the prisoner and his family. We did, however, ask each man whether he had discussed his problems (if any) with the prison welfare officer, and the replies are set out in Table XXIII (below). We excluded from this question attendance on a Board (i.e. Reception, Discharge, Review, etc.) at which the welfare officer would be one of a number of prison officials present and where the principal aim of the Board was not concerned with welfare matters. The question was intended to cover private interviews with the welfare officer, at whoever's instigation. It is also important to remember that in many cases it is possible that prisoners' welfare problems were dealt with by other

TABLE XXIII. *Interview with welfare officer*
(*Percentages*)

|  | Stars | Recidivists | Total |
|---|---|---|---|
| No, don't want to | 32·3 | 33·0 | 32·7 |
| No, no opportunity | 5·5 | 3·1 | 3·9 |
| No, they never help | 5·2 | 15·0 | 11·8 |
| Yes, he is helping | 14·9 | 14·7 | 14·8 |
| Yes, but he can't help | 23·7 | 17·1 | 19·4 |
| Yes, don't know if helping | 10·0 | 8·0 | 8·7 |
| Not yet, but will do so | 4·9 | 8·0 | 7·0 |
| Other | 3·4 | 0·9 | 1·7 |
| Total | 100·0 | 100·0 | 100·0 |
| Number of prisoners | 328 | 325 | – |

members of the staff, in particular the governor, assistant governors, or chaplains. Where such is the case the information is not knowingly included here, though in some instances it may well be that the prisoners were confused about who was, and who was not, a welfare officer.

In general the comments about prison welfare suggested that men had very little faith in this relatively recent innovation within the penal system, and it seems likely that this negative attitude resulted in fewer men admitting to having seen the welfare officer than was probably the case. Welfare officers were asked how many of the men in our sample they had interviewed, and the figure given was 71·8 per cent, compared with 42·9 per cent of prisoners claiming to have seen the welfare officer. Since the welfare officers' questionnaires were completed at a later date, it can be assumed that those prisoners who had not had an opportunity to see him and those intending to do so, had by then seen him, thus increasing the number to 53·8 per cent. Furthermore many men are not interviewed until about a month before their discharge, and this may possibly account for much of the remaining discrepancy of 18·1 per cent.

We have attempted, in this chapter, to give an account of the condition of those prisoners in the study who were serving sentences of imprisonment for a *criminal* offence. There is nothing in the data which was obtained to suggest that this was in any way an abnormal population. They appeared to share many of the characteristics of those unmarried offenders to be found in penal institutions, though they tended to be slightly older than the latter.

The most striking fact about these interviews was, perhaps, the degree to which men in prison perceive the situation in the world outside selectively, and in particular perceive it favourably. They thought of those outside as persons with whom their relationships were, if not good, at least tolerable, though there were of course men who recognized that their marriages were in a parlous state, and who were in no mood to think favourably of their wives.

Although it is not possible to account in all cases for the existence of this roseate picture, it seems likely that the fact of separation itself produces an emotional realignment. Many of these marriages, as will be seen later, were undergoing severe stress before imprisonment, a situation produced in part by the delinquent and/or irresponsible behaviour of the husband, and in part by the fact that the wife had problems of her own which the husband was unable or unwilling to handle. Detention in legal custody, whilst creating many acute problems for the prisoner, at least relieves him of many of his obligations in the outside world.[1] He may well have failed in the past to be a good provider, but at least in prison it is socially recognized that he cannot, by definition, provide for his family, and hence he cannot have his behaviour in this role unfavourably evaluated. Moreover despite the often superficial expression of a negative self-image, there is an underlying tendency to regard himself as a 'wronged' person—one of the results of the deprivations of imprisonment,[2] and in some cases a consequence of the manner of his conviction. The effect of casting himself in a passive role is to create a feeling of virtue; after a while his recognition of his own faults tends to dim and he may come to think of himself as 'not such a bad fellow after all', a feeling which is reinforced by the need, in prison, to put on a 'face' for the sake of maintaining status amongst the other prisoners.

Other aspects of the separation may also be relevant, in particular the question of visits and letters, for although in 'open' establishments

[1] In a number of cases the inability to do anything about family problems itself creates feelings of severe anxiety and guilt amongst the prisoners, but these feelings are often mixed with relief, both because the pressure on them is removed, and because the amount of acting-out they can do in prison is limited by the conditions of security. They cannot turn to crime or drink to relieve tension, and it is more difficult to endanger family relationships.

[2] See Morris, T. and P., *op. cit.*

the position regarding contact between men and their families may be regarded as relatively satisfactory (provided the wife is not prevented from visiting by distance and/or expense), conditions in closed prisons have changed hardly at all since the early years of the century, when contacts with the outside world were considered a *privilege*, and formed an essential part of the system of rewards and punishments by which the authorities sought to control the behaviour of prisoners. The unsatisfactory conditions of closed visiting boxes and the relative infrequency with which letters may be received and sent,[1] or the limitations on length and the necessity for censoring, may acutely limit the sensitivity of response to this form of communication. In other words there are often structural constraints upon a relationship which is already unnatural, resulting in the prisoner not knowing with any degree of accuracy how his wife and family are faring in his absence.

[1] If the limitation on the number of letters allowed each week were removed, it is unlikely that there would be any great increase in the amount of correspondence, since the *majority* of prisoners and wives find it difficult to express themselves in writing. It would, however, reduce the number of misunderstandings which at present arise, by allowing a quicker flow of letters between them when domestic problems and tensions arise. Whilst facilities for extra letters exist—on application to the Governor—this requires an explanation to the authorities, whereas what is needed is the possibility to sit down and write when the anxiety is greatest, and to feel a sense of contact with the other person at a time when the relationship may be 'drifting'.

## Chapter IV

# THE WIVES

As with the prisoners, it is intended in the following two chapters to discuss exclusively the wives of star and recidivist offenders, that is to say, omitting civils; a total of 477 such wives were seen. In eight of these cases the interview was incomplete[1] and will not, therefore, be included in the analysis. Of the remaining 469 wives 256 were wives of star prisoners, and 213 wives of recidivists. Since many of them had been separated for a considerable period before the imprisonment, it has been decided to devote the present chapter exclusively to a discussion of wives living with their husbands at the time of arrest; the following chapter will relate to the separated wives. It will be remembered, however, (Chapter II, p. 28) that in some cases the woman interviewed was a common-law wife and the man had, in fact, a legal wife from whom he might be legally separated, or whom he had merely deserted.

The common-law wives were not large enough in number to treat as a separate category. Of the 256 wives of star prisoners, 215 said they were legally married and living with their husband, a further ten were common-law wives, and there were eleven wives where the marital situation appeared so uncertain as to be described as 'fluid'. They have been included in this chapter because the wives themselves considered the marriage to be still in existence. The total number of non-separated star wives is therefore 236.

As in the case of the prisoners, wherever the overall picture of recidivist wives and star wives is combined, the former have been given double weight. Of the recidivists 154 claimed to be legally married and living with their husbands, nine said they were common-law wives and the relationship of sixteen could be described as 'fluid', but they are included in this group. Thus in this chapter we shall be concerned with the wives of 179 recidivists.[2]

The wives of the remaining twenty stars and thirty-four recidivists will be discussed in the following chapter. Nor, in these two chapters,

[1] The remaining four incomplete interviews (see Chapter II, p. 35) were with wives of civil prisoners.

[2] For the purpose of simplification we shall, in future, refer to the two categories as 'stars' and 'recidivists' though in fact we are referring to the wives of such men.

do we intend to discuss discrepancies between the husbands and wives; these will be dealt with in a subsequent chapter.

In the initial stages of the analysis the replies of stars and recidivists were kept separate, and tests of significance were carried out on the basis of these figures. In the text, however, for purposes of simplification the results of the two groups have been combined unless they were found to be significantly different, or it was felt that to make a differentiation added point to a particular argument.

### BACKGROUND FACTORS

*Family composition and household structure*

Interviewers calling on these families were all immediately struck by the youthfulness of the sample. Table I sets out the age structure of the wives, and it will be seen that for both types of prisoner, the modal age of the wives is between twenty-one and twenty-nine, and over 50 per cent of all wives are under thirty. It will subsequently be shown (see page 79) that the majority of marriages have been in existence over five years, suggesting that early marriage is the norm for this group of wives:

TABLE I.   *Age distribution of wives*
(*Percentages*)

| Age | Stars | Recidivists | Total |
|---|---|---|---|
| Under 21 | 7·6 | 8·4 | 8·1 |
| 21–29 | 42·3 | 46·3 | 44·7 |
| 30–39 | 24·5 | 31·8 | 28·9 |
| 40–49 | 16·1 | 11·7 | 13·4 |
| 50 and over | 8·5 | 1·7 | 4·4 |
| No information | 0·9 | – | 0·6 |
| Total | 100·0 | 100·0 | 100·0 |
| Number of wives | 236 | 179 | – |

Whilst none of the husbands was under the age of twenty-one as such men do not usually serve a sentence of imprisonment in an institution for adults, the same is of course not true in the case of the wives; a rough comparison with Table I, Chapter III, shows a tendency for the husbands to be slightly older than the wives, but presents no unusual distribution.

Whilst it is probable that relatives and friends outside the household of the prisoner are affected in some way by his imprisonment, it is certainly true to say that all those actually living in the household will be affected to some extent. This research is concerned primarily with the effect on wives and children, but others are likely to be affected by a collective stigma, by the attitude of neighbours, by material problems and probably by considerations of what will happen when the prisoner returns to the community. There was virtually no difference between stars and recidivists so far as household size was concerned; 21·7 per cent contained three people and 20·5 per cent four people; 2·2 per cent of households contained ten or more people, and if we assume the figure to be the minimum one of ten in each case the average household size would be 4·2 persons, excluding the prisoner himself.[1]

Many of these households contained parents, siblings, adult children, whether married or not, and grandchildren. Table II sets out the number of children living in the household and *dependent* upon the wife:

TABLE II.   *Number of dependent children in household\**

*(Percentages)*

|  | Stars | Recidivists | Total |
|---|---|---|---|
| None | 14·4 | 14·0 | 14·1 |
| 1 | 23·7 | 22·3 | 22·8 |
| 2 | 25·3 | 23·4 | 24·2 |
| 3 | 21·2 | 15·6 | 17·8 |
| 4 | 9·2 | 10·0 | 10·2 |
| 5 | 2·1 | 6·1 | 4·5 |
| 6 | 2·1 | 5·0 | 3·9 |
| 7 or more | 1·7 | 3·4 | 2·7 |
| Total | 100·0 | 100·0 | 100·0 |
| Number of families | 236 | 179 | – |

\* *All* children in household who were dependent upon the wife at the time of interview are included, e.g. step-children and illegitimate children as well as the legitimate children of the marriage.

It will be apparent from this table that there is a slight tendency for the wives of recidivists to have more children, though the difference is very marked only amongst those with five or more children.

In addition to these dependent children living with their mothers (or step-mothers) 11·9 per cent of wives had a total of 128 dependent children living away from home. Well over half of these were in the

[1] Complete information relating to household composition was obtained, and would be available for further analysis. However it was felt that for the purposes of this particular research the demographic information set out should be kept to a minimum (consistent with the requirements of the research design).

care of the local council and almost a quarter lived with relatives. Only 4 per cent of those living away were in correctional institutions.

Although a record was kept of the religious affiliation of the husbands, this was unfortunately not done in the case of the wives. When planning the research we were not aware of the extent to which 'mixed' marriages might create difficulties. Although we have no statistical data on the number of such marriages, reference will be made later to the fact that they may result in a considerable amount of conflict within the marriage.

The ethnic origin of the wives was recorded, as in the case of the husbands, but was of no special significance; 93 per cent of wives were born in England and Wales, and only three of the wives interviewed were non-white.

Most of our sample lived in large cities, in many of which there are known to be considerable problems of housing. The following table gives an indication of the geographical distribution of the sample in terms of residence, and compares it with the distribution of the total population of England and Wales:

TABLE III. *Area of residence at time of interview**

*(Percentages)*

| Area | | Total population of England and Wales |
|------|------|------|
| Northern | 10·8 | 7·0 |
| E. and W. Ridings | 17·6 | 9·3 |
| N. Midlands | 6·0 | 8·0 |
| Eastern | 1·3 | 8·2 |
| London and S. Eastern | 25·2 | 24·0 |
| Southern | 5·2 | 6·1 |
| South Western | 1·6 | 7·3 |
| Wales | 6·8 | 5·6 |
| Midlands | 6·0 | 10·3 |
| North Western | 19·0 | 14·2 |
| Total | 100·0 | 100·0 |
| Number | 594 | |

* These figures are broken down into the standard regions used by the Registrar General in the Statistical Review of England and Wales for 1961, with the exception of the fact that the whole of Wales is here treated as one region.

These two sets of figures are not strictly comparable, since our own distribution relates to *family units*, whereas the Registrar General's information relates to *total population*. However one might expect any discrepancies of this kind to be equally apparent in all the regions, and the fact that they are not suggests that other factors play a part in accounting for the differences. The most noticeable discrepancy is the over-representation in our sample of families from the East and West Ridings of Yorkshire, and this becomes even more striking if one takes into account other parts of the north, i.e. the Northern and North Western regions. At the time of the research there was considerable unemployment in these areas and a good deal of acute poverty. There is little evidence to suggest that crime is caused by poverty, but it is probable that an empty pocket contributes to it, not only by providing a motive, but by providing the leisure to plan crime with others in similar straits.

By contrast the Midlands and North Midlands regions are under-represented in terms of prisoners' families, although the difference is much smaller. These two areas were conspicuous for their affluence and full employment at the time of the research.

The other noticeable differences between our own distribution and that of the general population are in the Eastern and South Western regions. These are two predominantly rural areas and it is a well-established fact that crime, and the opportunity to commit offences, is primarily a feature of urban rather than rural life.

It is sometimes suggested that a family is evicted when the husband gets into trouble, or as a result of imprisonment, so that we sought information from wives about their accommodation both before and after imprisonment. A total of 28 per cent had in fact moved since the imprisonment; their reasons for so doing are set out in Table IV below:

TABLE IV. *Reasons for moving*

*(Percentages of wives who moved)*

|  | Stars | Recidivists | Total |
|---|---|---|---|
| Could not afford rent | 6·3 | 19·6 | 14·8 |
| To avoid gossip | 7·9 | 8·9 | 8·6 |
| Evicted (non-payment of rent) | 6·3 | 7·1 | 6·9 |
| Evicted (pregnancy) | – | 1·8 | 1·1 |
| Evicted (other reasons) | 18·9 | 16·0 | 17·1 |
| Parents invited me | 9·4 | 1·8 | 4·6 |
| To be near parents (wife's wish) | 6·3 | 10·7 | 9·2 |
| Better opportunities for work | 4·7 | – | 1·7 |
| To avoid loneliness | 3·2 | 5·4 | 4·6 |
| Other | 52·1 | 19·6 | 31·4 |
| Number of wives who moved | 63 | 66 | – |

Totals do not add up to 100 per cent since some wives gave more than one reason.

'Other reasons' for *eviction* referred most often to the fact that the wife previously lived in a 'tied' house, or one which was connected with her husband's job, such as the coal board or the police force. Sometimes it was a caravan on a site connected with the job, as in the case of a chef at a country pub, or a flat over a shop or business. Slum clearance, the landlord wanting to sell the house, or the fact that the children made too much noise were also cited as reasons for eviction. It can be said that whilst the only cases of eviction which occurred *directly* as a result of imprisonment were those where the house went with the husband's job, in the majority of other cases there was some connection, the crisis of imprisonment precipitating the move.

The general category of 'other', although large, was very varied; overcrowding, furniture taken back, admission to mental hospital, condition of probation that wife should return to her parents, wife sent to a training centre for mothers and children, such were a few examples.

However it should not be assumed that because 28 per cent of wives moved, their conditions after removal were necessarily worse than before. A very high proportion of these (42 per cent) went to live with their parents and 28 per cent were re-housed in unfurnished rented accommodation, either by the local council or privately, and in many such cases the physical conditions were greatly improved. The remainder went to hospital, to residential jobs, to friends or to furnished rooms.

At the time of interview 70 per cent of all the wives seen lived in flats or houses which they were either renting or buying, and a further 20·8 per cent lived with relatives. The fact that such a high proportion live with their parents, and in particular that so many return to them in times of crisis, would seem to support the material relating to kinship ties reported on by Young and others.

In general there was very little difference between stars and recidivists regarding type of accommodation, but an exception to this was to be found amongst those who were buying their own houses. The number of star families so doing was significantly higher than the number of recidivist families $[\chi^2 = 12\cdot07; 1 \text{ d.f.}; P < 0\cdot01]$.

There appeared to be a little overcrowding: stars averaged 0·81 persons per room (excluding bathroom and toilet) and recidivists 0·99 persons per room; the national average for 1961 is 0·68.[1]

The majority of families did not appear to be living in particularly unsatisfactory conditions, though it would probably be true to say that where conditions *were* bad they were appallingly so, and interviewers learned to take an old mackintosh with them, even on hot days, as a precaution against sitting on filthy chairs, or suffering

[1] *Annual Bulletin of Housing and Building Statistics for Europe*, UN, Geneva, 1962.

the depredations of sticky fingers, wet nappies, or sick children. Assessments of material furnishings and home conditions were made by the interviewers, and whilst precautions were taken to avoid interviewer bias and to ensure that assessments were made according to the standards appropriate to the usual life style of the social group to which the family belonged, any evaluations must necessarily be subjective. Some 18 per cent lived in conditions of considerable dirt and squalor, though it should be pointed out that such conditions were probably in no way specific to prisoners' families, and a similar number might be found in any random sample of families in the areas concerned. It is noticeable, however, that the domestic standards amongst the wives of recidivists were noticeably less satisfactory than amongst those of stars [$\chi^2$ for trend $= 10\cdot67$; 1 d.f.; $P < 0\cdot01$].

The picture in relation to material furnishings was similar and whilst most families lived in fairly comfortable circumstances, the conditions of recidivists' wives compared unfavourably with those of stars [$\chi^2$ for trend $= 11\cdot42$; 1 d.f.; $P < 0\cdot01$]. It must be borne in mind, however, that a number of wives were living with their parents and it is therefore the standards of the parents that are being assessed in those cases.

It seems legitimate to conclude that whilst a specific prison sentence does not result in a noticeable deterioration in material living conditions, repeated sentences, as might be expected, result in a gradual deterioration of this kind.

It seemed likely that the length of separation from their husband would be an important factor in the degree and type of adjustment made by families. This information is set out in Table V below:

TABLE V. *Length of separation at time interview (including time on remand in custody)*

(*Percentages*)

| | |
|---|---|
| Under 1 month | 4·0 |
| 1 month under 3 months | 16·8 |
| 3 months under 6 months | 19·3 |
| 6 months under 1 year | 26·7 |
| 1 year under 18 months | 16·3 |
| 18 months under 3 years | 13·6 |
| 3 years and over | 3·2 |
| Total | 100·0 |
| Number | 594 |

Eighty-two per cent of the wives interviewed had been married for three years or more, the majority of these for over five years. Furthermore a total of 67 per cent had known their husband for at least a year before marriage, so that the relationships we are discussing in this chapter are, for the most part, of long duration, though as will be seen later many of them had been punctuated by periods of separation, not necessarily associated with previous imprisonment.

### FINANCE

Apart from housing, and very closely connected with it, the biggest practical problem for wives was thought to be a financial one, since the breadwinner had been removed from the home. Wives were therefore asked the amount and sources of their income:

TABLE VI.   *Sources of income*

(*Percentages*)

|  | Stars | Recidivists | Total |
|---|---|---|---|
| At work (full- or part-time) | 38·5 | 25·1 | 30·2 |
| National Assistance | 73·3 | 82·1 | 78·5 |
| Living with relatives | 9·3 | 16·2 | 13·4* |
| Material help from relatives | 51·2 | 26·8 | 36·5 |
| Family Allowance | 52·9 | 63·6 | 59·3 |
| Lodgers | 0·8 | 2·8 | 2·0 |
| Rent reduction | 3·0 | 3·3 | 3·2 |
| Pension | 1·7 | 1·7 | 1·7 |
| Help from welfare agencies (voluntary and statutory) | 46·1 | 37·4 | 40·8 |
| Private Income | 0·4 | – | 0·2 |
| Savings | 4·2 | 1·1 | 2·4 |
| Other | 7·2 | 5·0 | 5·9 |
| Number of wives | 326 | 179 | – |

Totals do not add up to 100 per cent since most wives had more than one source of income.

* This figure is discrepant with the information set out on p. 78 above. This arises because some wives lived with their own, or their husband's family, but considered that they derived *absolutely no material benefit from the situation*, often complaining that in fact it cost them more than would otherwise be the case.

A closer examination of this table indicates some interesting differences between the wives of stars and those of recidivists. In the first instance, proportionately more wives of star prisoners go out to work than is the case with recidivists [$\chi^2 = 8\cdot30$; 1 d.f.; $P < 0\cdot01$]. It also appears that proportionately more stars' wives receive help from both sets of parents than do recidivists' wives [$\chi^2 = 8\cdot79$; 1 d.f.; $P < 0\cdot01$]. The number of women who claim to receive help from social agencies, whether statutory or voluntary (other than national assistance and family allowances) is surprisingly small, and this will be discussed again later in the general context of welfare. At the moment we would merely point out that, despite considerable probing, wives certainly did not disclose all their contacts with welfare agencies when asked the question in respect of income. This seems to indicate that material help provided in this way is not looked upon as a source of income unless it is a regular amount given weekly, although help from relatives *is* so regarded. Similarly items which we subsequently learned had been sold or pawned to add to their liquid capital assets, were not listed under 'other'.

In order to assess the amount of weekly income, only the following items were included: (i) declared earnings, (ii) national assistance (including rent allowance), (iii) family allowance, (iv) lodgers, (v) pension, (vi) relatives (including contributions from children at work and/or ex-husband), (vii) private income, (viii) other *regular* weekly income.

TABLE VII.    *Amount of weekly income*

(*Percentages*)

| | |
|---|---|
| Under £3 | 2·7 |
| £3 under £5 | 15·8 |
| £5 under £7 10s 0d | 39·4 |
| £7 10s 0d under £10 | 27·9 |
| £10 under £20 | 12·1 |
| £20 and over | 0·8 |
| Don't know | 1·2 |
| Total | 100·0 |
| Number of wives | 594 |

Assuming that the wives are representative of those of the married prison population, comparison with Table VI, Chapter III, p. 52, showing husband's earnings before imprisonment indicates that most families experience a very considerable reduction in *income*. It is often suggested, by some sections of the public, that families are better off when the husband is in prison. These figures suggest quite the opposite, at any rate from a financial point of view. Whilst it is true that there is one fewer mouth to feed, other regular weekly expenditure is unlikely to be reduced to any marked extent. It is, however, not possible to compare these figures accurately since 38·4 per cent of men were not working at the time of arrest. However, assuming that their only regular sources of income were national assistance and family allowances it can fairly be assumed that their average weekly income would be about £8. Table VII above indicates that 58 per cent of these wives are in receipt of an income of under £7 10s 0d per week, and this would seem to suggest that many of them must be experiencing real poverty. We shall later be discussing this proposition in more detail when relating income to expenditure.

It was thought that families might underrate the amount of assistance they received from the National Assistance Board, and we therefore checked this information with the Board. Of those receiving national assistance only 4·5 per cent gave inaccurate information, and a further 0·7 per cent of wives could not be traced by the Board. In these cases of misinformation the amount received was usually correct but the period over which it had been received was incorrect. This would appear to be a fairly genuine type of mistake, possibly due to misunderstanding of the question, rather than to a deliberate wish to misinform us. Of those who could not be traced, this situation mainly arose from the fact that they drew their national assistance money under another name due to a complicated marital situation. We found only one instance where the Board was being deliberately misinformed; in this case the wife lived with her husband's parents but drew national assistance in her own home area, leading them to believe that she was still living there. As, however, she continued to pay the rent of the flat, she could see no reason for not claiming as though she lived there. It is sometimes hinted that wives may 'cheat' the NAB, or exploit them: we have virtually no evidence of this, and only in one or two cases did we find wives not admitting to the Board that they worked, or possibly had a lodger.

Any true assessment of reduction in income is, however, a complicated issue,[1] and it would probably be more realistic to compare the wives' present income with the amount of housekeeping money they claim to have received before their husband went into prison.

On the basis of such figures, 55 per cent of the wives were receiving a sum of £7 10s 0d, or less for housekeeping before imprisonment, so that the difference in *their* income [the wives] does not appear to be so great as is suggested by the comparison of Table VII above (present income) with Table VI in Chapter III showing the amount the husband claimed to be earning. This suggests either that the husbands made exaggerated claims about their earnings, or that they kept a rather large proportion of such earnings for themselves, and gave their wives much less than they earned. Data relating to housekeeping allowances before imprisonment indicate that many wives were in very poor financial straits before imprisonment; on the other hand it is likely that their husband paid for a good many 'extras' when at home (rent, and similar essentials seemed always to be paid by the wives), and the above figures represent the basic weekly mini-

[1] For a discussion of assessing family income and expenditure see Grad, J.C., 'The Comparisons of Family Income in Social Surveys' (unpublished).

mum. This was self-confessedly so for the many (usually recidivists) who made an irregular but welcome income by their nefarious activities.

Asked whether they considered themselves financially better or worse off since their husbands' imprisonment, 22 per cent claimed to be better off. However the great majority undoubtedly missed the extras which their husband provided, and this possibly accounts for the fact that over half the wives said they thought he provided for them 'very well'. The fact that more recidivists' wives than stars' wives thought they were better off [$\chi^2 = 7 \cdot 90$; 1 d.f.; $P < 0 \cdot 01$] probably arises because they were now in receipt of a regular income which they were able to control, whereas before imprisonment many of them received irregular sums from their husband, and were often asked for some of it back half-way through the week. Generally speaking star prisoners showed a more responsible attitude towards their work and to the amount and regularity of money they gave their wives.

If these families were experiencing great financial strain it might be thought that they would find it necessary to pawn or sell things: the practice is more widespread amongst stars' wives, 28 per cent of them having pawned or sold goods compared with 16·4 per cent of recidivists' wives [$\chi^2 = 7 \cdot 33$; 1 d.f.; $P < 0 \cdot 01$].[1] About half the goods disposed of were the property of the wife and/or children, and the remainder were equally divided between goods owned by the husband and those that were jointly owned. Most wives had only sold or pawned one or two items, but one said she had pawned two wedding rings (her own and her mother's), six wrist watches (her own) [*sic*!], an electric 'Teas-made', her nine-year-old boy's clothes 'the moth would have got in them anyway' (the next boy was only aged five). She had also *sold* two fur coats (her own), a bedroom suite, bed settee, kitchen cabinet, two other beds, radiogram, two wirelesses and curtains. She claimed to have been evicted by the landlord for owing £200 and had been separated from her husband for six years of a ten-year sentence. She admitted to having been 'on the game' (with her husband's permission) during most of his sentence, and of her marriage said 'We couldn't have got on weller'. Certainly both her own and her husband's interviews confirmed this, though how or why she put up with his continual drinking bouts and affairs with other women would require a much greater insight than we were able to obtain in one interview.

How did the wives spend their money? Rent, rates and mortgage repayments did not appear to constitute a very high proportion of their expenditure: 53 per cent paid under £2, and a further 18 per

[1] It might be argued that this does not necessarily indicate that stars' wives suffer more financial strain, but merely that they have more goods to pawn or sell.

cent paid none. This latter group were usually living with their parents and contributed (if at all) only for their board. There was no difference in expenditure on these items between stars and recidivists.

The pattern of income and expenditure is shown in Table VIII (below). Expenditure includes insurance, clubs (clothing, Christmas, holidays, etc.) gas, electricity, coal, TV rental, HP,[1] credit sales, tallymen and other regular weekly outgoings other than food, rent and rates.

TABLE VIII.   *Weekly income and expenditure (excluding rent and rates)*

*(Percentages)*

| Income | Under £1 | £1 under £2 | £2 under £5 | £5 under £7 10s 0d | £7 10s 0d and over | No Information | Total |
|---|---|---|---|---|---|---|---|
| Under £3 | 2·4 | 0·3 | – | – | – | – | 2·7 |
| £3 under £5 | 5·0 | 5·6 | 4·7 | 0·3 | – | 0·2 | 15·8 |
| £5 under £7 10s 0d | 2·5 | 15·0 | 20·7 | 0·9 | – | 0·3 | 39·4 |
| £7 10s 0d under £10 | 1·5 | 6·0 | 17·6 | 1·8 | 0·7 | 0·3 | 27·9 |
| £10 under £20 | 0·7 | 0·7 | 8·5 | 2·0 | 0·2 | – | 12·1 |
| £20 and over | 0·2 | – | 0·4 | – | 0·2 | – | 0·8 |
| Don't know | 0·2 | 0·3 | 0·5 | – | 0·2 | – | 1·2 |
| Total | 12·5 | 27·9 | 52·4 | 5·0 | 1·3 | 0·8 | 100·0 |

Number of star wives           236
Number of recidivist wives   179

Bearing in mind that to these figures must be added the rent and/or mortgage payments there is some indication that many of these families are living in conditions of considerable poverty, and that there can be little left over for food, let alone household goods and cleaning materials.

Table VI, p. 80 (*supra*) indicated that 30·2 per cent of wives were working at the time of interview. The number who claimed to have been doing so before their husband's imprisonment was 25·5 per cent.[2] Furthermore, whilst the difference between star and recidivist wives at work is significant *during* imprisonment (see p. 80 *supra*), there was no significant difference between the two groups at work *before* imprisonment [$\chi^2 = 1·33$; 1 d.f.; N.S.]. Those wives who were

[1] For a separate analysis of the amount of weekly HP payments see p. 87.
[2] National figure for married woman at work is 35·5 per cent (see f.n., p. 65, Chapter III).

working during the separation were not necessarily the same ones who did so before; 14·6 per cent started to do so only after their husband's imprisonment, and 9·7 per cent gave up work at that time. Furthermore 8 per cent changed from full- to part-time work, and 6 per cent from part- to full-time work, there being no difference between stars and recidivists amongst those who changed.

Changes in work pattern, so far as we can tell, are related largely to domestic matters (and in particular to family size), coinciding with job opportunities. For example if a woman is asked to do part-time domestic work by a prospective employer, and if she can make suitable arrangements for child-minding, she will tend to go. Had no one approached her, it is unlikely that she would have bothered to go looking for work. Nor is the situation static, and an interview later in the year might have produced quite different answers. Data from the intensive sample confirm that those wives who want to find work do so, whereas those who have no such desire find the appropriate means to justify not doing so, depending upon their personality.

Some 60 per cent of those wives who worked were doing unskilled work, mainly as domestics; a further 19 per cent did semi-skilled work, usually light engineering or machining.

Most working wives said that they went out to work in order to buy essentials; some said it was to buy 'extras'. Only 13 per cent said they liked it, and generally this was because it gave them something to occupy their minds during their husband's absence, rather than because they actually liked the work. A very few of those who went out to work before the imprisonment and continued to do so, did so because their husbands could not, or would not, work; one did so 'because the doctor advised it, for nerves'.

Those who did *not* work mostly said it was because they had young children; quite a few said their husband disapproved of their working. Those who went out to work and had children were asked who looked after them, and the replies were fairly equally divided between those who worked only in school hours, those whose children looked after themselves, and those whose children were looked after by friends or relatives *outside* the home. Very few children were looked after by friends or relatives *inside* the home. We had anticipated that more wives living with relatives or friends might go out to work than those living alone. However this proved not to be the case and we found virtually no difference: 34·3 per cent of wives living with relatives or friends worked, and 37·6 per cent of those living in their own home did so. Nor can this be accounted for by the presence of relatives or friends in the wife's home (i.e. parents living with *her*), since we have no instances of this in our sample.

Since certain geographical areas may present better opportunities for women to work, a distribution was obtained by area of residence. However, a breakdown of this kind involved very small samples in many of the cells and we do not think the information of much value. However, it did appear that fewer wives went out to work in the north and north-east of England, a situation which may reflect the fact that most work done by prisoners' wives is domestic, and there are fewer opportunities for this type of work in the depressed north. Furthermore, as mentioned earlier, the question of whether these wives work or not has, we believe, little to do with external factors such as where they live, and is related much more closely to personal and domestic matters.

### Families' Indebtedness

In view of the low income on which the majority of these families manage, it might be expected that they would have a considerable amount of debt. It has been mentioned earlier (see Chapter III, pp. 67–9) that the prisoners were often in debt before coming into prison, and it seemed unlikely that the wives would be able to pay off these debts during their husband's sentence.

Wives were asked what goods they had on hire purchase at the time of interview; as in the case of the husbands, many were confused about the difference between HP, clubs, and mail order purchases. So far as possible only items on HP are included in Table IX, but it is conceivable that under the heading 'other', which mainly covers clothing, some of the purchases may have been made through clothing clubs, tally-men, or mail order firms.

TABLE IX.   *Goods on HP at time of interview*
*(Percentages)*

|  | Stars | Recidivists | Total |
|---|---|---|---|
| Furniture/furnishings | 41·1 | 39·7 | 40·2 |
| TV/radio | 12·7 | 15·1 | 14·1 |
| Domestic appliances | 27·1 | 22·3 | 24·2 |
| Car/motor cycle | 3·8 | 2·8 | 3·2 |
| Other | 30·9 | 39·7 | 36·2 |
| Nothing | 30·9 | 26·8 | 28·4 |
| Number of wives | 236 | 179 | – |

Totals do not add up to 100 since many wives had more than one item on HP

Additional items included under 'other' were: books, bicycles and toys, and in one instance a mink stole, 'because we were going out somewhere on New Year's Eve and hadn't the cash at the time, so that was the only way I could have it'.

Table IX (p. 86) shows that 28·4 per cent of wives had nothing on HP; of those *with* goods on HP, 45·6 per cent said payments were in arrears at the time their husband went into prison, the amount of debt being directly related to the type of goods (e.g. most arrears were for furniture, which was the item most often bought on HP).

If their memory of the situation was accurate, the number of wives in arrears appears to have increased considerably during the period of imprisonment, since 61·4 per cent of those with HP commitments were in that position by the time we interviewed them, mostly for sums of £25 or less. This increase in part reflects their general attitude to HP which will be discussed in Chapter XI, but it also probably represents sheer financial hardship.

The amount spent by wives on HP is included in Table VIII (p. 84 *supra*) showing total weekly expenditure, but we have extracted this item and the following tables show the amount spent weekly on HP according to income:

TABLE X.    *Weekly HP expenditure by income*

(*Percentages*)

| Income | Expenditure | | | | | | Total |
|---|---|---|---|---|---|---|---|
| | Under 5s | 5s under 10s | 10s under £1 | £1 and over | Don't know | No H.P. | |
| Under £3 | 0·2 | 0·3 | – | 0·2 | 0·7 | 1·3 | 2·7 |
| £3 under £5 | 1·0 | 1·5 | 4·4 | 3·7 | 0·5 | 4·7 | 15·8 |
| £5 under £7 10s 0d | 1·7 | 7·9 | 9·2 | 10·0 | 0·5 | 10·1 | 39·4 |
| £7 10s 0d under £10 | 1·0 | 5·2 | 9·2 | 6·7 | 0·3 | 5·5 | 27·9 |
| £10 under £20 | – | 0·8 | 2·2 | 6·0 | 0·7 | 2·4 | 12·1 |
| £20 and over | – | 0·2 | – | 0·2 | – | 0·5 | 0·8 |
| Don't know | – | – | – | 0·3 | – | 0·8 | 1·2 |
| Total | 3·9 | 15·9 | 25·0 | 27·1 | 2·7 | 25·3* | 100·0 |

Number of star wives       236
Number of recidivist wives   179

* The discrepancy between this figure and that appearing in Table IX arises as a result of the confusion between HP, clothing clubs, etc. Items may be included in Table X which are not strictly HP and which are *not* included in Table IX.

Wives were asked whether they, or their husband, owed money other than for HP arrears. The replies were not wholly satisfactory, since many wives admitted knowing that their husband *had* debts, but disclaimed knowledge of the amount. Others said they were sure their husband owed money, but could give no details. Whilst it is likely that ignorance between husbands and wives over money matters is a usual working-class pattern, we think that amongst our sample this ignorance is unusually marked owing to the erratic work habits (and therefore earnings) of the husbands. Furthermore those who make money on the fringe of crime do not appear normally to discuss this with their wives, nor do they discuss the amount spent on cars, drink, and gambling, or other activities in which they indulge separately from their wives.

Sixty per cent of the sample owed money other than for HP, the amounts being in some cases very high—usually for business debts. Although it is noticeable that stars owe much larger amounts than recidivists (average of £141 for stars with debts compared with £77 for recidivists; $t = 2 \cdot 81$ P $< 0 \cdot 01$), this does not necessarily imply a

TABLE XI.  *Debt other than for HP*

(*Percentages*)

|  | Stars | Recidivists | Total |
|---|---|---|---|
| Rent/rates | 21·2 | 23·4 | 22·5 |
| Fines | 10·6 | 24·0 | 18·6 |
| Gambling debts | 0·8 | 4·5 | 3·0 |
| Money lender | 3·4 | 5·6 | 4·7 |
| Loan clubs | 3·0 | 4·5 | 3·9 |
| Insurance | 3·4 | 8·4 | 6·4 |
| Relatives/friends | 18·2 | 14·5 | 16·0 |
| Gas, electricity, food bills, etc. | 19·0 | 20·7 | 20·0 |
| Income tax | 2·1 | – | 0·8 |
| Bank overdraft | 5·9 | 2·1 | 4·4 |
| Other | 12·7 | 13·4 | 13·1 |
| No debt (or only HP) | 40·6 | 38·5 | 39·3 |
| Number of families | 236 | 179 | – |

more serious financial situation for the family. A recidivist offendee with few material assets and irregular work habits may find it morr difficult to repay £50 than would a star prisoner who owed £500, but who owns capital goods he can sell and has every possibility of earning a regular income from his work. Furthermore, many of those with large debts have, in fact, been made bankrupt and are not particularly *concerned* about the fact that money is owed. Some deliberately set out to defraud the hire purchase companies and again are simply not concerned about their debts. Nor are recidivists *necessarily* particularly concerned about debts, though their wives may be. They tend to adopt a somewhat unrealistic attitude, assuming either that by the time they are discharged from prison the debt will somehow have 'disappeared', or alternatively that one day soon they will make a really 'big tickle' and pay off all their debts and live in luxury for the rest of their lives. On the whole it is only when the wives owe money for rent, rates, electricity or gas bills that there is any real concern.

It is interesting to note that whilst there are considerable differences between stars and recidivists in relation to money owed for fines, ($x^2 = 12\cdot48$; 1 d.f; $P < 0\cdot01$) and gambling depts ($x^2 = 4\cdot24$; 1 d.f; $P < 0\cdot05$) there is no discrepancy when such essential items as rent, rates, gas, electricity and food are concerned. The relatively large amount of debt for these important items underlines our earlier comment that many families are in considerable financial difficulty. These are expenses which most of them regard as of first importance when budgeting, and they are not items which wives would tend to put aside and pay reluctantly when other less essential goods had been obtain. The fact that there is debt for these items, in particular rent, usually indicates real hardship.

Approximately two-thirds of those who had no HP commitments were in debt for other items, and just over half of those *with* goods on HP had no other debt.

Thirty per cent of those in debt blamed their husband's improvidence, but if to this figure is added those who blame his criminality, drinking, gambling or laziness, the total reaches 66 per cent. It is probable that some, at least, of those who blamed their husband's unemployment could also be added to this larger group, since, as we shall show later, unemployment amongst these men was often by choice rather than by necessity.

Sixteen per cent of wives said the debts had arisen because their husband had borrowed money to start a business. A considerable number of these men dislike working for a 'boss' and so attempt to set up in business on their own. Unfortunately, even if technically equipped to do so, they are usually under-capitalized and do not have the required business ability. The result is frequently failure, and they turn to crime to try to repay their debts. Other offenders who also set up on their own and often fail are pressed into doing so by their wives, usually for status reasons. We find this happens particularly when wives begin to compare their husband unfavourably with their [the wives'] more successful fathers.

Many wives describe their husband as improvident: 'He just fancied a car and went in and bought one. He asked them to take it back but they didn't.' Wives, generally speaking, do not appear to enquire too deeply where things come from, and many say they are afraid to try and stop their husband getting into debt, since this would be nagging, and would simply result in the man spending more time outside the home.

### PROBLEMS DURING IMPRISONMENT

Wives were asked to say what particular difficulties and problems had arisen (if any) during their husband's imprisonment. It is not easy to say which, if any, of these problems arose directly as a result of imprisonment, but we believe that even where they were present beforehand they were usually exacerbated by the separation. Table XII sets out the type of problem experienced:

TABLE XII.   *Type of problem*

(*Percentages*)

|  | Stars | Recidivists | Total |
|---|---|---|---|
| Money | 44·8 | 39·6 | 41·6 |
| Loneliness (including sexual frustration) | 36·4 | 30·7 | 32·9 |
| Shame, remorse, guilt | 4·2 | 4·5 | 4·4 |
| Housing | 13·1 | 17·9 | 16·0 |
| Children (management or absence of) | 35·1 | 33·5 | 34·1 |
| Health | 11·8 | 12·8 | 12·4 |
| Hostility in the community | 8·4 | 3·3 | 5·4 |
| Fears re adjustment on discharge | 26·7 | 20·6 | 23·1 |
| Fears husband will try to come back | 4·2 | 5·5 | 5·0 |
| How husband managing in prison | 6·3 | 3·9 | 4·9 |
| Other | 14·0 | 10·6 | 11·9 |
| None | 4·2 | 8·9 | 7·0 |
| Number of wives | 236 | 179 | – |

Totals do not add up to 100 per cent since this was an open-ended question and when coding, an assessment was made of up to three of the most serious problems in each case.

A further analysis was made to ascertain whether the type of problem changed according to the length of separation, but this did not prove to be the case.

So far as money is concerned, although the difference between stars and recidivists is not significant, we feel that the fact that more stars' wives cite this as a serious problem ties up with some of the other comments we have made in this chapter. For example we suggested (see p. 83 *supra*) that significantly more stars' wives pawned or sold goods; similarly significantly more recidivists' wives thought themselves better off since they now received a regular income which they were able to control. The fact that significantly more stars' wives both go out to work, and receive help from their parents (see p. 80 *supra*), and yet find money a severe problem, confirms our view that because recidivists' wives are more used to facing financial crises, they are less likely to see money as a problem specifically connected with imprisonment. This is to some extent true of most problem areas as will be seen by reference to Table XII—only housing is clearly more of a problem for recidivists' wives.

Apart from money, the largest problem area for both star and recidivist wives relates to managing the children, or in a few cases to the fact that they are absent, having been placed in institutions, generally as a result of an incestuous relationship with the father who is now in prison. Difficulties such as truanting, enuresis, refusal to eat (or incessant eating), sleeping badly, fretting, clinging, and general behaviour problems are usually not seen by the wives as being directly connected with the father's imprisonment. In one family an eight-year-old boy became very difficult to control when, after six months, he discovered the whereabouts of his father. On being found by a friendly policeman tampering with car locks, he declared his intention of joining his father in prison. Amongst recidivists' families, where imprisonment is often part of the pattern of life, the problem of controlling children single-handed is very real. Some mothers are afraid that the children will get out of hand, and so they become abnormally severe and restrictive. Others give up altogether and simply wait for father to come back and administer punishment, often using this as an [empty] threat. The failure of the wives to see the children's problems from the child's point of view (or to admit to there being problems *for* the child) is perhaps one of the most striking findings of the research, though we are not suggesting that it is in any way particular to prisoners' wives. The problems of the children are seen simply in terms of their nuisance value to the mother.

A problem very frequently mentioned is loneliness, including sexual frustration. Most wives who mentioned loneliness said that they missed their husband in the evenings and at nights, or when the children play up and there is no one to discipline them. 'I miss him like. I was in bed with my sister the other night and I was asleep like, and I forgot, and I said "move over Jimmy", and he wasn't there'; or, 'I get fed up sponging and worrying, down in the dumps, usually in the evening when I've a chance to sit down and think about it. The next day I wonder where it's all going to end. . . . I can never put on no weight. I miss my husband in the evening or when the boy plays up.'

Such wives often express fears that men will 'pester' them sexually because it is known that their husband is away. They say they are frightened to go out in case gossip gets back to their husband. Others are very ambivalent about other men, feeling that they need other men to 'want' them, but fearing their husband's wrath when he comes out. Many wives have fears about adjustment on release, particularly if the husband is a drinker or violent. They are especially frightened of having more children, but are usually unwilling to attend family planning clinics, or afraid of them. 'I went down to the planning place once, but the thing they gave me to wear made me sick every time I wore it, so I don't now.'

Housing, whilst constituting a difficulty for a sizeable proportion of the sample, was largely a problem for two reasons; either the wife was living with her parents and they were not prepared to have her husband there on his release, so that the problem would be severe on discharge; or the wife lived in unsatisfactory conditions—and did so before the imprisonment—and felt that unless they could get more suitable accommodation, her husband would be forced back to crime.

Twelve per cent of wives mentioned ill-health[1] as a major source of difficulty. Table XIII sets out the symptoms of various family members as reported by the wives. They were asked to include past and present symptoms if they were still in any way incapacitating. As in the case of the husband's questionnaire, the category 'highly strung' includes 'nerves', where medical or psychiatric treatment had been (or was being) given. If there had been no treatment, the symptoms were included under 'other'. A great many wives said their husband was 'mad'; however unless he had received psychiatric treatment, or there was definite confirmation of psychosis on his prison record, the symptoms were included under 'other', as was, for example, the wife who said her husband was 'ruled by the moon'.

The figures given show that wives reported considerably less illness amongst their husbands than did the men themselves. We think that there was a tendency amongst prisoners to exaggerate symptoms in order to account for irregular work patterns, and equally a tendency to under-estimate such illnesses on the part of their wives, since they often felt their husband's symptoms were a convenient excuse for his failure to work.

There is evidence from other studies[2] to confirm that so far as illness is concerned, the wife reports less than do individual family members when speaking about themselves.

Table XIII indicates that a high proportion of wives were (or had been) receiving medical or psychiatric treatment for 'nerves'. In the report of the Government Survey on Sickness (1957) referring to 1950, the prevalence of nervousness and debility was given as $5 \cdot 4$ per cent for males and $14 \cdot 8$ per cent for females. Whilst this figure approximates to our own findings for males, it is well below the figure we have for females. Taylor and Chave[3] question the validity of the Government Survey, since they too found the figure well below their own findings; however the problem of classifying and coding

---

[1] For a discussion of illness amongst recidivists see West, D. J., *op. cit.*

[2] Cartwright, A., 'The Effect of Obtaining Information from Different Informants in a Family Morbidity Survey, *Jnl. App. Stats.*, Vol. VI, No. 1.

[3] Taylor and Chave, *Mental Health and Environment*, Longmans, 1964.

data of this kind is difficult and may account for some of the discrepancy.

Twenty-five per cent of wives said that general anxiety was the main problem in relation to illness in the family, and a further 16·5 per cent said it caused additional expense—treatment, diet, hospital visiting, etc. 8·4 per cent said it was a problem because it resulted in unemployment.

TABLE XIII.   *Illness in family*

(*Percentages*)

|  | Wife | Husband | Children |
|---|---|---|---|
| Skin complaints | 3·7 | 2·4 | 0·7 |
| Hernia | 0·3 | 0·9 | – |
| Nervous breakdown | 3·7 | 2·9 | 0·1 |
| Highly strung | 24·5 | 4·7 | 2·0 |
| Concussion | – | 0·3 | 0·1 |
| Chest ailments | 5·2 | 5·7 | 4·1 |
| Epilepsy | 0·7 | 1·8 | 0·3 |
| Tumours | 0·3 | 0·3 | 0·1 |
| Migraine | 2·7 | 3·4 | 0·3 |
| T B | 1·8 | 0·2 | 0·2 |
| Psychosis | 1·2 | 2·4 | 0·1 |
| Diabetes | – | 0·2 | – |
| Paralysis | 0·3 | 0·3 | – |
| Loss of limb or sight | 0·7 | 1·8 | 0·2 |
| Deafness | 1·2 | 0·9 | 0·3 |
| Sinus | 1·3 | 1·8 | 0·2 |
| Kidney disease | 0·3 | 0·7 | 0·4 |
| Duodenal/peptic ulcer | 1·5 | 5·0 | 0·1 |
| Mentally retarded | 1·2 | 0·5 | 2·7 |
| Other | 18·9 | 14·6 | 5·9 |
| None | 50·2 | 59·2 | 82·6 |

| | |
|---|---|
| Number of stars | 236 |
| Number of recidivists | 179 |
| Number of children | 1,495 |

Percentages do not add up to 100 since some people had more than one illness.

Since so many mothers mentioned their children's behaviour as a serious problem, it might be expected that many of them would truant, or appear before the Courts. Possibly because so many of the children were under school age, or under the age of criminal responsibility, this proved not to be the case. Only seventeen children of stars (3·4 per cent of the total at risk) and thirty-two children of recidivists (3·6 per cent of the total at risk) had been before the Courts, the great majority of these having been placed on probation.

Five had been to borstal and one to prison. This latter is a case where the family are extremely well adjusted to the husband's criminality, except in so far as the children misbehave. The wife exerts a great deal of energy in fighting the police on behalf of both her husband and children. Eight per cent of the parents in the total sample had delinquent children who had appeared in Court. A further seventeen children had started truanting since their father went into prison, and four did so both before and since. On the other hand, thirty children used to truant but no longer did so, though it is not suggested that their stopping was connected with the father's imprisonment.

HELP WITH PROBLEMS

*Financial*

The most widely used of the welfare services was, as might be expected, the National Assistance Board. Table VI, p. 80 (above) indicates that fewer stars' wives (73·3 per cent) than recidivists' wives (82·1 per cent) were in receipt of national assistance at the time of interview. The difference is significant at the 5 per cent level [$\chi^2 = 4·00$; 1 d.f.; $P < 0·05$].

Data were collected in order to ascertain to what extent the wives' use of national assistance coincided with their husbands' imprisonment. We found that the very great majority of wives who claim assistance do so as soon as they become separated from their husbands, though in some 11 per cent of cases they appear to have been receiving it *in their own name* before the imprisonment. This is usually because the husband was 'on the run' for some time before being caught, or was known by the NAB to keep the money himself so that payment was made direct to the wife. Where the wife has not been receiving national assistance for the whole period of the separation (5·4 per cent of cases), it is generally due to the fact that she was working for part of the time, but gave up owing to ill-health, children, or some change in the family circumstances.

Of those on national assistance, 28·9 per cent claimed to have difficulties with the Board. The type of difficulties they experienced suggested that in one way or another wives felt they were being treated as though something of their husbands' criminality must of necessity have rubbed off on them. 'Too inquisitive'; 'don't believe you'; 'treat you as though *you* are a criminal' were typical of the replies, though the most frequent complaint, particularly amongst recidivists' wives, was that the Board did not give enough 'extras'.

We also asked those wives in receipt of national assistance whether they felt they were treated differently from others on national assistance, because of their status as prisoners' wives; 11·1 per cent said they definitely felt this and a further 6·2 per cent felt it, but said they had no evidence, while 14·6 per cent of wives were unsure about it.

There appeared to be little evidence of *real* difficulty between the officers of the NAB and the wives, but it seemed that in a large number of cases considerable lack of tact was shown by the officials. One wife said that to go to the NAB made you feel as if you were begging, and she added 'When the man came down and I said my husband was in prison he said "He's not much good to you in there is he?". He shouldn't say things like that, it's not very nice, is it?' There is undoubtedly a great disparity between one officer and another, not only in the distribution of discretional grants, but also in their general handling of applicants. There would appear to be a genuine need for a regular grant for capital goods (e.g. clothes and household equipment) possibly based on the length of separation.[1] Where clothes are given it is for children under school age, and wives are referred to the Education Department for a grant for school uniform. They are often reluctant to ask, however, since they are afraid that the school authorities will find out the whereabouts of the husband, and they feel the child may suffer.[2]

There appears, in some cases, to be an undue emphasis on getting wives, often with young children, to go out to work. This was confirmed in the intensive sample where such pressure was usually unsuccessful and caused great resentment. One wife, aged forty, who genuinely wanted to work but was under medical treatment, put it this way:

'I'm on a book and they come round every six months, just a routine check-up to see if I'm still getting treatment. Some of the men are very nice, but there's just one or two that say "well it's public money", and it makes me so mad. I wouldn't be drawing it if I were able to work. It's just an existence, you get nothing extra. These men, they're just clerks, it's a job for them. I suppose if I spoke to a manager it would be better. This man that came round after my heart operation said he knew someone who's had an operation the same time as me, and was working now. I told him she hadn't had thirteen months on her back or a kidney operation straight after a heart operation, and all the worry with my husband on top of it. He made me depressed, I can tell you, as if I wasn't depressed enough.'

One wife felt affronted when asked to put her new baby 'on the counter' to be inspected to see if she needed 'extras'. We have many such

[1] See Wilson, H., *Delinquency & Child Neglect*, Allen & Unwin, 1963.
[2] This applies equally to free school dinners. On one occasion where a child was being victimized, the headmaster gave out in assembly that anyone found doing so in future would be punished.

examples of hurtful remarks; no doubt some of these wives, particularly those of genuine first offenders, are hypersensitive, but we
believe that there should be a closer check on the way some officers
handle their clients. A wife, aged thirty-four, told the interviewer 'A
man came yesterday from the NAB, and when he was gone I broke
my heart. I'd applied for a clothing grant, I've six children. . . . He
looked at my line-full of washing and he said "It doesn't look as
though they're short of anything".' He added that anyway she couldn't
*need* anything since she'd had a grant of £7 10s 0d for clothing the
previous year!

There are a few examples of wives who say the officers are better to
them when their husband is in prison: 'you don't have to fight for
your money like you did before', or 'the lady seems to feel sorry for
me'.

Most wives said they would prefer to draw their money on a
Friday rather than a Monday—they say it would be easier to plan.
Even those wives who had no complaints were often very reluctant to
ask for extras. A wife with six children under the age of six had only
two beds, but said she wouldn't ask for another 'in case they refuse'.

We found no families getting less than the statutory minimum, but
there appeared to be wide differences over the use of discretionary
grants, including rent allowances. A great deal of resentment centred
round grants for clothing: many area offices sent applicants to the
WVS for second-hand clothing, and this was universally criticized
as 'unwearable', 'fit only for rags', etc. Other areas (the minority)
gave clothing grants, about which there were no complaints.

### General Welfare (*Statutory and Voluntary*

Wives were asked with which welfare agencies they had been in touch.
We have reason to believe that information obtained in reply to this
question is incomplete (largely based on evidence from the intensive
sample and because, for example, families with children in care
would often omit to mention contact with the Children's Department). This arises, we think, for three reasons:

(*a*) A genuine confusion about what welfare organizations do, and
an inability to differentiate between agencies, especially as
between statutory and voluntary. A social worker, from whatever agency, or department, is seen as 'the welfare lady', so that
callers from different departments may often be assumed to
come from the same place.

(*b*) A desire to underrate the amount of help given by community
services, largely because of resentment about the type of help
given.

(*c*) Genuine forgetfulness.

Table XIV sets out agency contact so far as wives were able and willing to tell us:

TABLE XIV.  *Agency contact*

(*Percentages*)

|  | Stars | Recidivists | Total |
|---|---|---|---|
| Probation Officer | 29·2 | 33·5 | 31·8 |
| FSU | 0·4 | – | 0·2 |
| NSPCC | 5·9 | 14·0 | 10·8 |
| Housing Department | 12·3 | 18·4 | 16·0 |
| Almoner | 4·2 | 6·1 | 5·4 |
| Children's Department | 8·0 | 11·7 | 10·2 |
| Health Visitor | 15·7 | 28·5 | 23·4 |
| Education Department | 15·2 | 18·4 | 17·1 |
| WVS | 18·2 | 26·8 | 23·4 |
| Child Guidance Clinic | 0·4 | 0·6 | 0·5 |
| SSAFA | 5·2 | 3·3 | 4·0 |
| FWA | 0·8 | 0·6 | 0·7 |
| Church Welfare Organizations | 5·9 | 7·3 | 6·7 |
| CAB | 2·6 | 3·3 | 3·0 |
| Prison Welfare or After-care | 20·3 | 20·1 | 20·2 |
| Other | 10·2 | 7·3 | 8·4 |
| None | 34·7 | 27·3 | 30·2 |
| Number of wives | 236 | 179 | – |

Totals do not add up to 100 per cent since many wives were in touch with more than one agency.

Of those who had no contact with an agency, the majority said this was because they did not know whom to contact. To the prompt list supplied by the interviewer, 'never 'eard of 'em' was a frequent response. It was thought that the amount of contact might be related to the amount of time the family had been separated and there does in fact appear to be a slight increase in the number of agencies contacted after a separation of between one and three months, but apart from this the amount of use made of agencies appears to remain fairly static. What is very apparent, however, is the greater and earlier contact with agencies made by recidivists' families: the difference is particularly striking in relation to the NSPCC and the Health Visitor. Furthermore those families who *do* have contacts with welfare agencies tend, in recidivists' families, to be in touch with a wider range of agencies. It should, however, be borne in mind that this does not necessarily imply more *frequent* contact; about this we have no information and our data may simply mean that recidivists' families 'do the rounds' and try everyone once.

D

Even bearing in mind the likelihood that the use of social agencies is underestimated, the fact that 30 per cent of wives claimed to have no contact with them seems remarkably high. Their reasons for not doing so will be referred to later.

One of the most striking features shown by Table XIV is the fact that so many wives are, or have been, in touch with the probation officer. Whilst it is true that some of these contacts are necessarily short-lived, since they may have been confined to one home visit in order to report to the Court on the home conditions of a man on remand in custody, or regarding a prisoner's home leave, the potential of such contacts is very high indeed, since probation officers are likely to know a good deal about both the husband and the family, particularly if the man has been on probation previously. Probation officers could form an important link between the two parties during the sentence.

The fact that so many wives are in touch with the health visitor is largely due to the fact that they have young babies and have received statutory visits from her. Contact is also normally made with a health visitor if the younger children are taken to the child welfare clinic.

So far as the WVS is concerned, many wives are referred to them by the NAB for clothing in lieu of receiving a grant. Similarly most contacts with the Education Department are in order to obtain free school meals or clothing grants for school children. As has been mentioned earlier, many more would like to use this service were it not that they feel it may be taken out on the child, or that this would point out their child from others and it would soon be discovered that the father was in prison. Sometimes the Education Department will give some help with clothing, but say that the uniform is unnecessary. Strictly speaking this may be true, but when everyone else comes in uniform, the child that does *not* is immediately noticed and frequently suffers as a result of being 'different'. The pressure seems to be applied by both teachers and other children.

The fact that so many wives, particularly those of recidivists, are in touch with the NSPCC does not necessarily imply neglect of children: we found a number of families where the representative of that organization called regularly in a friendly way and gave advice or help. These contacts had usually started when the husband was at home and might have been reported by a neighbour for allegedly maltreating his children. Although it was also true that a number of neighbours had reported the wives after the husband's imprisonment, in most cases the children were not suffering from any cruelty and the NSPCC officer kept a friendly eye on the family.

Twenty per cent of wives said they had had some contact with prison welfare or after-care, mostly in the form of a parcel at Christmas, or very occasionally help with the fare for a visit. Only a small percentage said that 'someone had come round' at the request of their husband, and if anyone *did* call, it was never anyone directly from the prison, so that the caller could give no information about the routine of the prison or its rules, nor give first-hand news of their husband. This information differs from that given by the prison welfare officers themselves; they claim to have arranged for home visits to be paid to 27·4 per cent of wives, and to have put 12·6 per cent in touch with a social work agency. As mentioned earlier we think that wives certainly underestimated the amount of contact they had with welfare agencies, particularly if, as was probably the case with prison welfare, someone called to see them but took no further action other than reporting back to the prison. This would probably be considered so useless by many wives that they would either genuinely forget about it, or not consider it as a welfare contact. Another reason for the discrepancy arises, we think, from the fact that prison welfare officers almost always use other agencies, particularly church organizations and the wvs, to do the visits for them. In these circumstances wives may have included the contact under either of these headings, not considering it to be part of prison welfare (with some justification). What *is* important is that most wives did not know that there was a welfare officer at the prison. The feeling of isolation and lack of contact with anyone at the prison will be discussed again later; the almost universally expressed view of these wives was that they were left alone and ignored. All felt someone should visit them to see if they were all right: 'They seem to forget all about you when your husband goes away. You hear all about what they're doing for the prisoners, but they don't seem to care about those left at home. I think the Government should help you and give you something, not just *leave* you.' These views, expressed by a working wife aged twenty-eight, are very typical of the sample, both stars and recidivists. Almost half the wives interviewed thought that more should be done to help them, mostly by welfare agencies, though 7 per cent thought relatives and friends should have done more.

Wives were asked what kind of help they had received from the various agencies, and the replies are set out in Table XV (see p. 100).

The category 'treatment' includes such action as taking children into care, or rehousing a family. 'Other' includes visits prior to the granting of home leave, also offers by an agency to try to help but where nothing had been done by the time we saw the wife.

Wives were asked to what extent they considered the agencies concerned had been useful. There was a marked tendency for those who used more than one welfare service to regard them all in the same way, that is all useful or all useless. In general views were fairly evenly distributed, about half the wives saying the service was very useful or useful and half saying fair or useless. There were, however, some exceptions to this: housing departments were more often than not found to be useless, a situation which doubtless reflects the acute housing shortage in urban areas, rather than the failure of individual housing officers to offer help. Nor did wives think much of the children's departments, but again this probably reflects their resentment, or at

TABLE XV.   *Type of help by agency*

(*Percentages*)

| | None given | Advice | Finan- cial/ material | Treat- ment | Put in touch with someone else | Other |
|---|---|---|---|---|---|---|
| Probation Officer | 7·6 | 10·1 | 5·2 | 0·8 | 5·7 | 5·9 |
| FSU | – | 0·2 | 0·2 | – | – | – |
| NSPCC | 1·5 | 3·5 | 3·2 | 0·7 | 1·5 | 1·5 |
| Housing Department | 7·9 | 0·7 | 3·9 | 0·3 | – | 3·2 |
| Almoner | – | 0·7 | 2·4 | 0·3 | 0·7 | 1·8 |
| Children's Department | 1·3 | 1·6 | 4·7 | 1·2 | 0·5 | 1·6 |
| Health Visitor | 2·5 | 13·8 | 3·0 | 0·7 | 4·0 | 1·3 |
| Education Department | 0·5 | 0·5 | 16·3 | 0·2 | 0·5 | 0·2 |
| WVS | 3·9 | 0·5 | 18·5 | – | – | 0·5 |
| Child Guidance Clinic | – | 0·5 | – | – | 0·2 | – |
| SSAFA | 0·8 | 0·5 | 2·2 | – | – | 0·5 |
| FWA | – | 0·3 | 0·3 | – | – | – |
| Church Welfare Organi- zation | 0·3 | 1·5 | 3·9 | – | – | 1·2 |
| CAB | 0·3 | 1·5 | 0·3 | – | 1·0 | – |
| Prison welfare or after- care | 2·9 | 4·2 | 8·2 | – | 1·8 | 4·0 |
| Other | 1·8 | 1·2 | 4·2 | 0·3 | 0·2 | 1·0 |

| | |
|---|---|
| Number of star wives | 236 |
| Number of recidivist wives | 179 |

Totals do not add up to 100 per cent since some wives gave more than one answer, and others did not apply for help.

best ambivalence, at having their children taken into care. The education departments gave little satisfaction, but it might legitimately be said that they had little that was tangible to offer, since their opportunity to help this particular group of wives was largely confined to free dinners and school uniform. Prison welfare was heavily criticized, mainly because of the complete lack of personal contact: visits by other organizations and food parcels were regarded as far too impersonal and failed to establish a feeling of unity with their husband in prison.

At the other end of the scale, probation officers tended to be well thought of, as did the NSPCC. Furthermore, although not widely used, those who had contact with hospital almoners were usually well-pleased with the help they received.

### FAMILY FUNCTIONING

A surprisingly high proportion of our sample of both husbands and wives had been married before, particularly bearing in mind the relatively youthful age-grouping and the fact that they had been living with their present spouses for quite long periods.

TABLE XVI. *Previous marriages*

(*Percentages*)

|  | Stars | | Total | Recidivists | | Total |
|---|---|---|---|---|---|---|
|  | Yes | No |  | Yes | No |  |
| Husband | 8·5 | 91·4 | 100·0 | 19·0 | 81·0 | 100·0 |
| Wife | 8·5 | 91·4 | 100·0 | 16·2 | 83·7 | 100·0 |

Number of stars       236
Number of recidivists    179

As mentioned earlier (see p. 79 *supra*), the great majority of couples in our sample had been married, or living together, for three years or more. In order to obtain some practical assessment of the stability of the present marriage we asked the wives whether either partner had *deliberately* left the other during the time they had been together, owing to marital friction:

TABLE XVII. *Frequency of separations during marriage*

(*Percentages*)

|  | Stars | Recidivists | Total |
|---|---|---|---|
| Frequent separations of more than 1 week duration | 7·7 | 12·3 | 10·4 |
| Frequent separations of a week or less | 1·2 | 3·9 | 2·9 |
| Occasional separations | 21·5 | 26·8 | 24·6 |
| Left just prior to imprisonment for first time | 0·4 | 2·8 | 1·8 |
| Never | 68·9 | 54·1 | 60·6 |
| Total | 100·0 | 100·0 | 100·0 |
| Number | 236 | 179 | – |

It is apparent that if the stability of marriage can be judged by the criterion of frequency of separations, the marriages in our sample are far from stable. This view is confirmed by the replies to a question asking how they got on with their husbands. Although 60·6 per cent of wives had not separated at any stage during the marriage, only 50·7 per cent said they got on very well, or very well indeed. 26 per cent said they did not get on at all well, and 22 per cent described the situation as 'fair'. Furthermore, we have evidence to suggest that there is considerable instability in the marriages of many who have never had a period of separation. One wife who had been married for over five years without separation said she got on pretty well with her husband 'but then I don't see him much as a rule you see—just see him tea-time, and then he's off again at night you see. . . . He wouldn't stay in and watch the telly . . .' After serving five months of his present three-year sentence for housebreaking, his wife found out that he'd been having affairs with twelve or more women and was keeping one permanently in another flat in town. When she thought he was working he was with other women and living off crime. She then started going with other men 'not permanent like', and also started divorce proceedings, but dropped them when her husband, after a long fight, agreed to the divorce going through! Her attitude to the future was full of doubts, 'I'm frightened it won't work out you know and I don't want to add to the family in the trying out process. I've got a lot to forgive him, and he's got something to forgive me, but to be on equal footing with him I should go out on the streets.'

TABLE XVIII.   *Attitude to marriage at time of interview*

(*Percentages*)

|  | Stars | Recidivists | Total |
|---|---|---|---|
| Stronger than ever, miss him a lot | 24·5 | 15·6 | 19·1 |
| Quite happy about it | 47·0 | 35·1 | 39·9 |
| Occasionally regret it | 6·3 | 15·0 | 11·5 |
| Often regret it | 15·2 | 24·5 | 20·8 |
| Other | 6·7 | 9·4 | 8·4 |
| Total | 100·0 | 100·0 | 100·0 |
| Number | 236 | 179 | — |

It is somewhat surprising, therefore, to find that when asked how they felt about their marriage at the time of the interview, so many appeared satisfied (see Table XVIII *supra*).

This reflects, we think, a very strong desire to believe that life will be different when the man comes out. In order to keep going, even wives whose husbands have been inside many times, seem to *need* to think that he will change. It also reflects the loneliness of the wives: even a bad husband is better than no husband. Finally it suggests a great deal of tolerance towards their husband—even if they don't get on, it's better than having no one, and quite a few wives said they missed their husband knocking them about: they were used to it, it was part of home and family life.

This rose-coloured view of their husband *as* a husband is also reflected in their assessment of him in his various social roles. Furthermore, a surprising number of wives who said they didn't get on too well with their husband, nevertheless regarded him as a *good* husband, father, and worker. Of the 54·4 per cent of recidivists' wives whose views of the marriage varied from 'fair/average' to 'not at all well', 49 per cent said he was a good husband, 55 per cent said a good father and 71 per cent said a good worker. Of the 40·5 per cent of stars' wives in these categories, 57 per cent said he was a good husband, 58 per cent said a good father and 83 per cent said a good worker.

Almost all the husbands were considered by their wives to be good friends (of other people), a fact about which they were not wholly pleased, suggesting that he was 'too good', by which they meant that he gave away too much money, helped them too often (even to the extent of helping them to commit offences), and spent too much time with them in pubs at the expense of his family.

The fact that so many wives (81·6 per cent) described their husband as a good worker is, perhaps, the most surprising of all, since so many of the men worked irregularly and, as will be seen later, failure to work is both a major source of conflict in the home and a major source of concern for the future. It can possibly be explained by pointing out that a great many wives who described their husband in these terms, qualified the statement by adding '*when he works*'. Of the so-called 'good workers' the wives themselves admitted that 17·9 per cent of stars and 48·8 per cent of recidivists did not work regularly.

Amongst both stars' and recidivists' wives, by far the most frequent reason given for their husband's irregular work pattern was the fact that 'he doesn't like work'. Some wives said that there was no work available, or that their husband always lost his job when his criminal past was discovered. Rather fewer said it was due to illness, drink, or because he was a professional criminal.

An attempt was made to find out whether areas of conflict were present in the marriage before imprisonment, and if so what kind of situations resulted in friction. We made it clear to the respondents that we were interested only in situations engendering real *conflict*; if behaviour was not approved of by the wife, but she nevertheless tolerated it, and there were no overt clashes, then we did not consider this to be an area of conflict for purposes of this question. We can therefore assume that any mention of friction is an indication of real conflict causing considerable distress to one or both partners in the marriage.

TABLE XIX. *Areas of conflict in marriage before imprisonment*
(*Percentages*)

|  | Stars | Recidivists | Total |
|---|---|---|---|
| Finance (disagreements over spending) | 16·5 | 17·3 | 17·0 |
| Finance (shortage of money) | 19·5 | 34·6 | 28·6 |
| In-laws (disagreements *over*) | 15·7 | 15·6 | 15·6 |
| In-laws (disagreements *with*) | 14·4 | 11·7 | 12·8 |
| Work | 22·4 | 38·0 | 31·8 |
| Health | 10·6 | 12·3 | 11·6 |
| Drink | 20·3 | 32·4 | 27·6 |
| Gambling | 5·9 | 7·8 | 7·1 |
| Child-rearing | 17·3 | 14·5 | 15·6 |
| Sex | 19·9 | 15·1 | 17·0 |
| Jealousy | 20·7 | 32·4 | 27·6 |
| Other | 41·5 | 45·8 | 44·0 |
| Number of wives | 236 | 179 | – |

Percentages do not add up to 100 per cent since many wives mentioned more than one source of conflict.

The major source of trouble under the category 'Other' appears to arise from the fact that the men go out with their 'mates' at night and in general behave 'like they were single'. Also included under 'other' are the wife's objection to her husband's criminal activities (though this is by no means so frequent), and religious differences.

The fact that for both stars and recidivists work is the most frequently mentioned cause of conflict is not surprising in view of the poor employment record of so many of these men (see also Chapter III, pp. 48 ff.). This is closely linked with shortage of money and disagreements about how it should be spent. Drink is an important factor in conflict and is resented for a number of reasons other than the actual imbibing of intoxicating liquor. It uses money which the wives feel should be spent in other ways and it is usually done at the pub or club with mates or other women, whilst the wife has to remain at home with the children (or get into trouble for leaving them). Drinking in pubs is often a forerunner to planning future criminal activities and also leads to meeting other women. Finally it frequently results in the men returning home late and making what are felt to be, and often appear in fact to be, excessive sexual demands on their wives. As will be seen from Table XIX sexual adjustment is also a major source of conflict, partly because wives fear further pregnancies and partly because in many cases the sexual demands of the husband far exceed the expectations of the wife. Conflict surrounding the use of contraceptives is particularly noticeable where only one partner is a Roman Catholic.

A number of wives who mentioned health as an area of conflict did so because this prevented their husband from working, and resulted in his being around the house all day. In some cases it caused additional expenditure, and sometimes the wife considered her husband to be mad and this was thought to account for general dissatisfaction and inadequacy in many aspects of the marriage.

Jealousy was often combined with drink, for the reasons mentioned above. However quite apart from drink, the number of men who freely admitted that they went with other women was extremely high, though this information was not in fact sought from them.

Bringing up the children appears to cause a fair amount of friction, usually because one parent or the other spoils the children. Religious controversy is also a source of trouble here.

In-law trouble more often than not centres round the wife's parents who are felt to be 'too interfering', or to whom the wife turns too frequently. If the husband spends much time out of the home, the wife tends to spend an increasing amount of her time with her parents or relatives and the husband resents this: his wife should remain at home, even if he is out. Sometimes, however, it is the husband who remains very much attached to his mother, and any firmness by the wife (e.g. any attempt to stop him committing offences, or drinking, or to force him to work) results in his returning to his mother, who accepts him back with open arms and does not exert similar pressures.

In addition to asking the wives their own estimation of family

TABLE XX.   *Interviewer's assessment of family relationships*

*(Percentages)*

|  | Prior to imprisonment | At time of interview |
|---|---|---|
| Relationship warm and stable | 43·7 | 50·4 |
| Some friction/tension | 40·5 | 28·3 |
| Marriage on rocks | 14·1 | 15·8 |
| No reliable data | 1·5 | 5·4 |
| Total | 100·0 | 100·0 |

| | |
|---|---|
| Number of star wives | 236 |
| Number of recidivist wives | 179 |

relationships, we also asked the interviewers to make assessments of the position before imprisonment and at the time of interview. In making these ratings, interviewers were instructed not to go beyond the limits of the data, but to piece together in an intelligent way such additional hints and information as might have arisen in general conversation (see Table XX p. 105).

The interviewers appear to see some overall improvement at the time of interview, but it is our opinion that this reflects the wife's *desire* for improvement to which we referred earlier (see p. 102 *supra*), and her unwillingness to consider that problems which existed in the relationship before imprisonment may well continue to do so.

WIFE'S PICTURE OF HUSBAND'S CRIMINALITY

Accurate information about their husband's criminality is markedly lacking amongst most wives. Whilst the majority knew whether or not their husband had had a previous conviction, or been 'in trouble with the police', they rarely knew the extent of his criminal involvement, and they grossly underestimated the number of his previous prison sentences. Table XXI (below) sets out the number of previous convictions (not necessarily imprisonments), as reported by the wives; in Chapter III (Table VII, p. 53) we set out the *actual* number of previous convictions for the total sample. Whilst the two tables are not strictly comparable, we have no reason to believe that the pattern of convictions amongst the 'paired' couples was in any way different from those prisoners whose wives we did not see, and by looking at the two tables it will readily be seen to what extent wives underestimate their husbands' criminality.

TABLE XXI. *Husbands' previous convictions (juvenile and adult) as reported by wives*

(*Percentages*)

| Number of convictions | Stars | Recidivists | Total |
|---|---|---|---|
| None | 48·2 | 2·8 | 20·8 |
| 1 | 25·0 | 13·4 | 18·0 |
| 2 | 8·9 | 7·3 | 7·9 |
| 3 or more | 17·8 | 76·4 | 53·1 |
| Total | 100·0 | 100·0 | – |
| Number of wives | 236 | 179 | – |

It might be thought that girls would not willingly or easily marry men with previous criminal convictions, but this does not appear to be the case since of the 359 who had been convicted before marriage, the wives knew about it in 67 per cent of cases. Many were convinced that marriage would 'change him'.

Whilst 1·7 per cent of wives said that one or other of their parents had a criminal record, a much larger number (11·2 per cent) had siblings in this category. Their husbands, on the other hand, came from families with a good deal more criminal experience: 11·2 per cent had parents with a criminal record, and a further 23·7 per cent of wives were uncertain on this point. So far as the husband's siblings were concerned, 20·3 per cent were known to have had brothers and/or sisters convicted at some time and in a further 10·7 per cent of the cases the wife did not know. Since some families contained more than one child in trouble, the total is likely to be somewhat higher than the wives suggest.

Forty-eight per cent of wives said their husbands' or their own friends had been in trouble with the police, though most counted *some* 'straight' people amongst their friends. Nor was this situation confined to recidivists, and many stars' wives admitted that *all* their friends had been in trouble.

There is virtually no difference between the families of husbands and wives when it comes to mental hospital admissions, nor is there any significant difference between stars and recidivists in this matter. The numbers in all cases are fairly small; 4·2 per cent of parents and 4·2 per cent of siblings in the case of the husband's family and 4 per cent of parents and 3 per cent of siblings in the case of the wife's family. There were a number of instances where aunts and uncles or cousins had been treated, but no record was kept of these; nor were suicides in the family included in our questionnaire, though where this had occurred wives often told us and it might have been useful to ask this question.

Turning to the present sentence, we tried to establish how the wives felt about their husband's conviction and about his being in prison. They had some difficulty in distinguishing between these two aspects of the situation, but we tried, as nearly as possible, to separate the two, and to see whether the type of offence affected their attitudes to conviction and imprisonment. Feelings about conviction were to include feelings about justice of conviction, length of sentence, fairness of trial, degree of husband's guilt and the wife's feeling of personal involvement—not only with the particular crime but with her husband's criminality generally—how *concerned* she is. So far as the question about imprisonment is concerned, we aimed particularly to probe for feelings of shame or disgrace.

We believe from our experience with the intensive sample that feelings both about conviction and imprisonment fluctuate very considerably over the period of separation, and that this fluctuation is not necessarily connected with the length of separation, though there is a tendency for certain feelings to be present both at the very beginning of the separation and at the time of conviction, and again just before the sentence ends. However, in the main, changes in feeling may be experienced as a result of day to day events and matters only loosely connected with the imprisonment, as well as by events which are closely associated with it. For example, if a wife has had bad news from her relatives, or simply feels ill and needs a sympathetic ear, she may feel very angry about being left and feel that her husband has been unjustly treated. Seen on another day when she feels well, and has perhaps had a letter from her husband, or a pleasant visit, the same wife may feel better able to see the justice of his sentence and also be sorry for him locked up.

Dealing specifically with the wives' feelings about *imprisonment*, feelings of shame predominate and 67 per cent mention this, there being no apparent difference between stars' and recidivists' wives. However, we feel that this requires some comment, since interviewers in both extensive and (as will be seen later) intensive sample, were impressed by the fact that so little shame was apparent, and where it *had* existed, it very rapidly disappeared. We believe wives often *fear* gossip rather than experience actual hostility, and they start by being ashamed of what people will say. Gradually the wife becomes reassured; most stars' wives told us that at the beginning they were ashamed, and did not dare go outside the house. So far as recidivists' wives were concerned, shame meant something rather different: the loss of status in not having a man around. Shame, too, is more often experienced for the children than for themselves. Furthermore, there is a difference between shame and disgrace; one star wife expressed it well: 'It's not a very nice thing . . . nothing to be proud of. I'm not *ashamed* of him at all, he tried to do the government [forgery of national insurance stamps], he didn't go around beating up old ladies. There's a certain amount of disgrace, isn't there? I think the war years have changed things, broadened people's minds rather. I don't think people at work [hers] would worry if they *did* know, they're not nosey. . . .' Her description of her feelings at the time of his arrest is vivid: 'Your mind goes blank and your mouth sort of dries up and you can't swallow. It was horrible. I'll never forget it, but you can laugh at a few things now, but at the time it wasn't funny.'

Mays[1] refers to lack of shame/stigma and suggests it may be related to the fact that the families mainly live in old urban areas, where a crime-tolerant and delinquent social atmosphere prevails.[2] The other feeling most frequently mentioned was 'I miss him';

[1] Mays, J., 'Delinquency Areas: A reassessment', *British Journal of Criminology*. Vol. 3, No. 3, January 1963.
[2] See also Chapter I, p. 22, *supra*.

36·8 per cent of wives said this, and again the view was shared by both stars' and recidivists' wives. One wife commenting that she missed her husband said: 'It's bad enough when the Lord has them, but worse when they're alive'.

Many recidivists' wives said they were 'used to it', and about 16 per cent of stars' and recidivists' wives thought it terrible for their husband to have to be in prison 'with real criminals'. This often applied where men were in for white-collar offences, petty larceny and some sex offences, none of which were regarded as really criminal—'it's not like knocking an old lady on the head, is it?'. A number of stars' wives thought their husband should not be in prison, 'it isn't necessary'. Some expect prison to 'improve' their husband, 'prison may make a man of him', or 'it will teach him to shoulder responsibility'. A star wife said it had 'done him good, he's taken his GCE, he didn't have a chance before'.

Further analysis in terms of type of offence showed that the wives of sex offenders tended to suffer feelings of shame and to be pleased their husbands were inside. Shame was also the feeling which predominated amongst the wives of those in for white-collar offences. The wives of those in for murder or manslaughter thought it terrible for him, mainly because it involved a life sentence.

Turning now to the wives' feelings about *conviction*, there are considerable differences between stars' and recidivists' wives. More of the former feel a sense of injustice about the conviction [$\chi^2 = 8·23$; 1 d.f.; $P < 0·01$]. Similarly more stars' wives feel the *sentence* to be unfair [$\chi^2 = 8·9$; 1 d.f.; $P < 0·01$]. A large number of recidivists' wives (55·3 per cent) thought their husband 'deserved it', and 15·8 per cent said they were angry at being left to manage on their own.

In general it seems that there is much more resentment about their husband being caught and put in prison than about his criminal activities. A thirty-two-year-old wife with four children put it this way:

'I've got so used to it by now. This is the third three-year straight off he's had. That means he'll be away for six years, and that's not counting all the two years, eighteen months, one year and nine months and everything else he's had. I reckon I've just got hardened to it. I just wonder how much longer it's going on for, because I can't stand much more. . . . I've wasted enough of my life on him as it is. Everyone here knows all about it, I reckon the whole neighbourhood knows [laughs]. They read it in the South London Press. It doesn't worry me, them knowing. They all think I'm a bloody fool to stand by him. When I went up to the trial the Judge said in Court "How much more can this woman stand? For the sake of your marriage and your wife and child I'll only give you three years".'

Broken down by type of offence, feelings of injustice regarding the sentence were expressed largely by those stars' wives whose husbands were in prison for either a white-collar offence or a sex offence. White-collar offences were not regarded as 'criminal' and sex offenders tend to receive extremely long sentences which wives compared unfavourably with sentences given to men committing other types of offence. Amongst recidivists' wives feelings of injustice about the sentence tended to be felt by the wives of men in for larceny and receiving—offences which did not involve the use of violence and were therefore regarded as relatively unimportant. Most wives of those in for murder or manslaughter thought the conviction and/or trial unfair. In view of the tendency for many Courts to be lenient towards motoring offenders, it is perhaps interesting to note that wives whose husbands were inside for such an offence usually thought he deserved it.

A number of wives complain about the judges: 'he looked tired or bored by the end of the day', or as one wife put it: 'they shouldn't have such old judges'. Complaints about legal aid are very frequent and it is generally thought by wives that you do better if you pay.

What did these wives consider to be the cause of their husband's criminality?

Although the wives gave the reasons indicated in Table XXII, (see p. 111) few had enough insight to know that there must be some *underlying* cause, for example it may have been true that offences were committed when the husband was drunk, but the problem still remained—why did he drink? We feel that although a number of wives were able to recognize the deeper implications of their husband's criminality, they were not able or willing to put these underlying causes into words, since they themselves were frequently involved, for example if they were sexually frigid, or very demanding, or nagged a good deal.

Although so many wives described their husband as being 'easily led', where we interviewed wives whose husbands had been involved in the same offence, the other woman's husband was always to blame! There were certainly many very inadequate, weak men, in the sample; often they took to the pub and to drink for consolation, and there met others, often equally inadequate. With a few drinks inside them they would together drift into some petty criminal activity, making no real attempt to avoid getting caught. A thirty-year-old wife with six children said she didn't know why her husband committed offences:

'I don't know, I don't know what comes over him anyhow. It's just his mates that he goes with . . . he's easily led. They suggest things and he doesn't like to refuse. He did it for me and the bairns, he didn't do it for himself. I blame the NAB this time [second imprisonment], I told them so. What with him coming out of prison and not being able to get a job. And the national assistance gave him £5 to keep us and the five children [sixth child born during present sentence] so Jamie said "don't worry luv, I'll get the money from somewhere", and that was it.'

TABLE XXII. *Wives' views of causes of criminality*
*(Percentages)*

| | Stars | Recidivists | Total |
|---|---|---|---|
| Desire for money (greed) | 17·8 | 25·1 | 22·2 |
| Gambling | 2·1 | 1·1 | 1·5 |
| Drink | 11·4 | 24·0 | 19·0 |
| Easily led | 28·8 | 32·9 | 31·2 |
| Ill-health | 4·2 | 3·3 | 3·7 |
| No work available | 0·8 | 2·8 | 2·0 |
| Lazy | 1·3 | 6·7 | 4·5 |
| Professional or habitual criminal | 0·8 | 12·8 | 8·1 |
| To help family | 12·7 | 15·1 | 14·1 |
| Unable to earn enough | 3·8 | 3·9 | 3·9 |
| Unsatisfactory childhood | 8·5 | 11·2 | 10·1 |
| Wife's fault (too demanding) | 10·6 | 3·3 | 6·2 |
| Sexual aberration | 3·8 | 0·6 | 1·8 |
| Family relationships generally | 11·0 | 5·6 | 7·7 |
| Cannot keep a job because of criminal past | – | 4·5 | 2·7 |
| Mental instability | 8·9 | 7·8 | 8·2 |
| Business failure | 3·0 | 0·6 | 1·5 |
| Don't know | 8·9 | 5·6 | 6·9 |
| Has not done wrong | 7·2 | 4·5 | 5·5 |
| Other | 16·1 | 7·8 | 11·1 |
| Number of wives | 236 | 179 | – |

Percentages do not add up to 100 per cent because most wives gave more than one reason.

A twenty-three-year-old wife with three children and a very inadequate husband thought maybe he preferred prison:

'I've no idea, I think it must be something that comes over him. What makes me think that was when they came for him at twelve at night and took him for questioning, and when I went down he had a strange expression on his face, as though he was pleased with himself for getting back in. He did me mum's electric meter and my gas meter, and while he was out he took £17 from his aunty's. I don't know what he did with it, I never saw any of it.'

One small, but possibly interesting, fact emerged on both the extensive and intensive samples, namely the number of husbands who go into prison as their wives approach the end of a pregnancy.[1] It seems as though they are unable to tolerate the additional responsibility that the birth may bring with it.

If men are to return to their families and to resume marital relations, there can be no doubt that the amount and degree of contact they maintain with their family will be of great importance in deciding the pattern of the marriage in the immediate future;[2] one of the major complaints of the wives was that they knew so little of what was *happening* to their husband. It might also be thought that the maintenance of good communications between husband and wife would result in the husbands having a more accurate knowledge about how their wives were managing at home. It became apparent in the course of our interviews that, in view of the very long distances which many wives have to travel in order to see their husbands, there was not *necessarily* any connection between marital disharmony and failure to visit. There was little apparent difference between stars' and recidivists' wives in the matter of visiting; 60 per cent said they went every time their husband sent a visiting order, 34 per cent said they did not, and 6 per cent said their husband sent no orders. The fact that he did not do so did not necessarily indicate an unwillingness to see his wife, merely a recognition of the fact that circumstances made it impossible for her to visit, and such men usually claimed an additional letter in lieu of a visit.

The primary reason for not visiting was the expense involved, though distance alone was a factor when it involved travelling with many young children. Only $11 \cdot 4$ per cent of all wives said it was because they preferred not to.

At the time of the research, the NAB was empowered to make a grant for a visit once every six months (this has since been increased to once a quarter), but the grant is a discretionary one, and although we do not know of any cases where wives did not receive such a grant on application, we did find that many wives (and husbands) were unaware of these facilities. We were also told that in some instances the number of children for whom grants could be issued for visiting was limited. Visitors from London to the open prison at Leyhill (Glos.) are well-served by a coach which makes the journey weekly at a very reduced price, but this is unfortunately an exception, and although the price is modest compared with normal means of travel, it must still be exorbitant to some wives (£1 return). Visits to some

---

[1] See Blood, R. O., 'Resolving Family Conflicts', *Jnl. of Conflict Resolution*, June 1960, pp. 209–19.

[2] A further discussion of visiting appears in Chapter X dealing with welfare, pp. 259 ff.

prisons, in particular The Verne at Portland, were often almost impossible, particularly if a cross-country journey at the home end were also involved, or if there were a number of young children to be taken, or found a home for the day (and night since many return journeys could not be undertaken in a day). For a few wives this was the greatest problem of the imprisonment; one, for example, who had to travel from Hertfordshire to Lancashire, thought that it was the two-and-a-half-year-old boy who suffered most from not seeing his dad. Living on national assistance of £5 17s 6d a week and with a rent of £2 12s 8d per week, she found the journey impossible except when the NAB paid. This is only one of the extremely large number of similar cases, and whilst the majority of wives had larger general problems to contend with, many of them felt very strongly about the inability to visit their husband once a month as the regulations permit.

In open and medium security prisons, facilities for visits are often such that once there, wives can spend a considerable amount of time with their husband in relatively pleasant surroundings. This is not the case for the majority, however, particularly in closed institutions where pressure of visits, especially at week-ends, is such that no additional time can be granted, however great the distance travelled. It is sometimes possible to have 'two visits in one' if a wife has far to come, but this then means a gap of two months without a visit.

We have also come across a few women who have genuine fears and phobias about travelling on trains and coaches, and who never visit their husband if he is transferred to a distant prison. Arrangements for transfer on compassionate grounds seem to vary considerably between different institutions. There are some governors who will informally ring up the governor of a similar type of institution in another part of the country, to enquire whether an 'exchange' can be arranged in order to place a man nearer his home. However, the greatest unhappiness results from the 'bulk' transfer system, whereby large numbers of men are sent from one establishment to another, merely to ease over-crowding, and with little consideration of domestic issues. Once there, a man finds it very difficult to get nearer home again. Welfare officers sometimes go to considerable lengths to help, but are successful only in relatively few cases. A petition has to be submitted to the Home Secretary and is accompanied by the comments of a governor or assistant governor. Even if, as seems usual, the man's story is confirmed by the prison authorities, there is generally a paragraph to the effect that the man's training and rehabilitation will *not* be affected by his staying in the present establishment, and this seems often to be the critical factor when a final decision is made by the Home Office.

Wives bitterly resent the 'closed' visiting conditions still so prevalent. Speaking through a glass partition is felt to be degrading as well as not being conducive to a pleasant atmosphere. There was one particular exception to complaints regarding visits: conditions at Wakefield prison were very greatly appreciated.

One star wife, living in Cheshire, whose husband was in prison in Gloucestershire asked: 'why should *my* husband be all that way away so that I can only visit him every six months? This chap [recidivist] who was in it with him has only gone to Stafford and his wife only pays 6s 9d fare to go, *and* she gets a long visit.' A wife whose husband had been transferred from Wormwood Scrubs to an open prison far away described visiting conditions in the London prison as 're- volting . . . dirty desks and dirty floors. And there were hundreds of women in the waiting-room and only *one* lavatory and no hand basin. After all the government pressure about hand-washing and polio. And it couldn't cost much to put a mirror up. A woman wants to look something when she goes up there. And the warders can be so rude and tough to the visitors—why be unpleasant to visitors? It's like martial law there . . . I was terrified.'

Most wives who visit their husbands take the children with them, though not always *all* the children are taken each time. Only 14·8 per cent of wives never took their children. In the main this was because the parents considered visiting conditions in closed insti- tutions to be unsatisfactory, this may occur even when the children concerned *know* their father is in prison.

Thirty-eight per cent of wives said that their children had no idea that their father was in prison, a further 12 per cent said that only the older children knew, and 2 per cent said they were doubtful. Bearing in mind that many children can read simple words by the age of five, and since the word 'PRISON' in capital letters is written outside the entrance to each establishment, it seems unlikely that so many children are in fact, wholly ignorant. The effect of this pretence is two-fold: children have to repress their feelings about their father, and at the same time have to support the mother when she invents reasons for his absence. One mother said her boy thought his father was 'a sheriff in a toy shop' because, as a first offender, he wore a red star on his uniform sleeve. (This despite the fact that the prison was a maximum security establishment with massive front entrance and locked doors throughout.) Another mother said her child thought his father was 'at school, learning to be clever'. Five-year- olds are often puzzled by uniforms and keys, but 'awkward' questions are answered by a simple denial.

As might be expected from children who show frequent signs of disturbed behaviour (see Table XII, p. 90 *supra*) most of them miss their father a great deal, and talk about him a lot. A fair number (9 per cent) fret inwardly and miss their father, but are reluctant to talk about him. Most of those who did not want him back (4 per cent), or seemed uninterested (9 per cent) were cases where the father was in prison for incest or sexual assault on the child concerned.

The majority of wives (80 per cent) said they wrote to their husband weekly—the maximum permitted. 4·2 per cent wrote fortnightly and 8·2 per cent never wrote; the remainder were irregular correspondents. Wives greatly resented the fact that their husband could only write one letter a week, since this often created difficulties with in-laws. They felt a man should be allowed to correspond with both wife and parents without one or the other being deprived. There was also some resentment (though much less acute) about censorship of letters, one wife commenting 'The Governor himself reads all the letters and I wish he'd be quicker about it'.

### CONTACTS IN THE COMMUNITY

Data appearing in the early part of this chapter indicate that wives appear to get a great deal of financial and material support from their families, in many cases living with them. We found, however, that this was not always indicative of good relationships between them, since parents often gave such help, but remained (or became) hostile towards their son-in-law. One mother for example, whose daughter lived with her, became very unpleasant after the husband's imprisonment and charged 25 per cent interest on the money borrowed by her daughter in order to visit the husband.

A wife aged twenty-six with two children under five lived with her mother and three siblings, none of whom would speak to her. They were not on good terms before the imprisonment, but the parents had become more unpleasant since, despite the fact that the daughter paid £3 for being there. Her in-laws, too, refused to have anything to do with her, or her husband, since the arrest, 'I've got no company at all. Sometimes I go to bed at 7.30 now I've got no one to talk to.' The mother does not want her there and completely refuses to have the husband there on discharge. It was, in fact, because of the impossible housing situation that the wife 'allowed' her husband to commit his offence in order to try and get £100 key money. Unfortunately for them he was caught and the wife now feels very guilty; he got a one-year sentence although it was his first offence and she had expected he would get put on probation. Not all parent/child relationships are as bad as these cases; even amongst hostile parents the majority are more subtle, and whilst giving a great deal of support and help, exert a good deal of pressure on their daughter to leave her husband. It was often difficult for wives to answer questions about their relationships with parents (and to a lesser extent with in-laws)

since there was a great deal of ambivalence in the relationship.
Bearing in mind that the answers are greatly over-simplified, the
following table gives some indication of their own assessment of their
relationships in the community.

TABLE XXIII. *Relationships in community (stars and recidivists combined)*

*(Percentages)*

| | Sympathetic/helpful, generally favourable comments | Unsympathetic/ hostile, generally unfavourable comments | Don't know husband in prison | Does* not apply |
|---|---|---|---|---|
| Own parents | 62·0 | 12·6 | 4·0 | 22·5 |
| Siblings | 69·2 | 11·9 | 7·9 | 15·3 |
| In-laws | 44·5 | 25·9 | 5·7 | 25·5 |
| Friends | 73·1 | 9·4 | 5·4 | 19·0 |
| Neighbours | 59·8 | 20·8 | 15·1 | 16·6 |
| Minister of Religion | 17·6 | 1·8 | 30·2 | 43·7 |

Number of star wives 236
Number of recidivist wives 179

* No contact before or since imprisonment.
Totals do not add up to 100 per cent since, where more than one person is
involved, i.e. parents, siblings, etc. they may have different views and this fact
has been recorded in both columns.

We frequently found it difficult to separate the categories 'neighbours' and 'friends': in some cases the two were identical, in others
the wives did not really know what was meant by the term 'friend'.
One woman, when asked if her husband was a good friend replied 'he
hasn't any friends, I'm his friend'. In general wives seemed to feel
that they were friends if they stuck by you, hence the large number
who said they were friendly and sympathetic: had they not done so,
there was a tendency no longer to see them as friends. On the other
hand, a great many said that they had no friends. We also found
that hostile behaviour and lack of sympathy by immediate *neighbours*
was far more wounding than similar attitudes from others; this
arises from the fact that the neighbours are, by definition, there all
the time—next door—you cannot avoid them, so that the influence
they have on your day-to-day life is in some respects greater than that
of relatives and friends.

One wife complained that if your husband is a criminal, the
neighbours often think you are too. On one occasion a neighbour's
child fell over and our interviewee bandaged her leg, only to hear the
child's mother say to another neighbour 'You wouldn't think that
sort of person would act like that'. And the wife commented to the
interviewer, 'You'd think I was going to let her bleed'.

An attempt was made to try to compare the amount of social activity in which wives were engaged before imprisonment with the amount and type of activity at the time of interview. In this we were not wholly successful however, since most wives were unable to give an adequate account of their activities before the separation. The data which follow, therefore, whilst based on the information collected from direct questions on the subject, are supplemented by impressions gained from general statements made during the interview, and are not really suitable for statistical analysis.

About 8 per cent of families in the sample appeared, before imprisonment, never to go out anywhere and to have no social contacts. The imprisonment of the husband now meant that quite a number of these wives were able to go out, having been prevented previously by their husbands' refusal to allow it. In general there was a very considerable reduction in such activities as going to the pub, to clubs, and dancing, and a marked increase in home-centred activities, such as talking to neighbours, watching television, knitting or sewing. There was also an increased amount of visiting of family and friends, and relatively little change in the amount of cinema-going. A little over 17 per cent of wives said they now attended church functions and about 42 per cent regularly went to Bingo. 7 per cent of wives attended concerts or lectures from time to time.

What seems to be important, however, is the degree to which particular wives felt isolated or otherwise. We interviewed a number of women who contrived to lead a quite active (if somewhat reduced) social life and yet who felt lonely and isolated by comparison with the past. Others whom we interviewed, seemed content to remain quietly at home and appeared not to suffer from lack of communication and social activity. So many wives complained that their husband took them out only once a week, if at all (whereas the men themselves went out nightly), so that they were used to being left at home. It seemed, however, that they nevertheless felt very lonely, because when not in prison their husband turned up some time during the night, and at week-ends; now they had no one even to wait for.

## THE FUTURE

How did these wives see the future, what hopes did they have for their husband so far as criminality was concerned, and what hopes for their marriage?

It has been suggested earlier that many wives see their husband in a very positive way when he is absent, and need to feel that all will be well when he returns. Bearing in mind that so many recidivists in the sample (and a considerable number of stars) had a long history of criminal activity, it is perhaps surprising to find that 36·5 per cent of wives of *recidivist* prisoners claimed to be sure that their husband would 'go straight' on discharge. A further 33·5 per cent were unsure and 16·8 per cent of such wives were certain he would get into trouble again. 70·3 per cent of stars' wives were sure *their* husband would 'go straight'.

Wives were asked whether they would have their husband home on release. Many who replied 'yes' said that this was a decision which had been reached after a lot of wavering, and it seemed likely that many would continue to waver until the man was released. A young common-law wife of nineteen explained:

'I'm going with someone else at the moment, and my parents think a lot of him . . . you see they'll cut me off if I go back to Jim. There's no future in it for me with Jim. He says he's got a divorce coming through but I don't know for sure . . . then again it would be three years for the divorce, and he's got no one else to turn to. I'm the only one he's got . . . I wish there was some future for me with him because I still think a lot of him . . . I don't know what the right thing to do is. My mother would like me to marry Harry, the lad I'm going with. I like Harry a lot, but if I married him I'd always have Jim on my mind, wondering whether I should have waited for him. I wrote to him on Sunday saying I thought it would be better not to see him again. I don't know how he's took it, I know he'll of took it bad, but I don't know how bad. I wouldn't like to hurt his feelings in any way. My parents liked him at first and even offered to help pay for the divorce, but I let them down by going to live with Jim, and then when he got into trouble, that finished it. I've got no one to talk to, I'm really confused . . . there's Jim pulling on one side and my family on the other, and there's Harry wanting me to stay with him. I think I worry too much about things . . . I worry about hurting people so I finish up with *nobody*, and it's *me* who gets hurt in the end.'

We felt fairly confident that in the great majority of cases the wives would in fact have their husbands back, largely because the decision *not* to have them back is so much more difficult to make. There were some who said they would have their husband back under certain conditions (only in one instance was this conditional upon their moving from the district), but again we felt these 'ifs' to be somewhat unrealistic, and it would probably be justifiable to add them to the 'yes's'. It had been thought that the type of offence might affect any decision about the future, and this information is set out in Tables XXIV (*a*) and (*b*) below.

Although many men were in prison for more than one offence, in considering their wives' attitude to the future in these tables we have taken only the most serious offence in each case. Furthermore, in some cases the total number of offences is so small that too much weight cannot be given to the results. However, there is no significant difference between stars' and recidivists' wives in their general willingness to have their husband back [$X^2$ for trend = 3·24; 1 d.f.; N.S.], nor is there any significant difference between the two groups of

TABLE XXIV(a). *Willingness of stars' wives to have husband home by type of offence*

(*Percentages of each type of offence*)

|  | Yes | No | Don't know | Total | No. of offences |
|---|---|---|---|---|---|
| Murder/manslaughter | 80·0 | 10·0 | 10·0 | 100·0 | 10 |
| Sex offences | 82·5 | 15·0 | 2·5 | 100·0 | 40 |
| Offences with violence | 88·4 | 8·3 | 3·2 | 100·0 | 96 |
| Offences without violence | 86·2 | 9·3 | 4·6 | 100·0 | 43 |
| White collar offences | 100·0 | – | – | 100·0 | 40 |
| Motoring offences | 85·7 | – | 14·3 | 100·0 | 7 |

Number of wives   236

TABLE XXIV(b). *Willingness of recidivists' wives to have husband home by type of offence*

(*Percentages of each type of offence*)

|  | Yes | No | Don't know | Total | No. of offences |
|---|---|---|---|---|---|
| Murder/manslaughter | 100·0 | – | – | 100·0 | 4 |
| Sex offences | 50·0 | 50·0 | – | 100·0 | 20 |
| Offences with violence | 85·4 | 11·5 | 3·1 | 100·0 | 192 |
| Offences without violence | 76·0 | 16·0 | 8·0 | 100·0 | 50 |
| White collar offences | 91·4 | 8·6 | – | 100·0 | 70 |
| Motoring offences | 81·8 | 18·2 | – | 100·0 | 22 |

Number of wives   179

wives when the type of offence is taken into consideration. Even in the case of sex offenders, where there would appear to be some difference, this is not significant [$\chi^2 = 3·64$; 1 d.f.; N.S.].

Bearing in mind the amount of conflict which existed in the marriage before imprisonment, we wanted to know what wives felt would be the greatest difficulty for *them* when their husbands returned (see Table XXV p. 120).

Although so many wives mentioned drink as a contributory factor both to conflict within the marriage (Table XIX, p. 104), and to criminality (Table XXII, p. 111), it is noticeable that relatively few of them consider that their husbands' drinking will be an important problem for them on discharge. However, we believe that in this question drink has been recognized as a contributory factor to bad marital adjustment, bad family relationships, and poor work record, etc., and that therefore those items have been mentioned more frequently than has drink alone. Once again the problem of work is far and away the largest single problem, over 29 per cent;

TABLE XXV.   *Greatest problem for wife on discharge*

(*Percentages*)

|  | Stars | Recidivists | Total |
|---|---|---|---|
| Husbands' work | 33·0 | 27·3 | 29·6 |
| Marital adjustment | 18·2 | 14·0 | 15·6 |
| Family relationships generally* | 12·3 | 8·9 | 10·2 |
| Debt | 3·4 | 3·9 | 3·7 |
| Drink | 0·8 | 6·1 | 4·0 |
| Gambling | 0·4 | 0·6 | 0·5 |
| Housing | 5·5 | 11·7 | 9·2 |
| In-laws | 0·4 | – | 0·2 |
| Wife wanting divorce | 5·9 | 11·7 | 9·4 |
| Other† | 11·4 | 18·4 | 15·6 |
| No problems | 16·1 | 10·0 | 12·4 |
| Wife not affected (won't have husband back) | 1·3 | 1·1 | 1·2 |

Number of star wives      236
Number of recidivist wives   179

Totals do not add up to 100 per cent since some wives mentioned two problems of equal severity, usually linked.
* This refers to relationships outside the marital one, i.e. involving other family members, usually children.
† Most frequently fears that husband will insist on returning and will injure them.

wives feel that if only their husbands worked regularly, most of their problems would be solved. One twenty-five-year-old wife commented that the greatest problem for *her* was 'finding something for him to do with his time until he gets a job. He misses the company at the prison very much.'

Marital adjustment is a very important aspect of the discharge situation and one which is possibly not greatly considered by social workers who may be in touch with the prisoners or their families. There is a tendency to concentrate on the practical problems: job and money, and whilst these are obviously of great importance, it is probably unwise to treat them in isolation from family, and in particular marital, relationships. Previous research experience in prison and in similar situations of separation such as the army had suggested that men experience very considerable doubts and fears about the sexual side of marriage on discharge, and our evidence is that these fears and anxieties are paralleled in the wives. Closely associated with these fears of sexuality, there is often the feeling that they will be like strangers to each other. This is particularly true of some stars' wives who feel they have learnt to manage on their own and acquired a new independence which was quite unexpected; they are concerned about giving this up when their husband returns. There is also much anxiety about how the children will react, even those who miss their father a great deal: they may resent his return, especially if they have been sleeping in a bed with their mother, or if there has been any sexual relationship between father and child. In many cases of incest the child has been removed from the home, but this is not necessarily the answer, since wives often want both their husband and their child at home. One wife whose husband was in prison for interfering sexually with his twelve-year-old step-daughter said she wanted him back, but added 'the law says he can't come. If there's any way round it, I'll have him back'. For her, the worst problem would be 'knowing he's free, and not knowing whether I can be with him. I know I *can't* be now, but when he's free and moving about . . .'

Wives were fairly evenly divided about whether they would, or would not, need help from an after-care organization when their husband came out. If help *were* needed, it was largely felt to be in order to assist him to find work. Many said 'no' because of their previous unsatisfactory experience with after-care organizations and about 21 per cent said they didn't know anything about such organizations. Others who said 'yes', felt they wanted someone to 'steer him right'.

The following case history is included not because it is particularly typical, but because it illustrates so many of the difficulties and problems that have been discussed in this chapter and of which a few, at least, are present in almost all our families. More particularly it illustrates the indecision and confusion which so often exist and which a statistical analysis such as we have carried out, fails to bring clearly to mind:

Mrs Smith[1] was a housewife of thirty-four and she had three children, aged eight, seven and five. She and her husband had been legally married for over ten years, but about two-and-a-half years ago she had left him to go and live with her sick mother, an old-age pensioner. She had done so because she had become very frightened of her husband: he frequently had 'funny moods' and would fix his eyes

---

[1] All names used throughout this report are fictitious.

on her and stare. He had several odd habits, particularly when drunk; on one occasion he had demanded that she should undress and then he had slashed her between the legs with a razor. She said he had a history of cruelty to animals, pouring hot fat over dogs, beating dogs with chains, etc. Shortly after the razor attack she had left him, but her husband had visited her frequently at her mother's house and she had visited him. When her husband was released on bail prior to his present imprisonment, he had lived with his wife at her mother's home. During the time they had been parted, the husband had been living with another woman, who, since the imprisonment, had given birth to a baby. This woman said the prisoner was the father of the child and had asked the *wife* if she would like to adopt it. The prisoner had denied being the father.

Mr Smith was serving an eighteen-months sentence for larceny, housebreaking and a motoring offence. At the time of interview he had served five weeks of the sentence. Aged thirty-one, he had previously had a number of fines, been once on probation, once in borstal and three times in prison. Mrs Smith said he got into trouble because he was unemployed and had no money to buy the children any shoes. There were debts for rent, and the husband had unpaid fines; Mrs Smith blamed her husband's unemployment for these, and did not herself mention money as a problem. Her main worry was where they would live when he came out of prison. The house they lived in before the separation [and where Mr Smith had continued to live with the other woman afterwards] was due for demolition and she supposed that they would be rehoused. Although she said she hadn't really decided to return to her husband, she talked about having to move to the new house, as otherwise her husband would have nowhere to put their furniture and he would have no home. Her mother was bitterly opposed to a reconciliation, but Mrs Smith was anxious to 'give it a try'. 'I just hope he changes his ways when he comes out; stop all these funny goings-on. All the funny things he does when he comes home at night.' Although living with her mother, the latter was described as unsympathetic and hostile, 'she told me I shouldn't have got married, and she's very difficult to get on with now'.

Mrs Smith thought her husband would probably get into trouble again and wanted 'someone to visit us and advise us . . . to see that everything is all right'. She did not know who this should be.

Mrs Smith said she missed him. 'I never go out at night now because they'll say I'm looking for a man. I don't like people saying things to me, it sort of shows me up because I don't come from a bad family, and kiddies at school have been saying things to our children.'

The findings of this chapter indicate that the wives interviewed were in the main young, and living on an income which rarely allowed for more than the basic necessities of life. Most of them were to a certain extent in debt and financial problems were experienced in almost all cases, often quite severe. They had usually been married for some considerable time, but the relationship frequently contained severe conflict and was peppered by separations, particularly so far as the wives of recidivists were concerned. The areas of tension within the marriage centred largely round the husband's failure to work regularly, with consequent financial strains, sexual dissatisfactions accompanied by promiscuity, drink, and intra-family conflicts. During the period of imprisonment wives tended to receive a good deal of support from their family of origin, though this was not always accompanied by a sympathetic attitude to the daughter or her marriage. Apart from financial considerations, the management of children was the subject of most difficulty during imprisonment. Wives led a somewhat restricted social life during the imprisonment and complained of loneliness and sexual frustration, though stigma and shame tended to wear off quite rapidly. Whilst recognizing that serious problems existed in the marital relationship, they were frequently very tolerant of these and needed to believe that life would change for the better upon their husband's discharge. The most widespread *practical* cause of conflict both before imprisonment and to be anticipated on discharge, was their husband's failure to work. There was a fair amount of contact with social agencies, principally the probation service, but the contact was often short-lived and the help given rarely extended beyond practical advice and material aid which, though extremely necessary in many cases, was insufficient if family relationships are considered, even loosely, to be connected with the husband's criminality. Wives were extremely limited in the amount of contact they had with their husband during imprisonment, largely owing to the long distances and expense involved in travelling to see him, nor do conditions in many prisons facilitate the continuance or maintenance of good family relationships.

*Chapter V*

# THE WIVES SEPARATED BEFORE IMPRISONMENT

The questionnaire administered to separated wives contained many of the same questions as were asked of wives living with their husbands. However, a number of questions dealing with the situation at home immediately before imprisonment were irrelevant and therefore omitted, and eleven questions relating specifically to the separation were added. In order to avoid a series of repetitive tables, it is proposed, in this chapter, to indicate briefly in which aspects the two types of family were similar, and to give more detail about the ways in which they differed and our interpretation of these differences.[1] As stated in the previous chapter, of the 256 wives of star prisoners whom we interviewed, twenty claimed to be separated. In the case of the recidivist wives of the 213 interviewed thirty-four wives said they were separated according to our definition of the term (see Chapter II).

## BACKGROUND FACTORS

There was no great difference in the age structure of the separated and non-separated wives, the modal age of both groups being between twenty-one and twenty-nine, and as in the case of the non-separated wives, 50 per cent of the total sample were under the age of thirty.

An apparent difference in the size of household between the separated and non-separated groups can be shown, by the technique of analysis of variance, to reflect the greater proportion of recidivists in the separated group, and the greater size of household for the recidivists: the difference in size of household between separated and non-separated is not significant [$F = 0 \cdot 2$; 1,465 d.f. N.S.] whilst the difference between star and recidivist families is significant [$F = 9 \cdot 1$; 1,465 d.f.; $P < 0 \cdot 01$].

The separated wives had noticeably fewer children dependent upon them than did those living together [$F = 12 \cdot 2$; 1,465 d.f.; $P < 0 \cdot 01$], but there was no difference between the wives of separated

[1] Detailed tables as in Chapter IV are available should future research workers wish to make use of them.

stars and recidivists in their number of children [$F = 0 \cdot 5$; 1,465 d.f. N.S.].

Wives were asked how long it was since they had lived permanently with their husbands. The information given in Table I (below) usually includes the period the men had been in prison on their present sentence, since in many cases the wives did not know *when* he went in, though in $85 \cdot 2$ per cent of cases they did in fact know that he was inside before we wrote to them.

TABLE I.  *How long since living permanently with husband*

|  | Percentages |
|---|---|
| 3 months under 6 months | $1 \cdot 1$ |
| 6 months under 1 year | $11 \cdot 3$ |
| 1 year under 3 years | $47 \cdot 5$ |
| 3 years under 5 years | $19 \cdot 2$ |
| 5 years under 10 years | $9 \cdot 1$ |
| 10 years and over | $11 \cdot 3$ |
| Total | $100 \cdot 0$ |

Number of star wives  20
Number of recidivist wives 34

It was suggested in Chapter IV (p. 78) that many wives return to their parents in times of crisis: amongst the separated families $39 \cdot 6$ per cent were living with parents at the time of interview, and this is significantly more than in the case of non-separated wives ($20 \cdot 8$ per cent) [stratified test $t = 2 \cdot 8$; $P < 0 \cdot 01$]. We have reason to believe that where wives do *not* have relatives able and willing to take them in, this fact plays an important part in preventing the physical break-up of the marriage, since, particularly if they have young children, the wives often have nowhere else to go.

There is very little difference between separated and non-separated wives living in rented accommodation [stratified test $t = 0 \cdot 8$; N.S.], however the number of non-separated wives who either own or who are buying their house ($10 \cdot 9$ per cent) is considerably higher than is the case amongst separated wives ($1 \cdot 1$ per cent) [stratified test $t = 2 \cdot 1$; $P < 0 \cdot 05$].

There is a little more overcrowding amongst separated wives, possibly due to the fact that so many live with their parents; the average room density for this group was $1 \cdot 05$ persons per room as compared with $0 \cdot 85$ in the non-separated sample. The domestic standards were similar to those existing in families living together, but the condition of material furnishings tended to be somewhat better. This we feel may also be connected with the fact that so many separated wives live with their parents, though similar conditions existed in some cases where the wife had a new 'man friend', who, although not necessarily living permanently in the home, contributed to its upkeep.

There was virtually no difference between the two groups of wives so far as length of marriage was concerned, the majority of couples, both star and recidivist, having lived together for over five years, most frequently for over ten years. Only eight couples separated within a year of marriage. Nor is there any significant difference in the amount of time the partners knew each other before marriage.

### SOURCES OF INCOME

There appeared to be a difference between the separated wives ($36 \cdot 3$ per cent) and the non-separated wives (30 per cent) who went out to work, but the difference was not significant [stratified test $t = 1 \cdot 64$; N.S.]. A factor which probably affects the ability to go out to work is whether the wives live with relatives or not (thus facilitating child-minding), and as we have indicated above, significantly more separated wives live with their parents. This is further confirmed by the fact that the majority of separated wives who worked said that their children were looked after by relatives or friends in the home, whereas in the case of wives living with their husbands, this form of child-minding was less often used (see Chapter IV, p. 85). However, although 26 per cent of non-separated wives at work lived with relatives or friends, and the figure for separated working wives was 40 per cent, the difference was not significant [stratified test $t = 1 \cdot 6$; N.S.]. As with the non-separated wives, the majority of separated wives went to work in order to buy essentials, and very few did so because they liked it; the great majority of those who did not work said it was because they had young children. There appeared to be a tendency for the separated wives to do more skilled work than the non-separated, but the difference was not significant: 56 per cent of the latter did unskilled work compared with 40 per cent of separated wives [stratified test $t = 1 \cdot 7$; N.S.]; the remainder were semi-skilled, skilled manual or clerical workers. This tendency might be explained by the fact that those separated wives who go out to work normally do so as an accepted and regular part of their daily life, and they can therefore undertake jobs which involve some degree of responsibility. As we suggested earlier (see Chapter IV, p. 85) many of the non-separated wives work only spasmodically, either when the opportunity presents itself, and/or when they urgently need to earn extra money, consequently they have less incentive to seek skilled or semi-skilled work.

However, the difference in source of income between the two

groups is even more striking if we consider national assistance payments: 79 per cent of those living with their husband received regular national assistance grants, whereas only 53·4 per cent of separated wives did so [stratified test $t = 4·2$; $P < 0·01$]. This cannot be accounted for solely in terms of the fact that more separated wives go out to work, and we found two other contributory factors. First the separated wife not infrequently kept house for her parents whilst they both went out to work, so that she received board and keep in exchange for household duties and was not drawing national assistance. Second, we found that 17 per cent in the sample of separated wives were cohabiting regularly with another man, and wholly supported by him. On the other hand, whilst there is a significant difference between *non-separated* stars and recidivists receiving national assistance (see Chapter IV, p. 94), amongst separated families the difference is not significant [$\chi^2 = 0·24$; 1 d.f.; N.S.].

Not only did more separated wives live with their parents, but even those who did not do so received considerably more financial or material help from them; there was little difference between the two types of family when considering the amount of help received from in-laws.

Both groups of wives drew family allowances to the same extent, but a noticeable source of income in the case of separated wives was from 'lodgers'. This arises because no special code was available on the schedule to account for the man with whom a separated wife might be cohabiting at the time, and such persons were included under the general heading of lodger. In some cases, owing to the fact that the prisoner did not admit to being divorced, we found ourselves interviewing an ex-wife who had legally remarried. Even more complicated to sort out was an interview with a Jamaican girl whose husband (as he still claimed to be) was in prison on a charge of attempting to murder the man with whom his wife was then living. When we saw the wife, the other man was there, assuring us that he was in fact legally married to the respondent, and very resentful of our appearance. The wife, however, was most grateful for our visit and in addition to returning the card requesting an interview, had actually written a letter to say she would be pleased to see us. Like the prisoner, she did not seem to think they had been divorced. The interviewer finally convinced the 'second man' that she was not colour-prejudiced and the interview proceeded on most friendly terms, though with no final solution so far as the marital situation was concerned. Strictly speaking divorced wives should not have been included in the sample, but once having been allowed to conduct the interview, it seemed churlish not to continue with it.

Separated wives said they received considerably more financial or material help from both voluntary or statutory welfare agencies than did those living with their husbands [stratified test on proportion receiving help from statutory or voluntary welfare agencies $t = 2\cdot1$; $P < 0\cdot05$].

As with wives who lived with their husbands, the majority of separated wives had a weekly income of between £5 and £7 10s 0d, but there is an important difference in their *feelings* about the situation [stratified test on the proportion feeling better off $t = 2\cdot4$; $P < 0\cdot05$].

TABLE II. *Feelings about financial situation*

(*Percentages*)

| | Non-separated | Separated |
|---|---|---|
| Worse off than before | 67·5 | 22·7 |
| Better off than before | 22·1 | 28·4 |
| About the same | 10·2 | 12·5 |
| Don't know | 0·2 | – |
| Not affected by imprisonment | – | 36·0 |
| Total | 100·0 | 100·0 |

| | |
|---|---|
| Number of star wives non-separated | 236 |
| Number of star wives separated | 20 |
| Number of recidivist wives non-separated | 179 |
| Number of recidivist wives separated | 34 |

The fact that rather more separated wives feel themselves to be better off (see Table II above) arises, we believe, for three reasons: (*a*) they themselves have sole control of the family finances; although separated, when their husbands are out of prison a good deal of contact often existed between the couple, with frequent demands for financial or material help by the husband, particularly in order to buy cigarettes or drink; (*b*) when her husband is in prison the wife can claim maintenance through the NAB with no difficulty. When he is out, such payments as he makes are often erratic and irregular, resulting in the wife having to make frequent court appearances to try to obtain maintenance.[1] Under these circumstances payments by the NAB are not so easy to claim, nor are they handed out so regularly, since it first has to be established that the man has *not* paid; (*c*) almost 40 per cent of separated wives returned to live with relatives when their marriage broke up, and although they usually support themselves and their children to a large extent, the extended family provides a sense of security and frequently contributes materially. In particular parents and adult siblings provide clothing and toys for

[1] A fuller discussion of this problem will appear in Chapter IX dealing with civil prisoners.

the children and help with 'extras' such as holidays, cigarettes, and presents.

The weekly expenditure of the separated wives was very considerably less than that of wives living with their husbands, largely owing to the fact that they paid less rent: 34 per cent in fact paid none, as opposed to 18·3 per cent for non-separated wives [stratified test $t = 2·2; P < 0·05$]. So far as other expenses were concerned, there was not a great deal of difference, but on the whole separated wives had slightly fewer regular weekly commitments.

In general it is our impression that separated wives are better adjusted to living on a small income. They are able to assess their financial position more realistically than non-separated wives, and they gauge their expenditure accordingly. As has been suggested earlier, this is partly due to the *regularity* of the income (however small) and partly due to the greater degree of family help received by separated wives.

### INDEBTEDNESS

Fewer separated wives (51·9 per cent) had goods on HP than did those living with their husbands (70·8 per cent) [stratified test $t = 2·9; P < 0·01$], and those that did tended to have less heavy commitments. The difference was particularly noticeable in relation to television and/or radio, domestic appliances and cars. Hire purchase commitments for separated wives were confined almost exclusively to furniture and/or furnishings and clothes.

Furthermore, only 32·1 per cent of all separated wives said they were in arrears at the time of interview, the figure for all non-separated wives being 59·9 per cent [stratified test $= 2·1; P < 0·05$]. So far as other debt is concerned there is very little difference in the amount owed by the two groups, the bulk of the debt amongst separated wives being for rent and/or rates. Separated wives also appear to have slightly more debt to loan clubs, largely for clothes.

There are some very striking differences in the reasons for debt given by the two groups. Whereas amongst the non-separated group the husband's improvidence was considered the primary cause, amongst separated wives the two major causes were ill-health and the husband's failure to pay maintenance.[1] The fact that their husband was out of work and improvident was considered to be connected with the failure to pay regular maintenance. More separated wives get into debt as a result of unusual expenditure, such as funerals, Christmas time, birthdays, and, particularly in the north, Whitsuntide. A great many blamed their debt on their husband's criminality, pointing out that he had gone into prison owing money which they

[1] None of this group was, however, in prison for failure to pay maintenance.

E

felt morally obliged to pay off, though admitting that they were unlikely ever to do so.

## PROBLEMS

Separated wives appeared to have fewer problems than did those living with their husbands. We believe this reflects an attitude of acceptance to the separation; imprisonment was not a crisis for these women: on the contrary it sometimes improved the situation. Only a few separated wives were waiting for their husbands to return.

Only 7 per cent of non-separated wives said they had no problems, whereas the figure for separated wives was $20 \cdot 4$ per cent [stratified test $t = 3 \cdot 1$; $P < 0 \cdot 01$]. For those who *did* have difficulties, the aspects of their lives which were most affected were identical in the two groups: primarily money and secondarily handling the children.

Only two children of separated wives had been before the Courts for an offence, and a further two had truanted in the past but no longer did so. It seems that the children of separated wives are considerably less delinquent, or less evidently pre-delinquent than those of non-separated wives. As the numbers involved are extremely small, the results are not statistically significant [stratified test $t = 1 \cdot 5$; N.S.], but they do corroborate the findings of other researchers who believe that unsatisfactory relationships and a delinquent home may be more conducive to producing delinquent children than is a physically broken home.[1]

We have referred above to the fact that separated wives mentioned ill-health as a major cause of their being in debt. We compared the two groups from the point of view of those having serious illnesses and found that, according to the wives, $59 \cdot 1$ per cent of non-separated and 69 per cent of separated *husbands* had had no serious illnesses so far as their wives were aware; the difference is not significant [stratified test $t = 1 \cdot 3$; N.S.]. So far as the wives themselves were concerned, $50 \cdot 2$ per cent of non-separated suffered no illnesses, and 44 per cent of separated wives were so fortunate: again the difference is not significant [stratified test $t = 0 \cdot 8$; N.S.].

## HELP WITH PROBLEMS

*Financial*

Although fewer separated wives receive national assistance than is the case amongst non-separated wives, this is nevertheless the most widely used welfare service, and $53 \cdot 4$ per cent of separated wives were receiving regular national assistance at the time of our interview.

[1] See for example McCord, McCord and Thurber, *op. cit.*

There appeared to be no difference in the amount of dissatisfaction with the service experienced by the two groups, and both complained bitterly about the lack of 'extras'.

## Contact with statutory and voluntary welfare agencies

Not only did more separated wives receive material and financial help from welfare agencies, but in general such wives tended to turn to a wider range of agencies. (There is no evidence that the total amounts received were any greater.)

The type of agency most widely used closely paralleled the situation amongst the non-separated group: most frequently used were the health visitor, concerning young children [stratified test $t = 0 \cdot 9$; N.S.], and the wvs for clothing [stratified test $t = 0 \cdot 5$; N.S.]. Of separated wives, $15 \cdot 9$ per cent were in touch with prison welfare or after-care, but since many of these wives had been separated from their husbands for long periods before the imprisonment this may account for the relatively small number. This figure is in any case not significantly different from the figure for non-separated wives ($20 \cdot 2$ per cent) [stratified test $t = 1 \cdot 1$; N.S.].

### FAMILY FUNCTIONING

The majority of wives in our sample had been separated for over a year (see Table I, p. 125 *supra*), and gave reasons for the break-up of the marriage as set out in Table III.

TABLE III.   *Reasons for break-up of marriage*

|  | Percentages |
|---|---|
| 1. Wife deserted | 2·3 |
| 2. Husband deserted | 19·2 |
| 3. Mental instability of husband | 10·1 |
| 4. Prolonged separation due to Army service, etc. | 2·3 |
| 5. Husband's criminality | 38·4 |
| 6. In-law trouble (husband's family) | 12·4 |
| 7. In-law trouble (wife's family) | 2·3 |
| 8. Marriage never got going | 12·4 |
| 9. General irresponsibility of husband | 61·0 |
| 10. Husband's cruelty | 32·8 |
| 11. Sexual promiscuity of husband | 22·6 |
| 12. Drink, gambling, 'layabout' husband | 21·5 |
| 13. Mutual incompatibility | 6·8 |
| 14. Other | 8·0 |
| 15. Don't know | 2·3 |

Number of star wives        20
Number of recidivist wives  34

Totals do not add up to 100 per cent since most wives gave more than one reason.

It would probably be justifiable to take items 2, 9, 11, and 12 together, since most wives reported that irresponsibility included drinking, failure to work, going with other women, and in some cases gambling. It appears from the above table that the wives blamed their husbands almost exclusively for the break-up, and rarely saw themselves as contributing in any way to the situation.

Comparison with Table XIX, p. 104 in the previous chapter shows that areas of *conflict* within the marriages of non-separated wives are almost identical with those which cause the *break-up* of the marriages amongst separated wives. More wives in the separated group mentioned their husband's criminality as a cause of conflict— we believe that in the day-to-day life of those couples living together, criminality was less significant as a cause of conflict because it affected their daily life less obviously (and also because in many cases it provided extra income however small and irregular). In retrospect the man's criminality may become more important, but if a husband is out drinking and comes back and assaults his wife, or spends his time gambling and his money on other women, these are subjects likely to generate more unpleasantness at the time than the fact that he sometimes breaks into a house or factory—even supposing the wife knows about it!

When discussing the prisoners, we referred to the fact that there were so many 'shotgun' marriages, though we kept no systematic record of this information. We have a number of examples of extremely stormy marriages and great cruelty, but they are probably atypical, and the following case gives an indication of the more general pattern:

Mrs J. is aged twenty and works as a domestic in an hotel. She has two children, aged two-and-a-half and one-and-a-half and lives with her parents, grandmother, and schoolgirl sister. She knew her husband for about eighteen months before they married, when she was seventeen. She said of the break-up of the marriage 'Well, we were living with in-laws. I kept on about getting a place because I didn't get on with his parents and I left him on the grounds he wouldn't get a home for the children and myself. Well we didn't actually hit it off. We just didn't get on together. He didn't take much notice of the child at all. That got up my nose. After we were married he paid more attention to his mother than me and my child. I knew he'd been to remand home, but after he left I found out he'd been to Borstal and all that. He didn't bother about Joan [the first child]. I never got any money from him which made me more embittered than ever. It was quite a time before I found out, I just thought he's been in trouble the once, quite a few boys do when they're kiddies. I don't think we were really in love, it was just that I was in trouble

when we got married. I'm just worried in case either of them [the children] turn out like him. . . .'
After leaving him Mrs J. went to Court and her husband was asked if he wanted her back, but he said 'no'; at the time of interview he had just written asking her for a divorce.

Despite the fact that many couples have been separated for a long time, and despite the negative attitudes expressed towards their husbands in discussing the cause of break-up, this by no means precluded contact between the partners. 54 per cent of wives remained in touch with their husbands by correspondence, and 22 per cent maintained personal contact.

Separated wives appeared far more critical of their husbands in their familial roles (e.g. as husbands and fathers), as well as in relation to their work performance.

Our interviewers' assessment of the families suggests that in at least 16 per cent of the cases, the marriage was by no means 'on the rocks' before imprisonment and, in a further 4 per cent of cases, they considered that the relationship could be described as 'warm and stable' at the time of the interview. These are usually couples who were living apart at the time of imprisonment, but where the wife started visiting during the sentence and there is some likelihood that they will resume living together on, or soon after, discharge. We shall return to this later in the chapter.

WIFE'S PICTURE OF HUSBAND'S CRIMINALITY

Ninety-one per cent of separated wives said that they knew their husband had been in trouble with the police before the present sentence. Fewer separated wives whose husband had convictions prior to marriage knew about it at the time [stratified test $t = 2 \cdot 3$; $P < 0 \cdot 05$]. We have some reason to believe that the discovery of a criminal past played a more important part in the situation of conflict amongst the separated couples than among those living together, and, as mentioned above (see p. 132) that it subsequently contributed to the break-up of the marriage. Whilst we do not suggest that criminality alone was the cause of break-up, we think that if suitable opportunities for separation occurred in these families, the husband's criminality acted as a catalyst.

In so far as separated wives were aware of the situation (and they tended to know much less about their in-laws than did the non-separated wives) there was little difference in the extent of criminality existing in the families of origin of the two groups. In both cases the greatest degree of criminality was to be found amongst siblings.

Nor was there much difference between the two groups in the wives' estimate of the extent of their husband's criminal contacts, though the separated wives claimed to be less personally involved with such friends and acquaintances.

So far as the present sentence was concerned, the great majority felt that their husbands deserved it; whereas amongst non-separated wives this view was principally held by wives of recidivists, amongst separated wives it was also held by star wives. As might be expected a far larger number of separated wives were uninterested. Most separated wives were also uninterested about their husband being in prison, though the proportion who felt ashamed was about the same in the two groups. Many more separated wives were pleased that their husband was in prison.

There were some very noticeable differences between the two groups regarding the alleged causes of their husband's criminality:

TABLE IV. *Wife's view of causes of criminality*
(*Percentages*)

| | Non-separated | Separated |
|---|---|---|
| Desire for money (greed) | 22·2 | 24·9 |
| Gambling | 1·5 | 2·3 |
| Drink | 19·0 | 9·0 |
| Easily led | 31·2 | 23·7 |
| Ill-health | 3·7 | – |
| No work available | 2·0 | – |
| Lazy | 4·5 | 4·5 |
| Professional or habitual criminal | 8·1 | 13·6 |
| To help family | 14·1 | – |
| Unable to earn enough | 3·9 | – |
| Unsatisfactory childhood | 10·1 | 22·6 |
| Wife's fault (too demanding) | 6·2 | – |
| Sexual aberration | 1·8 | 4·5 |
| Family relationships generally | 7·7 | 6·8 |
| Cannot keep job because of criminal past | 2·7 | – |
| Mental instability | 8·2 | 11·3 |
| Business failure | 1·5 | – |
| Don't know | 6·9 | 18·1 |
| Has not done wrong | 5·5 | – |
| Other | 11·1 | 23·7 |

| | |
|---|---|
| Number of non-separated star wives | 236 |
| Number of separated star wives | 20 |
| Number of non-separated recidivist wives | 179 |
| Number of separated recidivist wives | 34 |

Percentages do not add up to 100 per cent because most wives gave more than one reason.

Table III, p. 131 (above) indicated that the husband's criminality was most frequently mentioned as a cause of the break-up of the marriage, and it was also considered important as a cause underlying debt (see p. 129 *supra*). It will be noted from Table IV (above) that a higher proportion of separated wives consider their husband to be a professional or habitual criminal[1] than do the non-separated wives, but the difference is not significant [stratified test $t = 0 \cdot 7$; N.S.].

A great many separated wives blamed 'other women' for their husband's criminality (included in the above table under 'other'). They suggested that another woman presses the husband to give her more money, and he then finds himself in competition for the woman with single men who have no family responsibilities. The only way he can satisfy her needs and keep his own home going is by turning to crime. In general wives were, perhaps understandably, very bitter and vindictive about the 'other woman', and blamed her for everything, even if she only appeared on the scene *after* the separation, or even where the wife admitted that her husband was 'an absolute brute'.

More separated wives suggested that an unsatisfactory childhood played an important part in the causation of crime [stratified test $t = 3 \cdot 2$; $P < 0 \cdot 01$]. It is our belief that many of these separated husbands were inadequate men who married because they 'had to', but never really became independent of their mothers. Many turned to their mother as soon as difficulties arose in the marriage and often received material help in the form of a bed, food and cigarettes, as well as a sympathetic listener to their complaints against their wife.

More children in separated families knew that their father was in prison: since in most cases the father was frequently and loudly blamed for the break-up of the marriage, as well as for all the other misfortunes that had befallen the family both before and since, there was some advantage to mothers in blackening his name further. We found very few cases indeed where there was an attempt, or desire, to maintain the image of a good father, in order to help the child's adjustment and development.

### CONTACT IN THE COMMUNITY

Since we were endeavouring to find out whether wives had become more, or less, isolated after their husband's imprisonment, this was not a meaningful question for the separated wives whose position in the community was more likely to have been changed, if at all, at the time of the original separation, rather than at the time of imprisonment. However, although no systematic data were collected, we did find that the amount of conflict between the wives and their

[1] For definition of these terms see Chapter III, p. 46 f.n. 3.

parents appeared to be very much less amongst separated wives than amongst the non-separated group; rarely did the question of dual loyalty arise.

## THE FUTURE

Separated wives were very much more pessimistic about the future criminality of their husbands than were the non-separated. Forty-seven per cent felt certain that he would commit further offences, and only 9 per cent thought he would 'go straight'; the remainder were unconcerned, uninterested, or unsure; only 11·9 per cent of non-separated wives thought their husband would commit a further offence [stratified test $t = 5·3$; $P < 0·01$].

Ten per cent of separated wives said they would be willing to have their husband back on release if he would come, and a further 4·5 per cent said that they would do so under certain conditions. Those wives who wanted their husband back were, however, not always those whose husbands wished to return to them. Sometimes circumstances had changed since the husband went inside, as, for instance, in the case of a mentally retarded woman, aged forty-seven, who suffered from a severe anxiety state, and whose mother had died during the husband's present sentence. She was unable to go out on her own, and her life centred round her educationally sub-normal daughter, aged eighteen, and her dog. Fortunately she had good and helpful neighbours, but in order to survive emotionally, this wife badly wanted her husband back. He sent her occasional visiting orders, and wrote regularly; at interview he said he 'hopes to go back' to his wife, and claimed to have given up the girl with whom he was previously living. He was discharged from the army as medically unfit and in prison he suffers from depression.

As in the case of non-separated wives, we asked those who were separated what would be the greatest problem for them once their husband was discharged from prison. Almost 50 per cent were adamant that they did not want their husband back and seemed secure in this decision. Approximately 39 per cent expressed great fear that their husband would return to the district on discharge and would physically injure them. One wife had been severely beaten outside a pub after her husband's last release, and she had intended to take him to Court for it, but he was inside again within three months. Another said 'Actually I'd be scared stiff he'd come up here. I'd be petrified. When he comes out, if he's been sitting in there blaming me he might come here. He never blames himself for anything like most normal people do at times.' In a few cases wives feared that their husband would return to his erratic or non-existent maintenance payments and their financial stability would again be jeopardized.

In the main we found no particular differences between this group of wives and those who continued to live together—however spas-modically and erratically.

On the whole the separated wives seem better adjusted to being alone, and, if affected at all by the imprisonment, seem to derive some benefit from it both financially (in so far as they now have a regular income) and emotionally, in so far as their husbands cannot assault them, or make demands upon them.

We have made no contribution to answering the question of why some families break up and others do not, nor, as will be seen in a later chapter, does our intensive sample throw much light on this problem. Both sets of families experience very much the same sorts of conflict, and it would seem to us that separation results from a combination of personality factors plus opportunity. We think that childhood experiences colour the expectations of both partners in the marriage, and the degree to which each is able and willing to tolerate deviance. At the same time, unless circumstances are propitious, it is unlikely that separation will occur, since the wife must have the security of a roof over her own and her children's heads before she can leave. On the other hand there are undoubtedly amongst our non-separated families a great many who *could* leave but do not do so, and whose personality is such that they derive satisfactions from what appear to be the most unsatisfactory marriages.

## Chapter VI

# DISCREPANCIES BETWEEN HUSBANDS AND WIVES

Had the resources of the research permitted, it would have been desirable to check the responses of each couple individually, in order to see to what extent the information collected was discrepant. To do this systematically would, however, have involved a very great amount of additional work in planning the research, and it was not thought that such a process would substantially improve the reliability of the material.

During the interviewing period, about 50 per cent of all the completed wives' schedules were read through and, where relevant, compared with the husbands' schedules; a note was made of any major discrepancies. This procedure was not carried out either scientifically or systematically, but it did suffice to give us some idea of the extent of possible disagreement between the two parties. Discrepancies, where they occurred, tended to be of three distinct kinds:

(a) Different interpretations of the same facts, e.g. where each partner blamed the other for the break-up of the marriage;

(b) Lack of knowledge by one or other of the partners, sometimes genuine, at other times probably more accurately described as an unwillingness by the couple to share information;

(c) Differences arising from one partner being willing to tell the interviewer the truth, and the other deciding deliberately to withhold it.

Only on one occasion were the discrepancies so great in all areas of investigation that our suspicions were aroused. In this case it transpired that the wife shared herself between two 'husbands' both of whom happened to be in gaol at the time of our interview with her. Since this fact was unknown to the interviewer, it was not possible to tell that the information the wife gave related to a different 'husband' from the one whom we actually saw!

In the preceding chapters we have excluded civil prisoners and their wives from the discussion, since it was felt that the prisoners themselves differed from criminal offenders in important respects, and that the problems experienced by their families might be expected to be different from those of other families, in view of the very short period of separation. We do not believe, however, that civil prisoners and their wives were in any way different from other persons interviewed *so far as their response to the interviewer was concerned.* Furthermore, such evidence as we obtained from checking schedules (see above) confirmed that the existence, or otherwise, of discrepancies related largely to whether a family was separated or living together at the time of the arrest, and in no way related to the type of offender. The comments in this chapter therefore include the 107 civil prisoners and their families whom we interviewed, and who will be discussed in detail in a subsequent chapter. Nor have we, for the reasons stated above, differentiated here between stars and recidivists.

It must, however, be borne in mind that we are discussing here only the 'paired' couples. We have no way of knowing whether the extent of discrepancies would have been any greater had we been successful in making contact with more wives. We are, therefore, concerned in this chapter with 576 couples as follows:

|  | Non-separated | Separated | Total |
|---|---|---|---|
| Stars | 236 | 20 | 256 |
| Recidivists | 179 | 34 | 213 |
| Civils | 66 | 41 | 107 |
| Total | 481 | 95 | 576 |

Although we have not compared individual couples systematically, we have nevertheless produced crude counts and compared the total responses of husbands and wives on all those questions which appeared on both schedules.[1] As a result of this work, we estimate that in approximately 1 per cent of cases the information given by one partner was so at variance with that given by the other, as to make it obvious that one or other had deliberately given inaccurate information. It was not always possible to know where the truth lay, and to some extent we were greatly helped in this by the police reports which were, particularly in the case of long-term offenders, available on the prison record. Access to these records suggested that it was by no means always the prisoner who was lying, or distorting—a view commonly expressed by those working in institutions, who doubt the value of 'outsiders' interviewing prisoners.

---

[1] We do not feel that it would be useful to publish tables from these data, but the counts are available for perusal by anyone wishing to undertake further research.

West,[1] for example, found that at least half of the men he interviewed were unreliable in their accounts of themselves, and he
refers to the fact that even the shrewd and experienced observer
may occasionally be misled, at least on factual details if not on
overall assessment. He adds that in many cases the 'outside informant'
(family member or information from old records) gave a different,
and usually more unfavourable picture than that derived from the
prison interview, and he continues: 'the need to see relatives in order
to assess properly an offender's personality was amply confirmed
by this experience'.

Possibly owing to the somewhat limited nature of the information
we sought to obtain from prisoners, we would by no means put the
figure of unreliable informants as high as West. Nor do we believe
that the information obtained from wives was *necessarily* more reliable; the interviews with them were, however, much more exhaustive
both in terms of subject matter and time, so that a far better opportunity existed for assessing reliability. Our experience in the intensive
sample, however, made it clear that wives who were not willing to
give a truthful picture of the situation were able to sustain a fictitious
one over a long period, and in a number of instances the truth only
began to emerge at the third interview.[2]

In a few cases, where the wife was in a mental hospital, it was
often impossible to obtain reliable information from her, but we
were fortunate in having the co-operation of the hospital authorities
who gave access to records and who either discussed the case with
the interviewer, or wrote to us.

### AREAS OF DISAGREEMENT

As might be expected, the greatest discrepancies centred round the
marital relationship. There was, in the main, close agreement about
their marital status at the time of imprisonment, apart from the fact
that six men claimed to be legally married and living with their
wives, whereas the wives said they were separated. Where separations
existed, the couple were not always agreed as to whether there was a
legal separation, or otherwise, and, as has been mentioned in the
previous chapter, in some cases the prisoners claimed to be unaware
that a divorce had been granted.[3] There were a few discrepancies

---

[1] West, *op. cit.*

[2] It must, however, be borne in mind that the method of collecting data was
quite different in the two samples. In the intensive sample much less emphasis
was placed on fact-collecting in the initial interviews. For a further discussion see
Chapter VII.

[3] These men were usually recorded as 'separated' on their prison record, and it
is possible that they did not always realize that we differentiated, for purposes of
the research, between separations and divorce.

regarding the legality of the marriage, eight more prisoners than wives saying that they were not legally married. We have referred earlier to the fact that it became necessary to include a further category of 'fluid' when coding this question, and we found that coders used this category more for wives than for husbands. We feel this is largely due to the much more intensive questioning of the wives which allowed us to see more clearly the pattern of marriage at the time of arrest.

Whilst the number of husbands and wives claiming to get on 'very well indeed' was identical, there was a marked tendency for husbands to claim a better relationship with their wives than vice-versa. We have discussed what we believe to be some of the reasons for this in Chapter III (p. 71 *supra*). The more favourable light in which husbands see the marriage is also reflected in the discrepancies regarding conflict within the marriage. In almost all aspects the husband greatly minimized the existence of conflict, as compared with the wives. The more negative attitude of the wives appears again in response to the question regarding future plans: whereas 126 wives said they would not have their husbands back, only eighty-eight prisoners said they would not be going back to their wives.

Amongst separated couples there were major discrepancies regarding the reasons for the break-up of the marriage; perhaps naturally, each blamed the other. Where in-laws were said to have caused difficulty, it was always the family of the other partner.

Contrary to what might be expected, where information was discrepant regarding the length of time the partners had known each other before marriage, or before living together, such discrepancies were considerably greater amongst the *non*-separated group. We find it difficult to account for this, since there was very little discrepancy in either group regarding the actual time they had been living together.

Apart from the marital relationship, the major discrepancies between husbands and wives centred round the previous criminal history of the husband. There was a very marked tendency by the wives to underestimate the number of their husband's previous convictions. Since this information was checked against the prison record, we can confirm that the wives are either unaware of the true situation, or were unwilling to disclose it to the interviewer. More husbands than wives said that visiting in prison was regular. This question was asked only of the non-separated couples, but whereas fifty wives said they did not visit because they did not want to, only twenty-five husbands gave this as a reason for their wives not visiting. Furthermore, far more husbands than wives said their children visited.

Amongst non-separated families most husbands knew in what

type of accommodation their wives were living, though in a few cases wives had been rehoused by the time we saw them. Amongst separated couples this information was a little less accurately known, though if one took the total sample of prisoners (as opposed to the paired couples), an important reason for our inability to make contact with the separated wives might well be the fact that the husband gave us inaccurate information regarding the whereabouts of his wife. Separated husbands did not always know whether their wives lived with relatives or on their own, and sometimes suggested that they were living with another man. In order to avoid embarrassment interviewers were normally told if it was thought that another man might be living in the house, but more often than not they could find no evidence of this and the position for these few remains uncertain.

When asked to describe the husband's job, both partners tended to raise its status, though this was much more noticeable amongst the wives. Many seemed unaware of the fact that their husband was unemployed, and those that did know often said it was because no work was available, although many admitted that it was because he didn't *like* work. The men were certainly more accurate in giving information about their employment, or lack of it, and more often said it was because they were habitual or professional criminals. Most non-separated men knew whether their wives worked or not, but seemed to think that more satisfactory arrangements had been made for looking after the children than was actually the case.

Husbands were, on the whole, totally ignorant of any contact their wives may have had with welfare organizations, other than the National Assistance Board. However, as mentioned earlier (see Chapter III, p. 65) we do not think this in any way surprising since welfare is usually considered a 'woman's affair'. Although we have only very little systematic information on the extensive sample regarding role performance and decision-making within these families, the indications are that husband/wife roles are separate and clearly defined and that domestic arrangements are very much the province of the wife, except on the question of disciplining the children.[1] One question specifically about decision-making produced interesting results: very often, when wives claimed to have made the decisions, their husbands disagreed and said that they were *joint* decisions. However, when the husband claimed to have made the decisions, or if *he* said they were jointly made, the wives agreed, and there were no discrepancies.

Husbands also underestimated the amount of help their wives received from their own families, and over-estimated the amount

[1] A more detailed discussion of these matters will appear in Chapter VII dealing with the intensive sample.

received from the husband's family. Husbands rarely mentioned that their wives received family allowances, although there was almost complete agreement about the number receiving national assistance. We made no attempt to ask the husbands the amount of assistance their wives received.

Husbands could give relatively little information about the hire purchase commitments of their wives. They were vaguely aware that household goods were bought in this way quite regularly, but were unable to say whether they had been paid for or not. Far more husbands than wives said they had cars or motor cycles on HP, but this can be accounted for by the fact that by the time we saw the wife such items had usually been repossessed.

Although there was almost complete agreement about the extent of HP arrears (if any) at the time of arrest, there were major discrepancies concerning the amount of other debts, and this could not be accounted for by the delay between interviewing husbands and wives. Husbands greatly under-estimated the amount of their debts: whereas only 218 wives said they had no debts, 304 husbands thought this to be the case. Wives appeared to owe far more in rent, to friends, for gas and electric bills and to loan clubs than their husbands were aware of, or were prepared to admit. Nor were the husbands aware of the extent to which their wives pawned or sold things, particularly those belonging to the husband. We believe that it was the normal practice of the majority of these men to give their wives whatever amount they saw fit, and in many cases this varied from week to week, and they made no enquiries as to how their wives managed on this. Wives, on the other hand, were too frightened to tell their husbands when payments were in arrears, a situation which was very much reinforced by the imprisonment since wives did not want to 'worry' their husbands.

Possibly this chapter gives a somewhat distorted picture of the population we are studying, since we have here drawn particular attention to the discrepancies. By so doing we may have given the impression that there is a great deal of discrepant material. We think that in any circumstances of separation we should probably have found a similar pattern amongst a comparable group in the general population, since much of the discrepancy could more justly be termed ignorance due to breakdown of communication.

We would estimate that amongst non-separated couples, there are approximately 9 per cent whose relationship was extremely tenuous, and where the husband was unwilling or unable to give an accurate picture of the home situation, and where he was aware that the description he gave was a false one. There are also probably about 5 per cent of the wives who gave an unduly optimistic account of the situation.

However, the information given by both partners is not generally discrepant in the majority of cases, and with the exception of a marked tendency, particularly by husbands, to over-estimate the happiness of the marriage, we were impressed by the degree of congruence that existed. This was equally true of those couples who got on well and those who did not, though again in the latter cases there appeared to be considerable bias in assessing the *reasons* for conflict.

We have suggested that apart from marital relationships, the other aspects of these interviews which contain marked discrepancies are the wives' lack of awareness concerning the past criminality of their husbands, and the husband's lack of awareness about how his wife is managing in his absence, and in particular lack of awareness about their joint financial indebtedness. We use the word 'awareness' with considerable caution since we are doubtful whether they are in fact as ignorant as they would have us believe. The answers to these questions may reflect the same need to repress unsatisfactory conditions as do some of the exaggerated claims to a successful and harmonious marriage.

*Chapter VII*

# THE INTENSIVE SAMPLE

INTRODUCTION

In an earlier chapter of this report dealing with methodology and procedure (Chapter II, pages 29 ff.), we discussed our purpose in including in this survey a longitudinal study of a relatively small number of families. In this chapter we propose to examine the material collected from this intensive sample in the light of the theoretical discussion in Chapter I. We have established certain patterns of family functioning and shall discuss these and give illustrative case summaries. Before proceeding to this aspect of the analysis, however, we include some general facts about the sample, a comment on interviewing, and a brief description of the characteristics of the men and their wives.

Methods of selecting and interviewing the prisoners are described in Chapter II and we mention here only the fact that fifty star prisoners and fifty recidivists were seen, serving sentences of between fifteen months and two years. These time limits were imposed in order to allow us to visit the wives at least four or five times during the sentence, and once after the man's discharge.

None of the 100 men seen refused to be interviewed, but two Indians spoke so little English that a satisfactory interview was impossible. One gave permission to see his wife but we were unable to trace her; the other showed signs of gross disturbance during the interview and begged us to find his wife whose whereabouts he did not know; in this we were unsuccessful.

In order to complete the sample within a reasonable space of time, residence in the London area was interpreted very widely in all directions; few were obliging enough to live in the London postal district, most lived at the farthest point on the most outlying estates of North London or Essex, far away from the cafés and snack bars which might have provided sustenance and kept up the morale of the interviewer during the long hours of waiting for the wives to return home. Some lived in suburban villas, shrouded in net curtaining and complete with china ornaments on the window ledge, others lived in tenement blocks, or the peeling decrepit rooms of houses fit only for demolition. Nor, as might be expected, did they have much to offer in the way of home comforts when we *did* see them, though the lush, over-scented, over-heated flat of a prostitute supplied comfort, if of a rather nauseating kind.

The number of wives with whom we were able to make contact on our first visit totalled sixty-five; the reasons for not seeing the remainder are set out below:

| | |
|---|---|
| Husband refused to give permission | 11 |
| Wife moved outside the London area | 3 |
| Wife's address unknown to prisoner | 5 |
| Wife refused interview | 7 |
| Wife non-co-operative* | 9 |
| Total | 35 |

\* These wives agreed to be interviewed and appointments were made, but despite repeated call-backs it was never 'convenient' to see them, and attempts to do so were finally abandoned.

### INTERVIEWING

Interviews with the wives on the intensive sample were free-ranging and, from a methodological standpoint, were diametrically opposed to the closely structured questionnaire used for the national sample. Particularly in the initial interview, the emphasis was on the establishment of a good relationship between the wife and the research worker, since it was our intention to return at three-monthly intervals until shortly after the husband's discharge. Subsequent interviews became more specifically focused in order to cover all the items on the check list. The areas of interest were similar to those covered by the questionnaire used on the extensive sample, but information was collected in much greater depth. In addition the emphasis in this sample centred round family relationships and changing patterns of adjustment during separation. By including a visit after the husband's release we hoped to learn something of the effect of imprisonment on the families and of their plans for the future. It was, of course, necessary to guard against the inherent dangers which such informal interviewing methods entail, namely that the situation becomes so informal that it ceases to produce relevant information, or the interviewee manipulates the worker and turns the interview into a social visit, resulting in considerable contamination of the data.

Very extensive notes were taken at nearly all the interviews, with as much verbatim recording as possible, and only very rarely did this appear to inhibit the wife. In the few instances where she was hostile at the first interview, no notes were taken in order not to prejudice the relationship, and where undue distress was experienced during an interview, the notebook was discreetly closed. One wife, a professional prostitute, insisted on dictating slowly whenever pencil and paper were produced, with the result that it was always necessary for these interviews to be written up later.

Reports of each interview were written within a few days and notes made of any gaps in the information required. Although the interviews were all carried out by one research worker, frequent discussions took place between the investigators for purposes of clarification and interpretation of the material obtained. At the final interview a brief questionnaire was used which was really no more than a check list of factual matters, and which was designed to avoid the possibility of gaps in the information. Wives were generally very co-operative; where there was initial distress or anxiety, the fact that we should have an opportunity to obtain information on a subsequent visit proved of great value, since it allowed us to delay the discussion of emotionally loaded topics until such time as the wife was able to tolerate it. In three instances wives subsequently wrote to express their appreciation of the matter-of-fact attitude of the research worker, and suggested that an opportunity to talk, without too much painful probing on the part of the interviewer in the early stages, had been a helpful experience. Very few wives showed any hesitation in discussing their most intimate affairs. The majority were friendly and very quickly accepted that we could offer no material help. In some cases they had probably answered our initial letter asking to see them in the hope of getting help, but when they realized that we were there only to collect information, they did not seem unduly disappointed.

Some wives became concerned about the research workers' health during the severe winter, and one, in addition to the usual tea, provided hot-water bottles for her hands and feet resulting in chilblains! Several wives helped to dig the car out of the snow and one insisted on plying her with alcohol 'to keep out the cold'. It has been suggested that much of the success of this type of interview depends upon the interviewers' own 'flow of energy, sympathy and understanding'[1] and the work done with these families bears out the fact that when these qualities were at a low ebb the interviews suffered greatly.

Rarely were wives seen alone throughout the whole interview;[2] in most cases there were children present and this proved very valuable in enabling us to observe their relationship with their mother. The presence of relatives, friends and neighbours allowed us to obtain information about current attitudes to criminality in the wider society of which our families form part. Mothers of prisoners were able to give useful information about their sons' past pattern of behaviour. Where we thought it advisable we were, with one exception, able to arrange for a private interview with the wife; in that

[1] Zweig, F., *Labour, Life and Poverty*, Gollancz, 1948, p. 4.
[2] See also Chapter II, p. 38.

particular instance she felt secure in the interview situation only if surrounded by relatives and neighbours. However, even in this case we saw her on one occasion with only her grandmother present, instead of the usual protective *entourage*, and at that interview we were able to discuss freely all the more personal problems and those of family relationships, which were previously inhibited by the presence of so many people.

In one family where the wife lived with her mother-in-law, the latter was very hostile to the research; she denied her son's guilt (although the wife had admitted it) and caused the wife considerable embarrassment. Domineering mothers, or mothers-in-law, were certainly a problem, but by arranging subsequent interview situations to meet our own needs, this difficulty was largely overcome and the advantages of meeting friends, relatives and children were considered overwhelming.

Although it was intended to see each wife regularly at three-monthly intervals until after the husband's discharge, this proved impracticable, partly because it took much longer than we had anticipated to draw the sample[1] and partly because only one interviewer was available instead of two as originally planned. In addition, the wives often proved extremely difficult to trace; they would move home without leaving a forwarding address, or would forget to be in at the pre-arranged time, thus necessitating frequent call-backs. Appointments meant little to many of them; a wife might arrive home an hour late and not mention the fact, or she might be found at home later in the day and make no reference to the fact that she had been out. One wife who suffered great anxiety and feelings of shame, deliberately tried to avoid the research worker, but never had the courage to tell her not to call (she nevertheless managed to express her hostility quite effectively by appropriating the interviewer's gloves!).

Up to the time of the husband's discharge fifty wives remained in the sample and had been visited regularly. The remaining fifteen were 'lost' to the research for the following reasons:

### After the 1st Interview

1 declined 'fed-up with questions'.

1 left to live with husband's parents in Malta (information checked).

3 moved after the first call; left no forwarding address and attempts to trace them were unsuccessful.

1 was continually evasive and attempts to interview her were eventually abandoned (this wife had in any case been separated from her husband for five years).

[1] See Chapter II, p. 33.

*After the 2nd Interview*

1 declined further interviews.

1 husband successfully appealed against conviction and was released.

1 wife emigrated to Australia.

1 divorced her husband between our first and second interview.

A further five wives were seen at least three times but were finally lost to the research as the result of moving home and our attempts to trace them were unsuccessful.

Of the fifty families with whom we remained in touch throughout, fourteen were not seen after the man's release from prison, either because they preferred us not to call, or because they moved from the district. In the former cases the question of a joint interview with the husband had been put to the wife on the last occasion when she was seen alone and we knew that she was not keen on the idea; in such cases we did not press the matter if we received no reply to our letter asking permission for a final visit. In the remaining thirty-six instances the wives were seen after the husbands' release and the interview included the husband in all cases where he had returned to live with his wife.[1]

Terminating the interviews presented considerable problems for the research since many of the families had become greatly attached to the interviewer. Although research visits were not very frequent, wives were able to communicate with the research worker at times of particular crisis and a letter or telephone conversation seemed often to relieve anxiety or tension. Many families required help after their husband's discharge, mainly with marital problems and those of family adjustment generally; only in one case was the situation really critical, but our attempts to put the wife in touch with either a doctor or a social worker were adamantly refused by her.

## GENERAL CHARACTERISTICS OF THE PRISONERS AND THEIR FAMILIES

In most respects these families closely resembled those interviewed on the extensive sample, and who have been described in much detail in Chapters III, IV and V of this report.

Whereas in the extensive sample it proved possible, by the addition of a category 'fluid', to differentiate between the separated and the non-separated wives, these terms proved far less meaningful in the intensive sample. By getting to know the wives better over a long period we found that marriages that had appeared stable at the time

[1] Three husbands were not seen because they lost remission during their sentence for an offence against prison discipline, and were not released until the research interviews were finished.

of the first interview may have been punctuated by periods of separation, whereas families who might have been defined as separated by the terms of reference as set out in Chapter II may well have resumed the marital relationship since imprisonment, or have had a very erratic pattern over many years. For example, one man and his wife were legally separated and although not living together at the time of his offence they had been doing so a month previously. They were in touch during the remand stage but there was no further contact for eighteen months. When the interviewer finally visited the wife two months after the husband's release, it was found he had been home for six weeks but had gone again; the wife expected this pattern to continue indefinitely.

In some instances the husbands' and wives' statements did not tally and there was no way of telling which was correct, since the prisoner was seen so soon after conviction there was rarely a police report on his prison record which merely noted the man's own statement. One man, for example, said he was not legally married since his wife already had a husband from whom she was not divorced; his wife, on the other hand, persisted throughout the interviews in maintaining that she was legally married and that her first husband was dead. We have some reason to believe the husband since all the other information he gave us was correct (in so far as we were able to check it) whereas the wife was always evasive and a somewhat unreliable informant. So far as we were able to judge the marital status of the wives actually seen was as follows:

TABLE I.   *Marital status*

|  | Legally married living together | Unmarried but living together | Separated* | Marital situation fluid | Total |
|---|---|---|---|---|---|
| Stars | 26 | 4 | – | 1 | 31 |
| Recidivists | 21 | 3 | 3 | 7 | 34 |
| Total | 47 | 7 | 3 | 8 | 65 |

* Only those who were unequivocably separated are included here; others appear under marital situation fluid.

Two couples had been married for less than one year and fifteen couples for more than twelve years. The majority of recidivists had been married for under five years and the majority of stars between five and eleven years, although in both groups most men and their wives were under the age of thirty. The recidivists tended to be noticeably younger than the stars, a fact which may account for the shorter duration of marriage. Looking at the duration of marriage in terms of the number of years at risk (i.e. after the age of sixteen) there is a marked tendency for recidivists' wives to marry sooner than stars' wives. There were eleven families in which one or both partners had been married before.

Sixteen wives were pregnant at the time of their husband's arrest though only ten husbands appeared to be aware of the fact when we saw them.

All but five of the families in the sample had children of the present or a previous marriage, though in five instances the children were not living at home before the husband's arrest, either because they had married and moved away, or because they had been adopted. In two further instances the children were away at boarding school (in one case a special school for asthmatics) but they returned home during the holidays. The average size of family was almost the same for stars (2·3 children per family) and recidivists (2·2 children per family).

Most families had at least one child under school age, and since the majority of interviews took place after school hours they were frequently held against a background of bawling toddlers and 'Cisco Kid' on television, neither of which did the mother attempt to modify. A further complication was the reluctance of many mothers to tell their children the truth about their fathers' whereabouts; they seemed to assume that children could not tell the difference between a hospital and a prison, let alone a ship and a prison.

Shouting, swearing and cuffs around the head were the most frequent ways of dealing with unruly behaviour, combined with frequent threats that the research worker would 'take you away', or 'tell daddy'. Advice was often sought, but only in order to reinforce the use of physical punishments. The father of one boy who became actively delinquent during his father's absence and showed other signs of disturbed behaviour, such as enuresis, and aggressive attacks on other children as well as on family members and pets, told us that the boy had greatly improved since his return owing to stern discipline and 'a few good hidings' which, had they been given earlier, would, in his opinion, have 'stopped all this nonsense before'.

Physical neglect or cruelty to children was very rare amongst these families, but ignorance or denial of possible emotional difficulties was almost universal.[1]

A total of twenty-one families changed their address at least once during the husband's sentence, fourteen recidivists' wives and seven stars' wives. Of these three star and four recidivist wives moved directly as a result of imprisonment, though not *necessarily* to less satisfactory conditions. A further seven were lost to the research as a result of their moving without trace (two are known to have gone abroad) and one wife was rehoused by the local council. These seven

[1] A more detailed discussion of the children will appear later in the chapter.

families had housing problems before the imprisonment and their move could in no way be linked to the separation; a further six families moved frequently but could be described as 'itinerants' before the husband went into prison; this was part of their somewhat disorganized pattern of life.

The number of previous convictions amongst the recidivist group varied widely; at one extreme a young man who had been to approved school and Borstal only, and at the other, a man of thirty-five with several juvenile convictions, numerous fines and nine prison sentences on his record. The majority had nevertheless started their criminal career early in life and had siblings who were also known to be offenders. Amongst stars, however, there tended to be more genuine first offenders than was the case in the extensive sample, and twenty-four of the fifty men seen had no criminal record, nor had any of the stars been in prison before.

The fact that length of sentence was a vital factor in the selection process resulted in the type of offence being unrepresentative either of the prison population as a whole, or of the extensive sample. Table II shows the type of offences for which they were serving sentences:

TABLE II.  *Type of offence*

|  | Violence against person | Sexual offences* | Offences against property with violence | Offences against property without violence | Fraud/ embezzle- ment, etc. | Total |
|---|---|---|---|---|---|---|
| Stars | 2 | 3 | 4 | 30 | 11 | 50 |
| Recidivists | 4 | 3 | 24 | 14 | 5 | 50 |
| Total | 6 | 6 | 28 | 44 | 16 | 100 |

* For purposes of this research we have included in this category men living on immoral earnings, and corruption of public morals.

Work patterns amongst the prisoners were very erratic and although recidivists had a far worse work record than stars, many of the latter were also unemployed at the time of arrest and others worked only irregularly. The majority of those who were in work were earning between £10 and £15 per week and the only three men who claimed to be earning over £25 per week were all recidivists who readily admitted that this included criminal earnings. It is impossible to say what proportion of those unemployed were living solely 'off the labour', but it seems reasonable to assume that they were very few. However, although few had actually saved money from criminal earnings in order to provide for their families in case of imprisonment, some wives were certainly better housed and clothed and had more opportunity for going out and about as a result of such ill-gotten gains. One man who *had* in fact saved, had done so in order to take a holiday in Spain. This money was saved by his wife throughout the sentence and on his discharge they went there for two weeks. (The husband subsequently complained bitterly of the heat and the food and vowed he would never go back!) When money had been put aside before imprisonment the wife rarely touched it, usually seeing it as something for them both to use on his return, either to tide them over until her husband obtained work, or until he returned to crime.

Twenty-two wives were either working full- or part-time at the time of their husband's arrest. They worked mainly as domestics or in factories, though two were secretaries and two were prostitutes. With the exception of these two latter categories all earned under £10 per week. The prostitutes by contrast were extremely well off.

With the exception of these few who earned well, the families showed acute anxiety about money. Often it was not simply due to a shortage of it, but because they were unused to the responsibility of apportioning it. Although we found that the norm was for the husband to hand over a weekly sum and for the wife to handle it, the ultimate *responsibility* was always seen as the husband's. This was no longer possible when he was in prison, and the additional responsibility fell on the wife and caused anxiety. This fact was particularly noticeable when the husband was released; even though he usually went on National Assistance, and the family income was increased by only very little, the relief for the wife was disproportionately great.

Apart from hire purchase arrears, forty-eight families were in debt at the time of the husbands' imprisonment, twenty-two stars and twenty-six recidivists. An interesting difference between the two groups lies however in the amount and type of debt involved. The recidivists almost all owed less than £25 and for such items as electricity, gas, rent arrears, money borrowed from friends, gambling debts and fines. Although some stars had similar debts, the majority owed well over £25, and in eight cases the amount involved was well over £100. These large debts were all due to 'business failures'.

The financial situation of the families was rarely very much different at the time of the husbands' release though in the more disorganized homes there was usually some deterioration; for example one wife had got behind with the rent and had not told her husband who was faced with an eviction order a few days after his release. However, even if the day-to-day situation appeared to be about the same, there was a subtle worsening in so far as there was usually an acute shortage of clothing and household equipment. Whereas the wives used to buy from clubs and tally-men when their husbands were at home, they had been forced to buy second-hand clothes, or get them from charitable organizations, during his imprisonment; furthermore, it was the husbands who used to 'rig the kids out' at regular intervals, and they missed this greatly.

There was little pawning or selling, largely because there was not much to pawn or sell, and great resentment was shown if the NAB officer suggested selling anything. This was not true of all families however, and the Cox family were completely feckless. Before the husband's arrest their financial situation was very precarious and they had pawned most of their furniture, but they had nevertheless bought a second-hand car two months earlier. During the sentence Mrs Cox's attitude to money became increasingly unrealistic and she was perpetually seeking help from welfare agencies in order to pay off rent arrears, redeem pawned articles and buy clothes for the children. On one occasion the interviewer was present when the rent man called, and when Mrs Cox told him she hadn't any money, he simply replied 'if you haven't got it you haven't', shrugged and walked off. Mrs Cox then owed £6. She paid tally-men only if they made a fuss at the door and when one firm wrote her an unpleasant letter she wrote back pointing out that she was a very good customer and they could 'bloody well wait for the money'; she added with a smile 'and I've not heard any more'. She borrowed every week from neighbours and so long as no one was pressing her for repayment, did not consider that she had any debts. More and more goods were pawned and the round of social welfare agencies from whom money was sought grew wider and wider. When her husband came out of prison Mrs Cox freely admitted that they had plenty of debts. It was always difficult to get details, but she knew she was at least two weeks behind with the rent, she hadn't paid the milkman for weeks and weeks (she had also borrowed £5 from him) and she had bought a complete set of new clothes to take to hospital with her the day following our interview. However, debts were not regarded as a problem by either husband or wife; this was the way they had always lived and would undoubtedly continue to do so.

Two wives with good jobs saved money, and a third was able to pay off some of her husband's debts, although she slackened off as the sentence proceeded. Most wives received a great deal of financial help from their own families and often those of their husband. Money received in this way was always considered as a gift and not as a loan, even where it was not easy for the parents to manage. There was very little borrowing other than the odd ten shillings or a pound to last through the week, much less than when the husbands themselves were at home and borrowed from friends. The less intelligent wives really believed that if the NAB money was paid on a Friday instead of a Monday they would have no financial problems!

Hire purchase arrears fell into a somewhat different category from other debts, in that wives, particularly those of recidivists, were far less concerned about them, especially if the money was owed before the husbands' imprisonment. One wife had bought a cooker on hire purchase six months before her husband's arrest, paid the deposit and omitted to pay any further instalments. She had heard nothing from the firm concerned who, it was rumoured, had gone bankrupt; she did not expect to pay anything more. In another family, where the wife was actively connected with her husband's criminal activities, a radiogram worth £400 had been bought just before his arrest, and only the deposit was paid. They planned to keep it during the imprisonment without paying further on it, and thought they could do so by pretending to the firm concerned that it had been stolen. This brought the police round, and knowing the wife well, they threatened to arrest her if she didn't 'come clean' and tell them where it was hidden. She had already spent three days in prison on remand before being cleared of the housebreaking charge with her husband, and she did not relish the idea of a return visit!

Star wives were rather more concerned about their debts generally, and the arrears tended to be of a shorter duration. Most tried to pay off any arrears and to continue payments if only 2s 6d per week. However, one charming, but completely feckless woman of fifty had convinced herself that she did not owe anyone anything and she conducted a long correspondence with several firms on the basis that she was not responsible for her husband's imprisonment, and, as she was living on national assistance, of course could not pay. She conveniently forgot that the arrears had mounted up before her husband's arrest.

The majority of wives visited their husband during his sentence[1] and, where there were children, invariably took them, although not necessarily all at the same time. Even those couples where the relationship was very strained mostly made some attempt to see each other. Of the nine wives who never visited, five were already separated before the imprisonment, two marriages were in the 'fluid' category, and in two cases distance, combined with the wife's own emotional difficulties and mental health, made visiting impossible.

Of those who visited, nine did so only intermittently; three of these said it was due to distance and expense, four said it was due to instability of the marriage, and one wife who claimed to have committed the crime for which her husband was sentenced (and we have every reason to believe her) dared not go at first, then became diabetic and was hospitalized and finally had a baby [her husband's]. Towards the end of the sentence she began to visit him, but after a

---

[1] See also Chapter III, p. 72 and Chapter IV p. 113 for a disscusion of visiting.

while the husband refused to send visiting orders and we witnessed a severe deterioration in the marital relationship. Unfortunately the wife moved (possibly with her husband) as soon as he was discharged, and we were unable to trace their whereabouts. One other wife who only visited occasionally said she was 'too lazy' and in any case claimed that her husband did not like her visits as they were too upsetting.

The wives' feelings about visits varied a great deal, as did their comments on the arrangements provided. 'Closed' visits were regarded with horror, particularly by star wives. Not being able to touch one another and the bewilderment of young children under the conditions of the 'closed' visit were the main complaints. Shortage of time was another factor; clock-watching prevented relaxation and at times couples found themselves inhibited from any kind of communication. There was some criticism of prison officers for being unnecessarily officious, and particularly in some prisons wives complained that they were treated 'as if *we* were the thieves'. Those families whose visits took place in 'open' conditions found them to be very different. The time limit was far less rigid and families were able to sit round tables in comfort and have a cup of tea. In summer they were able to walk round the grounds of 'open' prisons and there was space and opportunity for the children to talk and play with their fathers. Such visits were clearly satisfying, and although some distress was inevitable at leaving, the wives usually felt much happier afterwards. 'Closed' visits, by contrast, often left wives feeling more miserable than ever.

The effort involved in taking children long distances (particularly in the appalling weather conditions experienced during the winter of the research, 1962–3) was tremendous; nevertheless it was generally considered worth the trouble, largely because mothers were concerned that young children should see their father often enough to remember him when he returned home. Some wives felt that prisons were not the sort of place to which a child should be taken, but this attitude was rare and much more general was the desire to keep as close a contact as possible between father and child.

### PATTERNS OF RELATIONSHIP

The pattern of relationship in any family is clearly a product of a variety of factors, but it is not intended in this Chapter to account for such patterns in the sense of discussing how they arise. What we have attempted is to construct a series of models for the purpose of illustrating those dynamic aspects of the family situation which we believe are relevant factors in understanding the modes of adjustment which follow upon the imprisonment of the husband.

It might be argued that the starting point in any analysis ought to be the consideration of the family *structure*. This we have rejected on the grounds that we are concerned primarily with the husband-wife relationship in the context of the nuclear family and this structural feature is common to all the families under discussion. Where the nuclear family is part of a joint or three-generational household, the fact may or may not have a bearing upon the relationship; as far as our data are concerned, membership of a joint household is only relevant in respect of certain husbands and wives who display what we shall later describe as the primary characteristic of immaturity.

It is also important to point out that in neither their structure nor their functioning are these families markedly 'abnormal'. They differ from 'ordinary' families in one important respect, namely the criminality and imprisonment of the husband, but apart from that there seems little reason to believe that they possess features which could not be found in any population of 'normal' families. Any other sample of sixty-five families with a similar social and demographic background would have produced similar patterns of relationships. Even the poverty, and dependence upon national assistance and other machinery of welfare is not unique to prisoners' families, but could be found among families in which the breadwinner has been made ineffectual or inoperative on account of hospitalization, serious illness or unemployment. We have, on the other hand, learned a little about the interaction of criminality and certain aspects of family life, but make no claim to have contributed much to the discussion of the 'causes of crime'. Nor do the data provide any satisfactory means of distinguishing between the crisis of separation and the crisis of imprisonment. We are concerned to demonstrate the ways in which the husband-wife relationship in the stage before imprisonment establishes a pattern, or sets subsequent limits upon, (*a*) the nature of the adjustment to separation and (*b*) the character of the relationship after discharge. It is around these two foci that the fortunes of the whole nuclear family will revolve.

Marital relationships are dynamic phenomena in that they adjust, adapt, flex and contort according to the nature of the social situation. It is impossible therefore to analyse such relationships except in terms of the general principles which can be identified and illustrated by reference to specific situations. These general principles have been inferred from our data and will be presented in the form of certain abstract primary characteristics which engender other subsidiary social processes. These processes are not mutually exclusive but may occur simultaneously. We do not claim to have discussed all the possible combinations, we have simply attempted to distinguish those processes which appear to be of major importance, or which we found to exist most frequently. Our conceptual apparatus is perhaps best illustrated in semi-diagrammatic form.

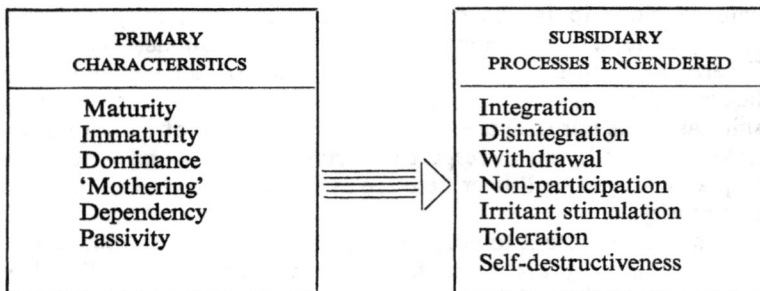

| PRIMARY CHARACTERISTICS | SUBSIDIARY PROCESSES ENGENDERED |
|---|---|
| Maturity | Integration |
| Immaturity | Disintegration |
| Dominance | Withdrawal |
| 'Mothering' | Non-participation |
| Dependency | Irritant stimulation |
| Passivity | Toleration |
| | Self-destructiveness |

We should point out that the distinction between withdrawal and non-participation lies in the fact that the former implies withdrawal from one situation (in this case the marital relationship) *into* another situation, possibly other women, drink, work, etc. Non-participation, on the other hand, implies an active decision to 'opt out' of a situation, but does not involve the substitution of another activity.

The primary characteristics are to be considered initially at an abstract level, that is independently of their specific manifestation in husbands or wives, as potentials for the determination of actual behaviour. In practice, they may vary in clarity and intensity, for example 'dominance' may be more marked in one individual's behaviour than in that of another whose behaviour has also been classified as dominant. Nor in any one individual will dominance occur in the same intensity in every sphere of behaviour, or in the same sphere on different occasions.

OPERATIONAL DEFINITIONS OF PRIMARY CHARACTERISTICS

(1) *Maturity*. This characteristic may be described as a condition of maximum personality growth. The individual has, in consequence of experience, developed a range of techniques enabling him or her to make decisions upon the basis of considered judgement, to adapt to change with a minimum of emotional disruption, and to tolerate frustration and critical or stressful situations without suffering a disabling degree of distress, or utilizing some alternative mode of compensation (such as withdrawal into mental or physical illness, or a frankly deviant pattern of behaviour).

(2) *Immaturity* represents to a great extent the converse of (1). The personality of the immature individual is comparatively under-developed and might be described as a form of social retardation. Experience has been of little relevance, and the individual has little

capacity for considered judgement or control over his reactive impulses, which develop as a consequence of frustration, stress or crisis. Such reactions as occur tend to be immediate, and repetitious of reactions to similar situations in the past, sometimes even replicating reactions which occurred in childhood. Aggression and withdrawal may be typical responses, although they may occur in a more subtle or sophisticated form than is normally observed in children. Deviant behaviour outside the home in the form of excessive drinking, gambling or sexual promiscuity may be the counterpart of such behavioural disturbances in children as enuresis, truanting, or over- or under-eating.

(3) *Dominance* is a manifestation of the patriarchal control of affairs. It is not necessarily to be thought of as a 'pathological' condition, in that certain forms of dominance in the family are culturally prescribed. For example the husband is expected to make important decisions affecting the course of family affairs and to assume responsibility for financial matters. Dominance, as will be demonstrated may, however, be either excessive or inappropriate in certain situations, and it is these forms, rather than the 'formal' dominance which is a culturally prescribed attribute of the male role, which are our concern here.

(4) *'Mothering'* is a phenomenon which occurs, as might be expected, mostly, though by no means exclusively, in women. 'Mothering' among men, though we found no examples in our sixty-five families, is likely to exist in conditions of acute role reversal. Essentially 'mothering' is supportive, protective and regenerative behaviour, an extension towards the husband of the maternal aspect of the female role. In this context it is inappropriate in that the female role is biassed in the direction of the maternal rather than the conjugal element. Frequently it may be the counterpart of dependency.

(5) *Dependency* has some features in common with immaturity, but is by no means synonymous with it. Rather it can be viewed as the continuation of the filial role which is appropriate to childhood. The dependent individual, like the child, makes few, if any, decisions of consequence. The dependent partner in the marriage may be able to play specific roles providing he or she is relieved of any serious responsibility. When faced with this, or with crisis in the absence of the protective partner, the consequences may induce a form of social or emotional paralysis, resulting in complete inability to control children or manage elementary financial affairs. Some dependency situations *may* contain a degree of latent hostility which manifests itself in temporary aggression, or such destructiveness as may obscure the fact of dependency from the casual observer.

(6) *Passivity* is a quality of response involving uncritical acceptance of events and the behaviour of others. The passive individual may be immature, or comparatively mature; what is important is his or her apparent non-involvement or non-reaction to behavioural or situational stimuli. This does not necessarily mean that the individual is unaffected by what happens, indeed the effects may be considerable. It may occur as the counterpart to dominance, as was most commonly observed, but may also exist in attentuated form as an element of dependency.

The primary characteristics which we have just defined tend to crystallize in certain ways in the marital relationship. These forms will now be described, and in the course of discussion the principal subsidiary processes engendered will be identified. Illustrative case material will be used at the end of each section. It is important to point out that these forms of relationship do not themselves imply either good, or bad, marital adjustment; that will depend upon the degree of congruence of norms and personality 'fit' existing between the partners; thus a dominant husband and a dependent wife are likely to be well-adjusted where their norms and personality 'fit' are good, whereas a similar type of relationship with bad 'fit' may result in bad marital adjustment.

## Group A *Dependent wife—dominant husband*

The major processes engendered in the wife by this situation are withdrawal and toleration: the wife tolerates her husband's criminality and his absence for the sake of a relationship upon which she is extremely dependent; at the same time she withdraws from the day-to-day demands resulting from being left on her own. Both these processes appear, from our interview material, to have been present before the separation, but withdrawal in particular became more marked during the imprisonment.

*Before separation:* Almost all decisions, including those most usually associated with female role playing (i.e. domestic activities and child rearing) are taken by the husband. He usually has a reasonably good work record (recidivists in this group tend to work quite well between sentences) and any contacts the partners have with people outside the family unit are normally confined to the husband's work situation. They tend to lead restricted social lives, and outings together, although frequent, do not normally involve other people. There is almost no visiting of friends or relatives unless through work; if the husband does meet acquaintances in the pub, it is when he leaves his wife at home.

*During separation:* For dependent wives the husband's departure is a real crisis, and a period of disintegration ensues, particularly if it is the first separation. Signs of considerable depression appear almost immediately and continue throughout the sentence. Such wives adjust to the separation extremely badly and show increased signs of personal deterioration—appearance, health—as the period of separation lengthens. Many get seriously into debt and few are able to maintain HP or insurance commitments. Rent arrears are seen as a real threat to their continuity of existence as a family and some very dependent wives are genuinely frightened of losing their homes. Most cannot bring themselves to look for work; occasionally they try a part-time job, but this is soon relinquished. Others, who may have worked before the imprisonment, may continue to do so, but make frequent job changes and do less and less work as the sentence progresses. Ill-health is the ostensible reason for their inability to manage during the separation.

Visits to their husband in prison, and to a certain extent letters, are intensely important to these wives, since they try to continue to use their husband in a supportive role and as a decision-maker. It is therefore unfortunate that the gradual deterioration of the wife both physically and emotionally often *prevents* her being able to make the effort to visit. For such families the question of physical distance from the prison is of great importance, since if the husband is sent far away from home, in order to visit him the wife is faced with very real practical problems of distance and expense; these exacerbate the more psychological problems which already contribute to the difficulty of visiting.

The children in such families tend to suffer a great deal through lack of direction from the mother and because, in her continuing need for dependency, she *uses* the children. She does this in two ways: in order to replace the husband as a support and decision-maker she pours out her worries to the children, who, particularly if young, are not usually in a position to meet these demands and responsibilities. On the contrary they often engender in the children a state of acute anxiety over such matters as money, their mother's health, and the possible problems when their father comes home. Secondly, the wives 'use' their children by displacing on to them the aggression they feel against the husband for having 'deserted' them, but which they dare not express to him. Since these wives had very little contact with adults outside the family before imprisonment, they have no one but their children to whom they can turn during the separation. Older children *may* be able to cope with these added demands and responsibilities, and the two examples given here will show how this can vary:

Mrs F. had five boys the oldest, Tommy, was at work, and although on licence from Approved School, seemed willing to contribute an

F

unusually large proportion of his earnings towards the family budget, and in addition assumed the father's controlling role *vis-à-vis* the younger children. Tommy was, in fact, the one stabilizing factor in Mrs F.'s life during the separation.

Mrs R., on the other hand, had four children living at home and had many problems with them. The oldest, an eighteen-year-old girl, frequently changed jobs after her father went to prison and finally gave up work for three months altogether, refusing even to register at the Labour Exchange so that Mrs R. could draw no national assistance money for her. Eventually Mrs R. told her husband who, on a visit, gave the girl 'a very severe talking to'. She made an effort and obtained a job which lasted only a few weeks. She then had a row with her mother and walked out of the home, announcing that she intended to marry. She went to live with her future in-laws, in some ways to her mother's relief since she was no longer responsible for keeping the girl. The marriage did not in fact take place until the father was released from prison.

Most of these dependent wives have always turned exclusively to their husbands for help and support if necessary and so, when he is away, they do not call on outside help; some even decline to go to the NAB. However, wives in this group are in general much more likely to be dependent on national assistance than wives in any other group, even where they have no pre-school children. If they take part-time work it undermines their health yet further and often causes additional anxiety for the children. One fourteen-year-old boy became very distressed at seeing his mother working late at night (she packed plastic flowers at home) and on one occasion when she started whilst he was still having breakfast, he created a great scene. The mother thought he felt a great responsibility now that his father was in prison and she recognized that this was bad for him. Nevertheless she often contrived to keep him home from school on the pretext that he had no shoes, but in reality so that he could keep her company.

Amongst this group of wives attempts were often made to manipulate the research worker, and to force her to make decisions, or 'do' something for the family. Where, as was the case in one family, many social work agencies *were* involved, this was because they called on her and she did not seek out their help. She dealt with the situation by becoming antagonistic and hostile towards them. Her refusal to co-operate took the form of deliberately withholding information and this resulted in agencies taking decisions which were in the main unhelpful. This then enabled the wife to castigate all welfare workers as 'useless and interfering'.

*After discharge:* There would appear to be no overt problems when the husband returns home. Wounds are healed overnight, but we have no knowledge of the extent of the scars, particularly on the future life of the children. The husband is accepted back into the home with relief by both wife and children. He takes over completely, sorts out debts, disciplines the children and generally dominates the household again. The wife is relieved and shows no signs of anger or recrimination. The husband is also welcomed back by relatives who had ignored the wife's difficulties during the separation and are anxious to make amends, since nothing is now demanded of them.

### 1st Case Summary for Group A

Mr R., aged 42, was serving an eighteen-months sentence for embezzlement. He had previously been fined, put on probation and served two prison sentences.

Our first interview with Mrs R. was delayed until Mr R. had been in prison for six months owing to the fact that three attempts to see her proved abortive.

Mrs R., aged about 38, lived in a semi-detached house on an estate miles from anywhere. Furnishings were extremely sparse, but the rooms were fairly clean and tidy. She lived there with her daughter of eighteen who worked as a shop assistant, a son of sixteen working in a factory, and two school-children aged fourteen and twelve. Another son was married and living away.

*At the first interview:* Mrs R. had recently been knocked down by a car outside the pub where she worked. She started working part-time when her husband went into prison. Mr R. suffered from a duodenal ulcer and had been off work until just before his arrest when he obtained work as an electrical engineer.

Mrs R. was very depressed throughout the interview and it was difficult to get her to talk. Her brother-in-law and his wife were present throughout; the former had a very 'inhibiting' effect on the proceedings and no one volunteered any information about anything.

Mrs R. found it very difficult to manage financially although she was in fact no worse off than before, since she got national assistance and family allowances as well as her earnings.

The whole family seemed to feel that the fact that Mr R. had got caught was just 'bad luck', and his brother remarked 'if you're short you've got to get it somehow'.

Mrs R. at first denied having contact with neighbours, but it later transpired that they called in regularly and were very friendly. She was also in touch with her own and her husband's family.

The R.'s had been married for eighteen years and she said she was very lonely without him. She looked physically ill and tired, and appeared to be trying hard to keep her depressive feelings under control.

*At the second interview:* Mrs R. was seen alone, but continued to be very reticent.

She had given up her job, which she found difficult to manage, and was now doing work at home putting plastic flowers into bags. This was very unremunerative and had made her fingers exceedingly sore, so that she hoped to give it up.

The rent was in arrears and she had pawned a number of items. She had also borrowed from a moneylender. Her exact financial position was extremely obscure and impossible to disentangle, but it was plain that she could not manage on the money she was getting and found it very difficult to budget. Mr R. when seen in prison had told us that his wife could not handle money and he normally controlled the family finances.

Mrs R.'s health had deteriorated and although she had always suffered from headaches she now had frequent migraines and was extremely depressed and irritable with the children. She was afraid to go to the doctor in case he found something really wrong with her.

The oldest girl had been causing a great deal of trouble[1] since her father's imprisonment and Mrs R. was quite incapable of controlling her in any way. The other children missed their father a good deal but she felt they did not suffer from his absence, apart from the eldest boy who was very irritable. Mrs R. certainly missed her husband's presence as a means of controlling the children.

She did not get on at all well with her mother-in-law who tended to blame Mr R.'s imprisonment on Mrs R.'s inadequacy particularly in financial matters; they nevertheless saw each other from time to time. She also saw her own mother somewhat irregularly. Neighbours were friendly, but apart from occasionally chatting to them in the street she now had no social life.

Mrs R. sought advice from the interviewer about financial matters; she showed herself to be worried and anxious but thought she would 'muddle through' until her husband was released and relied on him to sort it out then.

*At the third interview:* Mrs R.'s rent arrears had mounted so much that the National Assistance Board had started paying the rent direct to the Council for her and she was supposed to pay off the arrears. Other debts were also increasing and she explained that 'money seems to drip through my fingers'.

The daughter had left home after a row with her mother and was proposing to get married.

Mrs R. had started another part-time job at home, but had soon

1 For more details see p. 162, *supra*.

given that up as well. She seemed to feel she ought to work, but felt much happier at home not working.

She continued to visit her husband regularly and was taken there each time by her brother in his car. Mr R. had been ill in prison but Mrs R. was quite satisfied about the attention he received and did not seem to feel that his illness would affect him in any way once he returned. She was much more concerned about her own state of health and could apparently not tolerate the idea of her husband being ill and unable to control everything.

Contact with family and neighbours remained minimal. Mrs R. found it increasingly difficult to manage without her husband, both emotionally and financially, and relied a great deal on her children. She continued to keep them home from school for companionship and the attendance officer was a frequent caller at the house. He had, in fact offered to pay half the cost of shoes for the children if Mrs R. would go with him to buy them. She had not done so on the pretext that she would not be able to pay her share as the man would take them 'to a very pricey place'!

*At the fourth interview* (joint): Mr R. was seen alone at first. He told a good many lies and was very quick-tempered. He lashed out at the dog for no apparent reason and snarled at his wife as soon as she returned home. Any time Mrs R. tried to say something her husband interrupted and he bullied her throughout the interview. He considered the research worker was there for his benefit not his wife's.

He was not working, although he had been out of prison for over seven weeks, and blamed this on the fact that he told prospective employers that he had just come out of prison. He had borrowed a van from a friend he met in prison 'until I'm on my feet again'.

He had received an eviction notice six weeks after his return and took this down to the National Assistance Board where, he said, after 'shouting and raving' they apologized and admitted it was their fault for not paying in the money regularly.

All the tallymen were calling to collect their money now that it was known that he had returned, and he was sure he would 'soon put things right'.

The daughter had married and the son was working well. He had 'talked to' the two younger children who had been 'getting a bit out of hand' during his absence, and they were now all right. He was a strict disciplinarian and appeared to have little real feeling for the children.

Mr R. was very angry with his parents and brother for not helping his wife more whilst he was away, but was pleased that they were now rushing round to see *him*. In fact he appeared to blame his wife for not being helped even more than he blamed them for not helping her! He said he had given all of them 'a piece of my mind'.

Mrs R. had again taken on a part-time job packing plastic flowers; her husband thought this a good idea, since he was anxious to obtain money somehow. Money was very important to Mr R. and he seemed to see nothing wrong in obtaining it by illegal means if necessary; no one seemed to doubt that he would serve further sentences of imprisonment, but there was no question of his wife leaving him, so great was her need for him. She remained depressed but less so than during his absence.

### 2nd Case Summary for Group A

Mr Y., aged 39, was serving a two-year sentence for housebreaking. He had had twelve previous convictions, and been in trouble since childhood.

He had been living with Mrs Y, aged 40, for fifteen years; they were not married because Mrs Y. already had a husband. She lived in a tenement block in the city with her seventeen-year-old son and fourteen-year-old daughter. There was also a married son living away from home.

*At the first interview:* Mrs Y. was very tearful; she was a tense, anxious woman who could not manage on an income of £6 7s 6d which she earned at her full-time job. She had debts amounting to some £50. Although Mrs Y. insisted that her husband was a good hard-working man, Mr Y. had described himself as a professional criminal. It seemed likely that he spent most of the day out of the house and his wife assumed he was working legitimately, since he provided well for the family.

She complained of feeling 'completely broken—it is like if someone had died'.

*At the second interview:* Mrs Y. had given up her job and was doing a number of part-time domestic jobs. Physically her health had deteriorated, she complained of over-work and exhaustion.

She had no contact with any welfare organizations and refused to go to the NAB.

She remained lonely and depressed.

*At the third interview:* Mrs Y. was very tearful and reticent. Her main concern was her inability to manage financially, but she was firm in her unwillingness to go the NAB.

She was very resentful of everyone around her, but declined to discuss her problems with anyone. She had no contact with anyone outside the home except her employers. She appeared ill and under-nourished and had had to give up her job temporarily owing to ill-health. She complained of the worry of having to keep a home for the children.

She was visiting her husband regularly but was angry because, when she told him her troubles, he replied that he could do nothing about them. He laughed and joked a great deal on visits and she felt he failed to understand her difficulties.

*At the fourth interview:* Mrs Y. was so distraught that the interviewer remained only a few minutes, and during this time tried to give her a little reassurance. Her hair was all over the place, clothes awry, her face white and drawn and she was unable to speak in connected sentences.

*At the fifth interview* (joint): Most of the talking was done by Mr Y. who talked endlessly about his prison experiences. He had not taken a proper job, but provided adequately for his family and said he was 'all right down at the bookies'. Mrs Y. still did part-time domestic work, but had further reduced her working hours.

Mrs Y. did her best to pretend the interviewer was not there. Throughout our interviews with her she had tried to maintain the fantasy of a perfect marriage and a perfect husband, since she desperately needed both. With her husband present she was faced with the reality of the situation—a tough, jovial, but domineering husband who was a professional criminal, but to whom, as her children became older and grew away from her, she was increasingly bound by strong dependency ties.

Her health and general appearance had improved a little and she was content to let her husband 'take over' as he had before.

## Group B. *Mothering wife—dependent husband*

The major process engendered by this situation is stability, through mutual need; the extent to which the wife tolerates the situation to a large extent determines the degree of integration in the marriage. There are in this group, however, a number of families where both the partners are self-destructive within the relationship—they cannot decide what they want from each other and create situations of crisis which may result in temporary separation: this in turn causes them to miss each other and want to be together again.

*Before separation:* Husbands in this group are not socially inadequate; they have plenty of friends and are generally well-liked in the community. The stars amongst them usually have good work records and the recidivists, although they do not usually work, for the most part spend some time living more or less successfully off crimes for which they are not caught. It is only at home, in the relationship with their wives, that they are *noticeably* dependent. The wives are only sometimes older than their husbands, but even where they are not, they are often either the oldest child of a large family whom they mothered, or they have previously been married and have already brought up one family. They may be efficient, competent women, who, at least on the surface, appear to be ambivalent about their 'mothering' role; alternatively they may be extremely inefficient and incompetent in the management of day-to-day affairs, yet derive great satisfaction from the extension of the maternal role to their husband.

*During separation:* In this group there is some difference between star wives and recidivist wives. For the former, the crisis of separation is usually more acute; those who are good managers can feel protective towards their errant husband whilst those who are feckless and self-destructive continue to fluctuate in their attitudes towards him in much the same way as before the separation.

Wives of stars tend to suffer considerably throughout the sentence, largely because of their inability to 'get at' their husband and control the circumstances of his life. Such wives frequently write or telephone to Prison Governors and Commissioners enquiring about the well-being of their husband, or complaining about his treatment. The research worker was often approached in the hope that she would take up the cudgels on behalf of the wife, or that she might be able to manipulate the prison situation. The anxiety experienced by the wives concerning their husbands' well-being often results in their developing psychosomatic symptoms themselves. One wife became very tense and anxious when she discovered that her husband was receiving insulin treatment in prison. He had been suffering from diabetes for many years and she had nursed him by keeping him on a very strict diet. She regarded insulin as poisonous and convinced herself that he would never leave prison alive. She telephoned the research worker on numerous occasions and was finally persuaded that if she wished to discuss the matter, she should ring the Prison Governor. She feared doing this in case her husband was returned to a 'closed' London prison, because 'neither of us could bear his being locked in a cell'. The anxiety provoked by this situation resulted in the wife taking drugs and becoming very disturbed, and by the end of the sentence she had herself developed an ulcer. Free floating anxiety in these wives tends to fluctuate over the period of the sentence and appears directly related to their feelings about the well-being of the husband.

Visits to the husband in prison are not *necessarily* reassuring since the wife may perceive loss of weight or ill-health whether they exist in reality or not. The wives improve emotionally as soon as they can begin to look forward to their husband's return.

Couples in this group of star wives often have no children, or those they have are grown-up. Even where the children are still young, they probably suffer less than most children as a result of their father's imprisonment, since the mother is usually a 'good' mother, and aware of the children's potential suffering. She does not 'take it out' on the children, who are in any case more dependent on their mother than on their father.

Wives of recidivists in this group are less likely to see the imprisonment as a crisis, since they are more used to separation, and a period apart may effectively reinforce their maternalism. This situation may be compared with a mother's attitude to a child who has been away in hospital or at boarding school, and whose maternal feelings are thrown into relief when the child returns home. However, they often rely on their husbands for help in the house and with the children, in much the same way as a mother might expect her elder daughters to help. This is greatly missed during the separation and young children, in particular, may fret as a result of their father's absence.

Wives of both stars and recidivists have extraverted personalities and are well liked in the community. They expect, and tend to receive, a good deal of help from neighbours, friends and relatives. If it is not forthcoming, possibly because financial circumstances do not permit people to offer practical help, wives will seek it through social welfare agencies.

Husbands continue to play the part of the little boy *vis-à-vis* their wives during the sentence. Since dependency may be said to be a predominant feature of imprisonment, it serves admirably to reinforce the relationship they have with their wives. Both stars and recidivists derive a certain amount of enjoyment from the prison environment: the star prisoners are 'good' prisoners and are therefore selected by the staff as formal leaders (red bands, 'trusties', hut leaders, etc.), and although in such a capacity they are expected to accept a limited degree of responsibility and control, they have little real autonomy.

*After discharge:* Star wives tend to blame their husbands and to be *angry* mothers, although at the same time they are very glad to have them back. There is considerably less blame and anger in the case of recidivist wives; the emphasis here is on the 'naughty boy' returned, and they do not want to discuss it any more. Everyone is delighted to have the husband back; it is only in the marital relationship that readjustment presents problems, and the extent of these difficulties is hard to detect.

### 1st Case Summary for Group B

Although we believe this case to be typical of mothering wives and dependent husbands it is worth mentioning that the type of relationship described was not at all apparent to the research worker at the first interview, nor even at the second, but became increasingly apparent as we got to know the family better. This suggests that there are dangers in 'diagnosing' patterns of family relationship too soon, and that there is a need constantly to modify one's assessment as necessary.

Mr D., aged 31, was serving an eighteen-months sentence for larceny. It was his first offence.

Mrs D., aged 31, lived in a semi-detached house on a pre-war housing estate in Middlesex. It was a dismal area, very flat, with acres and acres of little grey boxes. The D.'s were buying the house which was poorly furnished, not very clean and the general impression was one of disorder and a singular lack of comfort.

The D.'s had three children, aged nine, six and five. The middle one had had polio and still limped. She had to be taken to and from school by pram and as she insisted on coming home to dinner this meant four journeys a day for Mrs D.

Before Mr D. went into prison the family were in very considerable debt. This had arisen largely as a result of Mr D. starting up his own plastering business some two years previously. Before this he worked for his father in the same line and earned well, but in recent months he had only been bringing home about £5 a week. Mr D. owed approximately £400 in business debts, but in addition Mrs D. owed about £40 on the house mortgage, and it was finally when they were threatened with eviction that Mr D. turned to crime.

*At the first interview:* Mrs D. received £8 5s 0d per week national assistance and 18s family allowance. Her outgoings were about 42s per week on house insurance, HP, TV, rental and clothes, and in addition she paid £14 2s 8d a month mortgage. A neighbour paid the instalments on her son's bicycle.

She was well liked by everyone in the district and received a tremendous amount of help from tradesmen who knocked odd bits off the bills each week and sent up goods without charging. Mrs D. found it quite overwhelming that people should be so very kind and said she didn't know how she would manage without it.

*At the second interview:* Mrs D. was managing extremely well. Whereas her husband had been frightened of asking the bank for a loan when their debts became so great, Mrs D. went straight to the manager and obtained one; he told her that repayment could wait until her husband came out of prison. Two months later she had a letter asking if she could start to pay back a little, and she was now paying back £1 per month. She had also been in touch with her MP in order to try and get her husband's sentence reduced, and although this had not succeeded, she was satisfied that the MP and the Home Secretary had at least taken time to think about the case!

Her national assistance had been increased by 1s a week (to £8 6s 0d) after a great deal of consideration, and Mrs D. was somewhat bitterly amused by this. Her debts had not increased; on the contrary she was doing her best to pay off as much as possible before her husband was released. She earned 32s 6d a week for domestic work in the evenings and 17s 6d working for a greengrocer who also supplied her with cheap fruit and vegetables. From time to time she obtained sewing jobs from friends and occasionally did washing for a couple of men living nearby. She was prepared to do anything at all in order to earn extra money to pay off debts and to buy food for the children.

As a result of overwork her health had deteriorated. She had lost three stone in the past eight months, but refused to go to the doctor as she said she had no time.

She had received a visit from a D P A representative and they were said to have told her that she was definitely a case they could help, but she never heard from them again. The N S P C C man had called and said it was a routine visit, explaining that they visited all prisoners' wives. She did not know how he found out about her, but was very pleased because he now visited once a month, and although he did not give her money he always brought toys and books for the children. The R S P C A man had visited her having been told that their Alsatian dog was being neglected. In fact he was simply moulting and they were quite satisfied. She had had a grant from the N A B for some children's clothes, but they would give her nothing for herself. The school authorities had sent her to the W V S for clothes for the older children, but most of these were too big or too old.

She was still being helped in small ways by neighbours, friends and tradesmen.

Mrs D. had a girl lodger who paid £3 a week for board and lodging but said she would shortly be leaving. A young boy who had lived with them previously, and whom she regarded as a son, had been involved in the offence with her husband and had been sent to Borstal. She was very disappointed that the authorities would not allow him to come to stay with her for his home leave.

Mrs D. had no social life outside the home, but received frequent visits from friends and neighbours. Her parents came over and brought food, but could not help her financially. Her brother was also in prison for the first time and this had almost broken her mother.

Mr D.'s family moved away from the district after his arrest because they could not bear the shame and disgrace. Mrs D. had remained in touch with them and went to stay there for a short holiday. Her father-in-law was on national assistance and they could not help her financially.

The children visited their father each month; the youngest boy showed signs of disturbance, having become enuretic; the GP said it was certainly due to father's absence and that it would clear up when he returned. The oldest boy had become extremely irritable and bad-tempered and was often very rude to his mother. Mrs D. was aware of how much they needed their father and did her best to help them, but her biggest problem was feeding them, especially as they refused to stay at school for free dinners, and she felt it was important not to add to their difficulties at this time.

She was resentful of the fact that it was herself and the children rather than her husband who was being punished for what he had done. At the same time she was concerned lest her husband did not get enough to eat in prison, though she realized that he needed to lose weight. Food was very important to Mrs D. and a never-ending topic during the interviews. She feared her inability to give enough to everyone, and she herself frequently went without.

*At the third interview:* The young man from Borstal appeared to be back again staying with Mrs D. having been released on licence, though to satisfy the authorities he was officially said to be staying with his mother. He was not working and said there were no jobs available.

Mrs D. continued to cope very well financially, and her debts had not increased. Her National Assistance had been increased by 7s to £8 13s 0d.

Her contact with the NSPCC man gave her a great deal of support, and he was planning to take the children to the pantomime. The 'woman from the DPA' had not returned and Mrs D. had asked the WVS for help with sheets; she did not know whether she would get them or not. She still received a lot of help from neighbours and tradesmen.

The youngest boy had developed a 'nervous rash' and she herself felt perpetually tired and worried. She considered that as she had slaved away for mere survival during her husband's imprisonment, he should be able to take a job on release *at once* in order to relieve the financial strain she had borne throughout. She also experienced some feelings of guilt that the young Borstal boy should have been mixed up in her husband's crime and by trying to prevent him staying with them she felt the authorities were depriving her of an opportunity to make it up to him.

*At the fourth interview:* Little change in the material situation, but Mrs D. was now preparing mentally for her husband's discharge. She was very insistent that he should earn a *regular* wage, and that he should work for his uncle. He, on the other hand, was still said to be hankering after his own business. Mrs D. said she would insist, however, since her husband had always been too vague and unrealistic: 'I've always made most of the decisions'. She had tried unsuccessfully to make him handle the money: 'I always had to nag him—I hate it . . . I've always dreamed of a nice house and freedom for the kids and he [Mr D.] always wanted a car. But somehow we've never had the chance.' She was very concerned because her husband 'seems happy' in prison—she felt he had settled down too well to institutional life.

*At the fifth interview* (joint): Mr D. had started work for his uncle a week after release. He still wanted to start up on his own again but Mrs D. was determined to try to prevent this. She still controlled the finances and gave her husband pocket money. She resented this and felt it was not *her* job, but dared not leave it to him, 'he's such a dreamer'. The debts were nearly all paid off. She was better physically and much less tense and tired.

The children had settled down well, but Mr D. commented that it was fortunate that it was not their mother who went away because they are much more dependent on her.

The ex-Borstal boy was still living with them and refused to visit his probation officer.

All their neighbours, friends and relatives had rallied round. Mr D. had dreamed of living in the country and running an allotment, but once again his wife brought him back to reality.

Mr D. was reluctant to talk about his pre-prison days though he was very anxious to talk about prison itself which he genuinely enjoyed, and he only came to life when talking of his experiences there. The strain of again being a breadwinner, husband and father was very great and this caused some tension between husband and wife. On the surface Mrs D. was delighted to have him back and all was well, but she had hoped that prison would change him and that he would become more responsible and realistic; it had certainly changed him, but in quite another way—he had had a taste of a kind of life he enjoyed and had not known before—a life with no responsibilities and where he was free to 'pipe-dream' all day.

### 2nd Case Summary for Group B

Mr E., aged 41, was serving an eighteen-months sentence for false pretences. He had never been in prison before, but had been fined three times and conditionally discharged once.

Mrs E., aged 49, a common-law wife, had been living with Mr E. for eleven years and was separated from her legal husband whom she refused to divorce; she claimed to have more power over Mr E. if she did not marry him!

There were two children of the union, aged ten and seven. Mrs E. had other children, none of whom lived with her, but all were said to like Mr E. Two of the boys had been in Borstal and one was in an Approved School.

*At the first interview:* Mrs E. had been working for some years as a canteen assistant at nights and intended to keep this job. She enjoyed it and got on very well with the people at work. Everyone knew about Mr E.'s imprisonment, but it made no difference to their attitude towards her. A neighbour gave the children their breakfast and saw them off to school.

Mrs E. looked tired and said her health was bad; she was due to go into hospital for a hysterectomy. She said her 'husband' suffered from nerves and dermatitis and was often unemployed on account of ill-health, but he helped her a great deal in the house and was very good to both her and the children. She enjoyed looking after him and did not resent her role as breadwinner.

Mr E.'s father was in a mental hospital and Mrs E. would have nothing to do with him 'he's a mental case you see'. Both his grandparents had been in mental institutions.

Mrs E. could not account for her 'husband's' criminality except by saying that he was easily led. She discussed it in terms of his being 'naughty', and added 'you can't do without money, can you?'.

Their financial position before his arrest was very precarious. Most of the furniture had been pawned and they had rent arrears, yet they had just bought a second-hand car on which Mrs E. maintained she would keep up the payments; nothing had in fact been paid for the past three months and the car was standing derelict outside.

Mrs E. had been to visit her husband; he was anxious and had cried throughout the time.

They had little social life before the separation (as Mrs E. worked at nights and Mr E. during the day there was little opportunity).

*At the second interview:* Mrs E.'s health had deteriorated and she had stopped work and was living on National Assistance. She had been to hospital for a minor operation but would not have the hysterectomy until her 'husband' was discharged.

Her financial situation was hopeless. She was paying nothing towards HP commitments and tallymen were only paid if they became too pressing. She borrowed money from neighbours each week. She said her electricity meter had been broken into and she was incensed because the police, to whom she reported it, wanted to take her fingerprints!

She was very concerned about the children who had been left with a neighbour whilst she was in hospital. She said they did not appear to be missing their father, though one of them had taken to wandering off.

Mrs E.'s eldest son by her legal marriage was now twenty-three and in the army. Her attitude towards him was very ambivalent and she roared with laughter when describing his latest escapade which was to get two weeks compassionate leave 'to come home and bury his mother'. Her attitude to both her 'husband' and her son was very similar: when either got into trouble she forgave them, but always added 'I'll kill him next time I see him'.

She no longer visited her 'husband' regularly as she could not afford it and felt too ill. When she had last seen him she was relieved that he had put on weight and his health had improved. She was very much concerned about their future sexual relationship once she had had her operation.

*At the third interview:* Mrs E. declared at the beginning of the interview that she no longer intended to live with Mr E. This state of affairs had arisen over a misunderstanding about his date of release, but so far as she was concerned he had lied to her and she wrote him a 'nasty letter'.

She was under the doctor for anaemia and was still worrying about the effect of the hysterectomy on her sexual relations with her 'husband'.

Mrs E.'s debts had increased but she said she hadn't any, by which she meant that, having written to everyone concerned telling them she was not going to pay, she regarded all debts as cleared.

Her son by her legal marriage was now in prison and she was very ambivalent about it. She was also very ambivalent about Mr E. She quite enjoyed the freedom of not having him around, but missed him since he did a great deal of housework for her. Throughout the interview she seemed anxious to impress the interviewer that she would not have him back, but it was equally clear that she had no intention of leaving him.

She recounted endless amusing stories of her relationships with neighbours, friends, and family, and seemed to thrive on creating difficult situations for herself about which she could subsequently complain.

*At the fourth interview:* Little change in her ambivalent attitude towards Mr E. She found the children more difficult to manage, both because they hadn't a father in the house and because of her own increasing irritability. She had made increasing contact with the children of her legal marriage; the two girls had been very helpful, and the youngest boy had now left his Approved School. One girl was married to an epileptic and Mrs E. would not talk to her because of this. She also got help from her brother.

Mrs E.'s health had deteriorated. So had her financial position. She had been given clothes for the children by the wvs.

Mrs E. visited her 'husband' from time to time. He had been moved outside London and the expense was too great to visit regularly. In addition they had rows whenever she did visit him and this upset her afterwards. Mr E. seemed to enjoy life in prison which annoyed her.

Mr E. had told her he had been offered money by a prison visitor to set himself up in business as a greengrocer and Mrs E. did not know whether or not to believe it. She desperately wanted to and said that life would be a lot easier for them all if he would only get a job and stick to it.

*At the fifth interview:* Mrs E. had expected her 'husband' on Home Leave but he had not appeared. Again there seemed to have been some misunderstanding, and she was extremely angry with him.

The children were at home because they had no shoes and the school authorities had promised to send some down.

She had received some help with rent arrears from a prison after-care organization, but the man had not been able to help redeem any of the items she had pawned, which included pretty well everything pawnable in the house. She was refused help by SSAFA and was very angry. The prison welfare officer sent her her fare to visit her husband on one occasion. The NAB also did so on one occasion, but although they paid the train fare, they did not pay the bus fares and this too angered Mrs E.

*At the sixth interview* (joint): Mrs E. had retired to bed and was enjoying being looked after by her 'husband'. Throughout all the interviews there had been considerable stress on Mr E.'s 'usefulness' in a domestic capacity. In this respect Mrs E. behaved towards him in much the same way as she might have behaved to a teenage daughter, expected to do her share of the chores.

Mr E. wanted to talk only about prison, and this consisted of a long tirade against the prison authorities, although he seemed to have been quite happy there.

They had decided to get legally married, but this in fact seemed most unlikely. Mrs E. said that if he still wanted to marry her after her operation she would be prepared to do so; Mr E. said it would be better for the children.

Both children were pleased to have their father back, particularly the younger one. Mr E. was much gentler with the younger one and obviously favoured him.

Mr E. had not yet obtained work. He insisted that a prison visitor was going to give him the money to start a shop.

Mrs E. had bought a pile of new clothes for going into hospital and they had acquired massive debts. However, neither of them regarded this as a problem.

They were both full of complaints about welfare and after-care, but whatever help Mrs E. got, she was always dissatisfied. Mrs E. also complained about the neighbours, although even during our visit numerous people popped in to say 'hello' and both seemed well-liked in the area.

Most of what this couple said had very little to do with reality, but it was very real to them. They were quite irresponsible about money, and heavily prejudiced about right and wrong, but both had a good sense of humour and played a cat and mouse game with their marriage, Mrs E. being the cat.

## Group C. *Dominant wives—passive husbands*

This pattern of relationship appears to engender a number of different processes: the wife's dominance may take the form of irritant stimulation—where the wife keeps pressure on the husband in many areas of life, or the wife may be extremely demanding and thrive in situations of conflict bordering on self-destruction. Families in this group fall within a continuum from the very closely integrated to those on the verge of disintegration.

In our discussion we feel it is useful to divide the wives roughly into two categories: dominance involving conflict and dominance involving no apparent conflict. Where conflict exists, it usually does so both within the home and outside.

*Before separation:* The most integrated families appear to exist where irritant stimulation on the part of the wife is apparently passively accepted by the husband. No overt conflict exists and the problem here appears to be the difference in expectations between husband and wife. The husbands are passive largely because they function to a great extent in a fantasy world, dreaming of what life might be like if they lived somewhere else, had another job, or even another wife. Their passivity is a form of withdrawal. They appear to have married women with high expectations, almost in the hope that this would make *them* stable. Both partners consider the marriage to be a very happy one: they share a common image of an ideal husband and marriage, but whereas the husband achieves this goal in fantasy, the wife persists in the belief that she can push him towards it.

Also well-integrated are those families where, although they appear much more disorganized, the wife is tolerant of what she feels to be her husband's failure, though persistently complaining of it. The husband is, for the most part, tolerant of his wife's dominance and his own feeling of inadequacy, but if and when life shows signs of becoming intolerable, he escapes from his wife's dominance by withdrawal, and turns to drink or gambling—if necessary to crime.

In families with much overt conflict, the wife's dominance is a form of self-destructiveness in much the same way as is her husband's passivity. Such families may be permanently beset by crises, but 'cope' so long as they are together (although the marriage itself may be punctuated by frequent self-imposed separations when one or other partner walks out). The degree of conflict in the family seems to be directly related to the extent of other forms of disorganization such as unemployment, drink, gambling and promiscuity, though which is cause and which is effect we cannot claim to know. In those couples where self-destructiveness is prominent, their behaviour is geared to bring about negative responses from all around them. Their apparent attempts to destroy the marriage are, however, usually superficial, and as soon as this is threatened the urge to be reparative reasserts itself since they have a real, if neurotically-based, need for each other.[1] The husband's offence may be part of this process of self-destruction, and prison, by providing a controlled environment, acts as a break. Crime in fact, may act as a means of maintaining a relationship which is built upon conflict. There are in this group some families which have disintegrated altogether and ended in separation and divorce.

One feature appears in all these situations; a direct relationship exists between the husband's criminality and the marital relationship: the dominance of the wife seems to reinforce the husband's feelings of insecurity or inadequacy and he turns to drink, gambling and other women, all of which in the long run are additional commitments which cannot be met, and crime is often the only apparent way out. If successful it reinforces his ego and provides money to cover debts; if unsuccessful it results in imprisonment, which provides an escape from the pressure of home life.

*During separation:* Wives in this group are usually extraverted personalities who, despite frequent rows in some cases, are well-liked in the community. Relationships with outsiders are usually initiated by the wife, but the husband is also popular, and imprisonment makes little difference to their pattern of social life.

Those wives whose marriage contained no overt signs of conflict make a very bad initial adjustment to the separation and suffer a great deal. They recognize the part their own behaviour has played in their husband's criminality, and they realize that the marriage was not as stable as they had believed. Wives who, at the first interview, talked of husbands who 'changed' unaccountably a year or so earlier, gradually begin to see how the difference in expectation between them contributed to this 'change'; however, this degree of insight soon passes. These wives make great efforts to take over the husband's roles, to keep the family together and to maintain financial stability.

Reassurance from the husband on visits and through letters is a great help to the wives, and each convinces the other that the marriage has been strengthened by the experience, since both have expiated their sins. Wives' attitudes to their husbands and to the marriage fluctuate a good deal during the separation and this to some

---

[1] See Eisenstein, *op. cit.*

extent appears to depend upon the recognition of their own guilt feelings.

Wives maintain contact with the wider family network and in some cases extend it. The husband is rarely condemned by relatives but is regarded as having been 'naughty and stupid' for having placed his wife in such a difficult and embarrassing position.

There is virtually no contact with welfare agencies amongst this group; this would have added to the embarrassment they feel through their own involvement in the situation.

We had very little opportunity to study the children in the group, since the mothers usually took pains not to have the children around when we visited. Mothers deny that the children are affected by the father's imprisonment, because they believe that *they* are more important to the children than is the father, and his absence is therefore immaterial. One wife said her children were 'doing better at school now that their father is away'. The atmosphere in the homes during our research visits would lead us to believe, however, that these children *are* affected, not so much by the father's absence as by the attitude of the mother: 'What a dreadful thing he's done, but we can manage without him'. This tends to inhibit the children from discussing the situation.

Where conflict is a prominent feature of the wife's personality the response to separation is very different, since the conflict situation is continued in their relationship both with the husband and with relatives, friends and children. Such wives are usually beset by financial problems during the separation, though they are rarely made anxious by these, and they seek a great deal of help from welfare agencies. Such help is considered a right, and is equally expected from relatives and neighbours.

The extent to which the children suffer varies, and depends almost exclusively upon the extent to which their mother acts out her conflicts in the home. They are used to her domineering and erratic behaviour which usually takes little account of their particular needs, but when their father is at home he acts as a break, and his passivity may lower the level of tension.

The more self-destructive wives endeavour to manipulate those who would like to help them and this tends to have the opposite result: people either give up trying to help since it is thought to be useless, or they become angry and hostile. For example, one social worker, no doubt pushed to the limit by her client's behaviour, on two occasions gave a wife inaccurate information about her legal position. She did so in order to try to persuade the wife to conform to what would normally be seen as reasonable behaviour, but which, from the wife's point of view, merely antagonized her further and made her even more determined *not* to conform. Nor was this an exceptional case; workers from both voluntary and statutory agencies used this method of persuasion with their clients, though it may be presumed that they were inexperienced members of staff.

*After discharge:* All wives in this group are glad to have their husbands back. Where there was irritant stimulation by the wife and no overt conflict, all seems well on the surface. The husband feels he has been inadequate and useless, but has paid for it and the wife is pleased to have him back because she needs a 'good' husband with whom to face the outside world. However, even a slightly more sophisticated acquaintance with these families after discharge suggests that the marriage is by no means improved and that the wife is likely to continue to blame her husband for a long time for what *she* has suffered.

The longer the husband remains at home the more the wife covers up any awareness that she might have had about her own part in the events which led up to the crisis. Wives show considerable anxiety about the kind of job their husband will take, and fears about losing their social position are uppermost. Concern about financial matters is minimal since this could be solved by the wife herself going out to work if necessary; this would give her yet another stick with which to beat her husband: 'look what you've done to me, first prison and now I have to work'.

When their husbands return wives also tend to develop minor physical ailments—headaches, mild depressions, insomnia. These sometimes start just before the release date and are treated by their GP with sedatives and tonics.

Older children find themselves in a rather difficult position, since they have been trained throughout the separation to see the suffering as their mother's. This results in some additional strain between father and child.

Where family relationships were reasonably well-integrated before separation, in so far as conflict was tolerated, husband and wife are happy to be together again and full of optimism and hope. They too are convinced that the marriage has benefited by the separation, and as witness to this they throw fewer saucepans at each other. Some wives become pregnant as though to indicate the arrival of a new era. Husbands return to work and try to limit their excesses—less drinking, fewer bets and flirtations only. Since these are forms of escape from the dominant wife it is not too difficult to limit them in the early stages of reunion. Their wives are usually extraverted and demonstrative women who can show plenty of affection, and this helps to make the husband feel needed and wanted and eases the relationship. The fact that all is well with the parents means that pressure is removed from the children.

Unfortunately we were not able to follow-up these families for very long after the husband's discharge, but assuming that no lasting change in personality had occurred, and basing our impressions on their past experience of similar situations, we are left with the very strong belief that it was merely a matter of time before the conflict was reactivated.

Where conflict is much more severe and the disruptive pattern continued throughout the sentence, it is often fortuitous whether or not the couple come together immediately on discharge. In one family where the wife had had a complete mental breakdown, she had been determined not to have him home, but although we did not see them together (the husband refused), we knew that they were in fact reunited and according to the wife were continuing their normal pattern of conflict. Another wife disappeared before the husband's release and we could not trace her, and a third suddenly packed up and left for Australia. However, the majority were reunited and continued the pattern of cyclical destructiveness, their deviant behaviour representing their way of solving problems.

Nevertheless the fact that some families exhibiting a similar pattern of relationship had actually separated or divorced suggests that there may be limits to the amount of conflict and destructive behaviour which can be tolerated.

### 1st Case Summary for Group C

Mr G., aged 38, was a genuine first offender serving an eighteen-months sentence for embezzlement.

Mrs G., aged 35, lived with her three children, aged fourteen, eleven and four, in a pleasant, well-kept, four-bedroomed, terraced house in South London. The area was not particularly attractive, but solidly respectable and with well-kept gardens.

She and her husband had known for some time that he would be charged with fraud, and so Mrs G. had taken a job as a receptionist/clerk. They had been married for fifteen years and the marriage had been happy for about the first eight years, during which time Mr G. had a regular, though poorly paid job. When he began to launch out on his own the marriage began to deteriorate. It was at this time too, that Mr G. gave up all his Church connections and voluntary work, though Mrs G. continued with them.

*At the first interview:* Mrs G. had now come to realize that she was partly responsible for what had happened since she had always nagged her husband and accused him of lacking ambition. As Mr G. became increasingly involved with his business, so he began to neglect his family, and his wife turned for companionship to the children and to friends, and the two drifted apart. When, about a year ago, Mr G. said he must go to the police and put the facts before them, the relationship began to improve and they were once again a 'happy family'. Mrs G. complained that no sooner had this happened than he was sent to prison. However, she was sure that the separation would strengthen their relationship.

Mrs G. denied that the children were in any way affected since they had in any case lost touch with their father when he started working so hard. [She forgot that she had earlier told us that there was a subsequent period when they were all happily reunited.] Any attempt to press her on this matter resulted in her becoming increasingly vague and evasive.

Mrs G. enjoyed going out to work and felt the children did not suffer: the youngest child went to a day nursery. She earned £8 per week and had 18s family allowance.

Both her own and her husband's family lived in the area and all were giving very active support. She also received support from neighbours and friends.

She was under the doctor for nerves during the year they were waiting for the case to come up, but normally she said her health was quite good.

Her main concern was loneliness. She saw the present situation as a 'punishment from God' for going against the laws of honesty and truth. She now felt she was covetous and her husband ambitious, although in the past she had always accused him of lacking ambition.

*At the second interview:* Mrs G. was maintaining regular contact with her husband by visits and letters, although he had been moved out of London. Her only regret was that she could not often see him alone as her mother-in-law insisted on going with her. Mr G. had always been very much dominated by his mother as well as by his wife.

She was receiving regular financial help from relatives; the NAB turned down her application as she was working. Mrs G. said she had 'changed' since her husband went away and she would go on working when he returned.

At this interview Mrs G. said the children had 'recovered quite well' and she was able now to admit that they were very upset at first.

She had had no contact with any welfare agency and would not welcome any, but felt that someone ought to have called from the prison to see how she was managing.

Her health had greatly improved and she no longer took pills. She was full of confidence about the marital relationship in the future, though a little disappointed that it seemed to have settled down and letters and visits had become more mundane now that the initial crisis of separation was over.

*At the third interview:* Between these two interviews Mrs G. had written to the interviewer asking if she could help by visiting other wives of prisoners. She thought it would be good for her to 'repay some of the damage' her husband had done.

She did in fact visit one woman on two occasions but found it rather more difficult than she had anticipated. At this interview the subject was not mentioned, but Mrs G. used the experience as a means of denying her own position as a prisoner's wife and treating the interviewer as a colleague, thus trying to avoid discussing her own family by means of a general discussion of welfare and prisons.

Mrs G. saw no problems for the future; she said her husband was returning to the Church and was happy about this.

She discussed the attempts made by her own family and herself to 'bring her husband up a step or two in the social class race', and said that his mother had always treated her son like a child and still did. Mrs G. talked about her disappointment that Mr G. did not settle at a steady job and she compared him unfavourably with her own father.

She thought the children were not suffering at all, in fact she added 'it is probably good for them and will teach them to stand on their own feet'.

*At the fourth interview* (joint): The atmosphere was somewhat tense and Mrs G. found it difficult to allow her husband to talk and she watched him carefully when he did. He seemed only concerned to talk about prisons and penology, and was intelligently critical.

The interview took place within a week of discharge and Mr G. was in touch with a number of firms about a job, but nothing was yet definite. Mrs G. was worried about this and was most anxious that he should find a *good* job. Mrs G. herself continued to work and her husband was agreeable, provided she was free during the school holidays.

No debts had accumulated during the separation and there were no financial problems: Mrs G. had received a lot of help from family and friends.

They both said that the experience of imprisonment had strengthened their marriage.

The eldest child had started truanting about a month before his father returned, but both Mr and Mrs G. emphatically denied that it was in any way connected with his father's imprisonment, although the boy himself said it was because other boys questioned him about his 'free dinners'.

*A fifth interview* was held with this family, since the first joint interview had taken place so soon after release. Mr G. had obtained a job as a works study clerk within three weeks of discharge. He was pleased and Mrs G. was also satisfied with the status of the job.

Mrs G. was still working, although her parents disapproved. Her health had deteriorated and her nerves were very bad. She was under the doctor. She described her symptoms as acute sensibility to noise, severe headaches and fits of depression.

The oldest boy was still being 'very difficult'. Mr G. described it as 'typically adolescent behaviour', but it included truanting and stealing.

Although Mrs G. was relieved that her husband had a white-collar job, and she found the joint income a help, she was still very much concerned about their social position and was putting pressure on her husband to get new curtains and a washing machine. Although she tried not to, she frequently reminded him of his imprisonment, and could not avoid telling him what a terrible time she had had by comparison with him.

Both were very anxious to help wives of ex-prisoners, and Mr G. was working for the Samaritans. They felt this to be a form of 'atonement'.

### 2nd Case Summary for Group C

Mr J., aged 28, was serving an eighteen-months sentence for house-breaking. He had been in trouble since childhood having graduated from Approved School to prison, and this was the second prison sentence since his marriage six years ago.

Mrs. J., aged 24, lived with three children, aged two years, sixteen months, and eight weeks, in an LCC flat in East London. She had moved to the flat after her husband's imprisonment, and owing to difficulty in tracing her whereabouts our first interview took place three months *after* her husband's conviction.

*At the first interview:* Mrs J. was living on national assistance and family allowances and found it very difficult to manage, although she had already approached a great many social welfare agencies and was receiving financial help from many of them. She was prepared to ask anybody and everybody for help and felt that she should be given enough to make life pleasant whilst deprived of her husband. She did not think she should suffer and thought welfare societies should both give more and give more frequently than they did at present.

Mrs J. said her husband was a good worker and gave her regular housekeeping money, but his trouble was gambling and this had become particularly difficult when someone opened a betting shop nearby. However he never gambled away *all* the housekeeping money. She spoke in deprecating terms of his inadequacy, but at the same time was obviously fond of him.

Mrs J. met her husband three weeks before he went to prison on the last occasion, and married him on the day he was released. She had previously been engaged to another boy, by whom she had a child at the age of fifteen; this child had been adopted.

Mrs J. said she was 'fed up' with the constant prison sentences and was adamant that she would not stick by him if he went inside again.

Most of the interview was, however, taken up by a discussion of her own difficulties, in particular her very erratic relationships with relatives and neighbours. She had rows with everyone, though being a somewhat volatile personality, such rows did not appear to affect her at all deeply. She considered an elderly man a few doors away to be 'not quite sane', he having accused her of being 'a dirty old whore', and similar epithets. Another neighbour she described as a 'Chinese chef with a reputation for interfering with little girls'. Her mother-in-law she described as 'a hard old bitch', and she had no contact with her own family. However, these relationships appeared to fluctuate and Mrs J. joined in the general pattern of visiting which seemed normal in the flats, if only to gossip.

Mrs J. spent much of the interview shouting at, slapping, and nagging the eldest child. The children had been told their father was at sea, and Mrs J. was sure they were not missing him at all. She had taken the oldest one to visit her father on one occasion, but this had been upsetting for both father and child and so she did not intend doing so again. Mr J. was said to be a good father who spent as much time as possible with his children.

*At the second interview:* the main difficulties centred round Mrs J.'s relationship with the oldest child. The girl was very demanding and constantly interrupted, but was ignored by her mother until she started screaming and kicking when she was told 'don't take liberties with me'—accompanied by a sharp blow or slap, to which the child's response was 'fuck off'. This scene was re-enacted countless times throughout the interview. In between times the child was threatened with a stick hanging on the wall which Mrs J. said she used when the child was 'worse than her usual bloody self'. The child clung to her mother wherever she went and some weeks ago had been found by a neighbour running naked and screaming round the courtyard because she could not find her mother who was watching television in a flat in the block opposite. The same child had later fallen down the concrete stairs with the pram containing the baby; the latter had been unharmed but the little girl had broken her arm; Mrs J. said she had soon got used to the plaster and was 'just as bleeding wild as usual'. Mrs J. complained bitterly that her husband was 'too bloody soft' with the children.

She was still finding lack of money a great problem and had lost a good many items in pawn, including her husband's suit, watch and camera, because she was unable to reclaim them.

She visited her husband regularly and his letters assured her that he would not get into trouble again.

Relationships with neighbours continued to fluctuate, with much abuse on either side, but Mrs J. nevertheless derived a fair amount of support from these somewhat negative relationships.

She was missing her husband a good deal and getting very irritable and depressed. She had in the past suffered from a nervous break-down but now refused to consult her GP, despite increasing tension. She derived a certain amount of support from attendance at the wives' club which had been formed at the prison.

*At the third interview:* Mrs J. was busy preparing for her husband's return. Debts were rather worse and she continued to ask for help on all sides, receiving a fair amount.

She had not visited her husband for some time because the children had been ill and the weather bad. Mrs J. recognized at this interview that the eldest child *was* in fact missing her father, by which she meant that the child had become virtually unmanageable. Her own behaviour to the girl was identical with that described at the second interview. Mrs J. seemed only interested in children when they were babies; though she was determined not to have any more children she was not prepared seriously to consider the use of contraceptives.

*At the fourth interview* (joint): All was well. Mr J. had obtained a job within three days of release and was quite happy about it. The debts were gradually being paid off, and neither of them were concerned about financial problems. Although Mr J. still spent money at the betting shop, he was managing to limit the amount quite successfully.

Mrs J. was pregnant and quite happy about it. Mr J. said 'let's have a big family and all at once', and Mrs J. grinned and replied 'I like babies'.

The children were easier to handle with their father home. His quiet and passive manner with them was a great relief after the tumultuous and often inconsistent behaviour of their mother. He did not use force on the oldest child and Mrs J. was relieved that she would soon be attending nursery school in the daytime. Mr J. thought none of the children had suffered during his absence—they were all too young.

None of Mr J.'s family had been near him, and although he visited his mother regularly he seemed indifferent to her.

The neighbours were the same as before—since this was an area of high delinquency, there was no question of shame or stigma.

Although Mr J. was a somewhat weak and inadequate man, he was a good deal calmer than his wife and seemed able to reduce her state of tension and restlessness. He was anxious to stay away from crime but seemed at least faintly aware that if life became too de-manding he would return to heavy gambling which would un-doubtedly land him in trouble again. 'I usually lost', he said, when speaking of gambling, but it seemed to be true of most aspects of his life.

### 3rd Case Summary for Group C

Mr K., aged 35, was serving an eighteen-months sentence for larceny. He had had a long series of previous convictions which included nine sentences of imprisonment, covering eleven years of his life. He was a weak man of rather low intelligence, but with a violent temper of which he was afraid.

*At the first interview:* Mrs K., aged 22, said she was living with an aunt, and not until the fourth interview did we learn that the 'aunt' was in fact her mother! She had put her six-months-old baby in care, so that she could go out to work when her husband was 'on the run' for six months before going into prison. Although Mr K. had told the interviewer that it was a common-law marriage, it was not until the second interview that Mrs K. admitted this.

Mrs K. had heavy debts, most of them HP commitments, for which she had been taken to Court. She also owed money to a friend. She worked as a garage attendant earning about £8–£9 per week, and was supposed to pay 30s for the baby and £4 to her 'aunt' for her keep.

They had never settled in one place for long, mainly living with odd friends and relatives, or in rooms from which they were often evicted. Mr K. worked from time to time between spells of imprisonment; according to Mrs K. he only committed offences when he was drunk and this had been a problem for years. All his friends were criminals. He was said to be 'accident prone' and had been knocked down by cars on seven occasions.

Mrs K. was herself illegitimate and at this interview denied having any contact with her mother. Mr K. came from a delinquent family, his 'wife' said they came together eighteen months ago because they were both 'looking for somebody to love'. For a brief period they had been able to give each other some stability, but as individuals they were too disturbed to maintain this and the marriage soon settled down to an erratic pattern of coming and going.

Mrs K. was a determined and forceful young woman who made all the decisions but these usually involved her in some additional form of difficulty—debts, pregnancy, crime, etc. Her 'husband' was quite happy to remain a persistent offender with a drink problem, and for the most part acquiesced in whatever his 'wife' said. He thought she might keep him out of prison because 'I can't say no, I just can't say it'.

Mr K. was said to be very jealous of his 'wife' who was so much younger, and there were major rows about his drinking.

Mrs K. knew a great many people in the area and her relationships with them were not affected by her 'husband's' imprisonment. Her employers did not know she was living with anyone, nor about the baby.

*At the second interview:* Mrs K. expressed concern about the baby in the home. She only visited him once every three months, and the child had developed asthma. At this interview Mrs K. gave a long and confused account of why she and Mr K. were not married, but said they would get married soon.

Her main problem was shortage of money. Everything would be perfect if only she could find a few hundred pounds.

The relationship with the 'aunt' had deteriorated, and she was not on speaking terms with the 'aunt's' husband.

Most of this interview was taken up by Mrs K. telling what she subsequently admitted was a pack of lies about her own family background and that of her 'husband'.

*At the third interview:* Mrs K. had been ill and she had had to give up her job. In addition she had fallen downstairs and cut open her head. She had no income whatever since she dared not go to the N A B, having told them so many lies in the past, nor could she draw sickness benefit for the same reason, nor unemployment benefit because her 'stamps are not quite up-to-date'—a gross understatement as it transpired!

Mrs K. had moved away from her 'aunt' a few weeks before her illness and was sharing a flat with a friend, though she spent a lot of time with the 'aunt' who helped her financially. She owed a month's rent but the landlord had not complained.

She had not seen her baby for the past six months because she had not paid the money for his keep and so was scared to go there.

At this interview we found out that Mrs K. had been in touch with the moral welfare officer for some considerable time—it was to her that the money for the child's keep was supposed to be paid, but she said 'she makes me terribly nervous and I'm scared of her'.

She had not seen her 'husband' for four months, and said this was because of the expense, as he had been moved to a prison outside London; later she claimed it was because she had met an American whom she had considered marrying, but whom she had finally given up. She said she was now missing the money he had been giving her, as he had bought her a lot of clothes, and a few weeks after they broke up had sent her £20.

She then wrote to Mr K. telling him all about it and he wrote back a 'desperate letter'. The prison welfare officer got in touch with her 'aunt' because Mr K. was 'creating chaos in the prison and was in a desperate state'. Mrs K. then thought she'd better give him another chance and realized she still 'loved him very much'.

Mrs K. had debts everywhere: Court orders for H P, money owed to her 'aunt', to friends, to the local authority, to the landlord. She did not, however, seem unduly worried about all this.

At the end of this interview (which had taken place in the 'aunt's' house) Mrs K. asked the research worker if she would drive her to Mrs K.'s own flat. In the car Mrs K. told her that one of the 'aunt's' two children was in fact *her* child, but not Mr K.'s.

She was very undecided about whether or not she would have Mr K. back when he left prison, she thought she might 'take off' on her own somewhere.

*Before the fourth interview:* A message came from the 'aunt' saying Mrs K. had gone up North as her adoptive father had died. Mrs K. later phoned herself to say that Mr K. was out of prison and working 'in the country' having been upset on finding that she was in Scotland when he came out. She promised to get him home for a joint interview a few days later.

On arrival, however, only the 'aunt' and her husband were in, and they talked for three hours. It was then that it came out that the 'aunt' was really Mrs K.'s mother. Mrs K. had conceived her first child at the age of thirteen, but that had been aborted. This occurred again a little later, and again at seventeen; this last time the baby was born and adopted by the 'aunt'. In addition Mrs K. had been in Court on a charge of grievous bodily harm, and on one occasion was brought home by the police having been found raped and exhausted on the common. Every time she got into trouble her 'aunt' had picked up the pieces. Mrs K. helped run a brothel on one occasion and had stolen all her life.

Mrs K. then met Mr K. and they had the baby and when Mr K. went to prison Mrs K. returned to her 'aunt', leaving her from time to time to live in furnished rooms. She had slept with a number of men other than the American during the present sentence and had finally been evicted for non-payment of rent.

*At the fifth interview* (joint): The 'aunt' was present most of the time and having been out to celebrate something, was drunk. Mrs K. went on telling fantastic lies throughout the interview: these Mr K. just accepted good-humouredly as fantasies. There was a lot of uncertainty about whether the baby should or should not come home; a large sum of money was owed to the council for his keep and Mr K. had promised to give £3 to the 'aunt' every week for her to pay to the authorities. However, so far his payments had been 'irregular'. He was said to be working 'for a friend, but on me own you know'.

The 'aunt', being drunk was much less controlled than usual and there were fierce exchanges between her and Mrs K. with the latter periodically slamming out of the room.

Mr and Mrs K. had been having terrible physical fights which Mrs K. usually won since she was the stronger of the two. She did not want to get married because it would give Mr K. a legal right to the baby. On the other hand *she* didn't want the baby and would rather he stayed in care. Mr K. wanted to get married, if only so that he could have legal custody of the child if and when his wife 'took off'.

Mr K. knew quite well that he would soon return to crime; he had already been 'approached' many times since his discharge, meanwhile he was managing to keep his drinking under control.

Together they were as mutually destructive as separately each was self-destructive.

### Group D. *Immature wife—immature husband*

In our operational definition of immaturity we have pointed out that aggression and withdrawal may be typical responses of the immature person and it is important to bear this in mind when considering this particular pattern of relationships. It comprises a group of families where the relationship is considerably less static than others we have discussed. This may be because immaturity amongst adults appears to bear some relationship to chronological age, so that toleration, which is the most obvious process engendered by the truly immature couple, may tend to lessen as time goes by. Where this occurs, the husband may withdraw from the marriage and fail in his responsibilities as a husband: if the wife remains immature such behaviour may be tolerated to quite extraordinary lengths. If, however, she gains in maturity over the years, it may result in her good adjustment to permanent separation.

Within this category we have information about families at various stages of the spectrum: some very immature couples share maximum toleration, are well-integrated and oriented to their families of origin; in many the wife is tolerant of her husband's irresponsibility and even complete withdrawal (resulting in periods of separation). A few wives seem to gain confidence during the imprisonment and to recognize their ability to manage on their own, and so no longer want their husband back. The fact that such a wide range of families fall within this group makes it rather more difficult than in other groups to discuss their patterns of behaviour and adjustment.

*Before separation:* The most outstanding feature of these families is their youthfulness, none of them being over the age of thirty. All tend to rely heavily on their families of origin, and the more immature couples are, in fact, not only dependent on their parents, but dominated by them. Husband and wife have never established a separate marital unit away from their parents, though within these limits the relationship is a good one.

Where immaturity is a less strong feature of the relationship, the wives are not dominated by their parents and would in fact be less dependent upon them had they married more mature men. The marriage is successfully established away from the parental home.

Marriages usually take place when the couple are very young (under twenty) and many of the wives have an inadequate father and become closely tied to their mother.

Couples have a good deal of social life together, using relatives or neighbours to baby-sit.

In the more immature but well-integrated couples, the husband normally works, though often in jobs which may border on the criminal world; betting shops, street trading, second-hand car dealing, etc. In less well-integrated couples, husbands tend to be weak and feckless and to have very poor work records. When life's responsibilities become too much for them they try working away from home, or they become ill, or they temporarily desert their wives. Judging by the way their offences are committed it seems likely that some, unconsciously at least, intend to get caught. Amongst this very large group where the husband withdraws, all those in the sample come from delinquent families and live in areas of high delinquency where such behaviour is accepted as normal.

*During separation:* It is doubtful whether imprisonment represents a crisis for these families, though it may do so initially in so far as the wife misses her husband. The effect is minimal, however, both materially and emotionally. Where the wife is in close contact with her own and her husband's family they take over the husband's roles and his absence is barely felt. Wives who are less dependent on their parents are usually able to manage reasonably well—if they get behind with payments it is for non-essential items rather than for rent or similar essentials and this causes no anxiety. The children are well looked after: since these are usually very young parents, most of the children are also extremely young and the wives do not normally consider them old enough to miss their father, though some complain of children fretting. In many cases other male family members are able to act as father substitutes.

Wives receive support, and frequently direct financial help, from their family. Where there is a close relationship with parents no contact is usually made with welfare organizations—no need is seen to exist. Even where family ties are less strong most wives do not use the welfare services apart from the NAB, not because of any intrinsic dislike of them, but because they do not feel the need.

In those families where the husband has tended to become irresponsible, this has sometimes led to a rift between the wife and her mother, so that the husband's removal to prison results in an improvement in that relationship. This may result in a good deal of renewed contact with other members of the extended family. Where wives were already becoming increasingly intolerant of their husband's behaviour before imprisonment, this renewed contact with their own family may reinforce their dissatisfaction and provide them with the necessary confidence to leave him. However, some wives feel that their parents are becoming too dominant, and there is some resentment of this, though they are reluctant to admit to such feelings.

Wives visit their husbands very regularly, sometimes regarding it as *the* social occasion of the month. Visits are enjoyed and seen as helpful, even when, as in two families, the time is spent in one long family row.

Possibly because of their extreme youth, this group of wives show considerable resentment at the more restricted social life they are compelled to lead. They never go dancing or to the pubs for fear that malicious gossip may get back to the prison and upset their husband.

*After discharge:* Prison appears not to have affected most of these families once they are reunited. The pre-separation pattern re-establishes itself with no complications; only where wives have returned to live with their parents does conflict sometimes arise over the decision to return to their own home. It is almost as though the husband had left for a day-trip; his wife is glad to see him, he returns to his (usually) delinquent friends and the children seem unaffected.

However, as we have suggested earlier, marriages falling into this pattern do appear to break-up more frequently than in groups showing other patterns of relationship. Some were separated before the imprisonment, but these couples tended to be older than others in this group; it seems that a wife will put up with her husband's withdrawal from responsibility for so long, and then, if the opportunity presents itself, will leave. They tend to justify the unsatisfactory relationship they have with their husbands in terms of its being better for the children. This is perhaps understandable since they themselves have frequently been deprived of a father, owing to death, divorce, hospitalization or 'working away'. Alternatively the husband grows tired of family responsibilities and 'takes off' with another woman who has no children. As we have suggested in an earlier chapter, so far as the wife is concerned, the opportunity to leave generally depends upon the existence of a family willing and able to offer a home.

Because these couples get on very well for much of the time and have much in common, breaking point is often long delayed, but we believe that in these marriages, where both are immature, the couple appear to have little real *need* for each other compared with the other types of marital relationship that we have been discussing where the need is very great, however neurotically based. Such needs as they have can be met independently by other people, the wife's by relatives, friends and children, the husband's by 'mates' and other women.

To show what we believe to be different 'stages' in the marital relationships of these families, we are giving three case summaries. In the first, though the couple are very immature and very closely tied to their parents, the marriage is quite stable. In the second, the wife is showing signs of dissatisfaction with her husband's irresponsibility, but her need for him is great and despite talk of leaving him it is clear that she will not do so, at any rate for the present. In the third family, separation is virtually complete though the wife is unwilling to accept the fact.

### 1st Case Summary for Group D

Mr L., aged 30, was serving an eighteen-months sentence for receiving. He had been on probation as a juvenile, and as an adult had been fined on six occasions under the Street Betting Acts, and had been in prison on one occasion.

Mrs L., aged 28, had two children, aged five and three. Although she had a council maisonette of her own, she lived with her parents, partly to avoid loneliness and partly in order that her mother could look after the children whilst she went to work part-time as a typist. She had worked for most of her married life and enjoyed doing so.

*At the first interview:* Mrs L. was seen at her in-laws' home. This address had been given to the research worker by the prisoner in order that his father should decide whether it would be all right for us to see Mrs L. It was the father-in-law that answered the bell and had the initial discussion with the interviewer and, presumably satisfied, he agreed that if she returned next evening he would have Mrs L. there.

Mrs L. was not overtly depressed or upset by her husband's imprisonment, but was very angry since she completely denied his guilt. Her mother-in-law was present for most of the interview and both she and Mrs L. were anxious to impress the interviewer with the fact that Mr L. was not a criminal. Mrs L. was reluctant to answer questions or talk spontaneously, leaving her mother-in-law to do most of the talking.

Financially she had no problems. The NAB continued to pay her £2 8s 0d per week, which included the rent of her maisonette, unaware that she was living free of charge with her parents. She earned £5 5s 0d per week and paid £1 to a day nursery for the youngest child. She had no debts and received a great deal of financial help from both families.

Both Mr and Mrs L. came from very close-knit families. They had been married eight years and both said the marriage was very

G

happy. Mr L. was described as a very good husband and father; the youngest child missed him a great deal and clung to his mother, and both missed their week-end outings with their father.

Mrs L. said she had been given tablets by her doctor since her husband went to prison.

*At the second interview:* Mrs L. was seen in her own mother's home, this time surrounded by parents, grandparents, and a friend. She had put on weight, looked younger and less sophisticated, and seemed to be reverting more to the role of daughter. She said her health had improved and she no longer went to the doctor or took pills. Her parents had a spare room in their flat and we were told that, although the L.'s had a home of their own, Mrs L. had never really left the parental home since her marriage, as she and her husband often stayed there for weeks at a time.

Mrs L. continued to work and to receive help from both sides of the family as well as from the NAB, who, she complained, asked too many questions! She no longer paid anything for the child in the day nursery. She would not consider asking any welfare agency for help even if she needed it, she would simply ask more of her family.

Mrs L. took the children to visit their father regularly, but said neither of them knew where he was, they thought it was a hospital. She went out a good deal with both friends and relatives. She expected no problems when her husband came out; he would return to work in a betting shop.

*At the third interview:* Once again Mrs L. was surrounded by relatives and friends, but when for a short while they were out of the room, she managed rapidly to tell the interviewer that she and her mother had not been getting on too well, but that she had decided to stay there because of the children.

Mrs L. and her family expressed anger that no welfare agency had been to enquire about their well-being, but added that she would not accept any help even if it were offered.

The children were now said to be not unduly affected; Mrs. L. felt this was because her own parents were adequate substitutes for their father. Mr L. had a car on HP when arrested and this was taken back by the firm; Mrs L. said the children missed the car more than they missed their father and she assumed that as soon as he was discharged her husband would buy another.

Mrs L. continued to visit her husband monthly and did not appear to mind the fact that other members of his or her family always went too.

*At the fourth interview:* After some time an aunt who was present left the room, leaving only Mrs L. and her grandmother. Mrs L. explained that she had always been much closer to her grandmother than to her mother. She said that it was a strain to live at home with her mother, but complained that she could not afford to live in her own home, as, although the NAB paid the rent, she would still have had to pay to live. The emotional ties to her home also appeared to be very great, though only the financial ones were discussed.

For the first time there was tacit admission that Mr L. did dabble in crime—though they still denied that he committed the present one.

No problems, Mrs L. was looking forward to her husband's return.

No joint interview was possible with this family. They did not reply to two letters; the interviewer called and saw the aunt who said Mr L. had been discharged and they had moved back to their own flat. She declined to give us the address and promised to give them a note if we wrote one. No reply to this.

## 2nd Case Summary for Group D

Mr M., a very youthful looking 22-year-old, was serving an eighteen-months sentence for housebreaking. He had been in trouble since the age of nine and first went to Approved School when eleven. Mr and Mrs M. had been married for two-and-a-half years and this was his third imprisonment during this time.

Mrs M., aged 19, lived with her fourteen-month-old son in a privately-owned tenement block in South London. She was a gay, alert girl with a reasonably bright flat.

*At the first interview:* Mrs M. was drawing £4 19s 0d national assistance and this was her only regular income. Her rent was 25s per week, rates 5s per week and another 10s was spent on clubs and HP. She had a number of debts (amounting in all to about £50) but regarded these as mainly her husband's responsibility and was not at all concerned even though the Electricity Board had threatened to cut off the power. She had a somewhat irresponsible attitude towards debts and HP payments—as long as she had the goods she wanted she was not concerned about who paid for them, nor how or when.

Mr M. had not done any regular work for two years, having been sacked when goods were missing from the warehouse where he worked. He would not go to the NAB because he did not like them, and he lived largely off what he could make from crime. Mrs M. worked until the baby was born, but did not propose to do so whilst her husband was in prison as this would set the pattern for when he returned: 'He'll retire to bed and I'll be going out to work'.

Mrs M. occasionally talked of leaving her husband if he did not give up crime, but in the next breath said she was very fond of him and she had married him 'for better or for worse'. 'It's just bad luck that most of the time it's for worse!'

She visited him regularly in prison and took the child each time. Mrs M. described the marriage as very happy—they rarely had rows, even though he would not work. Her husband was rather jealous and kept writing to tell her not to go out but to wait for him at home.

All the family were very healthy, though Mr M. complained of symptoms such as headaches, lumps in his throat and bad eyesight. His wife regarded these as 'imagination'.

Until the child was born they went out a lot together drinking and visiting friends, but this had been reduced lately. They had a lot of friends in the vicinity and many called on her during the separation.

Mr M. had two brothers in prison and Mrs M.'s father was also in prison at the time of this interview, and appeared to have been there on a number of previous occasions.

*At the second interview:* Mrs M. had moved to a slightly larger flat and the NAB were paying the additional rent. She received a good deal of help from relatives.

The NAB officer was very unpopular with Mrs M., having allegedly twice suggested that she should leave her husband: 'why worry about your husband, we're keeping you not him, aren't we, and I don't see why we should have to go on doing that'. Mrs M. had asked for a clothing grant, but this had been turned down.

Mrs M.'s debts had increased, but this did not bother her. The only payment she was determined to keep up was the provident cheque so that she could buy clothes for herself and the child.

She would not go out to work as she claimed this would leave her with less than the NAB gave her at present, since she would then have to pay her mother to mind the baby.

Friends and neighbours were friendly and helpful and she spent most weekends with her mother. She complained of being very lonely in the evenings.

She denied that the boy missed his father, but said he recognized him when they went on visits.

*At the third interview:* Little change financially, though Mrs M. had now been summonsed for non-payment of rates. She did not intend to appear in Court—'I can't pay so what can they do about it?'. She continued to keep up the provident cheque since she desperately wanted 'something new' and found it very hard to bear when her friends bought new clothes.

She now thought she might go out to work when her husband returned in order 'to help'. She was also now threatening to leave her husband if he did not give up crime, but obviously she had no real intention of so doing.

She continued to receive a good deal of financial help from her family.

Mrs M. was anxious to move to 'a nice modern flat somewhere', and believed this would cure her husband of his delinquency. He had been moved to a prison outside London and visits were now reduced to one every two months because of the expense.

Mrs M. found the baby a great 'nuisance'; she spent an increasing amount of time with her mother, and although looking forward to her husband's return, was at the moment happiest playing the role of daughter.

She thought she would like to return to the days when they had no children, and when both she and her husband worked. She certainly did not want any more children, but said later that if she did fall for one when her husband came home, maybe it would make him go to work!

*At the fourth interview:* (joint). Not only were Mr and Mrs M. present, but also two other 'cons', one with his wife. Most of the time Mr M. and his friend discussed prison with a certain amount of relish. Mr M. made no attempt to pretend that he intended to go straight, he saw no point in doing so: 'in society it's every man for himself and if the individual considers that the only way he can get on is by being a criminal that's up to him'. When asked about the effects on his family, Mr M. pointed out that if his wife didn't like it she could leave, but he knew quite well *his* wife wouldn't do so. He considered his son was too young to know about it and he would sort that problem out when he came to it.

Mrs M. was still anxious to move away to another area where her husband would not be with his delinquent friends, but Mr M. said that he would only move to another place in the same area, if at all—he certainly wouldn't go to a 'crummy new town'.

His attitude to welfare, and prison welfare officers in particular, was wholly negative and he would only co-operate fully with the interviewer when she made it clear that she was not there to help him, nor to try and change him.

The child had settled down quite happily and Mrs M., when reminded that last time she had complained of his being difficult, said she thought it was just because she was fed up at the time.

Mr M. had joined a friend in a removal business but was only working part-time and so had not told the NAB. Their debts were still high but neither was particularly worried about this. Mr M.'s friends seemed to be helping him out financially and there was little apparent shortage of money for pubs and similar activities, which obviously took up most of Mr M.'s time.

### 3rd Case Summary for Group D

Mr N., aged 28, was serving a two-year sentence for shopbreaking. He had been in trouble since the age of fourteen, having been twice in Approved School and twice on probation. He had served one previous prison sentence.

Mrs N., aged 22, lived with her two children, aged four years and four months, in a basement flat in a Victorian house in North London. It was spotlessly clean and well-furnished.

*At the first interview:* Mrs N. said she had been separated from her husband for a month before his arrest, and he had been living with another girl who had had a baby by him. During five years of marriage Mr N. had left his wife at least seven times, but always returned asking for forgiveness and promising not to do it again. She had on two occasions taken out a separation order, but both times this action had brought her husband back running, and she had dropped it. The marriage was said to have been happy until the birth of the first child (previously Mrs N. had had two miscarriages), and then her husband had begun to drink and go with other women.

Throughout the marriage they had moved frequently from her relatives to furnished rooms and back again, Mr N. leaving her each time there was a serious row.

Mrs N. had occasionally worked since their marriage to help out financially, but it had always caused trouble, since her husband disapproved strongly of wives working because he liked to think of himself as 'a big fellow'.

Since he had been in prison this time he had written asking her to forgive him and to write, but a few weeks later he wrote saying he had changed his mind and wanted a divorce. The other girl [whom Mrs N. knows] came to the house and removed all his clothes.

The oldest child was very upset by his father's repeated disappearances. Although Mr N. claimed to be very fond of the boy he seemed to have little idea of the distress he was causing him, though he had bought him a large number of toys to make up for his absence.

Mr N. had rarely worked, and never left Mrs N. with any money when he went off. She owed a great deal for furniture on HP, but felt this was not her concern, since it was all in her husband's name, and, as she was under twenty-one at the time, her father acted as guarantor.

Mrs N. earned a little money working at home, but managed mainly on national assistance and family allowances.

She said her husband had always been a terrible liar and very boastful. She now spent her time cleaning the house and looking after the children and was very lonely and wanted him back.

*At the second interview:* There was little change. Mrs N. was extremely ambivalent in her attitude towards her husband. She said she did not want him back, but half expected him to return and realized she would accept him if he did. She said she would not have the strength to reject him. She had intended to do so on many occasions but it had never worked out. Once she had made up her mind to hold a dramatic scene on the doorstep, but he usually returned when she was out, and on that occasion she found him in the kitchen eating cheese rolls, which so shattered her that she had been unable to have a row with him!

She remained very depressed and lonely, and had had to give up her home work as there was none available. She saw her mother occasionally, but the relationship was not a good one. It seemed that her mother had been very interfering in the early stages of Mrs N.'s marriage and had caused a lot of trouble, accusing Mr N. of taking away 'our little baby'.

Mrs N. in some ways preferred her husband to be in prison, at least she knew that he was not out in a pub or with another woman.

*At the third interview:* Little change. Mrs N. remained doubtful about whether or not to have him back. She was obviously still fond of him and seemed to want him back. The other girl had been round to see Mrs N. a few times 'in a terrible state', but Mrs N. explained to her that she could do nothing to smooth the path of *their* relationship. Mrs N. seemed well able to cope with these visits, seemingly in the hope that prison would change her husband and he would return to her and get a steady job.

*At the fourth interview:* Mr N. had been discharged and had returned to live with the other girl. He came on Sundays to take out his eldest son. Mrs N. could not bring herself to take out a maintenance order against him; she felt her husband would want to come back to her one day, when everyone else had rejected him, and she seemed willing to wait. She described herself as 'a sort of old-age pensioner's home'. She seemed to miss him a good deal more than on previous visits and although she recognized that it would be more sensible to divorce him, she also recognized that her need for him was greater than her desire to behave in a 'sensible way'.

*At the fifth interview:* Mr N. had in fact returned to his wife and stayed for six weeks. He had then left quite suddenly and she did not know where he had gone—it was not back to the other girl. She was very happy whilst he was there, except that during the last week he had been out every night drinking. However, she was quite willing to have him back at any time and on his terms, and she said that talk of divorce, or even separation, was really 'pie in the sky' until she was less tied to the children and able to work and 'make a new life'. She preferred to be around and available for her husband when he needed her. Since she was very fearful of becoming pregnant and her husband refused to allow her to use a contraceptive (or to use one himself) she was now taking the oral contraceptive.

Group E. *Mature wife—dominant husband*

The most noticeable feature about these marriages is the degree of tolerance exhibited by both partners towards behaviour which may usually be described as deviant. Neither is necessarily stable and well-adjusted as an individual, though he may well be, but within the marriage each behaves in a way acceptable to his own and his partner's norms and expectations.

The dominance of the husband in these families is not excessive or inappropriate, as is often the case in group A, but is more often the culturally approved dominance of the male role.

*Before separation:* A high proportion of the families in our sample are to be found in this group, and it is noticeable that both husbands and wives are considerably older than is the case with most of those we interviewed. Although one couple were both aged twenty-five, almost all the others were well on in the thirties, and many were over forty. They have usually been married for many years and the marriage seems to be based on the apparently genuine acceptance by one or other partner of the abnormal behaviour of the other (in some cases both are deviants). The husband's criminality in these well-adjusted families does not appear to disturb or distress the wife in any way, and it is interesting to note that this group includes the only two sexual offenders in the sample, as well as the two men in prison for living on immoral earnings.

*During separation:* The crisis for these wives is an emotional one, since they are deprived of an apparently stable relationship and a husband who provides well for the family both materially and emotionally. The wives are usually extremely competent, efficient women, and they adjust to the emotional deprivation by focusing on material problems. They strive hard to maintain the *status quo* materially, and appear to succeed. Where practicable they use family and friends to help in assuming the husband's roles.

The children are well looked after, and although they miss their father, no problems appear to develop—or if they do the mother denies them and the interviewer observed none. Some mothers in this group tell their children the reason for father's absence, others do not, but both appear to cope efficiently whichever line they take.

*After discharge:* These families present no apparent problems. The husbands are delighted with the way their wives have managed and they, in turn, are content to resume the relationship as before. Most of this group would undoubtedly continue their criminal activities as before, and seek no help from social work agencies. In two instances, one of incest and one of attempting to corrupt public morals, social workers were in fact involved, but it was interesting to observe how these families used the agencies constructively in order to obtain what they felt to be best for their needs.

Since so little was obtained in our interviews that could account for the husband's criminality, it was felt that we might have missed important clues. Particular attention was therefore paid to these cases in the hope that discussion between research workers might elicit some further explanation. However, we could detect nothing within the marital situation which could result in such behaviour, or if it did (as in an incest case where the wife was somewhat frigid) we could find no indication of damage to what appeared to be a very happy marriage.

### 1st Case Summary for Group E

Mr P., aged 44, was serving a twenty-one-month sentence for false pretences. He had his first conviction at the age of thirteen and had had a number of subsequent convictions and been in prison three times since his marriage, which took place twenty-five years ago. He had eight brothers and two sisters, most of whom had been 'in trouble' at some time or another.

Mr and Mrs P. owned the house they lived in; it was large, well-built and comfortably furnished and there was a warm family atmosphere about the place.

A married daughter lived upstairs with her husband and baby. A younger daughter of sixteen who had just started work lived with Mrs P.

*At the first interview:* Mrs P. was living off savings and from help she received from her husband's brothers. She had no financial problems since her own family were able to help her whenever necessary, and a relative would continue to run her husband's car sales and repair business whilst he was inside. There was no shortage of anything in the home and Mrs P. said she intended going out to work soon.

According to Mrs P., the marriage had been a very happy one and she had become increasingly determined to stand by her husband, although she saw little likelihood of his remaining out of prison for long. She felt he had been an excellent husband and a very good father, and had provided very well for the family. Although the earlier prison sentences had been difficult for her, particularly financially, she had never blamed him for these.

She had always shared her husband's social activities with the exception of one night a week when Mr P. went out on his own. They went out a great deal to the theatre, cinema, pubs and to visit friends and relatives. This type of activity was very much reduced when her husband was in prison. She preferred not to go out in case gossip got back to her husband, but although her family were visiting her a lot, no one could make up for the absence of her husband.

Mrs P. seemed to have a considerable amount of control over her daughter; she did not allow the girl to visit her father because she thought it would upset him; children are not able to put on a 'front' and be cheerful when they do not feel it, and Mrs P. considered this an important part of visiting. She did not feel that the children had been in any way affected by their father's criminality—she had never had any trouble with them.

*At the second interview:* Mrs P. had taken a job and was enjoying it—somewhat to her surprise. Despite the fact that she still received a good deal of help from various family members, she was nevertheless in a fair amount of debt. This was partly because she was determined to maintain her normally high standard of living during the separation, so that everything should be the same when her husband came out. She was quite unperturbed by her debts, they would soon be sorted out when Mr P. came home.

Her main concern was to see that the children were properly looked after (this included the married daughter and her family) and to see that they did not suffer in any way from their father's imprisonment.

Mrs P. did not in any way blame her husband for his criminality; they had done very well out of it financially and she was quite content. Her main feeling was one of relief that he had not got a longer sentence.

Her husband was due to be moved out of London and she had persuaded the prison Governor to allow her an open visit on the grounds that she would not let the children visit unless this was granted.

Mrs P. was effusive about her husband. Their only disappointment was that they had had no more children; they tried to adopt one but could not do so because of Mr P.'s record. She was tremendously proud of the children (she saw her daughter's child very much as her own) and felt that her husband's criminality was *her* problem and not the children's, and therefore they had nothing to worry about so long as she kept the home going as usual. At this stage the sixteen-year-old girl suggested to her mother that the children do in fact share the problem, but Mrs P. denied this.

*At the third interview:* Mr P. had been moved to Lancashire and as Mrs P. was working full-time she was only free to visit on Sundays and this was not allowed. She wrote to the prison commissioners about it, but they replied that they had insufficient staff and nothing could be done. However, she was subsequently granted a Sunday visit on one occasion. The reduction in visiting had had a bad effect on Mrs P.'s health; she was much more tense and anxious than on previous visits.

Mrs P.'s debts had increased, but she remained unconcerned, being quite convinced that her husband would be able to 'find' the money as soon as he returned. Her somewhat irresponsible attitude seemed to stem from the fact that whenever she had needed money in the past to pay off a debt she had only to ask her husband for it and it would materialize!

Mrs P.'s youngest daughter was now 'courting' and having 'had a good talk with him' Mrs P. was satisfied about the boy's honesty and respectability.

*At the fourth interview:* There was very little change. It became increasingly obvious that both Mr and Mrs P. shared a common system of values which accepted such criminal activities as might be necessary to ensure a reasonably good standard of living; there was nothing wrong with 'fiddling' the tax authorities, or doing a deal over stolen goods.

Visits remained a major problem since she had never again been given permission to visit on a Sunday. Getting away from work (where they did not know about her husband) on a Saturday had not been easy.

*Before the fifth interview:* (which should have been a joint one). Mrs P.'s daughter telephoned to say that her father had lost eight weeks' remission, but that her mother would like the research worker to visit as planned.

Mr P. had lost this remission for sending out unauthorized letters, and he was also accused of having tobacco sent in. He had been moved to a 'closed' prison in the North and although Mrs P. had visited him once, she would not be able to do so again as it was not worth going for forty minutes.

Mrs P. seemed more anxious than usual at this interview, and although we were not able to pin-point the cause of this, it seemed likely to be connected with the disappointment of not having her husband back on time.

*At the sixth interview* (joint): Mr P. had somehow resolved all his wife's financial problems; he was working with his brother and had opened a new car showroom. All their friends and relatives had come round to see them and everything was fine.

It was at this interview that we learned that Mr P.'s conviction in 1957 had been for living on immoral earnings. Mrs P. had withheld this information throughout our interviews with her, whereas Mr P. felt no need to do so. [We do not know whether he told us in order deliberately to embarrass his wife.] Mr P. said that the marriage did not break up at the time, though it nearly did so, but he had always liked 'a bit of life with the girls' and Mrs P. had been very good to him about it all. Mrs P. obviously felt very reluctant to talk about it. When she was out of the room Mr P. talked about sexual offenders in prison, and in particular about incest, and we obtained the impression that on these matters he is by no means the paragon of virtue that his wife had tried to suggest throughout our interviews. Nor did he make any bones about his intention to continue as a criminal: before he went into prison he had been doing very well and spending between £400 and £500 per week. Most of it went on parties and taking the 'boys' out drinking.

Mrs P. intended to give up work very soon, since they would no longer need the money. The eldest daughter and her family were going to live in the Midlands, which upset both Mr and Mrs P.

Mr P. talked in glowing terms of his wonderful wife, and there was much mutual admiration throughout the interview.

### 2nd Case Summary for Group E

Mr V., aged 25, was serving an eighteen-month sentence for conspiring with other persons to corrupt public morals; it was his first conviction. He made no attempt to deny his homosexuality, but denied this particular charge. He was a Eurasian and came to this country at the age of seventeen.

Mrs V., aged 25, lived in a terraced house in East London with her four children, aged five, three, two and one. They had just bought the house when Mr V. was arrested.

*At the first interview:* Mrs V. was busy redecorating the house. She was pregnant but very healthy.

The children were happy; they had been told their father was in hospital and accepted this. Mrs V. was very firm, but quite permissive, in her handling of them.

She did not discuss her husband's homosexual tendencies, but knew that his associates were involved in running a homosexual brothel. She was quite unperturbed about the nature of the charge and thought the whole thing was fixed by the police.

She had visited her husband regularly in prison, but was concerned lest he be moved out of London, in view of the difficulty of travelling long distances with four young children.

The V.'s had been married for six years, and had always been very happy. Mr V. was very fond of the children and his wife described him as a very good husband. He had worked hard in a clerical capacity, and although she described him as 'a lover of pleasure', she had no complaints. In order to earn additional money he played the piano in a club, but she felt he was doing this for her and the children. He also helped in the house a good deal. Just before his arrest he had become ill owing to over-work and had given up his job on his doctor's instructions.

Mrs V. was managing all right financially. She found the NAB very helpful, and got some help from her husband's family. Before her marriage she worked as a secretary, but had not done so since, on account of the children.

Her own family did not know of her husband's offence and keeping it from them was her only real problem. However, she was on very good terms with her husband's family and not at all lonely. As the V.'s had only recently moved to the present house she had no friends nearby; but her interests lay wholly in her home and family.

*At the second interview:* Mrs V. was managing very well. Neither she nor the children appeared to be missing Mr V. unduly. Visiting had become a problem since her husband had been moved a long way from London. She had no debts.

The Roman Catholic priest had been to see if she needed help, as had the Health Visitor who offered to help, but she declined both.

She had a lot of contact with her mother-in-law, and as her own parents lived in the Midlands, she had managed to avoid telling them. She wrote to them regularly.

The children appeared very healthy and happy and the interviewer had some difficulty in assessing how Mr V. fitted into this extremely well-adjusted family. Mrs V. was rather concerned about the effect of prison on her husband's morale. As far as she was concerned, the imprisonment would make absolutely no difference to her marriage.

*At the third interview:* Little change. Mrs V. had no problems—she handled everything with efficiency, calm and lack of anxiety. The midwife called during the interview and the relationship was a very easy one. Mrs V. had explained to the midwife on her first visit that her husband was in prison; since then it had not been mentioned. Her mother-in-law would live in the house when the baby was due.

*At the fourth interview:* No change. Mr V. was due out a week later and the whole family was tremendously excited. The new baby had arrived and all was well. Her husband had not been very happy in prison and she said the Governor had told him he should not have been sent to prison but given treatment. Since Mrs V. was quite satisfied with the sexual side of her marriage she seemed to have accepted his homosexual side, and decided that it did not affect her.

*At the fifth interview* (joint): After very considerable difficulty, Mr V. had persuaded the Ministry of Labour and the NAB to maintain himself and his family for twelve weeks whilst he took a training course. He had borrowed the money to pay for the course from his mother. Both Mr and Mrs V. were delighted, although it would mean some financial sacrifices for quite a while. Mr V. had won what he considered a major battle and had done so by attending a psychiatric out-patient department and being supported in his application by the psychiatrist. Even so the first attempt had been unsuccessful, and only when the psychiatrist pressed the matter was he given permission.

Relationships with Mr V.'s family remained excellent and, apart from the training course, there had been virtually no problems of readjustment.

Mr V. thought the second child might have suffered owing to his absence—he had become somewhat out of hand; however, he thought it might equally well be due to jealousy of the new baby. Mr V. had at first found the presence of so many young children rather irritating after the adult world of prison.

He had been considerably frightened by his sentence, and said he would be more careful to control his homosexual behaviour in future. He thought he would be more 'home-centred' instead of 'pleasure hunting'. However, within the family, both husband and wife seemed well adjusted to his dual sexuality.

### FAMILIES SEPARATED BEFORE IMPRISONMENT

Six of the families with whom we made contact on the intensive sample were separated before imprisonment.[1] In four of these cases the husband's personality was very similar: they were all recidivists, all under thirty, and with very irregular work patterns. They lived in a fantasy world, believing that one day they would really make money. They lied about everything, including their marital relationships. Two of them were living with other women by whom they had illegitimate children, and they asked the interviewer to see their common-law wife not their legal wife.[2] On release from prison both returned to their legal wives but only for a matter of days or weeks.

All the wives handled the separation differently; only one went back to her mother—whom she had never really left during six years of 'on and off' marriage. Every now and then her husband returned to spend the night with her, she became pregnant and he then disappeared. By this means they had at the time four children and it seemed likely that he would repeat the process on discharge from the present sentence.

This wife, and two others, seemed to need a husband, however inadequate and however unfaithful.[3] They complained about him bitterly but were unable to make a final break. Two of them started taking the oral contraceptive before their husband's release: although they said they did not necessarily expect him to return to them, they hoped he would.

These wives justified this kind of life in terms of it being better for

[1] Included in these six is one family where the wife was never actually seen, but only her mother.

[2] In one instance we saw both, but as they were in touch with one another this was not a satisfactory arrangement and we continued to see only the legal wife.

[3] See case summary, p. 198.

the children; they themselves had very disturbed home backgrounds. None of them had been unfaithful, or had serious boy friends.

Only one of this group of wives planned to divorce her husband. She dealt efficiently with the problem of separation, sent her children to nursery school, obtained work, and was busy teaching the children to hate their father.

The fifth couple had much in common with the four described above, except in so far as the separation at the time of imprisonment was less final, and there was some hope of reconciliation. However, as a result of pressure being put upon the wife, an immature girl of nineteen, by her very dominant mother who was full of hostility towards the girl's husband, it seemed unlikely that she would return to him. Unfortunately the mother finally persuaded the girl not to see the research worker any more since she obviously believed her to be encouraging the girl to return to her husband.

The sixth couple had been married for thirty-two years and before imprisonment were living apart in the same house. The wife had started divorce proceedings and the decree came through during the sentence. This couple had separated many times during the course of the marriage and we tried, unsuccessfully, to find out what had precipitated the final decision to divorce him. She told us she had always gone back to him previously on account of the children, but since all the children had been grown up for some considerable time this seems unlikely to be the whole explanation. We believe that the fact of his enforced removal from the house for a long period was the precipitating factor.

### CHANGES OCCURRING DURING SEPARATION

One of the primary objects in carrying out this work with the intensive sample[1] was to trace the impact of imprisonment on the family over time, since we did not expect patterns of family adjustment to remain static over the months of separation.

From a material point of view it is an incontrovertible fact that unless a wife regularly goes out to work and earns a reasonable wage, the financial position of the family deteriorates very considerably as the period of separation increases. Grants, as of right, from the NAB for clothing and household equipment should replace the existing discretionary payments, and if the Board wishes to encourage wives to go out to work, the amount they are allowed to earn before deductions are made from their grant should be increased, and better provision made for day nursery care.

The effect of this worsening in material conditions will depend to a large extent on the personality of the wife. Those who become depressed and anxious as a result of material deprivation also deterior-

[1] See Chapter II, p. 29, *supra*.

ate physically and mentally, and a vicious circle is created. For the most part, however, we were impressed with the way increasing material deprivation did *not* result in increased mental deterioration, though we feel it did contribute to physical ill-health. Wives did not eat properly, took on too much work, and the general effect of scrimping, saving, and making do was certainly one of the causes of symptoms such as 'nerves', insomnia, fainting and general lassitude which so many developed over time. Even so, we feel that the development of such physical symptoms more often derived from emotional deprivation, the increasing loneliness they experienced, rather than purely from a worsening of physical circumstances.

In some cases help given by families, neighbours, and friends tended to slacken off as the period of separation lengthened, but again this was not a frequent occurrence and appeared to cause little real concern to wives. They tended to rally round again as the time for the husband's release approached.

It is our feeling that for the most part any changes we witnessed were fairly impermanent. Wives *felt* better, or excited, or miserable, or angry, depending very much on such factors as how the children had been behaving, or whether they had had a good visit to their husband, or even on the weather. In other words, their feelings about life were, with some exceptions, determined by the same sort of events which determine the feelings of most people. There were no major changes in overall patterns of adjustment except amongst those wives who were very dependent on their husbands and who were unable to find a substitute. For these women there was a fairly obvious and constant deterioration.

### DISCUSSION OF INTENSIVE SAMPLE IN RELATION TO THEORETICAL CONSIDERATIONS OF CHAPTER I

#### (a) Prison as a crisis

Previous studies of separation have been discussed in terms of crisis theory (see Chapter I, pp. 19 ff.), and we have considered it reasonable to accept that imprisonment *is* a situation of crisis. However, it was our belief that the impact of the crisis on a particular family would vary according to whether the crisis was recurrent or unique, and according to the quality of family adjustment existing before imprisonment.

Examination of the material suggests that the recurrent/unique hypothesis is not important *except* in relation to physical separation. In other words imprisonment, since it involves involuntary physical separation,[1] produces a quality in the crisis situation which dis-

---

[1] It could be argued that at an unconscious level it is not involuntary since it may be used as a mechanism of escape from a difficult marital situation, but we are here discussing conscious behaviour.

tinguishes it in a most important way from many other types of crisis.[1] The extent to which families have, or have not, experienced other previous crises is, we believe, largely irrelevant unless they were crises involving involuntary separation. Even so the difference in impact tends to show itself chiefly in the early stages of separation; thus for star wives the initial impact of imprisonment was more critical than for recidivist wives, and it was noticeable that in both extensive and intensive samples the majority of complaints about lack of information as to what was happening, as well as lack of help and concern at the time of their husband's arrest, came from the wives of first offenders.

The second factor which seemed important when considering imprisonment as a crisis was that the impact would vary according to the quality of family adjustment existing before separation. Here again we find it necessary to modify our original views and we find that the impact appears to be determined to a much greater extent by the personality of the wife than by the quality of family adjustment. Thus for wives with strong dependency needs the crisis was very great and remained so throughout the sentence; for wives with relatively stable, well-adjusted personalities the emotional crisis was certainly present, but they were sufficiently well integrated to be able to handle the situation, and remain apparently undamaged by the experience.

However, the quality of family adjustment is itself directly related to the personality of the wife, so that it must inevitably affect the impact on her. For the immature wives we have referred to above (see Group D), the experience is rarely one of crisis, since they have always maintained a close dependent relationship with their own family, and have never transferred this dependency to their husband. So long as the family continue to provide support, the absence of the husband is of relatively minor importance. Similarly, for those wives in Group C, whose norms and expectations are at variance with those of their husbands, the experience may initially be one of considerable crisis (depending to a large extent on the degree of conscious guilt they have concerning their own part in the husband's criminality), but as such feelings diminish and are replaced by feelings of martyrdom, so the quality of crisis quite rapidly disappears.

We referred earlier (see Chapter I, p. 22) to the fact that the family might not *perceive* imprisonment as a crisis of both dismemberment *and* demoralization. Our material suggests that dismemberment is almost certainly a far more important factor than demoralization: where the latter is a crisis, it tends to result from

[1] In so far as contact between the couple is maintained during separation it is not by any means comparable with the crisis of death.

the husband's physical absence, rather than from any other aspect of imprisonment such as stigma, shame, guilt, loss of status, etc.

Shame and stigma were feelings experienced almost exclusively by star wives, and then only in the initial stages of the separation. At that time they showed a strong desire to stay indoors, feared meeting people and often told lies to neighbours and acquaintances regarding their husband's whereabouts. However, this very rapidly wore off and no wives in the intensive sample appeared to experience such feelings after the second interview.

Among recidivist wives, many of whom lived in areas of high delinquency, none appeared to suffer from shame or stigma, though there was often considerable anger at the way other children behaved towards theirs.

Loss of status was certainly perceived as a crisis for most wives, but again this seemed directly related to the physical absence of the husband rather than to his criminality or imprisonment. Amongst working-class and lower middle-class families it is the expected norm for women to be married, and inability to appear in public with a husband was felt to place them in an invidious position.

We had thought (see Chapter I, p. 23) that it would be amongst the children that we should find it possible to differentiate between the impact of imprisonment and that of separation. We were, in fact, unable to make a sufficiently systematic study of the children to enable us to develop this line of thought. One cannot but feel, however, that the long-term effect of the additional stresses and strains which separation from the father brings about is likely to be detrimental, and it would certainly be a worthwhile subject for future research. It is perhaps relevant to point out that, as far as we could ascertain, only two of the sixty-five prisoners had themselves a criminal parent, though a further 21 per cent were brought up in broken homes or in non-penal institutions and almost 1 per cent had a parent permanently living in a mental hospital. The McCords[1] report that the children of criminal fathers become criminal only when other factors, such as the instability of the mother, play a part, and they suggest that it is possible to show that simple imitation of the father is less important in producing criminality in the child than is *rejection* by the father.

If we are correct in suggesting that the effects of *separation* are intrinsically more relevant for the family than the effects of imprisonment the question remains, is it possible to distinguish between the effect of imprisonment and the effect of criminality? There would appear to be differences here between star and recidivist wives. Although all the first offenders in our sample were fairly soon

[1] McCord & McCord: *Personality and Social Systems: The Effect of Parental Role Model on Criminality:* ed. Smelser, Wiley & Sons, 1963.

transferred to open prisons where conditions were regarded as incomparably better than in closed institutions, criticisms of the penal system were widespread. Restriction on communication, lack of adequate welfare facilities and unsatisfactory medical attention for prisoners were matters which greatly affected the adjustment which the wife was able to make to the separation. Their husband's criminality was usually frowned upon, but tended to be regarded as 'stupidity' which certainly did not merit the appalling punishment which prison conditions entailed.

Recidivists' wives had become used to prison conditions; they complained bitterly but expected little else. Only if and when their husbands were moved to a prison some distance away were they seriously affected, unless they were in the fortunate position of having a relative able to take them to visit regularly. For wives who were short of money and had young children, the very real practical problems arising from visiting their husbands often constituted an intolerable burden, on top of the emotional problems engendered by physical separation.

Recidivists' wives had no real conception of their husbands' criminality in the wider context; so long as the men made money their wives were not too concerned where it came from—the error lay in getting caught, not in committing an offence. 'I shall leave him next time' referred exclusively to the next prison sentence, not to the next offence.

### (b) *Adjustment to separation*

Good adjustment to separation is defined by Hill[1] in terms of 'closing the ranks, shifting of responsibilities and activities of the husband to other members, continuing the necessary family routines, maintaining husband/wife and father/child relationships by correspondence and visits. Utilizing the resources of friends, relatives and neighbours and carrying on plans for reunion.'

Our material suggests that this definition requires some qualifications. In the first place, only if *all* the criteria set out by Hill are adhered to can we accept that good adjustment may be achieved. Some wives, particularly those who were dependent, passive, or immature, so completely closed the ranks and shifted the responsibilities on to other family members that they deprived themselves of essential outside contacts and the emotional strain on the various family members was clearly visible, particularly in the case of children. Wives often made excessive demands both financially and emotionally upon their own and their husband's family which sometimes resulted in friction between members of the extended family, as well as resentment by the wife if she felt she did not receive sufficient

[1] *Op. cit.*

help. Such wives would refuse to ask for national assistance or make use of other welfare agencies on the grounds that 'it is a family matter'. Where more use was made of welfare agencies they often provided a useful 'scapegoat' and feelings of resentment and anger were directed at them, rather than at other family members.

Even where the closed-ranks behaviour was an effective method of handling the separation, when used by immature wives it tended to result in their returning increasingly to the role of 'daughter' with the result that the chances of establishing a successful marital relationship away from the extended family when the husband was released, became even less likely.

Clearly the concept of adjustment to separation must include the question of the re-establishment of the family unit on discharge. In our experience it was amongst some of those families where the wife herself assumed responsibility and adopted the husband's roles, using only such outside help as she found necessary, that the chances of good readjustment seemed most likely.

However, whilst this was the case where the marital relationship was relatively stable during imprisonment—particularly Group E— such behaviour during the separation need not *necessarily* result in good lasting prospects on reunion. Whilst it is possible that, particularly amongst the older first offenders, the shock of imprisonment was sufficient to prevent them ever committing further offences, we do not have any evidence to suggest that the marital relationships will have changed, except possibly in a negative direction. Thus if good adjustment to separation is to include good adjustment on reunion, the behaviour of the wife during separation may be of less importance than the quality of family relationships existing *before* imprisonment.

Recapitulating what we have said above (see page 208), it seems that, for those families where imprisonment is a crisis, it is a crisis of *separation*. The impact of the crisis upon a wife will depend primarily upon her own personality and only indirectly upon the quality of family adjustment existing before imprisonment. We now suggest, similarly, that the degree to which the wife makes a satisfactory adjustment to separation is to a large extent a function of her own personality, but that once the husband returns, his personality becomes of equal importance in the situation, and the quality of readjustment will depend upon the personality fit of the two partners— a factor which is unlikely to have been changed by the experience of imprisonment.

Two wives with quite different personalities, but married to men exhibiting very similar behaviour, adjusted to the separation in diametrically opposed ways. In both cases the pattern of family relationships existing before imprisonment was resumed on discharge:

Mrs L. had been married for five years to a feckless layabout, by whom she had had three children. Her husband never worked, never provided for her, was unfaithful and spent most of his time either in pubs, clubs, and 'spielers' with his 'mates', or with other women. Mrs L. herself had a very unstable personality and the departure of her husband was a severe crisis. Both her own and her husband's family rallied round, as did friends and neighbours. She had no debts and her children did not show any overt signs of disturbance. Mrs L. was not even particularly in love with her husband and could see him clearly for what he was. Nevertheless she broke down completely under the strain of trying to manage without him. 'If the kids are bawling, and you're both rowing about it, he's *there* and he takes his share of responsibility.' Mr L. did in fact return to his wife but the relationship remained as tenuous as it had been before imprisonment.

Mrs C. lived with her two children, one aged four years and one four months. She was also married to an irresponsible, feckless man, who during seven years of marriage had left her five times, always to live with other women. Her relationship with her own family was not at all good, and she had no friends and complained of being extremely lonely. She was in debt and had Court orders pending, but apart from national assistance she received no help from anyone. Although very depressed, Mrs C. in fact handled the financial situation extremely well, and devoted herself to caring for the children, even though doubtful whether her husband would in fact return to her. When Mrs C. was seen three months after her husband's discharge we learned that he had actually returned—for six weeks—he had then disappeared completely. Her comment: 'It's better than being alone *all* the time.'

We suggest that it is the *internalized* focus of the crisis, and adjustment to it, which is important, rather than its external concomitants. The latter may help or hinder adjustment, but do not lie at the root of the problem. It will readily be seen that this proposition has important implications for those whose work it is to help the families of men in prison.

## Chapter VIII

# ADJUSTMENT TO SEPARATION[1]

The primary aim of the statistical treatment of the data derived from this study has been to arrive at a measure of the social and economic adjustment of individual families contingent upon the imprisonment of the husband.

In the initial stage, each of the 469 wives with whom completed interviews took place was rated on a 7-point scale for thirteen areas of adjustment:

(i) Housing
(ii) Finance
(iii) Wife's work
(iv) Use of, and satisfaction with, welfare agencies
(v) Use of, and satisfaction with NAB
(vi) Wife's attitude to marriage and future plans
(vii) Children's behaviour
(viii) Wife's contact with husband in prison
(ix) Children's contact with father in prison
(x) Extent of wife's social activities during separation
(xi) Wife's relationship with parents
(xii) Wife's relationship with in-laws
(xiii) Wife's relationship with neighbours and friends

It is important to stress that the '0' and '6' ratings on the scale have peculiar status: '0' represents data too vague to warrant classification in categories 1–5, while '6' represents 'criterion does not apply', usually, though not always, because the family was separated before imprisonment. For convenience of treatment therefore, the rating scale can be taken as a 5-point one, with the rank position '2' representing 'no change in a family situation'.

[1] The data in this chapter refer only to criminal prisoners. We do not consider that the sentences of most civil debtors were long enough for us to measure adjustment to separation and in civil maintenance cases the majority of wives were unaffected as they were separated before imprisonment.

The relevant part of the scale thus reads:

*Scale position*

1. Situation improves following imprisonment of husband.
2. Situation unchanged.
3. Situation deteriorates slightly.
4. Situation deteriorates substantially.
5. Situation deteriorates seriously.

Before discussing or interpreting the findings of each individual area, it is necessary to bear in mind that the scores do not in any way indicate the extent to which a *satisfactory* state of affairs exists in relation to a particular area. For example, a family may live in appalling housing conditions, but if this is in no way different from the situation before imprisonment, such a family would score '2'. The same score would apply if a family continued to live in the same house as before even if, in order to do so, the wife made considerable financial sacrifices and deprived the family of adequate food. On the other hand, a family that had been evicted at some stage of the separation might score '4', although by the time we saw the wife she might have made satisfactory alternative arrangements. Further references to such difficulties will be made when discussing each area separately.

*Area* 1: *Housing*

### TABLE I

| Score | Stars % | | Recidivists % | | Total % | |
|---|---|---|---|---|---|---|
| 1 | 3·3 | | 5·1 | | 4·3 | |
| 2 | 72·5 | | 63·3 | | 67·1 | |
| 3 | 8·6 | | 9·6 | | 9·2 | |
| 4 | 10·2 | | 12·4 | | 11·5 | |
| 5 | 5·3 | | 9·6 | | 7·9 | |
| | 100·0 | 93·8 | 100·0 | 81·6 | 100·0 | 86·2 |
| 0 | | 0·8 | | 1·8 | | 1·4 |
| 6 | | 5·4 | | 16·6 | | 12·4 |
| | | 100·0 | | 100·0 | | 100·0 |
| Number | 256 | | 213 | | – | |

It will readily be apparent that amongst both stars and recidivists the housing situation for the great majority remains unchanged. Even where change has occurred, there is virtually no difference in the situation for the two categories of offender [$\chi^2$ for trend on scores 1–5 = 2·81; 1 d.f.; N.S.]: however, where there has been change, for the most part it is for the worse. We feel that this may well reflect the general difficulty such families (and others) would experience if they were to try to find alternative accommodation.

A score of '3' indicates those families for whom housing is relatively satisfactory during imprisonment, but for whom it will be a major problem upon release of the husband.

*Area 2: Finance*

### TABLE II

| Score | Stars % | | Recidivists % | | Total % | |
|-------|---------|--------|---------------|--------|---------|--------|
| 1 | 9·5 | | 18·0 | | 14·5 | |
| 2 | 23·5 | | 22·5 | | 22·9 | |
| 3 | 39·5 | | 30·3 | | 34·1 | |
| 4 | 21·0 | | 14·0 | | 16·9 | |
| 5 | 6·6 | | 15·2 | | 11·7 | |
| | 100·0 | 93·5 | 100·0 | 82·0 | 100·1 | 86·3 |
| 0 | | 1·2 | | 1·4 | | 1·3 |
| 6 | | 5·4 | | 16·6 | | 12·4 |
| | | 100·0 | | 100·0 | | 100·0 |
| Number | 256 | | 213 | | – | |

Scoring in this area proved extremely difficult. There are families where it is difficult to find any real decrease in income, but where, particularly if the wife is a bad manager, the problem may be acute. Equally there are some families who have experienced a considerable drop in income, but if the wife is a good manager, no problems may arise. We have tried to base our assessment on the *facts* of the situation rather than the wife's feelings about it, and for this reason we feel that the pattern of adjustment scores in this area does not wholly corroborate the picture obtained during the interviews, where, without doubt, almost all wives found it difficult to manage. Our questionnaire asked for no precise information about criminal earnings, and it is possible that husbands provided for their wives in this way, but more importantly, we think it is the *responsibility* of handling the finances alone which made wives feel more deprived; this does not show adequately on our rating scale since we were primarily concerned with *actual* reduction in income.

It is interesting to note that, although the proportion of stars and recidivists whose financial situation remains unchanged (score '2') is much the same, the proportion of recidivists showing an improvement (score '1') in their financial position is significantly higher [$\chi^2 = 6·55$; 1 d.f.; $P < 0·05$] than the proportion of stars. On the other hand, amongst those whose position deteriorates grossly (score '5'), the recidivists' wives experience a greater deterioration than do stars' wives [$\chi^2 = 10\cdot41$; 1 d.f.; $P < 0\cdot01$].

*Area* 3: *Wife's work*

### TABLE III

| Score | Stars % | | Recidivists % | | Total % | |
|---|---|---|---|---|---|---|
| 1 | 3·1 | | 9·3 | | 6·3 | |
| 2 | 16·5 | | 9·3 | | 12·7 | |
| 3 | 48·5 | | 44·4 | | 46·3 | |
| 4 | 24·7 | | 25·9 | | 25·4 | |
| 5 | 7·2 | | 11·1 | | 9·3 | |
| | 100·0 | 37·3 | 100·0 | 24·9 | 100·0 | 29·5 |
| 0 | | 55·8 | | 59·0 | | 57·8 |
| 6 | | 6·9 | | 16·1 | | 12·7 |
| | | 100·0 | | 100·0 | | 100·0 |
| Number | 256 | | 213 | | – | |

It will be remembered that approximately 33 per cent of the wives went out to work;[1] most of them did so in order to buy 'extras' which their NAB grant was insufficient to cover. Only very few of them actually liked doing so; the majority would have preferred not to, but they needed additional money and were therefore content to go to work for a while. Such wives were given a score of '3'. There are, nevertheless, a great many wives (34·7 per cent) who were by no means happy to do so, even though it relieved some of the financial pressure. It is noteworthy that again the differences between stars and recidivists are insignificant. [$\chi^2 = 4\cdot54$; 4 d.f. N.S.]

Many wives felt that welfare and national assistance were synonymous and did not want either, since they both represented 'charity'. Some had had previous unpleasant contacts with welfare, and said either that they could not be bothered to try again or, since they felt anxious about rejection, acted as though they were indifferent. '0' has been used a good deal in this scale because it includes those who reject, or are indifferent to, welfare services, and it also includes those not wanting to ask, although perhaps needing help.

Table IV (see p. 218) indicates that there was a good deal of dissatisfaction about the welfare provisions, and that this view was shared by both stars' and recidivists' wives. In making assessments in this area, as well as in area 5 (see p. 218), special consideration was given to the wife's unfulfilled perceived needs, as well as to the degree of satisfaction experienced. Stars and recidivists show different pat-

[1] See Chapter V, p. 126.

terns of adjustment, the difference is due to the higher proportion of recidivists classified '2' [$\chi^2 = 9\cdot16$; 1 d.f.; $P < 0\cdot01$].

*Area* 4: *Use made of, and satisfaction with, social welfare agencies*

### TABLE IV

| Score | Stars % | | Recidivists % | | Total % | |
|---|---|---|---|---|---|---|
| 1 | 24·7 | | 22·0 | | 23·0 | |
| 2 | 11·4 | | 25·2 | | 19·8 | |
| 3 | 40·5 | | 28·5 | | 33·2 | |
| 4 | 8·9 | | 13·0 | | 11·4 | |
| 5 | 14·6 | | 11·4 | | 12·6 | |
| | 100·0 | 60·8 | 100·0 | 56·7 | 100·0 | 58·2 |
| 0 | | 34·2 | | 28·6 | | 30·7 |
| 6 | | 5·0 | | 14·7 | | 11·1 |
| | | 100·0 | | 100·0 | | 100·0 |
| Number | 256 | | 213 | | – | |

*Area* 5: *Use made of, and satisfaction with,* NAB

### TABLE V

| Score | Stars % | | Recidivists % | | Total % | |
|---|---|---|---|---|---|---|
| 1 | 17·3 | | 18·1 | | 17·8 | |
| 2 | 33·0 | | 35·6 | | 34·6 | |
| 3 | 20·0 | | 18·8 | | 19·3 | |
| 4 | 20·5 | | 20·8 | | 20·7 | |
| 5 | 9·2 | | 6·7 | | 7·7 | |
| | 100·0 | 71·2 | 100·0 | 68·7 | 100·1 | 69·6 |
| 0 | | 21·9 | | 15·2 | | 17·7 |
| 6 | | 6·9 | | 16·1 | | 12·7 |
| | | 100·0 | | 100·0 | | 100·0 |
| Number | 256 | | 213 | | – | |

In area 5 one is struck by the similarity of the situation as experienced by the wives of stars and recidivists [$\chi^2 = 0\cdot89$; 4 d.f.; N.S.]. A high percentage were 'neutral' in their views having experienced no particular difficulties with the Board's officials and not feeling that they were treated differently as prisoners' wives. However, a great many expressed dissatisfaction, and it was difficult to make a distinction between scores of '3' and '4'; although care was taken to try to achieve uniformity of coding, it would probably be unwise to consider these two scores independently of each other. Wives often had one very bad experience with a particular NAB officer, but regarded all other dealings with the Board as satisfactory, and they had no current complaints or unfulfilled needs at the time of interview.

*Area* 6: *Present attitude to marriage and future plans*

TABLE VI

| Score | Stars % | | Recidivists % | | Total % | |
|-------|---------|------|---------------|------|---------|------|
| 1 | 10·1 | | 4·9 | | 7·0 | |
| 2 | 55·6 | | 41·8 | | 47·4 | |
| 3 | 16·5 | | 24·7 | | 21·4 | |
| 4 | 10·1 | | 15·4 | | 13·2 | |
| 5 | 7·7 | | 13·2 | | 10·9 | |
| | 100·0 | 95·4 | 100·0 | 83·9 | 99·9 | 88·2 |
| 0 | | 0·8 | | 0·5 | | 0·6 |
| 6 | | 3·8 | | 15·7 | | 11·2 |
| | | 100·0 | | 100·0 | | 100·0 |
| Number | 256 | | 213 | | – | |

This is one of the areas in which differences between stars and recidivists are strong [$\chi^2$ for trend on score 1 to 5 = 14·05; 1 d.f.; $P < 0.01$]. The trend would seem to indicate that recidivists' wives are less willing to have their husbands back, though as we have stated elsewhere, this reluctance is usually fairly superficial and unlikely to be acted upon.

This area was particularly hard to score where sexual offences were involved, especially if they concerned an incestuous relationship, where the wife felt forced to make a decision between husband and child.

In general a score of '1' was given when the wife claimed to have stronger and more positive feelings towards her husband since the imprisonment, though these may in fact have been quite unrealistic and merely the result of the tendency to see their husband through rose-coloured spectacles, or the need to convince themselves that he would change.[1]

Area 7 (see p. 220), relating to the behaviour of the children, was difficult to assess since it was not always clear whether their behaviour had in fact deteriorated since the father's imprisonment, or whether such behaviour existed beforehand. It was therefore decided to score '2' unless there was definite evidence that change had taken place.

'3' was scored in those cases where there were signs of disturbance since imprisonment, but these were not regarded by the mother as

[1] See also Chapter IV, pp. 102–3.

*Area 7: Children's behaviour*

TABLE VII

| Score | Stars % | | Recidivists % | | Total % | |
|-------|---------|---|---------------|---|---------|---|
| 1 | 10·7 | | 7·1 | | 8·5 | |
| 2 | 43·4 | | 41·9 | | 42·5 | |
| 3 | 22·0 | | 32·3 | | 28·2 | |
| 4 | 18·5 | | 12·9 | | 15·1 | |
| 5 | 5·4 | | 5·8 | | 5·6 | |
| | 100·0 | 78·8 | 100·0 | 71·4 | 99·9 | 74·2 |
| 0 | | 15·8 | | 12·4 | | 13·7 |
| 6 | | 5·4 | | 16·1 | | 12·1 |
| | | 100·0 | | 99·9 | | 100·0 |
| Number | 256 | | 213 | | – | |

constituting any sort of problem. This score was also used in the relatively few cases when a child initially showed signs of disturbed behaviour, but adjusted quite quickly and adequately.

It must be borne in mind that many of the children were too young to have made much of a relationship with their father, particularly the children of those recidivists who had spent a good deal of their time in prison. Furthermore, since so many children were under school age, questions regarding truancy were of little value in scoring this area; similarly because they were under the age of criminal responsibility, questions relating to court appearances were largely irrelevant.

A score of '1' was used to indicate an improved situation which could arise from two extremely divergent pre-imprisonment situations:

(a) A family with fairly normal, happy relationships where, upon the father's imprisonment the children miss him but help their mother increasingly and assume additional responsibilities; or

(b) Where there were bad family relationships before imprisonment resulting in definite relief for the children when the father was removed from the home. Many incest cases came into this category, though in some such instances the father was deeply missed and the children showed signs of disturbed behaviour on his removal from the home. Under such circumstances a score of 3, 4 or 5 was used, depending upon the degree of disturbance.

The differences between stars and recidivists are insignificant except for category '3'. [$\chi^2 = 4·83$; 1 d.f.; $P < 0·05$.]

We think this can be accounted for by the fact that stars' wives were, on the whole, more reluctant than recidivists' wives to admit **to** problems with their children, and, as mentioned above, a score of '3' included all families where the mother gave evidence of disturbance amongst her children, but did not admit that it constituted a problem.

*Area* 8. *Wife's contact with husband in prison*

TABLE VIII

| Score | Stars % | | Recidivists % | | Total % | |
|---|---|---|---|---|---|---|
| 1 | 53·4 | | 55·9 | | 54·9 | |
| 2 | 30·3 | | 18·1 | | 23·0 | |
| 3 | 2·8 | | 3·7 | | 3·3 | |
| 4 | 8·8 | | 12·8 | | 11·2 | |
| 5 | 4·8 | | 9·6 | | 7·7 | |
| | 100·1 | 96·5 | 100·1 | 86·6 | 100·1 | 90·3 |
| 0 | | 0·0 | | 0·5 | | 0·3 |
| 6 | | 3·5 | | 12·9 | | 9·4 |
| | | 100·0 | | 100·0 | | 100·0 |
| Number | 256 | | 213 | | – | |

In this case a graduated scale is used ranging from '1', to indicate that all available letters and visits were used, to '5' where the wife never wrote or visited. The use of category '2' does not, however, imply any lack of desire to visit, but merely the fact that the wife is genuinely prevented from doing so by circumstances (expense, distance, illness, etc.). If there was evidence that the 'circumstances' were in fact being used as an excuse for not visiting a score of '3' was

*Area* 9: *Children's contact with father in prison*

TABLE IX

| Score | Stars % | | Recidivists % | | Total % | |
|---|---|---|---|---|---|---|
| 1 | 22·0 | | 21·5 | | 21·7 | |
| 2 | 27·5 | | 25·5 | | 26·3 | |
| 3 | 24·5 | | 26·8 | | 25·9 | |
| 4 | 17·5 | | 14·8 | | 15·9 | |
| 5 | 8·5 | | 11·4 | | 10·2 | |
| | 100·0 | 76·9 | 100·0 | 68·7 | 100·0 | 71·8 |
| 0 | | 19·6 | | 16·6 | | 17·7 |
| 6 | | 3·5 | | 14·7 | | 10·5 |
| | | 100·0 | | 100·0 | | 100·0 |
| Number | 256 | | 213 | | – | |

given. Stars' wives more frequently scored '2' [$\chi^2 = 8 \cdot 51$; 1 d.f.; $P < 0 \cdot 01$], but otherwise differences between the two groups were small.

Since most wives automatically took the children to visit their father, we included in this assessment the degree to which the children appeared to miss their father and to want to visit him.

It will be noted that there are, amongst both recidivists and stars, quite a high proportion of '3's'. This score includes children who were too young to know about the imprisonment, as well as those whose parents thought it unwise to take them. It also includes situations where, within the same family, one child missed the father and wanted to visit, but another did not. There was no significant difference between the two types of family in the children's contact with their father [$\chi^2 = 1 \cdot 46$; 4 d.f.; N.S.].

*Area* 10: *Social activity of wife during separation*

TABLE X

| Score | Stars % | | Recidivists % | | Total % | |
|---|---|---|---|---|---|---|
| 1 | 8·0 | | 9·1 | | 8·7 | |
| 2 | 27·8 | | 29·0 | | 28·5 | |
| 3 | 31·6 | | 37·5 | | 35·1 | |
| 4 | 25·7 | | 20·5 | | 22·6 | |
| 5 | 6·8 | | 4·0 | | 5·1 | |
| | 100·0 | 91·2 | 100·0 | 81·1 | 100·0 | 84·9 |
| 0 | | 1·9 | | 2·8 | | 2·5 |
| 6 | | 6·9 | | 16·1 | | 12·7 |
| | | 100·0 | | 100·0 | | 100·0 |
| Number | 256 | | 213 | | – | |

Scores in this area were based not only upon measurable reduction in social activity, but upon the extent to which wives felt lonely, or deprived of outside stimulation. It will be noted that there was in fact a considerable amount of deterioration, 62·8 per cent reporting less activity than before, as well as complaining of loneliness. When making assessments, particular consideration was given to the question of change, and the 5·1 per cent who scored '5' had become almost complete isolates *only* since the imprisonment.

A score of '1' was given in those cases where the husband had been very restrictive before imprisonment and the wives enjoyed their new-found freedom, many of them no longer wanting their husbands home.

There was no significant difference in the pattern of adjustment between the two groups [$\chi^2 = 3 \cdot 79$; 4 d.f.; N.S.].

*Areas* 11, 12 *and* 13: *Wife's relationship with Parents, In-laws, Friends and Neighbours*

## TABLE XI.  (*Parents*)

| Score | Stars % | | Recidivists % | | Total % | |
|-------|---------|---|---------------|---|---------|---|
| 1 | 37·0 | | 36·3 | | 36·6 | |
| 2 | 33·3 | | 32·2 | | 32·6 | |
| 3 | 15·3 | | 17·8 | | 16·8 | |
| 4 | 7·9 | | 10·3 | | 9·4 | |
| 5 | 6·3 | | 3·4 | | 4·6 | |
| | 100·0 | 72·7 | 100·0 | 67·3 | 100·0 | 69·3 |
| 0 | | 20·8 | | 17·5 | | 10·7 |
| 6 | | 6·5 | | 15·2 | | 12·0 |
| | | 100·0 | | 100·0 | | 100·0 |
| Number | 256 | | 213 | | – | |

## TABLE XII.  (*In-laws*)

| Score | Stars % | | Recidivists % | | Total % | |
|-------|---------|---|---------------|---|---------|---|
| 1 | 20·1 | | 11·7 | | 15·2 | |
| 2 | 28·4 | | 22·6 | | 25·0 | |
| 3 | 27·3 | | 36·5 | | 32·7 | |
| 4 | 9·8 | | 20·4 | | 16·0 | |
| 5 | 14·4 | | 8·8 | | 11·1 | |
| | 100·0 | 74·6 | 100·0 | 63·1 | 100·0 | 67·4 |
| 0 | | 18·8 | | 21·2 | | 20·3 |
| 6 | | 6·5 | | 15·7 | | 12·2 |
| | | 100·0 | | 100·0 | | 100·0 |
| Number | 256 | | 213 | | – | |

## TABLE XIII.  (*Friends and neighbours*)

| Score | Stars % | | Recidivists % | | Total % | |
|-------|---------|---|---------------|---|---------|---|
| 1 | 5·9 | | 7·8 | | 7·1 | |
| 2 | 39·0 | | 34·1 | | 36·0 | |
| 3 | 35·2 | | 36·9 | | 36·2 | |
| 4 | 13·1 | | 16·2 | | 15·0 | |
| 5 | 6·8 | | 5·0 | | 5·7 | |
| | 100·0 | 90·8 | 100·0 | 82·5 | 100·0 | 85·6 |
| 0 | | 3·1 | | 2·3 | | 2·6 |
| 6 | | 6·2 | | 15·2 | | 11·8 |
| | | 100·1 | | 100·0 | | 100·0 |
| Number | 256 | | 213 | | – | |

In general wives found much more active support from their own parents than from in-laws, friends or neighbours (see Tables XI, XII and XIII). There was some hostility between the wife and her in-laws, but in most cases this dated from long before the imprisonment. Furthermore, where such negative relationships existed, they constituted far less of a problem for the wife than did any hostility on the part of neighbours. In some cases the wife moved (usually to her parents) in order to avoid facing the neighbours, or to ensure that her children would not be subjected to taunting remarks. It was sometimes difficult to discern whether such fears were based on actual experience (when a score of '5' was given) or whether the wife had been fearful of hostility and had moved in order to forestall it.

There were no differences between stars' and recidivists' wives in their relationship with parents [$\chi^2 = 2 \cdot 24$; 4 d.f.; N.S.], or with neighbours [$\chi^2 = 2 \cdot 47$; 4 d.f.; N.S.]. The difference between the wives of stars and recidivists in their relationship with in-laws was, however, significant, but differences did not follow a trend as can be seen from the chi-square table:

| $\chi^2$ due to | d.f. | $\chi^2$ | Significance |
|---|---|---|---|
| Trend | 1 | $2 \cdot 55$ | N.S. |
| Residual | 3 | $12 \cdot 61$ | $P < 0 \cdot 01$ |
| Total | 4 | $15 \cdot 16$ | $P < 0 \cdot 01$ |

It should be noted that the collection of data on this question was by no means satisfactory for the construction of a rating scale since to obtain accurate scoring it would have been necessary:

(a) To distinguish between friends and neighbours, the two being by no means synonymous.

(b) To include siblings, grandparents and other relatives who in fact often gave active support where there were no parents, but who were excluded by the wording of the questionnaire.

### THE CONCEPT OF ADJUSTMENT

Having rated each family as indicated above, the problem remained as to how a satisfactory overall score of adjustment might be arrived at. The findings of the intensive sample, and an impressionistic view of the extensive sample, suggested that adjustment to separation might be a function of general total attitudes to a crisis situation. For this reason, and for purposes of simplification, it was decided that in order to obtain such an overall adjustment score for each family, a simple average of all the areas would be taken. We make no claim that this is a wholly satisfactory method, but since it seemed that any weightings given to particular areas would be quite arbitrary, it seemed a legitimate if somewhat artificial procedure.

Having in this way obtained an overall adjustment score for each family, we then wished to establish whether any particular factors in the environment could be shown to have particular relevance to good or bad adjustment.[1] The following list shows those items which it was considered might be most relevant.

    (i) Length of separation.
   (ii) Length of sentence.
  (iii) Type of offence.
  (iv) Husband's occupation.
   (v) Duration of marriage.
  (vi) Period known before marriage.
 (vii) Husband's previous imprisonments.
(viii) Wife's age.
  (ix) Geographical mobility of family.
   (x) Marital status at time of imprisonment.
  (xi) Wife's previous marriages.
 (xii) Husband's previous marriages.
(xiii) Family size.

Unfortunately none of these factors was related to the adjustment score with the exception of family size amongst the families of star prisoners (significant at the 5 per cent level). Thus amongst these families, the greater the number of children the more likely the family is to adjust poorly to the separation. Amongst the families of recidivists family size was not a significant factor.

The failure to find a relationship between these environmental factors and adjustment to separation suggests at least three alternatives: either our concept of adjustment as a function of general total attitude is an over-simplification, or the methods of devising rating scales were insufficiently precise, or, quite simply, it may be that there *is* no relationship. As will be seen from the details in Appendix D, further tests were carried out which suggested that the original method of obtaining an adjustment score by forming a simple average was inappropriate.

It was recognized that it would be desirable to take each area of adjustment in turn and analyse it separately against the environmental factors listed above. Unfortunately the resources of the research did not allow such an analysis to be carried out in its entirety, and it was decided to take what were felt to be the two most important factors affecting adjustment to separation (based on the data obtained from both samples), one relating primarily to intra-family situations and one relating primarily to material conditions,

---

[1] A full discussion of the statistical procedures involved in this aspect of the work is given in Appendix D of this report. Only the general findings appear in this chapter.

H

and to test these against seven of the original thirteen environmental factors.

The two areas of adjustment selected for further analysis were:

(ii) attitude to marriage and future plans
(ii) finance

The environmental factors selected from the original list were as follows:

(i) length of separation
(ii) length of sentence
(iii) type of offence
(iv) duration of marriage
(v) husband's previous imprisonments
(vi) wife's age
(vii) family size

The results of this analysis indicated that the only factor related to financial adjustment is the number of previous sentences served in adult institutions, and this is relevant in the case of both stars and recidivists. Since the greater the number of previous prison sentences the better financially adjusted the families appear to be, this suggests that such wives may be more used to making the necessary contacts with the NAB and other welfare organizations and possibly more aware of all the possible sources of income. Whilst the data from the interviews to some extent support this view, we feel that this situation also arises because each successive term of imprisonment tends to lower the standard of living and the expectations within the family. Thus they tend to reach a level of subsistence below which they cannot sink, and since they no longer try to maintain high standards, their adjustment is *relatively* good.

It must be stressed that because a family is better *adjusted* financially, this in no way implies that they are better *off* financially. We have reason to believe (see also Chapter IV, p. 83) that the wives of first offenders with relatively high incomes before imprisonment, find it hardest to adjust financially, since their commitments cannot always be disposed of easily when the husband ceases to be a breadwinner.

So far as present satisfaction with marriage and future plans are concerned, in the case of stars' wives the number of previous imprisonments is again significant,[1] and in the case of recidivists' wives, so is the type of offence. The fact that those wives whose husbands have never been in prison before are more satisfied with

[1] 18·6 per cent of stars in the sample of men interviewed had been in prison before (see Chapter III, p. 53), 4·5 per cent of the total sample having been imprisoned more than once.

their marriage is understandable, and the fact that recidivists' wives also approach significance on this variable confirms the strong impressionistic view that each additional prison sentence loosens the family ties, and relationships deteriorate. A prison sentence only very rarely causes a marriage to break up, but a succession of such sentences may produce this result. We know very little about the degree of tolerance shown by wives, nor when and why the breaking point occurs, though we have suggested elsewhere[1] that the opportunity to separate is at least a relevant factor.

It is interesting to see that for the wives of star offenders, the type of offence is not a significant factor affecting satisfaction with marriage, whereas, it *is* significant for recidivists. Where the husband is in prison for either a sex offence or a white-collar offence (fraud, embezzlement, etc.), the recidivists' wives are less satisfied with the marriage and less likely to have their husband back. Where the husband is in prison for murder, manslaughter, or a property offence not involving the use of violence, recidivists' wives show good adjustment in terms of satisfaction with the marriage.

By testing separately two areas of adjustment we have been able to isolate certain factors which are relevant to this process, and we feel that this points to the desirability of testing each area individually had the resources of the research been available. Furthermore, it confirms the view that our method of constructing an overall index of adjustment was not satisfactory and greater refinement is necessary. We think that any further work on such an index should make a much clearer distinction than was done in our own scaling procedure, between matters of fact and attitudes. It might then be possible to construct two overall indices of adjustment which would be more meaningful.

[1] See Chapter V, p. 137.

## Chapter IX

# CIVIL PRISONERS AND THEIR FAMILIES

Most of the men who go to prison do so because they have been convicted of a crime, and in the general discussion about prisons, prisoners, and prisoners' families it is often forgotten that there is another class of inmate which, though smaller in numbers, presents symptoms of social problems no less acute than those of the criminal population. The civil prisoner is the forgotten man of the penal system.

Civil prisoners, although they are a group distinct from criminal prisoners, differ among themselves in one important respect, namely that some are committed by the county courts for failing to pay debts, others are committed by the magistrates' courts for neglecting to maintain their wives and children, and yet others may be committed by the higher courts in the course of civil proceedings. The most important sociological distinction to be drawn is between the debtor and the maintenance defaulter, the former failing in his obligations as a consumer, the latter in his moral and legal obligations to his own kin. The technical problems involved in attempting to separate the two main categories of civil prisoner in each stage of this analysis were such that we have avoided doing so when presenting the statistical data, but have indicated such important differences as exist at the appropriate points in the discussion.

Imprisonment for debt is a ghost that haunts the modern prison system. People are no longer sent to prison as in Dickens' day, because they cannot meet their obligations: the Debtors' Act of 1869 abolished imprisonment for debt and those who go to prison now do so, not as debtors, but for contempt of a court order to pay, the court having decided that they have the means to pay, but are deliberately refusing to do so.

Most civil prisoners are kept in closed local prisons, though if their sentence is long enough, they may now be transferred to an open establishment. They do not wear the ordinary blue prison battledress, but wear a brown uniform reminiscent of that worn by captured Germans and Italians in World War II.

The number of civil prisoners is increasing every year. In 1952,

6,132 men were sent to prison other than for crime; in 1961 the figure had risen to 9,377, an increase of some 51 per cent. Of these 9,000 odd, 5,506 were committed by the county courts for debt; 2,854 were sent by the magistrates' courts for failure to pay maintenance, or bastardy orders, while 370 were imprisoned for non-payment of rates. The remaining 668 were sentenced for contempt of court, as nuclear disarmers refusing to be bound over to keep the peace, or were being held as aliens awaiting deportation. In our research we were not concerned with the last three categories, but only with the two main classes of civil prisoner, the debtor, and the man who fails to pay an order in respect of a wife and/or child.

The number of county court debtors rose steadily throughout the 1950's, but there is reason to believe that this rise was due to an expansion in the consumer section of the economy, accompanied by a greater volume of spending involving the use of credit, rather than to a decline in the standards of integrity in meeting economic obligations. Until 1958, on the other hand, the number of men committed to prison for non-payment of maintenance remained fairly constant. During 1957, a good deal of public attention was focused on the problem by Miss Joan Vickers, who introduced a Private Member's Bill in an attempt to provide money for the women and children concerned. Subsequently the Government itself drafted legislation which took effect in the Maintenance Order Act (1958). The Act attempted to keep such men out of prison and to provide money for their wives and dependants by legalizing a system whereby wages could be attached at source if the arrears amounted to more than four weeks. Unfortunately, because there are no statistics available at a central source relating to the number of attachment orders made by magistrates, there is no way of knowing how many more men there might be in prison were the Act not in force.[1] Whilst the number fell by almost one half after the passing of the Act, it is now gradually creeping up again, the 1961 figure being an increase of over 8 per cent on that of 1958. One major difficulty is that unemployment, often of a deliberate nature, and frequent changes of job accompanied by equally frequent changes of address, makes the task of tracing the men, and making contact with their employers extremely difficult.

Imprisonment for debt is essentially one of the last in a series of measures available to the creditor, and attendance by one of the research workers at three county courts in different parts of the country confirmed the general impression that every effort is made to keep debtors out of prison. Imprisonment is applied as a purely

[1] A plan for improving the Act was devised by the National Council of Women and discussed by the legal committee of the Magistrates' Association in January 1963 (see *The Times*, report 17.1.1963).

coercive measure;[1] if, after a committal warrant has been issued, the debtor pays the whole sum owing he goes free. If he pays part of it his period of detention is proportionately reduced. This applies equally after he has been received into prison, and indeed if he has money on him at the time of reception, this is taken from him and paid into court as though he had made the payment voluntarily.

## THE COUNTY COURTS

In order to see how the system worked in practice, and to gather the views of those concerned, it was decided to interview the judges and staff of three county courts in different parts of the country. From figures kindly supplied by the county court branch of the Lord Chancellor's Department (reproduced in Table I) it will be seen that comparatively few of those upon whom committal warrants are served are actually conveyed to prison. The figures relate to those courts committing to the prisons which were studied in the research, but as those prisons were chosen by careful sampling there is no reason to believe that these data are unrepresentative of the country as a whole.[2]

The figures show that debtors in different parts of the country do not go to prison in comparable proportions. The Cardiff area stands out as the one in which county courts make proportionately more committal orders than anywhere else. The lowest committal order rate appears to be London.[3] On the other hand the pattern is not the same when one considers the percentage of cases in which, once a committal order has been issued, the recalcitrant debtor is actually conveyed to prison. By this stage well over 90 per cent of the debtors in all areas have already paid up by some means or other, though Liverpool and London imprison more debtors *pro rata* than do the others in the sample.

The variation in the percentage of those who, once in prison, buy themselves out before their sentence has expired, is very considerable indeed: whilst 62 per cent buy themselves out of Manchester, only 17 per cent do so from Lincoln.

[1] Before a committal order can be made 'it must be proved to the satisfaction of the court that the person making default has, or has had since the date of the original order, the means to pay, and has refused or neglected, or refuses and neglects to pay' (Debtors' Act 1869.) Although technically there is no such thing as imprisonment for debt, we shall use this term for purposes of simplification, and since it is nevertheless the initial reason for their being in prison.

[2] Although seventeen prisons were visited, only eight of these are local prisons to which civil prisoners are taken on committal. The Lord Chancellor's Department were unable to break down these figures by sex. However, the *total* number of women committed by *all* county courts in 1961 amounted to only 171, and as we were concerned with only eight prisons in respect of civils, the number of women included in the figures for Table I must be very small indeed.

[3] All debtors in the London area serve their sentence in Brixton prison.

The data are not easy to interpret, for the issue of a committal order reflects in part the attitude of the court and in part the distribution of apparently unco-operative debtors. Clearly it is possible that the shock of imprisonment was sufficient to make the point which the judge had been unable to make, namely that the court was in earnest about what it had said, but it might have been thought that this phenomenon was at least as evenly distributed throughout different regions as the practice of paying up after the issue of a committal warrant, but before the debtor had been taken to prison. Buying out might be explained by differential access to 'emergency' funds, help from relatives and employers, and so on: thus the debtors from country districts served by Lincoln prison might have less money available than those in the Leeds area. But if this were true, poverty must be very much greater in the Liverpool area than it is in Manchester and, on the face of it, this seems implausible.

TABLE I. *Committal warrants issued and debtors conveyed to prison*

| Prison | No. of committal orders made in 1961 | Orders made per 100 thousand of population* | Orders issued | Debtors conveyed to prison | Percentage of col. iii | Debtors released before expiration of full term | Percentage of col. iv |
|---|---|---|---|---|---|---|---|
| | (i) | (ii) | (iii) | (iv) | (v) | (vi) | (vii) |
| Brixton | 16,200 | 426·3 | 11,380 | 615 | 5·4 | 223 | 36·0 |
| Cardiff | 28,276 | 2827·0 | 25,330 | 981 | 3·8 | 264 | 27·0 |
| Durham | 11,805 | 737·8 | 8,342 | 204 | 2·4 | 72 | 35·0 |
| Leeds | 31,887 | 1312·2 | 26,580 | 1,044 | 3·9 | 257 | 25·0 |
| Lincoln | 9,259 | 791·3 | 8,043 | 305 | 3·7 | 52 | 17·0 |
| Liverpool | 12,267 | 776·3 | 8,094 | 493 | 6·0 | 101 | 20·0 |
| Manchester | 22,390 | 914·1 | 17,996 | 657 | 3·6 | 412 | 62·0 |
| Winchester | 5,138 | 642·2 | 3,695 | 112 | 3·0 | 22 | 20·0 |

\* The population of the catchment areas of each prison.

The proportion of persons actually conveyed to prison is much more constant, which suggests that once applied, coercion has a more uniform effect. Once imprisonment ceases to be a threat and becomes a reality, then it loses its value, for there is little in the penal treatment of civil debtors that is rehabilitative, and as a form of deterrence it can only operate in respect of some future indebtedness which may never occur.

We do not know for sure how far those who go to prison do so in consequence of a genuine inability to pay, and how many do so out of sheer determination not to co-operate. As the law stands, it is only those who *wilfully* refuse to abide by the order of the court to make payment that are sent to prison, but from what we were able to see of civil debtors in prison, there seems reason to believe that many of them are simply so socially incompetent and inarticulate that they cannot adequately put the case as to their means before the court. In other words, their imprisonment is as likely to be a consequence of their lack of intelligence, or understanding of what is actually required of them, as it is of contempt for the order of the court.

Whilst there is general agreement that civil debtors ought to be kept out of prison if possible, discussion with the county court judges and their staffs suggested that there were considerable differences in the detailed aspects of the use of the legal machinery, particularly with respect to the length of sentences imposed. (This is of course no more than a reflection of the situation which obtains in respect of sentencing policy as a whole.) One judge commented that his court was dependent upon the quality of the debt collectors, but this appeared to be an expression of his own modesty, since it was thought that his humane and understanding way of dealing with debtors had some influence on the bailiffs and other staff of the court. The supervisor of bailiffs in this same court told us that 'to have a man in prison is seen by the bailiffs as an admission of failure'. At another court we were told that judges often hold different views privately from those they express in court. The view was generally expressed that there should be uniformity of practice in the operation of the machinery of the county courts, and equally, everyone was agreed that this was not so at the present time. In one court visited there is a flat rate of sentence, ten days irrespective of the amount owing; this fact is said to be well known amongst debtors and men are said sometimes to take two weeks' holiday and then go along to court, asking to do their ten days then and there!

Nevertheless, despite individual differences between courts, it seems clear from Table I that the threat of imprisonment does reduce the number actually imprisoned, whilst the number who buy themselves out early is comparatively high. On the other hand, sitting in court, it soon becomes apparent that the majority of debtors are very vague as to what is happening and about the extent of their obligations. Many seem to feel that if they do nothing the problem will somehow solve itself. This is wholly in keeping with the characteristics displayed by the debtors seen in prison.

But whilst for debtors both length of sentence and amount owed seem unrelated and appear to oscillate wildly, men sent to prison for arrears of maintenance are almost invariably sentenced to the maximum of six weeks, irrespective of the sum owed, which may be less than £100 or well over £1,000. These differences almost certainly arise largely from the uncertainty of prosecution for the latter group. Whereas the debtors seem in the main to live at home with their wives and families, and can be easily found by the officers of the court, men owing maintenance may be anywhere in the country. Some are found within a matter of weeks of being in arrears, while others may go for months or years before the police catch up with them, since they are so often without a regular home or job.

We have already discussed in Chapter II (see pp. 27 ff.) our method of sampling and selecting civil prisoners. The fact that those in prison for non-payment of maintenance are inside for longer than are the debtors (who frequently buy themselves out early), meant that the sample of civil prisoners contained many more non-payment of maintenance cases than debtors. Table II sets out the position regarding our contact with civil prisoners and their wives:

TABLE II. *Interviews with civil prisoners and their wives*

| | No. selected for interview | No. actually interviewed | Unable to contact wife | No. of wives actually interviewed | % of col. (i) |
|---|---|---|---|---|---|
| | (i) | (ii) | (iii) | (iv) | |
| Debtors | 54 | 52 | 12 | 40 | 76·9 |
| Non-payment of maintenance | 123 | 119 | 54 | 67 | 54·4 |
| Total | 177 | 171* | 66 | 107† | – |

\* Four men declined interview and two interviews were incomplete.

† 111 wives were seen but four interviews were incomplete and are not included in the analysis.

## THE PRISONERS

Earlier in this report we expressed some doubts as to the feasibility of distinguishing between the problems arising for prisoners and their families as a result of *imprisonment* and those arising out of *separation*. During the course of interviewing it became clear that civil prisoners differed in certain important ways from criminal prisoners; it was also our impression that their problems and those of their families were less likely to be connected with either imprisonment, or with separation, than was the case with criminal offenders.

Whereas 50 per cent of *all* criminal prisoners are under the age of thirty, only 25·7 per cent of civils fall into this category (see Table III p. 234); on the other hand 31·5 per cent of the civils are to be found in the age group 40–49, whereas only 14 per cent of criminal prisoners fall into this category. Although, as a result of a necessary aspect of sample design, the population of civils is not directly comparable with the sample of criminal prisoners, comparison with Table I in Chapter III confirms our belief that there are considerable differences in age structure between the representatives of the two groups of married prisoners in our study. Since, in any case, the *married* criminal sample tends to be somewhat older than the prison population as a whole, it will be seen that our civil prisoners tend to be quite unlike any other groups in respect of age.

TABLE III.  *Age distribution of sample of civil prisoners*
(*Percentages*)

| Age | Civil prisoners | Corresponding % in prison population of England and Wales, 1961 |
|---|---|---|
| 21–29 | 25·7 | 50·1 |
| 30–39 | 35·6 | 27·5 |
| 40–49 | 31·5 | 14·0 |
| 50 and over | 7·0 | 8·3 |
| Total | 100·0 | 100·0 |
| No. of prisoners | 171 | – |

While little or no data were available from the prison records, these being for the most part bundles of starkly blank paper, we were left with an overriding impression of the low mental calibre of these men. Both the staff and other prisoners regarded them as the dregs of the prison population. At one of the prisons set aside for civils, a man had been interviewed by one of the research workers and was found a quarter of an hour later being interviewed again on the same schedule by another worker. Both interviewers asked with some surprise if the man had not thought it odd being asked the same questions twice over in so short a space of time. 'No,' he replied, 'I didn't know it was the same.'

Apart from knowing little or nothing about the details of their indebtedness, or their financial position generally, they were often unable to give coherent accounts of their employment history. Where they were able to do so, they seemed to have been unemployed for long periods, and those who worked did so only erratically. Furthermore, they seemed to have been involved in a great many accidents, usually at work, and to suffer from a multitude of physical and mental troubles, not infrequently of a psychosomatic nature. In short, the civil prisoners appeared to be truly social inadequates, needing almost permanent support if they were to survive in the community. The characteristics of those in for non-payment of maintenance were frequently quite similar but their attitude to the debt was very different. They often claimed that their default was a matter of principle, although most of them rationalized the situation and said it was because their wives were living with other men, or the children they were being asked to support were not theirs. In fact they simply hated their wives and were stubbornly prepared to undergo an infinite number of prison sentences rather than pay a penny.

However, it is obviously insufficient to base our findings upon impressions, and we shall here be concerned with discussing the data collected in relation to civil prisoners. Except where otherwise stated, civil debtors and those in for non-payment of maintenance have been treated as one group.

## *Work*

Whilst 36 per cent of the criminal sample were unemployed at the time of committing their offences, the same was true of no less than 52 per cent of the civil prisoners. Bearing in mind that the two samples are not strictly comparable, it nevertheless appears that a very high proportion of civil prisoners have acute difficulties about work. These stem essentially from a combination of personality problems and psychiatric or physical disability, or from being the most vulnerable element in the labour market, for those who *were* working did so almost exclusively in an unskilled capacity.

TABLE IV. *Reasons for unemployment*

*(Percentages of unemployed)*

|  | Debtors | Non-payment of maintenance | Total |
|---|---|---|---|
| No work available | 9·4 | 15·8 | 13·4 |
| Ill-health (physical or mental) | 50·0 | 22·8 | 32·5 |
| Professional or habitual criminal | – | 1·7 | 1·1 |
| Work problem* | 31·2 | 38·5 | 35·8 |
| Other | 9·4 | 21·0 | 16·8 |
| Total | 100·0 | 100·0 | 100·0 |
| Number of prisoners | 32 | 57 | 89 |

* For definition see Chapter III, p. 48.

It is striking that approximately a third (29) of those unemployed gave ill-health as a reason for it, and an attempt was made to categorize these complaints which are set out in Table V (see p. 236).

As was the case among the criminal prisoners interviewed, the category 'other' when probed almost invariably related to some form of nervous complaint. If to these nineteen men are added those suffering from other troubles with a well-defined psychological component, such as skin complaints, 'highly strung', 'nervous breakdown', migraine, and duodenal ulcer, the total of those who might reasonably be regarded as in poor mental health rises still further. There were, among the civil prisoners generally, a relatively high proportion suffering from chest ailments, though this information does not appear in Table V unless it was cited as a cause of

TABLE V.  *Nature of illness resulting in unemployment*
           *(prisoner's views)*

| | |
|---|---|
| Skin complaints | 3 |
| Hernia | 1 |
| Nervous breakdown | 2 |
| Highly strung | 1 |
| Chest ailments | 9 |
| Migraine | 2 |
| Loss of limb | 2 |
| Deafness | 1 |
| Duodenal ulcer | 6 |
| Other | 19 |
| Total | 46* |

\* The total exceeds twenty-nine as a result of some men reporting more than one illness.

unemployment. This is not surprising, since bronchial ailments are concentrated in the smoke-polluted working-class neighbourhoods of industrial cities,[1] and many of these men had worked in the mines of South Wales, Durham and the Yorkshire coalfields and had been exposed to pneumoconiosis and silicosis.

Not only do relatively few civil prisoners work, but when they do so, they tend to remain in their jobs for fairly short periods and to earn low wages: only 15·8 per cent of those who worked had been in one job for twelve months, and over 60 per cent of them had an income of less than £10 a week, and this to support what were often very large families. The majority of these incomes were derived from social benefits and not from earnings at all, and in view of their low earning potential many of these men must be in a position where, low as they are, the benefits of the social services come close to providing them with a larger income than they could earn.[2]

*Previous convictions*

About 68 per cent of the civils had been to prison before,[3] either as

[1] See Susser, M. W., and Watson, W., *Sociology in Medicine*, 1962, p. 36.

[2] c.f. Wilson, Harriet, *Delinquency and Child Neglect*, 1962, pp. 56 *et. seq.*

[3] As in the case of the criminal population this information was checked against the man's prison record, but in the case of civil prisoners, background data were frequently incomplete and we cannot tell whether the information given by the prisoners is correct.

civil prisoners, or following convictions for crime, or for both at different times. This is not perhaps surprising, since the kind of life led by many of them is of the type that frequently produces situations where a man may get into some trouble for petty thieving, or for vagrancy. Almost without exception those in for non-payment of maintenance had been there before; indeed for many it was a yearly pilgrimage, since a man cannot be imprisoned more than once in any period of twelve months for failure to pay arrears. Only 15·8 per cent claimed to have had no previous convictions either as adults or juveniles.

*The prisoner's picture of his family*

As was indicated above (page 232) family organization is a major point of difference between the debtors and those in for non-payment of maintenance. The presence in the sample of this latter group produces an overall picture in which a very large proportion are no longer living with their wives. But taking the debtors alone, no less than 88 per cent were living at home with their wives to whom they were legally married. On the other hand, since one of the most common reasons given for not paying maintenance was the claim that they had another family to support, it is hardly surprising to find that about 14 per cent of civil prisoners were living with women other than their legal wives.

Where marriages had broken up, the kinds of reasons cited by all prisoners, civil and criminal alike, tended to be similar. The same problems about housing, in-laws, improvidence, infidelity and so on were quoted. But among the civil prisoners with broken marriages, it was those men who owed money to their wives, and were in prison for it, who expressed the strongest feelings of bitterness and hatred. The criminals who were living apart appeared to have far less marked antipathy towards their spouses or ex-spouses.

TABLE VI. *How prisoner gets on with wife (husband's views)*

(*Percentages*)

| | |
|---|---|
| Very well indeed | 8·8 |
| Very well | 26·3 |
| Fair/average | 10·5 |
| Good in old days, not so good now | 1·2 |
| Not so well | 0·6 |
| Have our ups and downs | 3·5 |
| Separated before imprisonment | 49·1 |
| Total | 100·0 |
| Number of civil prisoners | 171 |

The presence of so many men in prison for non-payment of maintenance meant that by definition a high proportion of civil prisoners were separated before imprisonment. However, those who were in prison for debt, as opposed to non-payment of maintenance, claimed to get on very well with their wives, whilst admitting that they [the wives] were often bad managers and improvident.

TABLE VII. *Areas of conflict before imprisonment (husband's views)*

(*Percentages*)

| | |
|---|---|
| Finance (disagreements re spending) | 17·5 |
| Finance (shortage of money) | 15·2 |
| In-laws (disagreements *with*) | 23·9 |
| In-laws (disagreements *over*) | 22·2 |
| Work | 15·8 |
| Health | 8·8 |
| Drink | 18·7 |
| Gambling | 4·7 |
| Child-rearing | 9·9 |
| Sex | 12·8 |
| Jealousy | 17·5 |
| Other | 30·9 |
| Number of prisoners | 171 |

Totals do not add up to 100 per cent since many gave more than one answer

It is, of course, not possible to compare these figures accurately with the criminal population, but a glance at the figures in Table XX, Chapter III, page 66, indicates very great similarities between the two samples although, as might be expected from a group of debtors, finance constitutes a greater cause of conflict than in the criminal group. The only other major difference is in respect of 'jealousy', and we have already indicated that marriages amongst civil debtors tend to be happy and to involve few extra-marital affairs. Where they have broken up, there is hostility rather than jealousy. If it is true that the areas of conflict between husbands and wives are similar amongst both criminal and civil prisoners, then we can probably discount the element of criminality as a causative factor in conflict—or at any rate suggest that it is of only minor importance.

One of the most striking differences between the criminals and the civils was in their views of themselves as people. The civils saw themselves as being, on the whole, pretty reasonable and decent fellows, a reflection one suspects of that same naïve view of the world, and of their part in it, that leads them to believe that somehow all will come right in the end about their debts. There was, however, little difference between the two groups—with the exception of the separated husbands—in their opinions about their wives. The same stilted comments about 'good managers' and 'wonderful mothers' was made by both criminals and civils alike, although in many cases, to be more than generous, this must have been wishful thinking.

More than 10 per cent of civil prisoners did not know where their wives were living, having been separated from them for so long. A further 4 per cent thought that their wives were living with another man, but did not know where. Twenty-three per cent said their wives were living with relations and 53 per cent in their own homes which they either rented or were buying.

We referred earlier in this chapter to the fact that civil prisoners tend to have large families, and details are set out in Table VIII below. Bearing in mind their low income, it is hardly surprising that they fall into debt: often they cannot afford even the necessities of life such as food and clothing.

TABLE VIII. *Number of dependants*
(*Percentages*)

| | |
|---|---|
| None | 1·8 |
| 1 | 9·9 |
| 2 | 18·1 |
| 3 | 25·1 |
| 4 | 17·5 |
| 5 | 14·0 |
| 6 | 4·7 |
| 7 or more | 8·8 |
| Total | 100·0 |

Number of prisoners 171

*The prisoner's picture of his indebtedness*

By definition civil debtors owe money, but in almost all cases they have other debts than those for which they are committed to prison. Indeed in some instances permanent debt is a family way of life. Such families enter into economic commitments which they have little hope of honouring either now, or at any time in the future, and often with little thought of their utility. It was noticeable that on this topic in particular the civil prisoner's blurred view of his responsibilities became quite opaque, and often he did not know which particular debt had resulted in his present imprisonment. Table IX (see p. 240), shows the extent of their debt, *excluding hire purchase arrears and amounts owed for wife or child maintenance.* These amounts should not be regarded as comprehensive, since they were merely those which the men could remember at the time of interview, in some cases after prolonged probing.

TABLE IX. *Amount of debt other than HP and wife maintenance*
(*Percentages*)

| | Debtors | Non-payment of maintenance | Total |
|---|---|---|---|
| No other debt | – | 58·8 | 40·9 |
| £1–9 | 5·7 | 16·8 | 13·4 |
| £10–24 | 30·7 | 6·7 | 14·0 |
| £25–49 | 23·0 | 5·8 | 11·1 |
| £50–99 | 21·1 | 4·2 | 9·3 |
| £100–499 | 11·5 | 5·8 | 7·6 |
| £500 and over | – | 1·6 | 1·2 |
| Amount unknown | 7·7 | – | 2·3 |
| Total | 100·0 | 100·0 | 100·0 |
| Number of prisoners | 52 | 119 | 171 |

While the criminal prisoners, in keeping perhaps with their more adventurously irresponsible mode of life, tended to owe quite large sums, the civil prisoners were in debt for what were quite often paltry sums, a fact which underlines their poverty and ineptitude generally. Almost 60 per cent of the *debtors* were in prison for failing to pay sums of £50 or less, and even among the wife maintenance cases only approximately 41% of those interviewed had other debts.

TABLE X. *Type of goods on HP at time of arrest*
(*Percentages*)

| | |
|---|---|
| Furniture/furnishings | 25·1 |
| TV/radio | 8·8 |
| Domestic appliances | 9·3 |
| Car/motor-cycle | 5·3 |
| Other | 18·1 |
| Nothing | 57·8 |

Number of prisoners 171

Percentages do not add up to 100 since some men gave more than one answer.

Civil prisoners tend to have fewer hire purchase commitments than might be supposed, bearing in mind that they seem less well equipped to stave off the beguiling ways and fast talk of high pressure salesmen. The category 'other' in Table X refers mainly to clothing, but it also includes a mass of items such as relatively expensive toys, books, encyclopaedias, electric razors, watches and other similar 'luxury' goods which have been 'taken on' almost without realizing it. One man, in prison for failing to pay for some 'general knowledge' books, was in fact illiterate and was under the impression that they had been some kind of free gift from the salesman who had left them at the house.

TABLE XI. *Reasons for debt and HP arrears*

(*Percentages of all civil prisoners in sample*)

| | |
|---|---|
| No work available | 5·8 |
| Unemployed (not wanting work) | 5·8 |
| Ill-health | 15·2 |
| Drink | 0·6 |
| Gambling | 0·6 |
| Pressure from HP salesmen | 4·1 |
| Wife's improvidence | 9·9 |
| Husband's improvidence | 5·8 |
| Other* | 30·4 |
| | |
| Number of prisoners in debt | 134 |
| | |
| Number of prisoners in sample | 171 |

* Under 'other' are included a great many wives who simply could not give a reason for their indebtedness. In other cases debts had arisen as a result of unusual expenditure such as funerals, weddings, or Christmas. Sometimes husbands or wives owed money because they had broken open their own gas or electric meters in order to pay the rent, or for food.

These alleged reasons for being in debt should be seen against the background of social inadequacy. Sometimes prisoners complained bitterly of their wives' improvidence, but could see little that was relevant to the situation in their own poor work record. It was not that they drank, gambled, or 'lived it up' as was often the case with criminals who were in debt, it was simply that they could not cope with financial matters, and even when they did not blame their wives, they tended to see the cause of their troubles as external to themselves, usually in the form of 'bad luck'.

One hundred and nineteen men were in prison for maintenance arrears, the sums owed ranging from a few pounds to many hundreds. Imprisonment was much less certain than in the case of debt, and depended largely on chance. The NAB have at times criticized the police for not picking up the men sooner, before the arrears have assumed gargantuan proportions, but many of these men deliberately chose work which involved travelling from one site to another in different parts of the country; they lived in lodgings and to trace them was a very time-consuming activity. Others deliberately avoided work in order to evade an attachment of earnings order, and many believed that if they were not earning they could not be brought to court for non-payment. Many wives complained that they had been forced to take proceedings against their husbands, having been told by officials of the NAB that unless they did so they would cease to receive benefit. The head office of the Board vigorously denies that this is ever the case, but it was a practice reported to us so frequently that we feel there is good reason to believe that at a local level it is undesirably widespread.[1]

TABLE XII.   *Prisoner's reasons for not paying maintenance*
(*Percentages of those in prison for non-payment of maintenance*)

| | |
|---|---|
| Will only pay if wife returns to him | 8·4 |
| Will only pay if allowed to see child | 7·6 |
| Will not pay 'on principle' | 16·8 |
| Cannot afford to support two families | 5·9 |
| Cannot get work | 22·7 |
| Will not work | 9·2 |
| Wife working so will not pay | 11·8 |
| Wife living with another man | 18·5 |
| Will pay for child but not for wife | 8·4* |
| Amount too high | 27·7 |
| Other | 24·4 |
| | |
| Number of prisoners | 119 |

Totals do not add up to 100 per cent since many gave more than one reason.

\* It is perhaps worth noting that they nevertheless paid *nothing* in fact!

Asked if they intended to pay in the future, 21 per cent said 'no', 28·6 per cent said 'yes', 12·6 per cent were doubtful, 37·8 per cent gave replies that indicated that there was little likelihood of their paying unless they won the pools or came into some other unexpected fortune.

*Prisoner's views of how wives manage financially*

Most civil prisoners were seen within a few days of their coming into prison; they were, however, extraordinarily vague about how their wives would manage financially in their absence. Those who were on national assistance before their imprisonment had little doubt that their wives would continue to draw this money. The remainder had rarely thought about the matter and more often than not assumed that their wives would manage for the short period of their detention on a combination of credit, good neighbourliness and good luck. Such information as we were able to obtain is set out in Table XIII below:

1 For a further discussion of this see Chapter X, p. 269.

TABLE XIII.  *How wives manage financially*

(*Percentages*)

| | |
|---|---|
| At work (part- or full-time) | 28·6 |
| National Assistance | 60·2 |
| Living with relations | 18·1 |
| Receiving material help from relations | 27·5 |
| Family Allowance | 45·6 |
| Material help from welfare agencies (statutory and voluntary) | 3·5 |
| Lodgers | 2·3 |
| Pension | 0·6 |
| Savings | 5·3 |
| Other | 8·8 |
| Don't know | 10·5 |
| | |
| Number of prisoners | 171 |

Totals do not add up to 100 per cent since most wives had more than one source of income.

Even allowing for the probable inaccuracy of this information, it can safely be said that imprisonment made very little difference to the income of these families, or to the source of such income. The debtors were in prison for a very short time and they had often been on national assistance before their imprisonment, so that their wives continued to draw it. Nor were the legal wives of those in for non-payment of maintenance affected; they continued to draw national assistance. A number of separated husbands did not know the whereabouts of their wives, nor how they lived, and the category 'other' amongst civil prisoners usually covered those wives who were thought to be living with another man.

*Welfare*

Virtually no information was available from the prison records on this subject; 49·6 per cent of the men interviewed said that they had not seen the welfare officer; of these it is probable that about 21 per cent had not been in the prison long enough to have done so. Welfare officers themselves were asked how many interviews they had had with the men in the sample. Since their forms were completed after we had left the prison, we had expected that the number of men seen would be greater than the number of prisoners claiming to have seen the welfare officer when we interviewed them.[1] However, welfare officers said they had not had interviews with 52 per cent of the men in the sample, and they claimed to have no record of a further 10 per

[1] This was the position amongst the criminal population (see Chapter III, p. 70.

cent of men. They had had one interview with 32 per cent and the remaining 6 per cent had had two or three interviews.

### Civil prisoners—a general discussion

Civil prisoners gave the impression of being representatives of a social problem group, of a submerged fraction of the population living either in primary poverty on account of large families and low earning power, or in secondary poverty on account of low intelligence and mismanagement, or as a result of a combination of such factors. We would describe civil prisoners as essentially *passive*; the majority believed that their debt would be cancelled by their imprisonment, and although it is true that a man may not be imprisoned twice in respect of the same debt, the creditors are still at liberty to pursue the debtor after committal and to seize any fresh assets that he may come to possess. So far as those in prison for arrears of maintenance are concerned, the majority seem to prefer imprisonment to paying money, the demand for which they have convinced themselves is unjustified or unreasonable.

In an unpublished study of civil debtors in Brixton Prison, de Berker[1] divides debtors into three categories. The first he calls 'bloody minded', and these are drawn exclusively from the wife maintenance cases, being those who refuse to make any effort to pay their debt. Their professed reasons for refusal we have set out in Table XII (p. 242) but in general it can be said that they feel rejected by their families, and such loyalties as may exist are to a new 'wife' and family if they have one.

A second category are also basically 'bloody minded', but, as de Berker puts it, 'conceal the fact by putting forward a barrage of reasons why they cannot pay'. These are sometimes fabrications, but in our experience more often arise from genuine social difficulties about which the man has failed to take any successful action, usually, we believe, on account of a basic lack of intelligence, commonsense, and drive. Such men are inherently passive, and have a wholly negative attitude to life. By the time they reach prison it is difficult to see in what way they can be helped. These are among the men for whom indebtedness is a way of life. They are resigned to it and see no escape. It is difficult to see how far 'bloody-mindedness' plays its part, though it is our impression that it grows with their debts. They, or their wives, appear to incur debt quite haphazardly, and without thought of the consequences, since the problem of repayment becomes increasingly unimportant as the actual possibility of payment recedes.

Thirdly there are those who, while socially incompetent, are

[1] De Berker, P., *Impressions of Civil Debtors in Brixton* (unpublished Departmental Paper).

genuinely worried about their debts, and who, within the limits of their meagre ability, have tried—at least in the past—to find a way out of the situation. These are the casualties of our society, whose breakdown has taken the form of debt.

In general we would certainly endorse de Berker's comments, which he readily admits are impressionistic, but we feel it important to stress the low level of intelligence and social functioning which we believe to exist particularly amongst the debtors, though perhaps less often amongst the maintenance defaulters. We were not able to subject these men to psychological testing, but it seems likely that, compared with the general prison population (excluding drunks and other categories of short-term prisoners whom we did not interview) they would compare very poorly in terms of mental capacity. Like de Berker, we found no example of a reasonable, intelligent, and socially competent man who, through genuine misfortune, had fallen into debt and landed in prison. Such men were to be found, however, amongst the *criminal* sample, who often possessed the skill and intelligence to try fraudulent ways of paying their debts.

From what we have said, it might appear that judges and magistrates, however sympathetic, have failed to do their work properly by sending some of these men to prison. We think that where the socially incompetent are sent to prison it is because the courts have few available means of finding out the relevant facts, this being particularly true in the county courts where debtors are concerned. Even in the magistrates' courts it is often difficult for a truly objective view of all the circumstances to be obtained, particularly where the evidence may be distorted by malice on the part of one or both parties in matrimonial proceedings.

But while the court may have little choice but to imprison the truly recalcitrant husband who will go to prison indefinitely if need be, the situation in the county court is very different. There is an urgent need for such courts to have the services of a trained social worker to make enquiries as an officer of the court, in the same way that magistrates can call upon the services of a probation officer. Such an officer could not only provide the court with socially relevant information and establish contact with social agencies already in touch with the family, but could perhaps do useful work in assisting so-called 'problem families', to draw their lives into some semblance of order.

Imprisonment for debt—or contemptuous failure to pay—is a social problem which has received very little attention in our society. Sending the debtor to prison is merely one of a series of courses open to the creditor: he can, for example, seek to attach the goods of the debtor and sell them to recover what is owed. It is, by and large, the poor man who appears in the county courts, while his more wealthy counterpart appears in the bankruptcy courts. Moreover, nearly all the debts which are brought to court are owed to business organizations, and almost all such creditors allow for bad debts just as large stores allow for shoplifting. But although some debtors are dishonest in incurring debts which they deliberately intend not to honour, it is also true that many firms enter into credit transactions without enquiring closely into the circumstances of the customer, preferring to get a sale at all costs. It might be a useful solution to the problem if the county courts had the power to adjudge the debtor a bankrupt, and so wipe out the debt if it appeared irrecoverable. If the court had such powers, the creditors would not then be able to pursue their debtors to prison.

The matter does not, however, end here, for even if imprisonment as a result of indebtedness were to disappear, there are still the very real problems attendant upon other processes. Execution upon the debtor's goods may mean the loss of his home or its contents. The effect of such an upheaval on family life is likely to be considerable and may be particularly disrupting to children. Although the number of such executions in the county courts runs into some thousands every year, we have little idea of their social consequences: indeed it is scarcely recognized as a social problem.

For the minority of debtors who are wilfully dishonest in failing to meet their obligations it should be possible to punish them in the appropriate way as *criminal* offenders—on grounds such as obtaining goods by false pretences.

Bearing these points in mind, it is difficult to see what, in the present state of affairs, can be achieved by sending debtors to prison, the manifest objective of coercion having been tried and found wanting. Quite apart from the space they take up in overcrowded prisons, and the inordinate time they occupy in being processed in and out for very short periods, they are a heavy burden on the taxpayer who has to keep both the man in prison and his family outside. Such money might be used to greater advantage by ensuring that adequate social work help is available in the county courts. Alternatively, if we are to continue to imprison these men, it would seem that almost any attempt to help them would be better than simply containing them in expensive custody, which is all that happens at present. The conditions under which civil prisoners are detained and the brevity of their sentences are wholly out of keeping with modern penology. Drake Hall is, in reality, no more than a relatively hygienic version of the Marshalsea and the Fleet. Classes in basic education to overcome illiteracy, and psychiatric attention to their many psychosomatic complaints could well form the basis of an initial training programme. Clearly, longer periods of detention would be needed, but there is no reason why there should not be legislation to deal with chronic or habitual debtors, and providing the opportunity for a prolonged period of retraining. Even men of low intelligence can be taught some skills, and it may be that lack of basic education creates an impression of low intelligence which is a distortion of the man's innate capacities. The experience of the Ministry of Labour's Industrial Training Units could be of considerable relevance here, and it might be an advantage if a Disablement Resettlement Officer of the Ministry were to be attached to the prison to assist in finding men jobs on release. It seems unlikely, from the experience of Drake Hall, that civil prisoners require maximum security conditions in prison, so that the possibility of setting up work camps could well be explored. The value to the prison system as a whole would be in training staff to deal with social problems in their most acute form, and allowing them to develop skills which, once acquired, would have value in ordinary prison work where reflections of the problems presented by civil prisoners are often to be found.

## THE FAMILIES[1]

As mentioned above (see Table II, p. 233), we shall in this section be concerned with 107 wives, forty being the wives of debtors and sixty-seven being the wives, or separated wives, of men in prison for non-payment of maintenance or affiliation orders.

The Brown family are very typical of the debtor group (though not often do they have quite so many children) and a highlighting of their problems may serve as an illustration of the points we shall subsequently be discussing:

Mr Brown is fifty-four and comes from Monmouthshire. He is not very bright and has two brothers in a mental hospital. It is Mrs Brown who makes all the decisions in the family. He was given a four-week sentence for a debt of £20 for clothing, though he himself was barely aware of the reasons for his imprisonment. He has been in prison on three previous occasions, each time for small debts.

Mr and Mrs Brown are very happily married and they have had twenty-four children during thirty years of marriage, though five of these have died. There are now six children living at home, two of them unemployed. The Labour Exchange tells the boy there are no vacancies and the girl has been told to 'come tidy', to which she replies 'we have a large family and I can't come tidy'. Our interviewer was of the opinion that neither child was anxious to find work. One other child is in an approved school; according to Mrs Brown this is for truancy.

[1] For purposes of simplification detailed tables as in Chapter IV have been omitted but these could be made available for further analysis.

Mr Brown has not worked regularly for many years and has been living on national assistance. He says this is due to ill-health: 'there's blood coming out of me, I don't think it's TB'. He is registered as disabled on account of a chest complaint and he also complains of migraine. During our interview with him he was very depressed and tearful and seemed genuinely concerned at the lack of clothing for the children. Describing his wife he said 'She'd help everybody. Easy going about the house, wonderful about the children. Never relaxes. Her whole art is looking after children.' Of himself, he says 'I'm the same, do anything for the children. We've done good in our times and we shouldn't have to suffer like this. I've never had enough wages to manage.' He wouldn't allow his wife to visit him in prison: 'I'm ashamed of it.'

Mrs Brown is enormously fat, suffers from varicose veins brought on through excessive child-bearing, though she does not complain of this. She supports herself and her six children on £8 5s 6d per week, which includes 10s from a married daughter. She pays £1 8s 1d per week rent and her regular outgoings for coal, gas, electricity, H P, etc., amount to £2 10s 6d per week. Apart from clothing clubs, Mrs Brown has a kitchen sideboard on H P as well as wallpaper, paint and brushes. When the present sentence has been served there is another court order pending for arrears on clothing. The Browns also have a fine of £4 outstanding for their son's non-attendance at school. They owe £5 rent and £18 for gas and electric bills. They both realize that *there is no way of clearing their debts*: 'We don't get enough money to live on.'

Mrs Brown feels very lonely without her husband 'It puts me off my food, I can't explain the feeling. I don't sleep at all, I just doze off and wake up again.' She has only one friend, and says she doesn't speak to her neighbours.

The family live in four rooms in a detached house and share the kitchen and bathroom. The interviewer described the condition of the home as dirty and disorganized, with the remains of meals lying around the room and unpleasant smells. Nevertheless Mrs Brown explained 'I always keep *this* room tidy, in case someone calls!'.

The Browns no longer ask for help, yet they regard it as their right and are indignant when they get none. Mr Brown's illness is blamed for their financial difficulties which are made worse by the unemployment of the two children who have left school. Another child collapsed from malnutrition a short while before we visited the family. However, despite all these problems the marriage is a very loving one and Mrs Brown has a most romantic attitude towards her husband: her watery blue eyes still sparkle for him.

As in the case of their husbands, the wives in the sample of civil prisoners were generally older than the wives of criminal offenders, only five (4·7 per cent) being under twenty-one. They live in larger households and have many more dependent children, with a result that there is more over-crowding amongst civil prisoners and home conditions are generally somewhat unsatisfactory. Ten families had a total of fourteen dependent children living away from home, five living with relatives, six in care of the county council, one in approved school, one in hospital and one at boarding school.

Despite the very short sentences their husbands were serving, five (4·7 per cent) had moved since their husbands had gone to prison, two were evicted, one could not afford the rent, one moved to her parents to avoid loneliness and one separated wife was rehoused.

### Finance and indebtedness

Having interviewed the husbands, we had expected that the majority of these families would be experiencing even greater poverty than did the wives of many criminals. This view was reinforced by the apparent squalor in which so many lived: 30 per cent of them lived in conditions which our interviewer described as 'dirty', or 'dirty and disorganized', and almost half of those interviewed had very little furniture; what they had was usually in a poor state. This expectation was fulfilled and we found that 68 per cent received an income of less than £7 10s 0d; bearing in mind that they tend to have a large number of children to feed and clothe, it is not surprising to find that once they start getting into debt, there is little chance of extricating themselves from it. Despite the fact that many had been separated for only a short time, those wives who lived with their husbands felt themselves to be very much worse off whilst the man was in prison, although in fact there was little or no apparent drop in income. We think this arose because the wives are often extremely bad managers and are very dependent on their equally ineffectual husbands. They felt their absence acutely and translated it into financial terms, quite losing sight of the fact that they might not have worked for years.

Since the sentences were so short few wives had sold or pawned goods. Those that had (12·2 per cent) were regularly in the habit of so doing, so that imprisonment served merely as a stimulus to behaviour which was part of the normal pattern of life.

As stated earlier in this report, it was originally thought that amongst civil prisoners would be found men with very heavy hire purchase commitments and arrears. In fact we found that more often than not the debt was not directly connected with hire purchase. On the other hand, as was indicated in Chapters IV and V, many criminal offenders had extensive HP commitments and arrears.

Twenty-four per cent of the families had no debts or HP arrears (excluding amounts owed for maintenance and for which they were serving a sentence of imprisonment). The amount of money actually owed by the remaining 76 per cent was comparatively small, most debts being under £10. The money was usually owed for rent or rates, gas or electricity, or to relatives and friends. Reasons given by the wives for their debt varied widely:

TABLE XIV.   *Wives' views of reasons for debt*
(*Percentages of those in debt*)

| | |
|---|---|
| No work | 27·1 |
| Drink/gambling/lazy | 17·2 |
| Ill-health | 19·7 |
| Husband's criminality | 1·2 |
| Wife's improvidence | 11·1 |
| Husband's improvidence | 24·6 |
| Too much HP | 1·2 |
| Husband can't earn enough | 9·8 |
| Husband doesn't give enough | 2·5 |
| Unusual expenditure | 1·2 |
| Don't know | 22·1 |

Number of families in debt   81

Totals do not add up to 100 per cent since many respondents gave more than one answer.

It is interesting that so many wives should mention their own improvidence as well as that of their husbands. Ill-health was an important factor amongst civil families. Those who said their husbands could not earn enough, or did not give them enough, were usually common-law wives whose 'husbands' could not, they felt, earn enough to support both families.

*Problems and help received*

In general it can safely be said that the underlying difficulties experienced by the wives of civil prisoners were quite unconnected with their husband's imprisonment, although in some instances the fact of separation was a critical one which added to their problems. We think this situation arises for three main reasons:

1. The period of the sentence is too short to account for the very complicated social and financial difficulties in which they find themselves.
2. Civil debtors have often suffered for many years as a result of financial difficulties. Imprisonment rarely adds to these (nor does it resolve them); on the other hand such men often come

from closely-knit family units where husband and wife are emotionally very dependent one on the other, so that the strain of separation may make the financial problems *seem* worse, though they change little in fact.

3. The separated wives of those in for non-payment of maintenance have usually been parted for some considerable time and have learned to adjust to the separation. Such women are virtually unaffected by the man's imprisonment. The common-law wives of such men are the only ones who may suffer, but again, since their 'husbands' rarely work (in order to avoid paying maintenance to their legal wives), they are rarely worse off and at most suffer from temporary loneliness.

The two major problems experienced by these wives were money (53 per cent) and managing the children (35 per cent). We commented earlier in this chapter that it was our feeling that all members of the families of civil prisoners were exceptionally prone to physical or mental illness. Data collected confirmed this view, particularly amongst the husbands, 60 per cent of whom suffered, or had done so, from some serious illness, the symptoms of which still affected them and the most frequent being chest ailments, ulcers and nervous troubles. Although only 9·4 per cent of the wives mentioned illness in the family as a serious problem, many more were gravely concerned about it, primarily because they felt it prevented their husbands from working, and consequently reduced the family income (see Table XIV, above). The wives' own ill-health caused considerable anxiety both to themselves and to their husbands, the latter being frequently called upon to help with household chores, etc. The poverty-stricken conditions under which they lived (socially as well as financially) considerably reduced the chances of recovery, particularly amongst the wives, since they were frequently undernourished and harassed.

Only 8 per cent of the wives were concerned about their debts, a situation which we believe arises largely from the fact that for so many of these families, indebtedness is a way of life from which they can never hope to escape. 73 per cent of wives of civil prisoners were receiving national assistance when we interviewed them and of these, 19 per cent said they experienced difficulties with the Board of one sort or another though this was largely because they thought they did not get enough extras. They made considerable use of the statutory social services (probation, health visitor, children's department, education department), but very little use of voluntary welfare services. 44 per cent claimed to have no contact with welfare agencies (excluding NAB) and those who *did* approach agencies were in general very dissatisfied with what they received. It was suggested in the previous chapters that the efficacy, or otherwise, of help, tended to be assessed by the recipients in terms of material or financial assistance. Only 35·5 per cent of the wives of civil prisoners claimed to be receiving such help (other than national assistance and family allowances). This figure would appear to be extremely low even if it is assumed that wives underestimate the amount of material help received. Yet these families seemed to have a very great need for financial as well as other kinds of help.

Although we have little concrete evidence to support this view, our interviewers felt that a good deal of discrimination existed amongst social work agencies between the 'deserving' and the 'undeserving' families. So many of the families of civil debtors appear feckless and unable, or unwilling, to help themselves, and they tend to exasperate the social agencies by their inability to profit by what has been done for them, or given to them.[1] This results in such families no longer asking for help, or refusing it when it is offered.

Mrs Hall is fairly typical of such wives, though not all are as aggressively disturbed.

She appeared to our interviewer to be on the verge of a nervous breakdown and told us this was the result of years of being shunted from one hostel to another and being separated from all her children in turn. She now lives in one small room with five of her children ranging in age from two to fifteen, while two other children are still in LCC homes. Mr Hall is now in prison because he owes the LCC £103 for the children's keep (a debt incurred in 1954 and which he has been paying off gradually as and when he obtained work). He gave himself up to the police after spending five or six months on the run, since he knew there was a warrant out for his arrest in connection with the debt. Mrs Hall is very indignant about her husband's imprisonment and blames his 'so-called friends' for not paying back the money he lends them. Of welfare she says: 'I don't want to see any of them, they're the ones who've taken my kids away from me. And the welfare officer at the children's home could have lifted the phone and had the warrant dropped against my husband any time. Then my husband could have got started on his new job [instead of going on the run] and we'd have been all right. If the welfare people had been as quick finding me a house as they were in taking my children away from me sixteen years ago . . . and if the bleeding welfare man from . . . had turned up at court like he was supposed to, my husband wouldn't be where he is. When my husband decided to give himself up he [the welfare officer] said he might not go to prison. Yes, if Mr bloody X had turned up in court like he was supposed, that man never kept his promise. If he so much as turns up outside this house in his big car he'll get the door slammed in his face. Even the blackies

[1] See history of Brown family, pp. 247 ff.

get bloody better treated than I do in my own country. If the welfare came round tomorrow and gave me £100 I'd throw it in their face. . . And I've had enough of living in one room and of the bleeding welfare and their promises. This is supposed to be a human race, but it's a daffy lot of wild animals . . .' This tirade, which continued on similar lines for some time, was accompanied by stamping up and down the room and wild gesticulations with a coat-hanger. When it was over Mrs Hall slumped exhausted into a chair and stared at the floor, a picture of misery.

### Family functioning

Forty-four per cent of the wives seen were legally married and living with their husbands—most of these were married to debtor prisoners. 19·5 per cent were common-law marriages and 36·5 per cent were separated and lived alone.

Despite the poverty, squalor, inadequacy and general social incompetence which characterized so many of the families of civil prisoners who *were* living together, the marital relationship was often warm and stable and very few civil debtors or their wives had been married before. 36 per cent of all wives said they got on 'very well', or 'very well indeed', and 18·7 per cent described the relationship as 'fair'. Our interviewers' assessment of family functioning confirmed this generally positive picture and suggested some improvement in the position at the time of interview, compared with the situation previously. However, we would feel that, particularly in view of the short duration of the imprisonment, such reported 'improvement' was a result of the wives' over-optimism about the marital relationship, rather than the result of any real change. It is also worth noting that there was a marked tendency for the wives to claim a better relationship with their husbands than vice-versa.[1]

Almost without exception those wives who lived with their husbands saw them as good husbands, fathers and workers (despite the fact that 50 per cent were unemployed and many of the remainder had very poor work records). As might be expected, however, the reverse is true amongst separated wives; they saw their husbands as bad in all these roles and tended to be either highly critical or very vindictive. In both cases their views were expressed in very black and white terms, and there was little to denote objectivity amongst either group.

Very few (9 per cent) wives actually living with their husbands regretted their marriage; conflict, where it existed, centred mainly round shortage of money or the man's inability or unwillingness to

---

[1] This is quite contrary to the findings of the criminal sample (see Chapter VI, p. 141), and is perhaps due to the fact that men in prison for a longer time need to keep a roseate picture of life outside in order to survive inside.

work. Even so, wives were often anxious to excuse their husband's failure as a breadwinner.

*Wives' views of husbands' conviction and imprisonment*

In 72 per cent of the cases, the wife said that her husband had had previous convictions either as a juvenile or as an adult, and 52 per cent reported knowing that their husbands had been in prison before, either on a criminal charge or for a civil offence. There were considerable differences between the wives of debtors and those of wife maintenance cases in respect of their attitudes to conviction and imprisonment. Debtors' wives usually thought the sentence unfair and maintained that their husband had done no wrong. Separated wives, on the other hand, felt that their husbands got what they deserved, though not all of them agreed with the wife who said 'put them [non-payment of maintenance cases] all in a salt-mine in Siberia!'. Wives in both groups felt ashamed and some said their husbands should not be mixed with real criminals. They nearly all thought that prison was no solution to the problem, and many wives resented having to prosecute their estranged husbands if the result were likely to be his imprisonment.

Wives whose husbands were in prison for non-payment of maintenance were asked why they thought he did not pay:

TABLE XV. *Wives' views of husband's failure to pay maintenance*
(*Percentages of wives of those in prison for non-payment of maintenance*)

| | |
|---|---|
| Cannot support two families | 32·8 |
| Will not work (lazy) | 17·9 |
| Not working (illness or genuine unemployment) | 1·5 |
| Out of spite to wife | 17·9 |
| Wife had own income | 1·5 |
| Greedy, likes to spend money on himself | 7·5 |
| Don't know | 20·9 |
| Total | 100·0 |
| Number of wives | 67 |

The question of separated wives obtaining payment of maintenance through the NAB when their husbands fail to pay does not strictly fall within our terms of reference, unless the husband is actually in prison. However, during the course of our research we heard so many complaints about the procedure that we feel it worth mentioning here. Once it has been established that the absent husband is not paying and cannot be traced, all is relatively plain sailing, and the NAB will pay, usually by means of a book of vouchers to be cashed weekly at the post office. If the husband has been ordered to pay the money into court this may involve the wife in weekly visits to the court to collect it, though in some areas the court officers will arrange for it to be sent. The difficulties are most acute in those cases where the man pays sometimes, but not regularly. This may involve the wife in countless visits to the court *and* to the NAB offices. In some districts liaison between the court officers and the NAB is excellent and arrangements to pay the wife are made easily. But in other areas there is virtually no contact between them, and the wives are left floundering between their two offices. Sometimes NAB officers are unwilling to give a full week's money at once; presumably this acts as a safeguard should the husband later decide to pay. But for the wife it means yet another visit to the two offices, and such journeys are often time-consuming, expensive, and demoralizing, especially if they involve taking young children.

Some streamlining of the system would certainly be desirable where the husband has not paid, and it should, for example, be possible for *all* court officers to be authorized to pay the money due out of public funds and then be responsible for reclaiming it from the NAB. The whole problem of wife maintenance is an area about which there is very little systematic information and research is urgently required with a view to amending the legislation as and where necessary.

There was relatively little visiting between the husbands and wives of civil prisoners, largely for two reasons: (*a*) the short period of detention was felt to make it not worthwhile, (*b*) expense and distance. The latter was particularly true in Drake Hall (Staffs), where wives usually had to travel from the Leeds area; and Cardiff, where transport in the Welsh valleys turned a prison visit into a major expedition. Of the sixty-six wives who might have visited their husbands, nineteen (28 per cent) felt the arrangements to be unsatisfactory and these were mostly in category (*b*) above. It must be borne in mind that wives of civil prisoners are not eligible for an NAB grant to visit their husband, since at the time of the research, such grants were made (if at all) only after the man had been in prison for six months.[1]

### The future

Apart from those already separated before imprisonment, only three wives of civil prisoners did not want their husbands back and hoped for a divorce.

Those who wanted him back for the most part thought that lack of work would be the greatest problem—as in fact it had usually been for a very long time. Like the husbands, however, the wives of civil debtors were usually passive and apathetic. They saw little likelihood

[1] Now reduced to three months.

of any change in their circumstances, nor any possibility of becoming solvent.

Earlier in this chapter we suggested that adequate social work help should be available to these families; it seems to us vital to improve their general state of health, for only if they are physically fit can they be expected to cope with the multitude of problems which assail them. It is, however, only fair to say that many of these families have had a very great deal of social work help over a very long period, and their failure is possibly a reflection on the *type* of help given, rather than its quality or quantity. It is our feeling that much more help of the kind given by the Family Service Units is required, and it is perhaps significant that only one family in our sample was in fact in touch with this particular organization.

The legal wives of those in for non-payment of maintenance were barely, if at all, affected by the imprisonment, and as in the case of the separated wives in the sample of stars and recidivists, they had usually made a fairly good adjustment to the separation long before the present sentence.

# Chapter X

# WELFARE

We have discussed in some detail the use of voluntary welfare agencies by the wives, and their attitudes to such services (see Chapter IV, pp. 94–101). Our experience with the intensive sample confirms the view there expressed, to the effect that wives tend to minimize the amount of help they receive, partly because only material aid is felt to be helpful.

Reference was made in Chapter II (p. 26) to the fact that discussions were held with a number of social agencies in the hope of obtaining general information regarding their experience of prisoners' families.[1] A brief summary of their views is reported below:

In the main their experience of prisoners' families was limited by the fact that relatively few such families are referred to them. The Family Service Units estimated that 10 per cent of all referrals were the families of prisoners, and the Church Army, which often has a representative working inside the prisons, suggested that in the London area approximately 300 prisoners' families a year were referred to them. Soldiers', Sailors' and Airmen's Families Association and the Family Welfare Association were unable to give figures, but both said the numbers were very small.

It was also difficult for agencies to say how the families got in touch with them; many wives certainly referred themselves, but some came through probation officers, the NAB, local prisoners' aid societies, doctors, the police, etc. Most agencies commented that prison welfare officers referred very few families. Referrals to the Church Army came mainly from prison chaplains.

The problems with which the families were faced varied widely, but those of a financial nature predominated. The difficulty of clothing young children was frequently mentioned, and in some cases difficulties arose as a result of financial commitments entered into before the husband went to prison. If approached by a social agency, finance houses were usually found to be sympathetic and prepared to make suitable arrangements for the payment of HP commitments on very reduced terms. The Family Welfare Association found that

[1] The National Council of Social Service prepared a special memorandum on the subject which is reproduced in Appendix E.

I

although financial difficulties were a major source of concern, family problems were equally represented. It was reported that matrimonial and other family problems are extremely difficult to handle by virtue of the husband's imprisonment, and there was considerable adverse comment about the lack of a reciprocal casework service within the prison. Similarly there was criticism of existing visiting arrangements, couples being left to tackle their own problems unaided. It was generally considered that matrimonial problems existed before imprisonment, but that wives were reluctant to talk about such difficulties, tending to see the pre-imprisonment period through rose-coloured spectacles.

Most of the families consulting voluntary organizations were on national assistance and it was generally held by the agencies that the efficacy of the Board varied greatly from area to area. One organization referred to marked differences in the Board's treatment of 'deserving' and 'undeserving' cases, not arising as a result of any intentional policy, but partly as a result of a natural process of selection and partly as a result of community pressures and attitudes. Other organizations pointed out that not only were there variations according to area, but that differences existed between individual NAB officers.

Recognition of the low-income housing shortage as a problem was common to most of the organizations, but opinions differed as to its importance. Only one organization felt that it was a central problem for the families; most recognized the need for better housing and thought it to be an aggravating factor when combined with financial troubles, but they felt it would be an over-simplification to suggest that it was a major factor affecting families of offenders. Eviction directly as a result of imprisonment was considered to be extremely rare, but it *could* occur as a result of non-payment of rent; whatever the underlying cause, whenever it occurred it was often seen as another step towards family disintegration.

Most organizations considered that the problems of prisoners' families were not very different from those of any other families where the breadwinner is absent, though it was recognized that, amongst offenders, work problems were almost universal even when out of prison.

Social work agencies were unanimous in their adverse criticism of after-care arrangements for prisoners and their families. Even where the man himself receives some help, the services for the families were considered quite inadequate. One casework agency commented with surprise that they never receive any after-care referrals, and others said that if cases *were* referred to them from prison welfare officers they found a noticeable lack of background information.[1]

[1] These points were later discussed with those responsible for the organization

Most of these comments and observations bear out the findings of the research material, and it is clear that there is virtually no attempt made at present to enable the family to be dealt with as a complete unit, to include the prisoner. There are, of course, exceptions to this rather negative state of affairs: for example one local authority health department receives notification from the prison welfare officer of all residents in the borough who are committed to prison; this department also co-ordinates all existing social services in an attempt to prevent the creation and deterioration of 'problem families'. Other schemes to help wives are slowly being tried out, but they remain the exception, and there is no doubt that the granting of help for families of prisoners is a haphazard affair, and virtually non-existent when the needs are emotional rather than financial. It is often in those cases where the offence is closely linked with family problems that help is most lacking or inadequate.

In an article by the author of this report[1] and based on the material collected for this research, stress is laid on the importance of including the family in any rehabilitative work carried out with the prisoner. We believe that as a prerequisite to such work, whether carried out by social workers inside or outside the prison, it is necessary to review existing conditions of contact between husband and wife. Rule 31 (1)[2] states that 'special attention shall be paid to the maintenance of such relations between a prisoner and his family as are desirable in the best interests of both'. According to Rule 34, (2) *a* and *b*, a convicted prisoner may send and receive a letter on reception and thereafter once a week, and receive a visit [if over age twenty-one] once in eight weeks.[3] However, a visit is still technically a privilege which can, at the discretion of the governor, be deferred until the expiration of any period of cellular confinement. An additional letter or visit may be allowed by the governor 'where necessary for his welfare or that of his family'. Since visits are normally only of twenty to thirty minutes' duration, we feel that the restrictions imposed on contact between husband and wife, par-

of prison welfare, who held the view that they themselves were disappointed with other social work agencies, insofar as they did very little to help these families. Furthermore they suggest that prison welfare officers are reluctant to give confidential information about prisoners to outside agencies because they cannot be sure who will have access to it.

[1] *Br. J. Crim.*, Vol. IV, No. 4, April 1964.

[2] Draft Prison Rules, 1964.

[3] Although prison rules state that visits should be once every eight weeks it has been common practice for many years for visits to be allowed once every four weeks after the first two months of the sentence has expired. No satisfactory explanation as to why the new rules should not be amended has been forthcoming from the Home Office, except that it is thought desirable to leave the eight-week rule in existence so that it could be imposed in exceptional circumstances.

ticularly those on visits, inhibit the good intentions implicit in Rule 31 (1). If, as has been suggested by others[1] the maintenance of contact between husband and wife is important in the post commitment career of prisoners, family visits should be given as a right and not as a privilege, and it should not be possible to withhold visits as a form of punishment. The fact that this sanction is rarely used confirms our view that it should be removed from the new Draft Rules.

Furthermore, we feel that there is a strong case for an increase in the permitted number of visits and the option to extend the period of the monthly visit where travelling makes more frequent visits impracticable. We would suggest that a reception visit be automatically allowed to each man, and that the present arrangement whereby it is necessary to apply to the governor for such a visit, be abandoned. Thus as soon as a man comes into prison, whether married or not, he would be given a visiting order to send out. Secondly we think that men serving sentences of six months or more should have their visits increased to two per month. Thirdly we think that men serving sentences of three years or more should not only have an increased number of visits, but that consideration should be given to the idea of extending present home leave arrangements. We feel that after two years imprisonment, men should automatically be entitled to spend a weekend at home, say once every six months, and only in genuine cases of security risk should such offenders be prevented from enjoying this privilege.

Previous work in prison by the author, and the findings of this research, suggest that men are frequently transferred from one prison to another even when it is known that family problems exist. It seems that the requirements of prison administration usually outweigh the needs of the family, sometimes in quite severe cases, and prison welfare officers frequently complained that their own recommendations advising against transfer were over-ruled. We believe that far more attention should be paid to family problems and to the welfare officer's comments before men are transferred, particularly if it is simply a 'bulk transfer' due to overcrowding, as opposed to transfer to a prison better able to provide suitable training facilities. Where transfer is inevitable, much improved provisions should be available to allow the family to visit, such provisions bearing in mind not only the expense of visiting, but the particular difficulties arising when young children are involved. Since the majority of wives are living on national assistance it should be possible to provide, as a right, a grant enabling the wife and children to visit *each* time a visiting order is received from the prison. Furthermore, since most of the wives who are not on national assistance have very limited incomes, there seems little reason why the arrangement

[1] See references Chapter I, pp. 18 and 19.

should not automatically extend to them. Under existing regulations the Board cannot pay the fares for a wife who is in full-time work; but under the Hospital Fares Scheme it is empowered to meet the fares of people going to hospital for treatment whether or not they are in full employment; they then reclaim the money from the Ministry of Health. It should, therefore, be possible to make similar arrangements for prisoners' wives, the money being refunded by the Home Office.

At present if a recommendation is received from a prison welfare officer, the Board will sometimes pay for an overnight stay if the distance involved is very great. But such schemes rely too heavily upon individual welfare officers and the existence of satisfactory communications between all concerned. It would be preferable if the regulations regarding grants for visits could be systematized, and a specific distance fixed, so that a wife visiting her husband in a prison further away from home than is laid down in the regulations, would automatically receive the fare and overnight subsistence for herself and any of her dependent children she wished to take.

Not only would it seem desirable to increase the *number* of visits, but it also seems essential to improve visiting conditions.[1] Closed visits should be abolished, and facilities for discussion of family problems with welfare staff made readily available when the wife comes to the prison. There was, amongst wives, unanimous approval of facilities at Wakefield prison, where the visiting conditions were very greatly appreciated, and where, in addition, the welfare officer and/or assistant governors were often well known to the families. Where this situation prevailed, wives were less anxious and better able to handle the separation; unfortunately in other prisons most wives were unaware that a welfare officer existed. At the last interview with each family in the intensive sample we asked both husband and wife whether they had seen the booklet which was specially written for distribution to families of prisoners. We found that no one had in fact seen it; this state of affairs may be understandable in the case of those recidivists whose lives are spent largely in prison, with short spells at home in between, but for those recidivists who have not been inside for some time, or not at all since marriage, and in all instances of first offenders, we consider that a copy should automatically be sent to the family as soon as the man is received into prison, preferably with a covering letter giving the name of the prison welfare officer with whom they can get in touch in case of difficulty.[2]

We believe that there is sufficient evidence—particularly from the intensive sample, to assert that what happens to a family during the

---

[1] Conditions are slowly improving and it is said that closed visiting will be almost abolished within the next year or so, except for serious security risks.

[2] Ideally a personal visit should be paid to the wife.

term of imprisonment will affect the husband *in* prison, and what happens to him inside will affect the family *outside*. Both situations will affect the adjustment made on his release. We feel that this has important implications for the welfare services, since existing provisions are designed to treat the husband and the family as two distinct entities, and even where social work provision, or casework, is provided for one or the other or both, there is virtually no communication between those giving the service.[1]

Our material also indicates that the pattern of family relationships existing before imprisonment was frequently one of severe conflict. By ignoring this situation, or by treating husband and wife separately, we are allowing the family to be reunited with all the old anxieties, tensions, and difficulties present, possibly exacerbated by the fact of imprisonment.

The role of the prison welfare officer seems to be crucial in this situation. When a married man comes into prison an assessment should be made of his family situation, and the relationships contained therein, and this information should be taken into consideration by other staff members responsible for planning his training. Wives should be encouraged to consult freely with the welfare officer throughout a man's sentence. Undoubtedly a few individual prison welfare officers have been in close touch with some families, and this will have varied according to their particular interests and how much time they have available for such work. To do this work properly, however, will mean that prison welfare officers can no longer remain exclusively *inside* the prison; they must be free to visit families and, where necessary, to make personal contact with other social work agencies. Inside the prison they must have far more time to devote to the husbands of those families who they feel have special problems of marital relationship, and they must spend much longer handing over a family to another caseworker on discharge.[2] Above all they must have *time to think*; the endless procession of men outside their door, and the scurrying round of lunch-time 'applications', leaves no time to stop and consider the real problems and what can be done about them. The sheer mechanics of handling so many receptions and discharges at present occupies nearly all their time.

Lytton[3] in his study of the post-release behaviour of prisoners,

[1] For a discussion of the need for casework with families and for greater exchange of information between departments, see *Guide for Co-operative Staff Work with Prisoners or Parolees and their Families Receiving Aid to Needy Children*, California State Depts. of Corrections and Social Welfare 1959.

[2] Ideally there should be sufficient prison welfare officers to enable them to stay in touch with a family for as long as necessary after discharge. Regionalization of prisons and the abolition of 'bulk transfers' would also be prerequisites to such a system.

[3] Lytton, D. F., 'Family Relations and the Post-Release Behaviour of Federal Prisoners', M.A. Thesis, University of Illinois, 1961.

refers to the importance of pre-release liaison work between the probation officer and the family. Our material confirms this finding, though in view of the different structure of prison welfare and after-care work in this country, we feel it should be done by the prison welfare officer, at least whilst the man is still in prison.

Earlier in this report[1] we discussed our contact with the prison welfare officers and the many problems arising from this part of the research. We feel, nevertheless, that it is important to include such information as we were able to obtain in this way, whilst at the same time stressing that any interpretation of the data should bear in mind the comments contained in Chapter II.

Welfare officers were asked to complete a questionnaire concerning all 824 prisoners interviewed: 328 stars, 325 recidivists and 171 civils. In ninety-six cases they were unable to supply any information (fifty recidivists, twenty-nine stars and seventeen civils), leaving a total of 728 men about whom data are available. We understand that where no information could be given, this situation arose largely either because men were transferred (with their records) before the welfare officer had time to complete our questionnaire, or alternatively because the man had recently been transferred to the prison where we saw him and his record had not yet arrived. *It is important to bear in mind that the figures given in this section refer to all three types of offender and do not include the ninety-six men for whom no data were available.*

Perhaps the most striking finding, though it may simply indicate the extent of pressure upon welfare officers, is that 39 per cent of the 728 men had not had a personal interview with the welfare officer.[2] It is, of course, possible that these men had taken their personal or domestic problems to others in the prison (governor, assistant governor, or chaplain) but we feel that if the prison welfare officer is to make a significant contribution to the training of men in prison, full reports of such interviews should be recorded in the welfare department. Only in one prison was such a procedure being attempted.

Many welfare officers told us that, owing to pressure of work, they did not normally interview a man until one or two months before he was due for discharge[3] unless a special request to do so came from the man himself or from someone in the prison. Of those who had had

[1] See Chapter II, pp. 39ff.

[2] A personal interview is defined as a private one lasting five minutes or longer. Interviews on reception, discharge or review boards at which the welfare officer may be present but which are not intended to deal with welfare or personal problems were excluded from this question.

[3] In the case of civil prisoners such interviews usually take place a week before discharge if the sentence is long enough, the day before in cases where men are only sentenced to seven days.

at least one interview, 35 per cent referred themselves, 18 per cent came as a result of the welfare officer asking to see the man, having been told he had problems; in only 1 per cent of cases was the approach made by the family outside.

Welfare officers were asked whether men had any problems of a domestic or personal nature, or whether any such existed before imprisonment. Their replies are set out in Table I below:

TABLE I. *Domestic or personal problems of prisoners as known to welfare officers*

|  | % of 728 |
|---|---|
| Financial | 38 |
| Housing | 21 |
| In-laws | 7 |
| Health (any family member) | 9 |
| Work | 12 |
| 'Nerves' (including all mental disturbances) | 6 |
| Drink/gambling | 7 |
| Bringing up children | 8 |
| Sex | 11 |
| Jealousy | 2 |
| Marital incompatibility | 5 |
| No information as not seen | 37* |

* The 2 per cent discrepancy between this figure and the 39 per cent mentioned above as not having been seen, can be accounted for by the fact that in 2 per cent of the cases the welfare officers were aware of problems although they had not actually seen the man privately.

These figures cannot be directly compared with the information obtained from our own interviews[1] since the above table includes both civil and criminal offenders and furthermore in our own data we have none in the category 'no information'. Nevertheless, it is apparent that much greater emphasis is laid on financial and housing problems in data available from welfare officers compared with our own findings, a situation which *may* arise from the fact that the more personal emotional problems are experienced by the 37 per cent about whom the prison welfare officers had no information. On the other hand, it may also arise because prisoners who *do* see the welfare officer, at any rate for the first interview, are more likely to talk about practical problems such as housing and finance, rather than about family difficulties. Apart from the pressure of work, we feel that the unsatisfactory conditions under which many welfare officers are often forced to conduct their interviews (in cells, on landings, or in offices with other staff members present) are not in any way conducive to discussing more personal problems.

[1] See Chapter III, Table XX, p. 66.

The fact that prisoners are often reluctant to talk about these matters may account for the fact that only 10 per cent of marriages were described by welfare officers as 'unstable', with a further 5 per cent said to be 'deteriorating'.

Information was sought regarding the type of help welfare officers had been able to give, and where none had been given, the reasons for this state of affairs. This information is set out in Tables II and III below:

TABLE II.  *Type of help given by welfare officers*

|  | % of 728 |
|---|---|
| General advice | 53 |
| Home Visit* | 22 |
| Selection for special training in prison (discussion groups, pre-release courses, etc. where not automatic) | 2 |
| *Special* introduction to employer, DPA, landlady, etc., on discharge | 15 |
| Other (including referral to probation officer or social work agency) | 11 |
| No action to date | 35 |

* Almost all these visits were carried out by a representative of the prison welfare officer working outside the prison, most frequently the Church Army, or WVS.

These figures do not add up to 100 per cent since more than one type of help might have been offered to the same man. Furthermore, the last figure in the table indicating the number of men who had not been offered help at the time of completing the schedules (35 per cent) differs from the 39 per cent mentioned on p. 263 *supra* as not having had a private interview with the welfare officer. This arises because it is possible for a welfare officer to take action in relation to a man with whom he had *not* had such an interview, but whom he might have seen on an interview board.

TABLE III.  *Reasons for inability to help*

|  | % of 728 |
|---|---|
| Prisoner declined help | 29 |
| Unhelpable (recalcitrant, professional criminal, mentally sick, etc.) | 2 |
| No facilities available | 1 |
| Other* | 11 |

* This category usually included men who had not at that time been seen for a discharge interview.

A statistical analysis of this kind necessarily obscures the fact that some prisoners and their families receive a great deal of help from

prison welfare officers, or in the case of families, through co-operation with other social work agencies. However, it is very apparent
that if the findings of our research are correct, there is a vast amount
of distress amongst prisoners and their families about which the
prison welfare officers are unaware.

*Poverty*

The information set out in previous chapters indicates that both
voluntary and statutory welfare agencies, including prison welfare
officers and after-care societies, spend a considerable amount of
time and money on prisoners and their families. But the fact remains
that the great majority of prisoners' families *live in conditions of
grinding poverty*. This is evidenced in Chapter IV and V, and it is no
answer to say that this situation was true *before* the man went to
prison. 58 per cent of the wives in our main sample are in receipt of
an income of under £7 10s 0d per week and almost 14 per cent of
wives living on that amount have three or more dependent children at
home.

Throughout this report it has been made clear that the personality
of the wife and the pattern of her family relationships are the crucial
factor determining how well she will adjust to the separation and
subsequent reunion. But it is certainly true that the emotional
problems which these wives face would be far easier to handle if they
were not permanently beset by the practical problems of finding
enough money to live on. 'Society may as well start with poverty
because it is identifiable, preventable, and it is society's business. The
other more personal, emotional problems will anyway be better dealt
with by women if they are not exhausted, impoverished, worried
about the rent, hungry and disheartened.'[1]

The first essential, therefore, is to meet the financial needs of these
families in a way which both removes them from a state of primary
poverty and which relieves them from the constant round of begging
for charity which they so deeply resent. Only after achieving a degree
of financial stability is it likely that families will be interested in
casework, though the two may go together. Wives complain of being
made to feel they should be grateful for any help given by voluntary
agencies; they feel strongly that they are not involved in their husband's criminality and should not be made to feel that *they* are
thieves. Even those wives who condone their husband's criminality
(as is the case for many recidivists' wives) do not feel guilty and
resent being patronized.

Without denying the useful work done by voluntary organizations,
often under extremely difficult conditions and with great goodwill,

[1] Lena Jeger reviewing *Fatherless Families* by Margaret Wynn in *The Guardian*,
February 10, 1964.

we suggest that once the State accepts responsibility for the families of those in prison by giving national assistance grants, then this responsibility should be extended to ensure that families receive the necessities that make life tolerable, and that this should be given as of right, not as a charitable gesture for which they should be grateful.

A recent publication[1] has canvassed the idea of a 'fatherless child allowance' to overcome the countless anomalies which at present exist and whereby the amount a child receives depends more upon the circumstances of his fatherlessness, rather than upon his actual need. It is not relevant here to discuss the advantages and disadvantages of such a scheme in general, but it may be relevant to examine it in the context of the prisoner's family. Here, we feel, there may be considerable disadvantages. The majority of men are in prison for under six months, and to label a child as 'fatherless' may merely add to his difficulties. If such a scheme were to be adopted, it should, we feel, be only applicable where the parents were separated before imprisonment and a court order for maintenance in existence; even in such cases we are not wholly convinced that it is right to label such children as 'fatherless'. Furthermore, unless the term 'fatherless' were to apply to *all* children when the father is away from home (including men sentenced for periods of a month or less) a situation might arise whereby the child of a separated couple would be better provided for than one where the father had gone to prison for a short term.

In our opinion the answer lies, at any rate for prisoners' families, in improved national assistance rates, which would include a reasonable amount for each dependent child, irrespective of age: the present assumption that between the ages of five and eleven, for example, a child should receive a basic allowance of 4s 6d per week less than he does between the ages of eleven and sixteen seems quite unrelated to the actual needs of the child. Again it seems quite unrealistic to think that a married woman under the age of twenty-one should need a smaller amount than a woman over that age, or that at eighteen she should need less than at twenty-one.

We have already suggested that national assistance grants for capital goods and equipment should be given automatically, as of right, and should be related to length of separation.[2] These should include grants for clothing for all members of the family. It should not be the case that some of the Board's officers send families to the wvs for clothing whilst others give grants: the former system is degrading and bitterly resented by the wives themselves. Furthermore, at present the parents of school children are referred to the

[1] Wynn, Margaret, *Fatherless Families*, Michael Joseph, 1964.
[2] Our findings wholly support the recommendations made in the Young Fabian pamphlet, *National Assistance: Service or Charity*, Howard Glennerster, 1962.

education authorities for their clothes, even where it is not a matter of school uniform. If a grant were given automatically by the NAB this would obviate the necessity of explaining their circumstances to yet another organization. Similarly the NAB grant should be large enough to cover school meals so that parents are not obliged to make application to the education department for free dinners, a situation which also reflects on the children since, when it is known by their peers that they get free dinners, they are pressed to explain why. If there are objections to this on grounds of using public funds, it should surely be possible for the NAB to devise a system whereby any expenditure which at present falls on local rates can be reclaimed by the Board. We have earlier suggested that similar arrangements be made for those wives whose husbands are irregular in making maintenance payments.[1]

Finally we believe that certain practices exist in some areas which are in direct contravention of the policy laid down by the NAB Headquarters and we think it important that careful check should be kept on these matters. We mention three in particular:

(i) Pressure on wives to go out to work: we believe that if NAB officers wish to exert pressure in this way (and in some cases it may be justifiable) it is important that the case be referred to an experienced social caseworker in order to try to create conditions favourable to the wife's accepting the idea of work as part of a general improvement of conditions, rather than having it imposed upon her by an NAB officer whose chief concern is the payment of grants.

(ii) Distinction being made between 'deserving' and 'undeserving' cases:[2] this type of distinction was referred to in different ways by both the CAB and the FSU. Our own material suggests that some officers carry their own prejudices and values into the families they handle, and that this may seriously affect any decisions regarding discretionary payments. In general we found that the families of first offenders are treated with more tolerance and less condemnation than those of recidivists.[3] The role of the NAB officer is certainly not an easy one: he may be handing out money to those he knows are successful thieves, and feel that others need it more. He has to face constant grumbling about the basic allowance, demands for extra money, sometimes from people whose houses still contain luxuries such as cocktail cabinets and hi-fi's (mostly on HP) which bear witness to the 'successful' crimes for which their husbands were not caught.

---

[1] See Chapter IX, p. 255.

[2] See also reference Chapter IX, p. 252. The tendency lies in the attitude of some officials who try to maximize their help to 'deserving' cases by suggesting additional grants, whilst with 'undeserving' cases they adhere strictly to the basic scale.

[3] Those working at NADPAS Headquarters have expressed the view that the work of NAB officers in handling prisoners' families has greatly improved over the past year.

He frequently works in depressing and gloomy areas and he must often meet despair, anger and self-pity. He needs to be an exceptional person to avoid becoming either a judge of behaviour or simply a clerk handing out money. Removal of the necessity for so many discretionary grants through improved basic allowances would greatly simplify the work of the individual officer, as well as making life more tolerable for the recipient.

(iii) Pressure on separated wives to take proceedings against their husbands for non-payment of maintenance has already been mentioned.[1] It is the Board's policy[2] to encourage an assisted wife or mother to take her own proceedings for maintenance. The theory underlying this policy appears to be that by so doing a woman may obtain an order for a greater amount than the assistance grant she has been receiving, and that it remains in existence as a source of income if she later ceases to need assistance. The Board can, under Section 43 of the National Assistance Act, 1948, apply to the court for orders against husbands and they do so where the woman concerned is 'unable or unwilling to exercise her own rights or because of other considerations in the case'. However, in 1962 only in 115 instances were orders against husbands taken out under Section 43, so that the Board is obviously successful in persuading the vast majority of wives to apply to the courts. In addition, the Board in 1962 took criminal proceedings in 406 cases, under Section 51 of the Act, against men who persistently refused or neglected to maintain their dependants with the result that their families had to be given assistance, and 200 of these men were sentenced to imprisonment.

We feel that most deserted wives are quite willing to take out orders against their husbands *so long as there is no question of this involving his imprisonment*, but they are very reluctant to do so if there is any likelihood of imprisonment resulting. It is quite possible that some element of misunderstanding arises between the wives and the NAB officers, in so far as the latter try to persuade wives to take out orders for their own good, but the wives, who usually have some difficulty in understanding the legal aspects of the situation, interpret this pressure as being a form of blackmail—if you do not take out an order we will not give you any more assistance. If our interpretation of the situation is correct, we nevertheless think it vital that the position should be made quite clear to the wife and that no pressure of this kind should ever appear to be exerted.

[1] See Chapter X, p. 242.
[2] See Report of the National Assistance Board for the Year 1962, Cmnd. 2078, June 1963.

## Chapter XI

# HIRE PURCHASE

In previous chapters we have referred in some detail to the hire-purchase commitments of offenders and their families, and to the amount of arrears which accumulate before and during imprisonment.

In Chapter IX we pointed out that in 1961 some 5,500 men were committed to prison by the county courts for debt, a comparatively small percentage of those upon whom committal warrants are actually served. They remain in prison for a very short time (an average of ten days) and tend to owe small sums, nearly three-quarters of them owing £50 or less. In the main they blame ill-health or 'bad luck' for their indebtedness.

Over 70 per cent of the wives in the sample of criminal offenders said they had goods on HP at the time of our interview with them, and about 43 per cent of them were in arrears. Only seven[1] men were serving sentences for larceny bailee, but if they themselves are to be believed, considerably more of those interviewed could have been doing so had they been found out. Most of these men (largely recidivists) regarded this practice as 'fiddling' rather than crime, and maintained that hire-purchase was 'too easy', so that if firms were foolish enough to allow one to obtain goods so readily, they could hardly expect their customers not to profit by the arrangement. Apart from the obvious advantages which accrued to them from the present state of affairs, prisoners were in general critical of the existing system.

We now propose to discuss the attitudes of prisoners and their wives[2] towards hire-purchase, and to look at the problem in the light of present legislation.

Some wives are very ambivalent; they protest strongly about hire-purchase, but make very great use of it: Mrs W. said:

[1] Figures in this chapter relate to persons interviewed and *recidivists have not been given double weighting.*

[2] Since we thought it possible that attitudes of husbands and wives might be at variance on this subject, the discussion concerns only the 'paired' couples, i.e. those where husband *and* wife were seen.

'I think it's awful . . . I detest HP. It makes things so dear with high interest. There's no competition, all these firms are run by Wolfenstein's [*sic*], and all these multi-millionaires who make their money on us poor devils. More people go to jail for HP than anything else, my husband is inside for it now.[1] Any man can go into a shop and get a washing machine, transistor radio, or fridge on hire, and then go straight in a pub and sell it. . . . I played Holy War with the chap who came here looking for a fridge and a transistor tape recorder. I'm a saleswoman myself [works part-time in shoe shop] and I like a good salesman; after all it's an art. I don't like anybody coming to the house selling things, I think it's atrocious. If you want anything you go out and look for it round the shops and have a nice afternoon out at your leisure.'

The debts in this family amount to some £700 or more.

Husbands and wives were asked to give their views on hire-purchase. Classifying the answers into three categories of positive, negative and equivocal, differences are not readily observable, but a further breakdown of the type of each response shows that, within each category of observation there are notable differences between husbands and wives. We think this can be accounted for by the fact that the wives are much more concerned in the day-to-day arrangements of HP, finding the money when the man comes to collect it, using the goods (cars are an exception to this) and dealing with salesmen. Table I (see p. 272) therefore gives the information in some detail in order to illustrate the point, and since we are only dealing with 'paired' couples who were asked an identical question, the crude figures are directly comparable.

Taylor and Chave[2] enquired of a sample of 1,422 persons whether they thought HP was a good or bad thing, and their results appear to differ markedly from ours, since they found 57·2 per cent thought it good, 19·7 per cent bad, 19·4 per cent gave equivocal replies, and 3·7 per cent said they did not know. Broken down by age, the figures are even more strikingly different from ours, since in the younger age group (16–34) which make up most of our sample, over 60 per cent of Taylor and Chave's sample thought it a good thing. This would appear to add weight to our belief that offenders, whether criminal or civil, and their wives, have somewhat special views about hire-purchase which are not at all representative of the population as a whole.

There has been a great deal of public discussion about what is termed 'high-pressure salesmanship'; in the case of the present

---

[1] Although he had in fact sold goods whilst still under H.P. agreement, he was actually serving a sentence for false pretences (forgery).

[2] *Op. cit.*

sample, it is our experience that this is not a severe problem and at most 2 per cent of wives complain of it. However, this does not mean that no pressure is actually exerted on the wives, merely that it is not necessary for the salesmen to exert it unduly. The preconditions for exploitation already exist when the salesman calls, in so far as there is present in most of the families we visited (*a*) a desire to keep up with the Jones' or to impress the neighbours and (*b*) a strong temptation to buy when someone calls at the door and offers something one wants (and maybe needs) on what appear to be very easy terms. We have given evidence elsewhere in this report to suggest that when goods are taken on HP by the majority of wives in

TABLE I.   *Attitudes to HP*

(*Percentages*)[1]

| | | Husband | Wife | Total |
|---|---|---|---|---|
| Positive views | Necessary | 8·9 | 24·2 | 16·5 |
| | Good, useful | 37·8 | 31·9 | 34·8 |
| | All right if used in moderation | 24·2 | 34·9 | 29·5 |
| | Salesmen all right | 0·7 | 6·0 | 3·3 |
| | Firms all right | 1·2 | 23·0 | 12·1 |
| Negative views | No favourable views | 79·1 | 37·8 | 58·4 |
| | Prices too high | 12·8 | 15·6 | 14·2 |
| | Dislike salesmen | 12·1 | 32·9 | 22·5 |
| | Firms unpleasant | 6·7 | 13·4 | 10·0 |
| Equivocal views | Too easy | 14·4 | 7·6 | 11·0 |
| | Better to save | 22·2 | 29·2 | 25·7 |
| | Don't know | 4·5 | 4·7 | 4·6 |
| | Number of stars | 236 | | |
| | Number of recidivists | 179 | | |
| | Number of civils | 107 | | |

our sample, they do not consider the total cost, nor even what it will mean each week: the only matters with which they concern themselves are the deposit, and possibly the first weekly payment. The rest is in the future and of little account. It would, however, be true to add that this attitude is very much more apparent amongst the wives of civil prisoners and recidivists than amongst the wives of stars.

The most frequent complaint about salesmen is their practice of leaving goods at the house, not coming back for them and another man calling weeks later to collect the money. This means that the wife has to be strong-minded about not using the goods (not to mention making sure they do not get damaged) and also quite firm in refusing to accept them when another man calls for the money.

One wife had nothing on HP when her husband went into prison,

[1] Percentages add to more than 100% since both husbands and wives were invited to give more than one opinion.

but had since taken on furniture and clothes and had arrears amounting to £1 2s 6d. She did not like HP and seemed able to cope with the blandishments of salesmen—she described it this way:

'I don't like it at all. You've more or less got to have what they've got, there's no choice at all, and things are much more expensive when you have them like that. I don't like paying it each week, you feel as if you're paying for nothing. I don't like buying clothes that way, they're worn out before you're finished paying for them. You can get cheaper things at the shops. The firms are O.K.; if I can't pay them for a week they understand. Salesmen are a nuisance. Once a salesman left a Red Cross box, bits of bandages and so on—while I was at work. He left it with my mother for me to see. It was 31s 6d, and before I got home my little boy had pulled some of the things out and I couldn't get them back, so now I've got to pay for it. So if they knock at my door I don't answer it—because you can never get rid of them. Once a canvasser left a ten-yard roll of curtaining for me to see. It was supposed to be 3s a week. Well, it *was* nice, and I was tempted because I need new curtaining, but I decided not to have it because I knew I couldn't afford it. Anyway no one called about it for weeks until one man came and said that I hadn't made any payments on the curtaining that I'd bought! Cheek! So I told him to take it back.'

Not all wives, however, are able to dismiss the salesmen so easily:

Mr C. was serving a month's sentence as a civil debtor; according to him he had a car on HP and twelve months previously asked the firm to take it back: 'They didn't, and the car was pulled to pieces by kids, so I sold it for scrap'.

Mrs C. was paying £3 a week for HP and clubs, as well as £1 per week to a moneylender and £1 a week for television rental; in addition she had HP arrears of £15 and £35 worth of other debts. She said this of HP: 'If it weren't for HP I don't know where I'd be. But when your husband's working and you get things, you don't realize that he might not be working one day and then where will you be? Like I am now. I wish I'd never got the things and I wouldn't be in the mess I'm in now, but there you are. But I think you pay through the nose for things. Like I went down to the warehouse for a new coat for my brother's wedding and I told the woman I didn't want to pay more than £8. I kept trying them on and I never bothered asking how much they were because having said that, I thought she'd know. But when the man came for the money next week he said it was eleven guineas, and I've seen it in a shop up the road for £7 10s 0d. They've [collectors] all hummed and ha'd about taking less payments. One of them said 2s 6d a week wasn't enough and I'd got to pay the lot. I only wanted to pay it for a month or so till my husband comes out, and then I'd go back to 10s. The other two men I've been with eight years and they're all right, they just said they wouldn't come for a month. They know I pay when I can. The other men are nasty when they come for the money, telling me I should pay and it's their bread and butter as well as mine, and it's their wages that they're collecting. I refuse salesmen, I'm in too much debt already. Last week I couldn't get rid of a man. I told him straight that my husband was in prison for debt! But he said that was all right and hadn't I got 2s 6d? They try and tempt you all the time. Like the man trying to sell me a rug. He had it down here on the floor and said he'd leave it there if I gave him 2s 6d as first week's payment. But you reckon up and before you turn round you're paying £1 a week. That's how I got into all this debt . . .' etc. etc.

Our interviewer notes at the end: 'Mrs C. is finding it very difficult to buy the barest necessities for the family, yet last week she bought £40 worth of special white "Whit-Week clothes" for her two daughters to walk through the streets in, and she said she would have to spend a lot more money for clothes for the four boys.' Since there were so many emotional problems in this family—disturbed children and friction between husband and wife, debt seemed to be almost a minor difficulty.

*Motor Vehicles.* Although only about 22 per cent of men interviewed admitted to having a car or motor cycle on HP at the time of arrest, we have reason to believe that the true figure is very considerably in excess of this, and the fact that the car had been repossessed since arrest, often resulted in their omitting to mention it. A car, for most of these men, represented a status symbol of extraordinary importance, and many of them freely admitted their intention of obtaining another as a major priority as soon as they were discharged.

From what we learned during the prison interviews in this research, and from an earlier study in Pentonville prison,[1] there is reason to believe that HP in relation to cars—and in particular second-hand cars, presents special problems. It is unfortunately true that a small section of the motor trade conducts its business on the basis of standards which are below those normally observed by the trade as a whole. Car salesmen who operate on bomb sites, or advertise 'cars bought for spot cash', not infrequently have closer contacts with the police than is the case with more reputable dealers. Two car dealers discussing hire purchase transactions made the following comments:

[1] *Op. cit.*

Mr S., aged 34, had been convicted of his first known offence. He described himself as a self-employed motor dealer, employing seven or eight men: 'I'm the adventurous type—how would you describe a motor dealer? I like to enjoy myself.' Our interviewer described him as 'over-ambitious, always changing his business in an attempt to better himself'. He was in prison for attempting to defraud, and owed between £2,000 and £3,000 in business debts. His view of how this arose was that his 'criminal activities resulted in the loss of legitimate business interests'. Asked his views about HP he said he had two views, depending upon whether he was the consumer or the salesman. For the consumer he said HP was 'a thing where people are easily led with it and they don't stop to think before they take on the commitments. They don't read the agreements and a lot of people don't understand the interest on HP'. However as a man whose whole business depended on HP he said it was 'quite good—you can't really lose on it, though some do, through getting into the hands of villains'. It remained unclear in which category he placed himself!

Mr F., aged 33, had also been convicted for the first time and described himself as large-scale self-employed, the proprietor of four car showrooms. The interviewer commented that he was 'an exceedingly loquacious, conceited, but very amusing man with a good line in sales talk. He was determined to make a fortune in four years and retire to his favourite seaside resort'. His whole business was run on HP though he claimed to have bought nothing this way himself. A letter on the prison record indicated that this was untrue and he had paid a deposit on a typewriter and never paid any instalments. He had been made a bankrupt in 1960, but although this was on his record, and his wife told us, he did not mention the fact. Of HP he said 'They are robbing the public left and right. It's a silly business, they put the responsibility on the public and the best part of them can't afford to pay for them. I've always found that the public don't know what they're letting themselves in for, and they don't worry what they're signing till it's too late. If there'd been no HP I wouldn't be here. It's a terrible mess. I'm here for paying the deposits on seven cars—people who couldn't afford the whole deposit and I inflated it'. His wife's description of his activities differed a little—she said 'he was getting paid for cars that were no good'. Her one fear for the future was that he would start all over again, or that they would find out about other offences which had not been taken into consideration. She said her husband was an only child who had always had whatever he wanted from his mother. He was a great gambler and went around with people much better off than himself.

Recent legislation has greatly reduced, though not wholly prevented, the sale of vehicles in an unroadworthy condition and the practice of concealing defects and misleading the customer is still a feature of glib salesmanship. Broadly speaking the problem is equally divided between the activities of dishonest dealers and those of unethical salesmen, but at the same time there is no shortage of potential buyers.

A central register of vehicles subject to HP agreement exists, but its effectiveness depends upon the use the dealer is prepared to make of it. A man prepared to operate on the fringe of crime can readily dispose of his existing car—which is still the subject of an HP agreement—and for a small additional sum can part-exchange it for a bigger and better vehicle, also on HP. This he can equally easily sell elsewhere for a larger sum of 'spot cash'. Clauses 23–27 of Part III of the Hire Purchase (No. 2) Bill currently before Parliament,[1] proposes changes in the arrangements concerning Vehicle Registration Books which should bring an end to this relatively profitable crime, by requiring that the hirer shall retain the Registration Book until payment is completed.

Clause 9 of the new Bill provides that the dealer shall be deemed to be the agent of the owner or seller (many second-hand cars are sold on commission for private owners) in respect of representations concerning the goods made by the dealer in the course of negotiations leading to the making of an HP agreement. This, together with Clause 11 of the Bill, should protect the hirer from some of the more blatant attempts to conceal defects.

The present law offers no protection to the hirer who, if he falls behind with the payments, may find that the vehicle is repossessed (though after one-third of the HP price has been paid this can only be done by court order); he can then be sued for the balance of payments outstanding and he may be charged a repossession fee. If the car is disposed of again by the owner, the erstwhile hirer may be liable for any loss sustained on this transaction. Owners are often anxious to dispose of the car and will do so at a very reduced price, knowing they can claim the difference in the form of 'depreciation' from the original hirer. The fact that so many of the hirers who become county court debtors are in an unsound financial state in the first place, suggests that there may be some thoroughly unscrupulous second-hand car dealers who batten upon such individuals, knowing the likelihood of their falling into arrears, as well as the advantages accorded to them as dealers in relation to the re-hiring or resale of the vehicle.

We must emphasize that these practices are confined to motor traders of the type whom we found in our sample, and who were by no

[1] July 1964.

means reluctant to give details of their activities, since they are proud of the fact that they are able to operate at such advantage to themselves and yet remain strictly within the terms of the law, if not within its meaning. Our comments should by no means be taken to refer in any way to the motor trade as a whole. However, the traffic in stolen cars and accessories is sufficient to suggest that there are a number of dealers of the 'bomb-site' variety who have at some time been involved in criminal activities.[1] It is a world of hard, sharp, and often unscrupulous dealing, and sometimes the county courts appear to be in the unenviable position of enforcing the rights of those who, though operating within the letter of the law, are openly contemptuous of its spirit.

*Proposed New Legislation in respect of Hire Purchase*

We are only concerned here with discussing the situation as it might affect the kind of man who goes to prison, either as a debtor, or in consequence of some criminal offence, whether as the result of a hire purchase transaction or not. It is important to point out that credit is an essential feature of any modern economy, and the progressive extension of credit is a concomitant of economic expansion and rising living standards. The vast majority of hire purchase transactions are properly honoured on both sides; indeed, hire purchase has lost much of the social stigma that it once had amongst the middle-classes, although the introduction by the banks of 'personal loans'—usually at more favourable interest rates than those charged by the hire-purchase finance houses—which enable people to buy goods outright, may well limit the number of middle-class hire-purchasers. Credit sales, and the system of 'provident checks' tend to be linked with the drapery and clothing trades, and to retain their almost exclusive market among the urban poor.

The ethics of hire purchase have long been subject to debate simply because the element of free contract which the agreement theoretically constitutes is in practice often lacking. The hirer is in a relatively weak position, in that he is less likely to be adept at resisting the pressures of the salesman than the latter is in applying them. But the problem really arises when the pressure is applied, not in order to get him to take something that he already wants and has sought out in a shop, but to take something that he does not really want and may not be able to afford, the salesman then attempting to minimize the magnitude of the financial commitment. This is particularly true in respect of the activities of itinerant salesmen who press their goods from door to door, and are skilled at manipulating social situations once they are inside the home.

That hire purchase is a profitable business and the majority of

[1] Sometimes by defrauding the H P companies themselves.

transactions honoured, may well be fortuitous, in the sense that the salesman himself does not stand to suffer from the debtor; the individual salesman paid on a commission basis is interested in making a sale, and the money is not owed to him, so that there is no incentive for him to be selective in initiating transactions. It is difficult to feel sympathy for those hire purchase companies that suffer from bad debts since they appear to make few enquiries about the agents they employ; the lot of the debtor, however, is likely to become increasingly wretched the more commitments he has; but what is more important, the community, and therefore the taxpayer, tends to become increasingly—and expensively—involved in dealing with the problems which stem from his indebtedness. The courts become involved if the goods are repossessed, or if an order for payment of arrears has to be made. If the man is sent to prison— admittedly for alleged contempt—the community has to pay to keep him there, and in all probability has to keep his family on national assistance at the same time. It is scarcely valid to argue that the debtor entered into the agreement as a free agent when his social competence may be so limited that he may be no more responsible in this sense than a juvenile.

The new Hire Purchase Bill[1] proposes a number of amendments to the 1938 Act, and some new requirements which provide improved legal safeguards for the hirer or party to a credit-sale agreement. Perhaps the most important of these are contained in Clauses 4 to 8 which give the hirer the right to cancel the transaction (within a certain time) if the document which is to become the agreement is signed at a place other than trade premises. This provides housewives who have succumbed to the blandishments of itinerant salesmen with the opportunity to change their minds, instead of bitterly regretting their weakness after the man has gone. The owner or seller of the goods must send the hirer or credit-buyer a copy of the agreement, stating this right, and the name and address of the person to whom notice of cancellation may be sent. This copy must be sent within seven days, and the hirer can cancel the agreement up to four days after its receipt. In practice, however, this may still put a premium on literacy, and if the name and address is not forthcoming until receipt of the agreement, the maximum time for doing anything about it is only four days.

In general we feel that the new Bill, while improving the position of the customer, is unlikely to reduce the number of men going to prison who have hire purchase troubles. In the first place, as we have indicated in Chapter IX, civil prisoners with hire purchase or credit-sale debts, or men likely to fall into this category, lead disorganized and socially incompetent lives and are frequently illiterate

[1] See footnote p. 276.

or of low intelligence. They will get into difficulties however protective the law, and a small number will go to prison so long as salesmen are prepared to involve them in credit transactions. On the other hand, the disparity between the number of committal orders made, warrants issued and men actually conveyed to prison—to say nothing of the number that buy themselves out—suggests that most of the existing sanctions against bad debt are comparatively effective. Whether the community, through its courts and public officials, should continue to enforce agreements which, it might be argued, were entered into by owners and their agents irresponsibly, is another matter. Quite apart from the point that they ought to investigate properly the credit-worthiness of their customers, or bear the risk, it could be reasoned that to encourage further indebtedness among the already gullible and feckless is like plying an alcoholic with liquor.

Secondly, although the Bill makes new arrangements for the possession of vehicle Registration Books it will only limit the possibilities of larceny bailee as far as *motor vehicles* are concerned. Those men in prison as a result of crimes against the hire purchase companies are unlikely to diminish in number, for the Bill does not make it any more difficult to obtain other goods like radio sets, vacuum cleaners and so forth, which can be illegally sold. Criminals who intend to defraud are possessed of great ingenuity, and are likely to continue to find ways and means of so doing.

Finally, there are a vast number of men who are in prison neither as debtors nor as perpetrators of hire purchase frauds. They may, however, have hire purchase debts and be in arrears. The new legislation clearly could not prevent them going to prison, but it is conceivable that it may protect their wives from avoidable indebtedness while they are inside. Anything which may alleviate their poverty and social difficulties ought to be welcomed.

Whilst HP cannot be said to be the basic cause of men going to prison for debt or as criminal offenders, it seems likely that it is an important *contributory* factor.

## Chapter XII

# DISCUSSION OF HYPOTHESES AND FAMILY TYPOLOGIES

In Chapter I (p. 23ff) we set out a number of hypotheses which we proposed to test in this study, and these will now be discussed in the light of data collected in both extensive and intensive samples:

1. Family relationships following upon conviction and imprisonment will follow a pattern set by family relationships existing before imprisonment.

In Chapter VIII details were given of the rating scale devised to measure the wife's satisfaction with her marriage at the time of the interview. A similar scale was also constructed to measure the degree of satisfaction existing before imprisonment. Since it was based upon retrospective information, the reliability of such a scale is necessarily limited. We relied largely on the wife's attitudes and are fully aware that these may become distorted during the period of separation. However, for this particular scale we also took note of information on the husband's completed questionnaire, and in addition a considerable amount of discussion took place between the coders in order to arrive at a degree of uniformity in interpreting the data. It was emphasized that the assessment was based upon *the extent to which conflict before imprisonment was actually felt by the wife to be a threat to the marriage at that time*. It was assumed that there might be families with severe conflicts, but that these were not necessarily felt to result in bad marital adjustment. Furthermore, our assessment was based upon the situation existing *immediately* before the husband's imprisonment, so that an adjustment score might be given indicating an excellent relationship with a common-law wife, even though the man might be separated from his legal wife.

The two scores measuring relationships before imprisonment and those existing at the time of interview were then compared for 256 star and 213 recidivist wives. We found that in 69 per cent of cases there was a high degree of coincidence:

> 35 per cent satisfactory relationships before separation and during imprisonment.
>
> 15 per cent fairly satisfactory relationships before separation and during imprisonment.
>
> 9 per cent much conflict in the relationship before separation and during imprisonment.
>
> 10 per cent separation before imprisonment and no contact during separation.

Total    69 per cent

The remaining 31 per cent were distributed as follows:

> 5 per cent satisfactory relationships before separation deteriorated during imprisonment.
>
> 8 per cent strained relationships before separation improved during imprisonment.
>
> 10 per cent strained relationships before imprisonment deteriorated during imprisonment.
>
> 8 per cent no reliable information.

Total    31 per cent

We feel that the claim to an improved situation was not always an accurate assessment by the wife; for example, one wife based her assumption that things had improved merely on the fact that she knew her husband would not be going back to the woman he was living with before imprisonment, and she therefore hoped he would return to her. In another instance the wife took out a separation order just before her husband's imprisonment, but although he persuaded her to withdraw it, neither of them was sure that they would go back to each other.

Our data also suggest that many relationships worsen for a short period after conviction, or even at some time during the sentence, for example, if gossip gets back to the prison linking the wife with some other man. Furthermore, whilst for most wives imprisonment is unlikely to produce *permanent* changes in the pattern of relationships, the stresses resulting from the separation make great demands upon the families' psychological resources and capacity for adaptation, which tend to result in periodic deterioration in the relationships between husband and wife.

In the intensive sample, where we were able to observe the pattern of relationships more closely, and were less reliant upon information given in reply to a structured questionnaire, we feel that the data strongly support the hypothesis.

2. Wives with wide kinship networks will seek additional support from them during the husband's imprisonment.

The discussion of this hypothesis relates solely to non-separated wives, since with those separated before imprisonment it is impossible to tell whether the help they receive is in any way related to their husband's imprisonment; on the contrary it is more likely to be related to the period when they first separated.

It is undoubtedly true that were it not for help from their families most wives would be seriously deprived, both financially and emotionally. The data on residence and moving reported in Chapter IV, p. 78, show that 42 per cent of non-separated wives who moved home after their husband's imprisonment returned to live with their parents; 36·4 per cent received financial help from their own and/or their husband's family, and even where they were given some help before the imprisonment this was considerably increased during the period of separation. Information given in Chapter IV, p. 80, showed that significantly more star wives receive help from both sets of parents than is the case for recidivists, though there is no significant difference between the two groups regarding actual residence with parents.

From Chapter VIII, Table XI (p. 223), it will be seen that wives show a distinct improvement in their relationships with their parents. Whilst the amount of contact with parents during the separation depends to a large extent upon the closeness of the relationship existing before imprisonment, we have ample evidence, particularly in the intensive sample, to suggest that there is a considerable renewal of contact with the wider kinship network.

Where parents were either dead, or living a long way away, there was much renewed contact with siblings. In the extensive sample we found no families where the wife was rejected by both her parents, however great the resentment towards the husband on account of his criminal, or irresponsible, behaviour. There were, however, cases where one or other of the parents was hostile. Had more systematic data been collected to include grandparents, aunts and uncles, cousins, etc., we feel that the hypothesis would be further confirmed, since wives often received much active support from these groups.

3. Utilization of the statutory and voluntary social services will be greater and more systematic amongst the families of habitual offenders than amongst those of first offenders.

The data reported in Chapter IV, p. 97, suggest that whilst recidivists' wives make *earlier* contact with more welfare agencies than do the wives of star prisoners, at the time of interview the proportion of each group having no contact with such agencies was almost identical (30·3 per cent of star wives, 27·3 per cent of recidivists' wives). Furthermore, although the wives of recidivists are in touch with a wider range of agencies this does not imply more frequent contact.

Whilst amongst non-separated families the wives of recidivists made significantly greater use of the NAB than the wives of stars (see Chapter IV, p. 94), in the case of the separated wives there was no significant difference.

We have pointed out elsewhere that no differentiation was made in the extensive sample between genuine first offenders and those merely in prison for the first time, or those re-classified as Governor's Stars.[1] This necessarily limits to some extent the value of the information relating to the use made of the social services. Such differentiation can, however, be made in the intensive sample, where, amongst thirty-one star prisoners, none had been in prison before and sixteen had no previous criminal record. The numbers are obviously too small to be really meaningful, but no apparent differences in fact exist in the use made of welfare services by genuine first offenders and those with previous convictions.

Much more systematic information would be required in order to test this hypothesis satisfactorily, but such evidence as we have does not support it. Furthermore, information derived from both samples suggests that the extent of contact with welfare agencies is not necessarily related to imprisonment, since it would be true to say that far more families of recidivists than stars appeared to be in touch with welfare agencies (including NAB) *before* the separation. This would seem to suggest that the criminality of the husband is merely one of a series of social problems exhibited by these families over an extended period of time.

4. The wives of prisoners with children of school age will seek employment, by contrast those with children under school age will not be employed, nor will those where there are children in both groups.

Tables I and II (see p. 284) set out the information regarding the work pattern of the non-separated wives in the extensive sample in relation to the age groups of their children.

Perhaps the most striking fact which emerges from these tables is that amongst wives of both stars and recidivists who go out to work and have only pre-school children, quite a high proportion do full-time work. On the other hand, where the wife has only school children, or children in both groups, the situation is reversed and most of those working do part-time work [stratified test $t = 3 \cdot 58$; $P < 0 \cdot 01$.] Amongst star wives our hypothesis would appear to be confirmed since only $11 \cdot 1$ per cent of those with only pre-school children and $12 \cdot 3$ per cent with children in both groups go out to work, compared with $70 \cdot 9$ per cent of those with school-age children and $69 \cdot 6$ per cent of those with no dependent children.

The $\chi^2$ table (see p. 284) shows the significance of the difference

[1] See Chapter II, p. 27, for explanation of this term.

between wives with children of pre-school age and those without. The table also shows the similarity of the two groups with pre-school children—those with *only* pre-school children and those who have children in both groups. There is also a similarity between those with school children only and those with no dependent children.

TABLE I.  *Work pattern of stars' wives by ages of children*
(*Percentages of wives at risk in each group*)

| Wives with:— | Only pre-school children | Only school children | Children in both groups | No dependent children | Total |
|---|---|---|---|---|---|
| Full-time work | 7·9 | 27·3 | – | 58·3 | 21·6 |
| Part-time work | 3·2 | 43·6 | 12·3 | 11·3 | 16·9 |
| No work | 88·9 | 29·0 | 87·7 | 30·4 | 61·4 |
| Total | 100·0 | 100·0 | 100·0 | 100·0 | 100·0 |
| Number | 63 | 55 | 65 | 53 | 236 |

TABLE II.  *Work pattern of recidivists' wives by ages of children*
(*Percentages of wives at risk in each group*)

| Wives with:— | Only pre-school children | Only school children | Children in both groups | No dependent children | Total |
|---|---|---|---|---|---|
| Full-time | 15·7 | 6·9 | 1·4 | 53·6 | 14·5 |
| Part-time work | 5·9 | 27·6 | 9·9 | 3·6 | 10·6 |
| No work | 78·4 | 65·5 | 88·7 | 42·9 | 74·9 |
| Total | 100·0 | 100·0 | 100·0 | 100·0 | 100·0 |
| Number— (unweighted) | 51 | 29 | 71 | 28 | 179 |

| $\chi^2$ due to | d.f. | $\chi^2$ | Significance |
|---|---|---|---|
| Difference between those with pre-school children and those without | 1 | 85·05 | $P < 0.01$ |
| Difference between those with pre-school children only and those with both pre- and school children | 1 | 0·02 | N.S. |
| Difference between those with school children only and those without dependent children | 1 | 0·01 | N.S. |
| Overall $\chi^2$ | 3 | 85·09 | $P < 0.01$ |

Amongst recidivists' wives the differences are much less marked, since 21·6 per cent of those with only pre-school children go out to work, compared with 34·5 per cent of those with school children only and 57·2 per cent of those with no dependent children.

In the case of recidivists' wives there is also a similarity between wives with *only* pre-school children and those with children in both groups, and such wives differ significantly from those with no pre-school children. There is also a just significant difference between those with only children of school age and those with no dependent children. The results are set out in the following $\chi^2$ table:

| $\chi^2$ due to | d.f. | $\chi^2$ | Significance |
|---|---|---|---|
| Difference between those with pre-school children and those without | 1 | 18·63 | $P < 0·01$ |
| Difference between those with pre-school children only and those with both pre- and school children | 1 | 1·67 | N.S. |
| Difference between those with school children only and those with no dependent children | 1 | 3·89 | $P < 0·05$ |
| Overall $\chi^2$ | 3 | 24·19 | $P < 0·01$ |

In the intensive sample, however, the hypothesis is not confirmed for either star or recidivist wives, and it is our impression that family size is a more important factor than the ages of the children in determining whether or not a wife goes out to work. As there is so little local authority provision for the care of young children it seems likely that the larger the family the more difficult it is for the wife to find relatives and friends to take charge of the children.

5. The adjustment of the family to imprisonment will vary with the type of offence, and with the extent of previous criminal experience.

As indicated in Chapter VIII, p. 225, it did not prove possible to devise a viable measure of total adjustment and it is therefore not possible to test this hypothesis in a way which would prove or disprove it statistically. However, we feel that a good deal of the information collected sheds a reasonable degree of light on this question and can usefully be discussed here.

One measure of the wife's attitude to her husband's imprisonment was felt to be her attitude towards the future. In Chapter IV, p. 119, data given indicated that there was no difference between stars' and recidivists' wives in their willingness to have their husband back, even if this was broken down by type of offence.

These data were not, however, wholly supported in Chapter VIII, p. 219, where families were scored for satisfaction with marriage and this index of adjustment was correlated with type of offence. Here we found that *recidivists'* wives were less satisfied with their marriages and less likely to have their husband back if he was in prison for either a sex offence or a white-collar offence. Amongst star wives, however, there was no significant difference according to type of offence.

We think this information is likely to be more accurate than that set out in Chapter IV, since in preparing material for that chapter, we carried out only a simple analysis of the replies to the question: 'Will you have your husband back on discharge?' against the type of offence he had committed. In Chapter VIII however, our assessment of the wife's future plans was based on a careful analysis of her replies to a number of additional, indirect questions.

Furthermore, the findings set out in Chapter VIII, p. 219, indicate that the number of previous imprisonments is related to the willingness of the wife to have her husband home. This is significant in the case of stars' wives and even amongst recidivists' wives there is also a trend in this direction, indicating that the more frequent or more prolonged the absence of the husband owing to imprisonment, the less satisfied does the wife become with the marriage, and the less willing to have him home.

Thus data from the extensive sample appear to confirm the hypothesis; however, so far as the intensive sample is concerned our overall impressions do not do so. The adjustment of a wife appears to depend more upon her own personality and upon the type of marital relationship, rather than upon either the degree of criminality of her husband or the type of offence.

*Family typologies*

In the intensive sample we were able to examine closely the different types of marital relationship and to observe the interaction between these and the crisis of imprisonment. This was obviously not possible with the extensive sample, so that all we were able to do with this group was to look carefully at both husbands' and wives' schedules in order to see in what overall way the separation appeared to affect the marital situation. In addition to data collected from husbands and wives, we also took into consideration the interviewer's comments regarding family functioning and relationships, and reports by outside informants (prison authorities, police, probation officers, etc.). The information obtained in this way is set out in Table III (see pp. 288–9) it refers to all criminal offenders in the extensive sample, both separated and non-separated; civil prisoners have been omitted.

It will be noted that although a high proportion of families are to be found in Group 1, this should not be taken to mean that these are necessarily conflict-free marriages. They are, however, marriages where conflict is tolerated, and it must be remembered that both husbands and wives tended to be over-optimistic about their relationship during the period of separation. Furthermore, where coders experienced some doubt about the stability of the marriage we tended to give the family the benefit of the doubt.

The fact that there are relatively few families in Group 2 arises largely from the fact that there were many wives who went through a period of severe crisis during the early part of the imprisonment (or when they first heard about the offence), but by the time our interview took place this critical situation had usually passed, and relationships were quickly resuming their normal pattern.

Group 3 contains those who thought that imprisonment might in fact improve the marital relationship, either because the wife thought it would prove such a shock to her husband that he would never risk it again, or because both partners felt they had been given a chance to reflect on the marriage and had come to the conclusion they would have to make a better job of it in the future. Those of us concerned in the analysis of the material felt somewhat sceptical about accepting these views as accurate and thought that this hope of improvement was somewhat unrealistic. However, if both partners held similar views we could do little else but record this fact.

Families in Group 4 really comprise the next stage from Group 1 in the process of deterioration. The conflict is not willingly tolerated, but usually the wife believes that she has to remain with her husband for the children's sake, a bad father being better than no father at all. We feel that for many of these wives it was also a case of a bad *husband* being better than no husband at all.

This material relating to marital relationships supports other data discussed throughout the report, indicating that family relationships of recidivist prisoners contain more conflict than those of stars. However, since we estimate that at most the marriages of 6 per cent of star families and 10 per cent of recidivist families may break up during the term of imprisonment investigated, we are left with four conclusions:

(i) Where marital relationships are good before imprisonment there is almost no likelihood of the marriage breaking up as a result of imprisonment (see Groups 1 and 7).

(ii) Where marital relationships are *seriously* strained before imprisonment there may be a break-up of the marriage, but the numbers are relatively small (see Group 6).

(iii) Where imprisonment is experienced as a severe crisis for the wife there is a tendency for marital relationships to deteriorate, but the marriage is unlikely to break up (see Groups 2, 4, and 5).

TABLE III.  *Family typologies*

(*Percentages*)

| Group | Stars | Recidivists | Total |
|---|---|---|---|
| 1. Families where good relationships before imprisonment remain unimpaired, or where a certain amount of conflict is tolerated | 43·3 | 29·5 | 34·6 |
| 2. Families where relationships good before imprisonment, but deteriorate as problems become intensified during imprisonment. Nevertheless marriage will certainly resume | 5·1 | 5·1 | 5·1 |
| 3. Families where relationships strained before imprisonment, the experience of imprisonment (or the fact that the crime has come out into the open) brings them together and the marriage may be improved | 13·3 | 6·1 | 8·8 |
| 4. Families where relationships strained before imprisonment, prison may bring financial or material difficulties, but also may bring psychological relief. Contact is maintained during imprisonment and the marriage is likely to resume as before. *Or* strained relationships before, little difference financially or materially, contact maintained and marriage will resume as before | 10·9 | 16·4 | 14·3 |
| 5. Families where relationships are strained before imprisonment and the separation is a severe crisis materially and emotionally, but the family will remain together because there seems no alternative | 9·4 | 9·8 | 9·6 |
| 6. Families where relationships before imprisonment were very strained. Prison may bring further financial and/or psychological stress and the marriage breaks up during imprisonment with little or no likelihood of resuming. *Or* it may bring relief and the opportunity to break up | 5·5 | 9·3 | 7·9 |

TABLE III. *Family typologies*—continued

*(Percentages)*

|  | Stars | Recidivists | Total |
|---|---|---|---|
| 7. Families where good relationships before imprisonment but little likelihood of resuming | 0·3 | – | 0·15 |
| 8. Families separated before imprisonment and where there was definitely no contact during imprisonment | 3·9 | 15·0 | 10·8 |
| 9. Families where husband/wife in complete disagreement about the situation | 8·2 | 8·4 | 8·3 |
| Total | 100·0 | 100·0 | 100·0 |
| Number | 256 | 213 | – |

(iv) Where marital relationships were strained before imprisonment the experience *may* result in an improvement in the situation. This is particularly the case for the wives of star prisoners (see Group 3).

With regard to this last group we must, however, repeat, that the evidence of the intensive sample suggests that whilst the couple *hope* their marriage will be improved, in many instances even the more negative aspects of the marital relationship seem to be based on deep-seated psychological needs which make any real changes in attitude unlikely.

K

## Chapter XIII

# SUMMARY OF THE PRINCIPAL FINDINGS

The main recommendations for action have already been given in the Foreword to this book (pp. 17), and a number of specific suggestions appear throughout the text. It remains to summarize the principal points of information which emerged as a result of the enquiry.

### THE PRISONERS

The fact that the national sample was designed to be representative of the married prison population as a whole, divided into sub-samples of stars, recidivists and civils, gives an opportunity for describing certain features of these groups to supplement the normal prison statistics. It should be noted that, with the exception of the civil debtors, men serving less than three months were excluded from the present survey.

Although married prisoners were found to be slightly older than the prison population as a whole, 40 per cent were still under thirty years of age (compared with 50 per cent in the total prison population). Fewer than 7 per cent of the sample were born outside the United Kingdom, the largest single category being those born in the Irish Republic (2·3 per cent of the total population). The majority of those from Eire were serving a first sentence of imprisonment. Only 1·6 per cent of all prisoners interviewed were non-white.

Of the prisoners, 36·4 per cent were unemployed at the time of committing their offence. Thirty-one per cent were unskilled or semi-skilled manual workers, with whom may be grouped the 12·5 per cent of small-scale self-employed men who were largely street-traders, bookmakers, scrap metal dealers, etc. Fewer than 10 per cent were white-collar workers. Recidivists had experienced significantly more unemployment than stars. The majority of unemployed were out of work for reasons other than the prevailing state of the labour market. Thirty per cent of the unemployed lived habitually by crime, 33 per cent presented psychiatric problems in regard to work and 21 per cent suffered from some form of mental or physical ill-health.

An attempt was made to assess prisoners' earnings when in employment, though it was not always possible to distinguish between legitimate earnings and income from crime. Those who were employed appeared to have earnings comparable with those of manual workers in the normal population.

Among the stars, 35 per cent had at least three previous convictions; for recidivists the comparable figure was 94 per cent; 18 per cent of the stars had previous prison experience, but not all the recidivists had extended institutional experience, only 50 per cent having been in juvenile institutions.

The bulk of prisoners had committed property offences. Offences involving violence, excluding murder and sex offences, were more common among recidivists. Of the prisoners in the sample, which it will be remembered excluded very short-term prisoners, 42 per cent were serving sentences of three years or more. (These figures are based upon the daily average population and *not* upon the number of receptions.)

Approximately a third of the prisoners reported broken marriages, the marital instability of recidivists being markedly higher than that of stars. Estimates of the quality of the marital relationship made by the men themselves were remarkably optimistic, and appeared unduly so in the light of later investigation. Hasty marriages were rare. (Over 80 per cent had been married for at least three years.) 50 per cent had known their wives for at least two years before marriage; many had previously lived together, the majority of such spouses being pregnant at marriage.

The prisoners reported that visits by their wives were limited by a variety of factors, primarily distance, expense, and the difficulties of travelling with young children. Only 54 per cent of wives visited on every possible occasion (i.e. monthly); 30 per cent of men claimed never to have sent visiting orders, the majority, though by no means all, being men separated from their wives. The system of 'bulk transfers', to relieve over-crowding in local prisons, created distressing problems for prisoners and their families, many of whom were unable to arrange regular visits, and sometimes no visits at all. Visiting facilities varied considerably from one establishment to another, and between open and closed prisons, the latter being relatively satisfactory. 80 per cent of wives corresponded weekly with their husband.

Approximately 70 per cent of stars and 80 per cent of recidivists reported serious marital conflict before imprisonment, in-law trouble, work (or lack of it), drink and jealousy (usually concerning other women) being most commonly mentioned. Nevertheless, the majority of men claimed that their wives tolerated their irresponsible behaviour most of the time.

## PRISONERS' WIVES

The following paragraphs outline the information obtained from interviews with those wives of criminal offenders who were living with their husband at the time of his arrest. This includes 236 wives of star prisoners and 179 wives of recidivist prisoners.

Like the prisoners, the wives tended to be youthful, with a modal age of between twenty-one and twenty-nine years: 8 per cent were under twenty-one and 50 per cent under thirty. Only 4 per cent were aged more than fifty. The average number of persons per household was 4·2, a figure which in some cases included parents, siblings, adult children and grandchildren, as well as the prisoner's wife and dependent children. 14·2 per cent of households were without any dependent children.

Most wives lived in large urban centres where housing problems were relatively severe. Comparison with the Registrar General's distribution of population by standard regions indicated that the East and West Ridings of Yorkshire were considerably over-represented in the present sample of non-separated wives (17·6 per cent of families compared with 9·3 per cent of the total population) as was the North-West (19 per cent of families compared with 14·2 per cent of the population). At the time of the research these areas were experiencing considerable unemployment and consequent poverty, which may have some bearing on the distribution.

An attempt was made to classify the most serious problems experienced by the wives during the period of separation, and it was found that 41 per cent regarded 'money' as a major problem. In all, 34 per cent quoted the management of children, 32 per cent loneliness and sexual frustration and 23 per cent fears concerning what would happen when their husband was released. Only 5 per cent were concerned with the hostility of the community and only 4 per cent mentioned shame or guilt feelings concerning their husband's crime and imprisonment. The incidence of these problems appeared unrelated to the duration of separation. The management of disturbed behaviour among children, particularly those of recidivists, appeared to be a very considerable practical problem, although most children were too young to be officially termed delinquent; we regard this as one of the most striking findings of the research and one meriting further systematic investigation.

Thirty per cent of the non-separated wives were in some form of full- or part-time employment; relatively more stars' wives went to work than did recidivists' wives. The majority had unskilled jobs of a domestic nature; 20 per cent had semi-skilled jobs, mainly in factories. Wives went to work primarily in order to meet essential commitments. For the most part those who did not do so said it was on account of having young children.

Seventy-eight per cent were in receipt of national assistance. 11 per cent of wives felt themselves treated 'differently' as prisoners' wives, though on balance there seemed little evidence of discrimination beyond some lack of tact on the part of Board officials. Particularly resented was the policy pursued in some areas of referring wives to the wvs for second-hand clothes rather than making a monetary grant, and some officials appeared to put considerable pressure on wives, even those with young children, to go out to work. No families were found to be getting less than the statutory minimum, but discretionary grants in respect of 'extras' were the subject of wide variation from area to area.

The number of women acknowledging material help from social agencies, other than the NAB, was surprisingly small, though this may be due to the fact that such assistance is not regarded as income unless received regularly. Bearing in mind the number of dependent children, the wives' incomes were low, approximately 60 per cent being in receipt of £7 10s 0d a week or less. When compared with husbands' earnings before imprisonment there is no evidence to support the view sometimes held that the families of offenders are better off while the man is in prison. On the contrary the indications are of considerable reduction in income, and in some cases acute poverty. Of the wives of stars, 28 per cent had sold or pawned property to solve financial difficulties, compared with only 16 per cent of recidivists' wives.

When questioned about indebtedness, many wives were unclear as to the difference between hire purchase, 'club' payments, and mail order purchases; 40 per cent of wives reported hire purchase commitments on furniture and 24 per cent on domestic appliances. Only 28 per cent had no HP commitments. Of those with goods on hire purchase, 45 per cent were in arrears at the time their husband went to prison and this had increased to 61 per cent by the time of the interview.

There was relatively little complaint about high-pressure salesmanship, but this was partly due to the fact that the pre-conditions for exploitation already exist when the salesman calls and it is not necessary for him to exert undue pressure. There are already strong social pressures to acquire more goods, and the temptation to buy is ever present when need is great. Sharp practices were the cause of considerable complaint, in particular leaving goods at the house and failing to return to collect them until they were likely either to have been used intentionally, or to have been damaged by accident.

The new Hire Purchase Bill provides improved legal safeguards for the consumer, but is unlikely to reduce the number of men going to prison who have incidental hire purchase troubles. For prisoners, the most that can be hoped from the new legislation is that it may protect their wives from avoidable increased indebtedness whilst they are inside.

While it was difficult to obtain precise information concerning other debts, it appeared that 60 per cent of the families of the sample owed money other than for HP. Families of star prisoners owed on average £141, compared with £77 for recidivists, though the consequences of such indebtedness might well be more severe for the recidivists who usually had fewer assets. Many star prisoners with large debts had, in fact, been adjudged bankrupt, and the families were relatively unconcerned about their debts. Recidivists' families also owed money for gambling debts and often had considerable outstanding fines.

Of the wives in debt, 30 per cent blamed the improvidence of their husband and 16 per cent attributed debts to business failure. A considerable number of husbands, disliking the role of employee, set up in businesses which were under-capitalized and their technical skills failed to compensate for their lack of business acumen.

Apart from the financial support already referred to, contact with social agencies appeared to be limited, partly through the wives' ignorance. On the other hand, 29 per cent of stars' wives and 33 per cent of recidivists' wives were in touch with a probation officer. This seems a potential contact between the family and the penal system with possibilities for useful development. The existence of a prison welfare officer was unknown to the majority of wives, although 20 per cent reported having received either a Christmas parcel or some help with the fare for a visit. The feeling of isolation from the prison authorities was most marked, and almost all wives felt that a visit from some official at their husband's prison would have been helpful.

The negative comments of so many wives concerning such social agencies as the Children's and Education Departments and the housing authorities in part reflects their own feelings about having to act in the role of suppliants before 'authority', which they saw as hostile towards themselves and their husband. Two notable exceptions were the Probation Service and the NSPCC, the latter organization being often most highly praised.

Some 29 per cent of wives reported that they suffered from a nervous condition for which they received treatment, and many more complained of 'nerves' but had not attended a doctor for this. A total of 50 per cent of wives suffered from some form of physical or mental illness.

A relatively high proportion of both husbands and wives in the sample had been married before, particularly the recidivists (husbands 19 per cent, wives 16 per cent). Separations of varying duration during the marriage were also common (approximately 30 per cent for stars and 45 per cent for recidivists). In spite of this, many wives felt optimistic about their marriage and saw their husband in sanguine terms despite the evidence of his previous behaviour. The commonest source of marital conflict mentioned by the wives was the husband's inability to work adequately, more striking among recidivists (38 per cent) than among stars (22 per cent). Trouble over other women was also frequent (21 per cent among stars and 32 per cent among recidivists). Another major factor was drink (20 per cent and 32 per cent respectively).

Feelings concerning conviction and sentence fluctuated throughout the period of separation. Most wives *feared* gossip, though relatively few experienced actual hostility from other people. Stars' wives reported feelings of shame at the time of conviction and sentence; shame among recidivists' wives was apparently more related to not having a man about.

Feelings of injustice about the sentence were most commonly expressed by stars' wives, particularly when their husband had received a long sentence for a 'white-collar' offence which they did not really regard as criminal, or for a sex offence. Recidivists' wives complained about long sentences for larceny and receiving which, because they did not involve violence, were regarded as unimportant. Most wives whose husbands were convicted of murder or manslaughter thought both trial and sentence to be unfair. Strikingly, in view of the general leniency of courts towards motoring offenders, most wives whose husbands were in prison for such offences considered the sentence merited.

In spite of their having, in some cases, long criminal records, the majority of wives desired to have their husband back on his release. The most widespread cause of concern regarding his return centred round the problem of his work, but there was also considerable overt anxiety about marital adjustment.

### SEPARATED WIVES

It was found that a number of the wives in the sample (twenty stars' and thirty-four recidivists' wives) were separated from their husbands. These did not seem to differ substantially from the non-separated wives except in the following respects: separated wives had fewer children dependent upon them; they were twice as likely to be living with parents; considerably fewer were receiving regular national assistance, in part due to the fact that they were often either housekeeping for their parents or cohabiting with another man; separated wives also received more financial aid from voluntary and statutory agencies than did those who were normally living with their husbands; they had fewer financial commitments, and were generally better adjusted to living on a small income.

The majority of these wives had been separated for a year or more, and the reasons given for the break-up of the marriage were identical with those enumerated as areas of *conflict* among the marriages still intact. In spite of the fact that separation before imprisonment had lasted for some considerable time, 54 per cent of the separated wives remained in correspondence with their husband and 22 per cent maintained personal contact through visits, though often these were only sporadic.

Most of the separated wives felt that their husband deserved his present sentence, and they claimed in the main to be totally uninterested in his fate. A great many separated wives blamed other women for their husband's criminality and there was a great deal of bitterness against them, even when the husband had been irresponsible thoughout the marriage. Separated wives were also more pessimistic concerning their husbands' chances of giving up crime. Half of them were adamant that they did not want him back on release, and many feared that he would return to the district and physically injure them.

### THE INTENSIVE STUDY

In addition to the national sample, contact was maintained with a sample of fifty prisoners' wives living in or near London over a period of eighteen months. Interviews took place at three-monthly intervals and where possible the final interview included both the released prisoner and his wife. Comparison shows that these families were very similar in background to those interviewed in the national sample.

In this part of the study special emphasis was laid upon family relationships and changing patterns of adjustment during separation. The main general conclusion that emerged was that the patterns of family relationship established before imprisonment tend to determine the wife's mode of adjustment to separation and that, as far as could be ascertained, the *status quo* is resumed upon discharge. Further systematic work is, however, needed to test this generalization.

Apart from family adjustment, there was an almost universal worsening of material conditions as time went on, but the extent to which this affected the wife depended largely upon her personality. For the most part increasing material deprivation did *not* result in increased mental deterioration, though it did contribute to physical ill-health; this was also made worse by increasing emotional deprivation, in particular loneliness and sexual frustration which resulted in symptoms of nerves, insomnia, fainting and general debility.

For the most part changes occurring during separation were fairly impermanent and depended largely on external events, and only those wives who were very dependent on their husbands showed obvious and constant signs of deterioration. It is suggested that it is the factor of involuntary separation which produced a crisis distinguishable from most other kinds of critical situation. Furthermore, the early stage of separation, especially for stars' wives, appears to be particularly critical. On the other hand, there is evidence that each additional prison sentence loosens family ties.

The impact of the crisis appears to depend more upon the personality of the wife than upon the quality of family adjustment; the more stable and well adjusted wives were better able to handle the separation whatever the husband/wife relationship might have been before imprisonment. Once the husband returns his personality becomes of equal importance in determining the quality of readjustment; since neither the personality of the husband nor that of the wife is likely to have undergone any great change during the period of separation, the pattern existing before imprisonment will probably be resumed.

#### CIVIL PRISONERS AND THEIR WIVES

Prisoners so far discussed had all been convicted of criminal offences. The enquiry also included interviews with 171 civil prisoners. These tended to be appreciably older than criminal prisoners, only 25 per cent being under the age of thirty compared with 50 per cent of the stars and recidivists.

Data obtained visiting county courts, combined with information provided by the Lord Chancellor's Department, showed that civil prisoners are not committed in comparable numbers throughout the country; not only is there considerable variation in the proportion of committal orders made, but the percentage of men actually conveyed to prison also varies widely. Again there are considerable variations in the proportion who, after being imprisoned, are able and/or willing to buy themselves out.

Two entirely different types of civil prisoner must be distinguished. On the one hand there are civil debtors who are committed, technically for contempt of court, at the instance of creditors, the court being satisfied that the debtor is able to pay. On the other hand there are those who have defaulted on maintenance payments in respect of their wives and/or children.

Civil debtors are on the whole characterized by social incompetence. They themselves were unable for the most part to give coherent accounts of their indebtedness, work records or financial position generally, suggesting that compared with criminal prisoners they suffered a remarkable degree of social and intellectual inadequacy. More than half (compared with 36 per cent of the criminal sample) were unemployed at the time of committal, a high proportion having psychiatric and physical disabilities as well as being unskilled workers and therefore amongst the most vulnerable element in the labour market in times of over-employment. When employed they tended to remain in jobs only a short while and to earn comparatively low wages. Two thirds had been in prison before, either as civil prisoners or on conviction for crime. Many appeared to have been in trouble for petty thieving or for vagrancy.

By contrast, the maintenance defaulters stood out, not as mentally dull or socially inadequate, but as exceptionally recalcitrant. Many of them hated their wives, and would go to prison rather than pay, while others claimed that because their wives were living with other men they were not morally obliged to pay maintenance. Many of the maintenance defaulters evaded arrest and imprisonment by frequently changing jobs and moving about the country, some deliberately avoiding work in order to evade an attachment of earnings order. For the majority of maintenance defaulters imprisonment was an annual experience, since a defaulter may only be imprisoned for this reason once in any period of twelve months.

Men in for non-payment of maintenance were by definition in a situation of family disorganization. Debtors, on the other hand, appeared to have a far more stable background, 88 per cent living with their legal wives. In both groups, where the marriage had broken up, the reasons were much the same as in the case of criminal prisoners, but the criminal prisoners living apart from their wives appeared to have far less marked antipathy towards their spouses than was shown by the separated or divorced civil prisoners. Debtors living with their wives appeared to get on unusually well with them in spite of the fact that they often recognized and admitted their wife's improvidence and bad management. Despite poverty, squalor and generalized social incompetence amongst the families of those civil prisoners living with their wives it was usually possible to discern a warmth and stability in most of the marriages which contrasted markedly with that found amongst the families of many criminal prisoners. Imprisonment was generally too short to have a marked effect on these families' problems, either material or psychological.

Civil prisoners had appreciably larger families than is common in the population as a whole, over 40 per cent having four or more children and 26 per cent having five or more. Bearing in mind their low earning capacity and frequent unemployment, it seems hardly surprising that many of them had fallen into debt often for such necessities as clothing.

The debtors tended to owe money other than that for which they had been committed to prison; such families appeared frequently to enter into economic commitments which they had little, if any, hope of honouring and with little thought of the utility of the goods obtained. Thus in addition to debts for clothing and furniture there were debts for encyclopaedias and expensive domestic appliances. For many, debt appeared to be a way of life, although 60 per cent of those in prison had been committed in respect of debts of £50 or less. Civil prisoners tended to have fewer hire purchase commitments than might be supposed, but they were often involved in credit sales and clothing club transactions. Although the majority of them were interviewed only a few days after being separated from their wives, most were extraordinarily vague when asked how their wives would manage financially. Imprisonment appeared to make little difference to the income level of these families; 60 per cent were on national assistance, and the majority of these had been so before the separation.

When inadequates are imprisoned for debt, it results not so much from a lack of sympathy on the part of the courts as from a lack of objective information. A social worker in the county courts, with a role analogous to that of the probation officer in the magistrates' court, could do much to remedy the situation. Moreover, the fact that the enforcement of liability in the county courts tends invariably to be on behalf of large business organizations who make allowances for bad debts, rather than individual creditors, suggests that the whole philosophy underlying the legal procedures in respect of indebtedness is in need of careful rethinking in the light of the social and economic facts.

Little is at present achieved by the imprisonment of civil debtors, for whom the prison régime is almost exclusively custodial, and for whom there are no adequate provisions for social training. In the case of maintenance defaulters imprisonment is purely coercive and shows little evidence of success as a deterrent. For the social inadequates longer periods of detention could form the basis of a programme of social and academic education and industrial training, along the lines of the disablement resettlement schemes operated by the Ministry of Labour. Experience gained with a vigorous training programme for civil prisoners could well be of benefit to the prison system as a whole.

In all, 107 wives of civil prisoners were contacted and interviewed. About 30 per cent of these were living in conditions of dirt and squalor; their poverty was considerably more acute than that found amongst the families of criminal prisoners. Half had practically no furniture and 70 per cent were in receipt of an income of £7 10s 0d a week, or less, which was totally inadequate, particularly in view of the large families that they tended to have.

Money and the control of children were cited as major problems by the wives of civil prisoners and all members of such families appeared to be exceptionally prone to various forms of physical and psychological illness (60 per cent of wives reported at least one such illness). In addition to national assistance these wives made considerable use of other statutory social services (probation, health visitor, children's and education departments), but little use of any voluntary social services. The impression was gained that the exasperating social incompetence of some of the more feckless families led certain social agencies to make a distinction between the 'deserving' and the 'undeserving' in the matter of giving help. Once help had been refused these wives tended not to seek it again. Many of these families were clearly in need of some intensive form of social work of the kind normally provided by the Family Service Units. It is evident that the great amount of assistance already being given by other types of social agency has failed to overcome the difficulties of these families.

The problems experienced by the wives of civil prisoners tended to be unconnected with the husband's imprisonment: (*a*) because the sentence was too short to account for such complicated difficulties, (*b*) because the problems had been of long duration, and (*c*) the separated wives had usually been living apart for a sufficiently long time to be virtually unaffected by the imprisonment.

### WELFARE AGENCIES

Both the extensive and the intensive sample produced evidence that prisoners' wives tend to under-estimate the assistance they receive from voluntary welfare agencies, partly because they normally regard only material aid as helpful. Discussions were held at the outset of the research with a number of agencies in order to obtain data concerning their experience of prisoners' families and these suggest that relatively few such families are ever referred to them. The Family Service Units estimated that no more than 10 per cent of their referrals were of prisoners' families and the Church Army, with representatives in a number of prisons, suggested that in the London area they handled only about 300 such cases a year. Referrals, when they did take place, were from a variety of sources including probation officers, the NAB and local prisoners' aid societies. Most agencies commented that comparatively few referrals came from the prison welfare officers. The problems dealt with were varied but predominantly financial. When approached by an agency on behalf of a prisoner or his family, finance houses were usually prepared to make reductions in hire purchase payments. Intra-family problems generally were widely reported and any matrimonial work done with the wife was said to be made extremely difficult by the lack of reciprocal social casework in prison. Visiting arrangements in prisons were heavily criticized.

Most families consulting the agencies were on national assistance, and it was generally held that there were great variations between different areas in the attitude of the Board's officials concerning discretionary payments. The acute shortage of low-income housing was also noted, but opinions differed as to its importance; eviction as a direct consequence of imprisonment was found to be rare, but could, and did, occur in respect of rent arrears which were part of a general financial problem. Most agencies considered the problems of prisoners' families to be indistinguishable from those of other families where the breadwinner was absent. Agencies were unanimous in their criticism of existing after-care facilities, and commented upon the lack of background information from prison welfare officers when cases were referred. The organizers of prison welfare, in turn, were critical of the voluntary agencies on grounds of the inadequacy of the assistance they gave.

The material collected in the course of research suggested that satisfactory rehabilitation of the prisoner must involve the family outside. As a prerequisite, it is vital to review the existing conditions of contact between husbands and wives and in particular the regulations and arrangements for prison visits and home leave. The question of the transfer of men to institutions away from their home areas in order to relieve over-crowding in local prisons should also be reviewed.

The results of the enquiry also emphasize the difficulties that may arise if the problems of husband and wife are handled by two different social agencies. In this respect the work of the prison welfare officer is crucial; the evidence shows, however, that, for a variety of reasons, prison welfare officers had only partial knowledge of the problems reported by the prisoners to our interviewers; 37 per cent had not had a personal interview with the welfare officer, and of those who were interviewed, just over a third had been seen at their own request. Welfare officers tended to emphasize the prisoners' financial and housing problems, in contrast to the research findings which stress more personal problems which the prisoners may have been reluctant to discuss with them.

General advice was given by the prison welfare officers in 53 per cent of cases, home visits were made (generally by Church Army or WVS personnel) in 22 per cent, and special introductions to employers, landladies, etc. on discharge in 15 per cent of cases. Where no help was given it was stated to be predominantly because the prisoner had refused it.

The great majority of prisoners' families live in conditions of acute poverty, a fact which tends to exacerbate the other difficulties that beset them, and they deeply resent the consequent need to 'beg' for charity. Various anomalies remain, such as the differences in rates for wives under twenty-one and for those over this age. Other variations in practice continue; for example, some NAB officials send wives to the WVS to obtain second-hand clothing whilst others make discretionary grants. The fact that the NAB allowance does not cover school meals exposes the family's circumstances to teachers and other children. Certain other practices are found which are in direct contravention of NAB headquarters policy: (*a*) there is still pressure on wives—even those with young children—to go out to work, (*b*) a distinction is made between 'deserving' and 'undeserving' cases, and (*c*) pressure is exerted on separated wives to take proceedings against their husbands for non-payment of maintenance, rather than the Board themselves taking proceedings for failure to support.

### FIVE HYPOTHESES

Finally a sequence of five hypotheses were tested. Of these, two were supported by the evidence:

1. Family relationships following upon conviction and imprisonment will follow a pattern set by family relationships existing before imprisonment.
2. Wives with wide kinship networks will seek additional support from them during the husband's imprisonment.

On the other hand, the evidence failed to support the other three hypotheses:

3. Utilization of the statutory and voluntary social services will be greater and more systematic amongst the families of habitual offenders than amongst those of first offenders.
4. The wives of prisoners with children of school age will seek employment, while by contrast those with children under school age will not be employed, nor will those where there are children in both groups.
5. The adjustment of the family to imprisonment will vary with the type of offence, and with the extent of previous criminal experience.

# *Appendix A*

## (i) *Information available*

At the time the sample was drawn there were forty-five prisons in England and Wales containing one or more of the required categories of men. Since the prison interviews were to be carried out almost exclusively by one person, it was decided to limit the number of prisons to be included to seventeen.

The official information available about the numbers of prisoners in each category in any prison does not distinguish their marital status, nor the length of their unexpired sentence. The selection of *prisons* was therefore based on the *total* numbers of male prisoners in each category at a given date. It is particularly important to note that this was a sample of the *male prison population* (e.g. daily average population) and *not* a sample of men coming into prison (e.g. receptions). The justification for this decision was that it would give a better picture of the nature and extent of the social problem existing at any given moment, which would in turn suggest the kind of permanent machinery which might be set up to deal with it in future.

Information was made available by the prison department of the Home Office regarding the number of male prisoners in the three categories as at May 30, 1961.

TABLE I

| Category of prisoner | Numbers of male prisoners as at May 30, 1961 | Size of sample | Sampling fraction (approx.) |
|---|---|---|---|
| Civil | 443 | 200 | 1 in 2 |
| Star | 6,260 | 300 | 1 in 21 |
| Recidivist | 13,504 | 300 | 1 in 45 |

## (ii) *Selection of prisons*

In view of the different sampling fractions for the three categories of prisoner, the simplest method of obtaining a sample of prisons would have been a separate selection for each category. This would have meant, however, that some prisons would be selected to give a sample for only one category of prisoner and others would be selected to give samples for only two of the three categories. Since it was important to limit the number of prisons in the sample, this design was considered to be uneconomic; a sample design was required which would give samples for all three categories of prisoner from each prison selected (providing of course, it had prisoners of all these three categories).

In order to achieve such a design, prisons were selected with probability proportional to the weighted sum of the numbers of prisoners in the three

---

[1] We are very much indebted to Mr T. Corlett of the British Market Research Bureau, upon whose recommendations the sample was designed; much of what appears in this section is the direct result of his proposals.

relevant categories. The weights applied to the category of prisoner were proportional to the sampling fraction for that category, the recidivists being given a weight of 1, so that the weight for stars was $2\cdot2$ and that for civils was $20\cdot3$. Thus the weighted sum ($N$) for a prison is given by—

$$N = R + 2\cdot2S + 20\cdot3\ C$$

Where $R$ is the number of recidivist prisoners in the prison
$S$ is the number of star prisoners in the prison
$C$ is the number of civil prisoners in the prison.

It can be shown that, with this method of selection, unweighted sample estimates can be used if the total number of prisoners selected from each prison within a stratum is constant; the number of prisoners in a particular category, however, should vary according to the proportion of such prisoners in the selected prison.

### (iii) *Stratification of prisons*

Before selecting the sample, all the prisoners were placed into one of six strata—open, closed central, local in conurbations, local in towns of over 100,000 population, local in other areas, and regional. The number of prisons to be selected within each stratum was arranged to be roughly proportional to the weighted sum of prisoners for the stratum. Information about the strata is given in Table II.

TABLE II

|  | (a) Total prisons in stratum | (b) 'Weighted sum' of prisoners | (c) Number of prisons to be selected |
|---|---|---|---|
| ALL PRISONS | 45 | 35,094 | 17 |
| Stratum:— |  |  |  |
| (1) All open prisons | 11 | 7,770 | 4 |
| (2) Closed 'central' prisons | 5 | 2,688 | 2 |
| Closed 'local' prisons: |  |  |  |
| (3) In conurbations | 8 | 11,986 | 5 |
| (4) In other towns of over 100,000 population | 7 | 4,502 | 2 |
| (5) In other areas | 10 | 6,281 | 3 |
| (6) 'Regional' prisons | 4 | 1,867 | 1 |

Since the 'weighted sum' for all forty-five prisons totalled approximately 35,000 and seventeen prisons were to be selected in all, this implied a selection of 1 prison for every 2,000 (approx.) of the 'weighted sum'. Three prisons were automatically included in the sample since they had a 'weighted sum' of this size or greater. In each stratum where more than one other prison was to be selected, the remaining prisons were listed in regional order, according to six geographical areas, and a cumulative sum was then formed of the 'weighted sums'. The required number of prisons was then selected from each group by systematic sampling with probability proportional to the 'weighted sum' for each prison. This technique thus incorporates into the design some degree of stratification by geographical region.

(iv) *The resulting sample of prisons*

In the case of civil prisoners in three prisons, this procedure resulted in the number of men to be interviewed being greater than the number of men in those prisons on May 30, 1961, and the calculated number was near enough to the actual number in three other cases to risk its achievement being impossible. Table III below shows the final sample:—

TABLE III *Number of prisoners selected*

| | Civil | Star | Recidivist | Total |
|---|---|---|---|---|
| **A.** *Open Prisons* | | | | |
| Drake Hall (Staffs) | 50 | 10 | – | 60 |
| Thorp Arch (Yorks) | – | 39 | 7 | 46 |
| Sudbury (Derby) | – | 45 | 3 | 48 |
| Leyhill (Glos) | – | 47 | 1 | 48 |
| | | | | |
| **B.** *Closed Central Prisons* | | | | |
| Wakefield (Yorks) | – | 30 | 3 | 33 |
| Parkhurst (I.O.W.) | – | – | 29 | 29 |
| | | | | |
| **C.** *Closed Local Prisons* | | | | |
| *In Conurbations* | | | | |
| Brixton/Wandsworth (London) | (27) | 14 | 3 | 44 |
| Strangeways (Manchester) | 19 | 5 | 22 | 46 |
| Armley (Leeds) | (21) | 4 | 25 | 50 |
| Walton (Liverpool) | (11) | 10 | 35 | 56 |
| Pentonville (London) | – | – | 56 | 56 |
| ii. *In other towns of over 100,000 population* | | | | |
| Preston (Lancs) | – | 38 | 16 | 54 |
| Cardiff (Glam) | 17 | 2 | 18 | 37 |
| iii. *In other areas* | | | | |
| Durham | (11) | 7 | 24 | 42 |
| Winchester (Hants) | ( 9) | 7 | 24 | 40 |
| Lincoln (Lincs) | (12) | 12 | 19 | 43 |
| **D.** *Regional Prisons* | | | | |
| The Verne (Dorset) | – | 30 | 15 | 45 |
| | | | | |
| Total | 177 | 300 | 300 | 777 |

NOTE: The number of interviews enclosed in brackets would need to be given double weighting in the analysis.

It had been intended to add 10 per cent to all the figures in order to allow for 'wastage' since it was feared that it might be difficult to establish contact with the families. In view of what has been said above regarding civil prisoners, it was only possible to add this figure of 10 per cent to the stars and recidivists, thus increasing the total by 60 to 837.

(v) *Selection of the prisoners*
Details of this procedure have already been set out in the main text (see Chapter II, p. 31).

# Appendix B

## STATISTICAL ANALYSIS

by G. Kalton

The sampling theory of stratified two-stage sampling leads to lengthy formulae for the sampling errors required in the tests of significance. The stratification causes a reduction in the size of the sampling errors; the closer a stratification factor is related to the subject matter, the greater the reduction of the sampling errors. Two-stage sampling, on the other hand, usually results in larger sampling errors than those that would be obtained from simple random sampling with the same sample size; the greater the similarity of the prisoners in one prison compared with the overall prison population (the intra-cluster correlation) the larger will be the increase in the sampling errors. Thus the two aspects of the design, stratification and two-stage sampling, act in opposite directions. In sampling general populations in this country the usual design is a stratified three-stage sample: here the increase in sampling error from the three-stage sampling generally exceeds the decrease due to stratification and in many cases the sampling error is between $1 \cdot 25$ and $2 \cdot 0$ times the sampling error that would have been obtained for simple random sampling with the same sample size.[1] In this case, however, it is felt that the stratification factors may be more closely related to the subject matter of the survey and also the intra-cluster correlation is likely to be fairly small, since the prisoners have no opportunity to choose the prison to which they are sent. In order to reduce the complexity of the tabulations required, and also to simplify the statistical calculations, it has therefore been assumed that the reductions in sampling errors through stratification are equal to the increase caused by two-stage sampling; in other words the tests of significance are carried out as if the selection procedure were simple random sampling. In particular, this has the great advantage that the chi-square test can be used. It has not been possible to investigate the validity of this assumption; if the reader feels that it is too optimistic, he could use a higher significance level than the usual 5 per cent level.

The double weight given to recidivists when the results for stars and recidivists are combined, has caused difficulties in the application of the random sampling formulae to tests of significance when the comparison is not between stars and recidivists: for example Chapter V is concerned with comparisons of separated and non-separated families. For such comparisons the sample of prisoners has been treated as a stratified sample with two strata, star prisoners and recidivists. (The other stratification factors and the two stages of sampling are still not taken into account.) The standard errors for the significance tests were calculated as for a stratified sample with two strata, one of which is given double weight.[2]

---

[1] For a full discussion, see Corlett, T., 'Rapid Methods of Estimating Standard Errors of Stratified Multi-Stage Sample: A Preliminary Investigation', *The Statistician*, No. 1, Vol. 13, 1963.

[2] See W.G. Cochran: *Sampling Techniques*, Wiley 1964.

# Appendix C

### COPY OF LETTER SENT TO LEGAL WIVES LIVING WITH THEIR HUSBANDS

Dear Mrs

I recently saw your husband in                    Prison in connection with a survey we are carrying out into what happens to a man's family when he goes to prison. Having heard your husband's views, we should very much like to discuss the matter with you as well.

Very little is known about what happens to the wives and children of men in prison and we should like to try to find out just how they manage, what sorts of difficulties arise, and whether any help they receive is adequate.

I wonder whether you would help us by allowing a lady visitor to come and talk to you in the near future about the problems as they affect you. Naturally all the information you give will be strictly confidential.

I enclose a card and stamped addressed envelope so that you can let us know whether a morning, afternoon or evening call is most convenient.

Yours truly,

### COPY OF LETTER SENT TO COMMON-LAW WIVES

Dear Mrs

I recently saw                    in Prison in connection with a survey we are carrying out into what happens to a man's family when he goes to prison. Having heard his views, we would very much like to discuss the matter with you as well.

Very little is known about what happens to the dependants of men in prison and we should like to try to find out just how they manage, what sorts of difficulties arise, and whether any help they receive is adequate.

I wonder whether you would help us by allowing a lady visitor to come and talk to you in the near future about the problems as they affect you. Naturally all the information you give will be strictly confidential.

I enclose a card and stamped addressed envelope so that you can let us know whether a morning, afternoon or evening call is most convenient.

Yours truly,

### COPY OF LETTER SENT TO SEPARATED WIVES

Dear Mrs

I recently saw your husband in                    Prison in connection with a survey we are carrying out into what happens to a man's family when he goes to prison. Having heard your husband's views, we would very much like to discuss the matter with you as well.

I realise that you have been separated from your husband for some considerable time but I should nevertheless be glad if you would help us by allowing a lady visitor to come and talk to you in the near future about the problems as they affect you. Naturally all the information you give will be strictly confidential.

I enclose a card and stamped addressed envelope so that you can let us know whether a morning, afternoon or evening call is most convenient.

Yours truly,

# *Appendix D*

## ADJUSTMENT TO SEPARATION[1]

Adjustment to separation was taken as a dependent variable and analysed with respect to a number of independent variables, which it was thought might be related to the degree of adjustment achieved by families. Separated families were excluded from this analysis, since their adjustment in many areas was quite unrelated to the husband's imprisonment and any overall adjustment score would therefore not be meaningful. If an area of adjustment did not apply for a non-separated family (i.e. if they were given a score of '0' or '6'), then a neutral score of '2' was used in forming the average. The total number of non-separated families for whom adjustment scores were available was 415. These independent variables chosen for this analysis were as follows:—

(i) Length of separation.
(ii) Length of sentence.
(iii) Type of offence.
(iv) Husband's occupation.
(v) Duration of marriage.
(vi) Period known before marriage.
(vii) Husband's previous imprisonments.
(viii) Wife's age.
(ix) Geographical mobility of family
(x) Marital status at time of imprisonment.
(xi) Wife's previous marriages.
(xii) Husband's previous marriages.
(xiii) Family size.

Table I (below) shows the analysis of this material, and it will be seen that in fact all the independent variables were unrelated to the adjustment score with the exception of family size amongst star families (significant at the 5 per cent level). Thus amongst non-separated star families the greater the number of children the more likely the family is to adjust poorly to the separation.[2]

The failure to find a relationship between the independent variables and adjustment to separation suggests at least three alternatives: either our concept of adjustment as a function of general total attitude is an oversimplification, or the methods of devising rating scales were insufficiently precise, or, quite simply, it may be that there *is* no relationship.

In order to investigate whether a simple average of the area scores was a reasonable way to describe the general total attitude, it was decided to form the correlation matrix for all the areas (see Table II below). For this purpose, the scale positions on each area were assumed to constitute not merely an ordinal scale but also an interval scale. Also, since histograms of the subjects' scores on the scales for the different areas were approximately

[1] This appendix should be read in conjunction with Chapter VIII, pp. 214 ff. where the statistical findings set out here are commented upon.

[2] In fact, this analysis was repeated for the separated families and despite the doubts about the usefulness of the overall adjustment score and the small number of families, the same results were obtained: for star families there was a significant linear regression—$F = 4.74$; 1,18 d.f.; $P < 0.05$—in the same direction as for the non-separated families, whilst for recidivist families there was no significant linear regression—$F = 0.06$; 1,32 d.f.; N.S.

normally distributed in each case, it was felt that product-moment correlations could be used. In forming the correlation matrix, the scale positions '0' (too vague to be classified) and '6' (criterion does not apply) were, as before, taken as being equivalent to a position of 'no change in family situation' and were therefore given a score of '2'.

The fact that the correlations in the above matrix were small,[1] and some

TABLE I. *Results of analyses of variance on the overall adjustment score.*
(*Non-separated families only*)

| Factor | Variance Ratio ($F$) Values, Degrees of Freedom, and Significance | |
| --- | --- | --- |
| | Stars | Recidivists |
| 1. Length of separation* | $F = 0·36$ (1,234 d.f.) N.S. | $F = 1·25$ (1,177 d.f.) N.S. |
| 2. Length of sentence* | $F = 0·42$ (1,232 d.f.) N.S. | $F = 0·02$ (1,177 d.f.) N.S. |
| 3. Type of offence† | $F = 0·45$ (4,231 d.f.) N.S. | $F = 1·78$ (4,174 d.f.) N.S. |
| 4. Husband's occupation† | $F = 1·55$ (10,225 d.f.) N.S. | $F = 0·52$ (8,170 d.f.) N.S. |
| 5. Duration of marriage* | $F = 0·01$ (1,234 d.f.) N.S. | $F = 1·53$ (1,177 d.f.) N.S. |
| 6. Period known before marriage* | $F = 0·03$ (1,234 d.f.) N.S. | $F = 0·41$ (1,177 d.f.) N.S. |
| 7. Husband's previous imprisonments* | $F = 0·25$ (1,234 d.f.) N.S. | $F = 0·12$ (1,177 d.f.) N.S. |
| 8. Wife's age* | $F = 1·73$ (1,232 d.f.) N.S. | $F = 0·10$ (1,177 d.f.) N.S. |
| 9. Geographical mobility* | $F = 1·73$ (1,233 d.f.) N.S. | $F = 2·03$ (1,176 d.f.) N.S. |
| 10. Marital status at time of imprisonment† | $F = 0·50$ (2,233 d.f.) N.S. | $F = 0·15$ (2,176 d.f.) N.S. |
| 11. Wife's previous marriages* | $F = 0·12$ (1,234 d.f.) N.S. | $F = 1·88$ (1,177 d.f.) N.S. |
| 12. Husband's previous marriages* | $F = 0·15$ (1,234 d.f.) N.S. | $F = 2·30$ (1,176 d.f.) N.S. |
| 13. Family size* | $F = 4·75$ (1,234 d.f.) $P < 0·05$ | $F = 0·52$ (1,177 d.f.) N.S. |

* A linear regression model was tested for each of these factors.
† A one-way analysis of variance was carried out for these factors.

[1] With an unweighted total sample size of 469, a correlation coefficient of less than $-0·09$ or greater than $+0·09$ is significantly different from zero at the 5 per cent level. The corresponding sizes for the 1 per cent level of significance are $-0·12$ and $+0·12$. Theoretically this approach should not be applied indiscriminately to every correlation coefficient in the matrix, but it may be used to give a rough guide to the significance of the correlations.

TABLE II. *Correlation matrix*

| Area | (1) Housing | (2) Finance | (3) Wife's work | (4) Use and satisfaction with welfare | (5) Use and satisfaction with NAB | (6) Wife's attitude to marriage and future plans | (7) Children's behaviour | (8) Wife's contact with husband | (9) Children's contact with father | (10) Wife's social activity | (11) Relationship with parents | (12) Relationship with in-laws | (13) Relationship with friends and neighbours |
|---|---|---|---|---|---|---|---|---|---|---|---|---|---|
| Housing (1) | - | | | | | | | | | | | | |
| Finance (2) | 0·0608 | - | | | | | | | | | | | |
| Wife's work (3) | 0·0936 | 0·0283 | - | | | | | | | | | | |
| Use and satisfaction with welfare (4) | 0·0909 | 0·1615 | 0·0847 | - | | | | | | | | | |
| Use and satisfaction with NAB (5) | 0·0784 | 0·2326 | -0·0546 | 0·2282 | - | | | | | | | | |
| Wife's attitude to marriage and future plans (6) | 0·0387 | -0·2006 | 0·0992 | -0·0072 | 0·0026 | - | | | | | | | |
| Children's behaviour (7) | 0·0250 | 0·1228 | -0·0492 | 0·4079 | 0·1364 | -0·0997 | - | | | | | | |
| Wife's contact with husband (8) | -0·0108 | -0·2102 | 0·0101 | -0·0117 | -0·0728 | 0·5129 | -0·1339 | - | | | | | |
| Children's contact with father (9) | -0·0662 | -0·0815 | -0·0018 | 0·0379 | -0·0749 | 0·3545 | 0·0317 | 0·5064 | - | | | | |
| Wife's social activity (10) | 0·0549 | 0·1437 | 0·0322 | 0·0740 | 0·1734 | -0·2956 | 0·2525 | -0·2972 | -0·1563 | - | | | |
| Relationship with parents (11) | 0·0274 | 0·0727 | -0·0004 | 0·0078 | 0·0775 | 0·0043 | 0·1101 | -0·0518 | 0·0274 | 0·1294 | - | | |
| Relationship with in-laws (12) | 0·1141 | 0·1546 | 0·0058 | 0·0992 | 0·1623 | 0·1201 | 0·0969 | 0·0385 | 0·0390 | 0·0755 | 0·0898 | - | |
| Relationship with friends and neighbours (13) | 0·0292 | 0·0940 | 0·0452 | 0·1390 | 0·1247 | 0·1290 | 0·0940 | 0·0835 | 0·1025 | 0·1208 | 0·0933 | 0·2260 | - |

of them were negative, confirms the view that the initial method of forming an overall index of adjustment was inappropriate. Any general factor of adjustment could only be a weak factor, but the negative correlations suggest that the first factor would not score positively on every area. A principal component analysis confirmed this prediction: the first factor accounted for only 18 per cent of the variance. It had sizeable negative weights (i.e. less than $-0.4$) on the areas relating to finance (area 2), children's behaviour (area 7), and social activity of wife (area 10), and sizeable positive weights (i.e. over $+0.4$) on the areas relating to present satisfaction with marriage and plans for reunion (area 6), contact with husband by wife (area 8), and by children (area 9). There appeared to be two poles on this factor, though it was difficult to see exactly what they consisted of. There was a slight tendency for families who were well adjusted in inter-family relationships to be badly adjusted on external factors and *vice-versa*.

TABLE III. *Analysis of variance on the finance adjustment score*

*(Non-separated families only)*

| Factor | Variance Ratio ($F$) Values, Degrees of Freedom, and Significance | |
|---|---|---|
| | Stars | Recidivists |
| 1. Length of separation† | $F = 0.05$ (1,232 d.f.) N.S. | $F = 3.39$ (1,172 d.f.) N.S. |
| 2. Length of sentence† | $F = 0.86$ (1,229 d.f.) N.S. | $F = 0.50$ (1,172 d.f.) N.S. |
| 3. Type of offence* | $F = 0.75$ (4,228 d.f.) N.S. | $F = 2.10$ (4,169 d.f.) N.S. |
| 4. Duration of marriage† | $F = 0.33$ (1,231 d.f.) N.S. | $F = 0.02$ (1,172 d.f.) N.S. |
| 5. Husband's previous imprisonments† | $F = 11.29$ (1,231 d.f.) $P < 0.01$ | $F = 6.89$ (1,172 d.f.) $P < 0.01$ |
| 6. Wife's age† | $F = 1.52$ (1,229 d.f.) N.S. | $F = 0.08$ (1,172 d.f.) N.S. |
| 7. Family size† | $F = 0.01$ (1,231 d.f.) N.S. | $F = 0.13$ (1,172 d.f.) N.S. |

† A linear regression model was tested for each of these factors.
* A one-way analysis of variance was carried out for this factor.

Two alternative methods of further analysis seemed possible:
(1) To form an index for each of the poles.
(2) To take each area in turn and analyse it separately.

In view of the low correlations even within the poles, the latter solution appeared to be the most desirable. Unfortunately the resources of the research did not allow such an anlaysis to be carried out in its entirety, and it was decided to take what were felt to be the two most important factors affecting adjustment to separation (based on the data obtained from both samples), one relating primarily to attitudes and one relating primarily to external factors, and to test these against seven of the original thirteen independent variables. The two areas selected were:[1]

(i) Attitude to marriage and future plans.
(ii) Finance.

The independent variables selected from the original list were as follows:

(i) Length of separation.
(ii) Length of sentence.
(iii) Type of offence.
(iv) Duration of marriage.
(v) Husband's previous imprisonments.
(vi) Wife's age.
(vii) Family size.

The results of these analyses of variance are set out in Tables III and IV.

TABLE IV. *Analysis of variance on the satisfaction with marriage adjustment score*

*(Non-separated families only)*

| Factor | Variance Ratio ($F$) Values, Degrees of Freedom, and Significance | |
|---|---|---|
| | Stars | Recidivists |
| 1. Length of separation† | $F = 0.37$ (1,232 d.f.) N.S. | $F = 0.28$ (1,174 d.f.) N.S. |
| 2. Length of sentence† | $F = 0.55$ (1,230 d.f.) N.S. | $F = 0.23$ (1,174 d.f.) N.S. |
| 3. Type of offence* | $F = 0.60$ (4,229 d.f.) N.S. | $F = 3.62$ (4,171 d.f.) $P < 0.01$ |
| 4. Duration of marriage† | $F = 0.75$ (1,232 d.f.) N.S. | $F = 1.83$ (1,174 d.f.) N.S. |
| 5. Husband's previous imprisonments† | $F = 14.94$ (1,232 d.f.) $P < 0.01$ | $F = 3.33$ (1,174 d.f.) N.S. |
| 6. Wife's age† | $F = 0.20$ (1,230 d.f.) N.S. | $F = 0.20$ (1,174 d.f.) N.S. |
| 7. Family size† | $F = 0.10$ (1,232 d.f.) N.S. | $F = 0.67$ (1,174 d.f.) N.S. |

† A linear regression model was tested for each of these factors.
* A one-way analysis of variance was carried out for this factor.

So far as finance is concerned, it will be seen that the number of previous sentences served in adult institutions is the only factor which is significant, and it is so for both stars and recidivists.

So far as present satisfaction with marriage and future plans are concerned, one independent variable is significant for star wives, namely the husband's previous imprisonments, and one for recidivists, type of offence.

These results suggest that it would be desirable to test each area of adjustment independently had the resources been available.

1 Wives who scored '0' or '6' (see p. 311 for explanation) on these two areas were excluded from the analysis.

# Appendix E

## Memorandum prepared by the National Council of Social Service

### NATIONAL CITIZENS' ADVICE BUREAU COMMITTEE

(in association with the National Council of Social Service)
26 Bedford Square, London, W.C.1

#### MEMORANDUM FOR PEP ENQUIRY[1]
#### THE SCOPE OF THIS ENQUIRY

Bureaux have recently been asked to provide material for a number of special projects and because this throws a heavy burden on bureaux which operate with small, mainly voluntary, staffs and because it was felt that the experience of each bureau on the problems of prisoners and their families would be limited, it was decided to circularize only a limited number of bureaux.

It was clear from the replies that some bureaux found it difficult in retrospect to give detailed figures of numbers of enquiries and full information about particular cases, since this would have involved them in a detailed search through past records.

The material collected does not show new types of problem. It is, however, interesting in that it illustrates clearly that bureaux can, and do, play a part in advising the families of prisoners during the husband's imprisonment and in supporting them over the difficult period of adjustment to new circumstances and guiding them to sources of help. Their need for this kind of assistance is perhaps very little different from that of other families faced with the need for similar adjustment for other reasons, though the attitude to their problems is likely to be different and there is perhaps less likely to be the kind of 'sympathy' for their problems amongst, e.g. neighbours and friends, which would ensure that they are directed to sources of advice and help (including the CAB) if these are not already known to them.

Nothing in the material provided by the bureaux suggests that there is any organized attempt to enquire from prisoners' families whether they are in need of any kind of help during the husband's imprisonment and it will be seen that one bureau is interested in this lack and is proposing to undertake some research locally into the situation.

CAB headquarters are receiving an increasing trickle of enquiries from men (and women) in prison, seeking advice either about their own problems or for their families, and a number of the latter have been put into touch with local bureaux.

It has become apparent to CAB headquarters that information about the function of the CABX could with advantage be made more widely known to prisoners themselves (and would no doubt be passed on by them to their families) and we propose to explore methods of undertaking this.

[1] In order to save space this memorandum has been slightly shortened and some of the case material deleted (P.M.).

We know that a number of local bureau secretaries are invited to give talks to prisoners shortly due for release from nearby prisons.

## Number of enquiries received from prisoners' families during the past year

Most bureaux found it impossible to answer this question in retrospect. Numbers mentioned ranged from one to thirty-five, some bureaux said that they received occasional enquiries from this group and the Manchester Family Welfare Association said that it was impossible to estimate how many of the total of 3,621 enquiries received during the year came from prisoners' families. They added that, in any case, in a number of families with which they were concerned over a long period the husband was in and out of prison. Other bureaux which are part of casework organisations commented that it was often difficult to separate CAB and casework cases.

## Length of sentence involved

Here again bureaux were unable to give detailed information in every case. Length of sentence mentioned was from one month to five or six years, but, on the whole, it seems that the sentences were mainly short-term, i.e. up to two years.

## Type of offence

It was clear that bureaux did not always know this and a number pointed out that although the information is sometimes volunteered, they would not ask for it unless it appeared to have direct bearing on the problem brought to the bureaux. In the case of sexual offences it often is relevant, since the problems brought to the bureau have a direct bearing on the offence, e.g. attitude of neighbours and family, effect on the children, etc.

Types of offence mentioned by bureaux include theft, burglary, embezzlement, fraudulent conversion, passing cheques which could not be honoured, sexual offences against children, failure to maintain wife, arson, infanticide, larceny, assault, malicious damage, traffic offences.

## The way in which families come into touch with the bureau

Many of the enquirers turned to the bureau of their own accord because it is known to be a source of advice and help, and some indeed had been in touch with the bureau on a previous occasion (i.e. before the husband was sent to prison). A number of bureaux remark that the families have said that they feel the bureau is the only source of advice and help for them.

One or two bureaux which are closely linked with a casework organization find it difficult to know in which capacity the enquirers approach them.

Bureaux also mentioned that families are referred to them by other social workers including probation officers, the National Assistance Board, local authority departments, prison welfare officers, local Prisoners' Aid Societies, doctors, the police, etc.

*Types of problem*

(*a*) *Financial difficulties and material needs.* Financial difficulty is mentioned by every bureau contributing material to the enquiry. This takes various forms but there are frequent references to the difficulty of clothing young children. Sometimes the problem arises as a result of financial commitments entered into by the prisoner before his sentence.

In most cases the family is on national assistance by the time it consults the bureau, though in a few cases application has not been made and it is the bureau which directs the family to this source of help. Even when the family is already receiving national assistance, however, they have sometimes not thought of turning to the Board for additional help when special needs arise.

It is clear too that a number of wives need help over budgeting to enable them to cope with the reduced standard of living during the breadwinner's absence. It is also pointed out that the family has frequently been in financial difficulties prior to the husband's sentence and has no resources on which to fall back.

There is frequent mention of the fact that most of the wives have young children or are pregnant and are therefore unable to seek work. It is mentioned that some, in order to support the family, take in a lodger who sometimes turns out to be the source of much trouble later on.

Where there are hire purchase commitments the bureaux are often able to make what some describe as 'the usual arrangements', i.e. to approach the finance house or retailer to arrange for temporarily reduced payments to be accepted, or for termination of the agreement and return of the goods if this is more appropriate or perhaps, again where appropriate, for a loan or grant from a suitable charitable organization. A number of the bureaux remark that when the first approach seems suitable and the circumstances are explained by the bureau, finance houses are usually sympathetic and prepared to make special arrangements. Bureaux are, of course, accustomed to dealing with this kind of problem and to the methods of approach to it, since the same situation arises from unemployment, sickness, death, etc., as well as where the breadwinner is in prison.

(*b*) *Accommodation.* Accommodation difficulties are mentioned as a recurring problem, sometimes caused or aggravated by financial problems —arrears of rent, rates, gas and electricity debts, arrears of mortgage, etc.

In some cases the local authority has a differential rent scheme which automatically benefits the family which is on national assistance because of the husband's imprisonment. In one case, however, a family were struggling to meet the normal rent because, in spite of the fact that the husband had written to tell the local authority that he was in prison and therefore not in receipt of his usual income, the authority had apparently failed to accept this as evidence of qualification for a differential rent. The intervention of the CAB was necessary in order to straighten the matter out.

In another case the wife had allowed the mortgage payments to lapse, had consulted no one about her difficulties and had failed to explain the situation to the building society. By the time the CAB was consulted (by means of a letter from the prisoner himself to CAB headquarters) the building society had foreclosed and the family were due to become homeless within a few days—only a few weeks prior to the husband's release from prison. At that stage CAB were unable to help because heavy arrears had accumulated, and since the family had been in difficulties on a previous occasion, the society were not prepared to make a special arrangement for a temporary period until the family were able to get on their feet again. A number of bureaux report that if approached at an early stage, building societies are often prepared to make temporary arrangements to accept 'interest only' payments.

Other requests received are for help in finding accommodation by wives who want to move to the town in which the husband is imprisoned in order to be near him and, in some cases, for help in finding accommodation in a quite new area. This may be so that when the father comes out of prison he can return to a district where he is not known, or, alternatively (particularly where the family relationship has not been happy, where there is a history of cruelty or where the husband has been guilty of a sexual assault on one of his own children) the family may seek help in moving from the district so that the husband will not be able to trace them on release.

The kind of help which bureaux can give with this type of enquiry is limited because of the difficulty of the housing situation generally but a number report that where the family is already in local authority accommodation, the latter are helpful and are sometimes prepared to arrange a transfer.

Some examples are quoted of landlords who have tried to evict a wife because of her husband's imprisonment, even though there are no rent arrears and no other tenancy difficulties. Where it is evident that the landlord has acted illegally, the bureau is able to ensure that the wife has legal advice and, if necessary, is helped to apply for legal aid.

Some accommodation difficulties result from eviction from a 'tied' house or flat as a result of the husband losing his employment on imprisonment.

Other examples are quoted where a family which has lost its home on the imprisonment of the breadwinner is subsequently rehoused and needs help in obtaining furniture for the new house or flat and in such cases the bureau is often able to enlist the help of other local organizations.

(*c*) *Matrimonial problems.* Matrimonial problems are frequently mentioned and here there is obvious difficulty in resolving matters whilst the husband is in prison. On this point one bureau comments: 'I really think the one letter a week system is bad. Many couples are on the verge of a domestic break when the husband is sent to prison. Instead of being allowed to put things right, matters are made far more difficult because of the difficulty of communication.'

A few wives seek advice about the possibility of divorce because of the 'stigma' of the husband's prison sentence on the children. On the other hand some bureaux comment that the wife makes heroic efforts to cope with the problems arising, and struggles to keep the home together for the husband's return.

Another bureau remarks that the reaction of the wives varies greatly and depends largely on the relationship built up in the family before the man was imprisoned. In a few cases, especially where first sentences are involved, the wives seem to share the attitude of the prisoner—that the offence was relatively slight and the judge biassed. In the case of recidivists, the wives seem more likely to break up the marriage or at least bear a grudge against the husband.

In some cases bureaux remark that the parents of the prisoner's wife bring influence to bear against the husband.

The marriage problems are obviously acute where the crime was a sexual one and in cases where the assault was against one of his own children, the husband's return is often dreaded.[1]

(*d*) *Management of children*. A number of bureaux say that mothers have difficulty with the management of the children in the father's absence, particularly where the mother is herself a weak character, or in the case of adolescent children. One bureau comments: 'We can only say that financial hardship appears to be the big problem though I must admit that I am fearful for the children, especially the young teenagers, left with a mother when the father goes to prison. The financial problems can be dealt with in one way or another but the boy or girl of 13–17 presents a serious problem to which I can think of no solution, especially if the mother is of a weak disposition which is often the case.'

Conversely, however, some bureaux comment on the fact that management of, and relationship with, the children is much easier when some fathers are in prison, and that wives dread their return.

*Difficulties of families where the breadwinner is in prison as opposed to families where he is absent for other reasons, e.g. death, desertion, divorce, etc.*

Bureaux make a variety of comments on this comparison. On the whole it seems that the problems themselves are often not very different, particularly the financial ones, but the attitude of the families is obviously different and has bearing on the problems. The financial help needed is usually of a temporary nature, whereas in cases where the breadwinner is absent for other reasons a more permanent solution has to be found.

There is usually a defined period that must be 'got through' until the husband's return (which may be dreaded or longed for). In the case of deserted wives, for instance, they often have no idea when their husband may turn up again, if at all, and even those who have a court order suffer from irregular payments and much uncertainty—the implication being that at least the prisoner's wife knows where she stands! Another comment made by a casework organization which has a bureau attached to it, is that often the only time of security for a prisoner's wife is when her husband is in prison and she gets the whole of the allowance from the National Assistance Board instead of having to rely on what he chooses to give her.

In the case of landlord and tenant and accommodation problems, the

[1] Data obtained from our research seems to indicate that this feeling is by no means universally held, and many wives would like to have both husband *and* child at home. In our experience it is the sometimes punitive attitude of social work agencies which normally prevents such a solution being possible (P.M.).

difficulties are usually a direct result of the husband's being in prison and would probably not have arisen had the husband been absent for other reasons.

### Attitudes of neighbours, relatives, etc.

These appear to vary—some bureaux suggesting that neighbours and relatives 'fight shy' or are actively unkind and others remarking that 'hostile' attitudes of neighbours are often imagined. There were however a number of comments made about the social ostracism suffered by families where the husband has been sentenced for a sexual crime.

It is remarked that the grouping of the 'they' and 'we' camps varies. Sometimes the neighbours are 'they' and the family and in-laws 'we' and on other occasions the opposite grouping applies. In a few cases the wife's parents are reported as unwilling to have anything more to do with either her or her husband.

There are a number of references to the effect of the father's imprisonment on children at school, especially where the case has received press publicity. A number of bureaux mentioned that wives appear not to mind for themselves the attitude of neighbours where this is unfriendly, but are concerned about its effect on the children.

### The help available from bureaux

The bureau's normal service is available equally to prisoners' families as to other members of the community. It includes making sure that they are aware of help available from both statutory and voluntary sources; that they are in touch with other organizations which may be able to help over particular problems, e.g. matrimonial, or the need for temporary material or financial assistance for a specific purpose such as clothes or toys for young children.

Moreover, the bureau itself is able to intervene for the inarticulate with local authority officials, landlords, gas and electricity undertakings, finance companies, building societies.

Bureaux remark that a wife who comes with a relatively simple problem (e.g. clothes for the children, toys for children at Christmas) often subsequently reveals other more complex problems. This is common CAB experience with all types of enquirer, i.e. once confidence is established and it is known that the bureau worker is sympathetic and competent, the family will reveal its deeper and more difficult problems and will continue to return to the CAB whenever help is needed.

### The help of other organizations

The bureau seeks the help and assistance of other organizations and officials whenever this is appropriate for a prisoner's family and in some cases it is clear that even though the bureau's function in a particular case is merely one of referral, the enquirer would never have found the right source of help for himself. One bureau linked to a casework organization, comments that although a good deal is done to help discharged prisoners, their experience suggests that services for the families of those committed to prison are inadequate. They propose to undertake some research locally as to whether there is need for some machinery for arranging to visit the homes of such families to guide them immediately to appropriate sources of help.

Even when a family is referred on, the bureau itself often gives a personal 'introduction' to the organization or official concerned, makes known its interest in the family and its readiness to help if other problems arise subsequently.

Long-term help is made available by casework organizations, many of which sustain families for long periods. Where a casework organization and a CAB are closely linked or are in the same town, it is obvious that there is frequent referral from one to the other.

Help of Children's Officers is also frequently sought.

A casework organization (linked with a CAB) comments as follows on the limitations of the Prisoners' Aid Society in their area: 'There is a Prisoners' Aid Society operating in this area which helps wives of men serving prison sentences. There are however many limitations to what they can do: they cannot help where the sentence is either very short or very long, and the money available for grants is small, so that £2 is usually their maximum grant. Also they have a very small staff, and actually at this moment have no one available at all to do this work and have notified us that they cannot do anything at all for wives for some months. In any case they do not provide the casework help which is usually so much needed, and we very seldom refer cases to them.'

L

# INDEX

accommodation, *see* residence
address, change of, 151 f.
adjustment—
  choice of factors affecting, 226
  to family separation, 20, 211, 214 ff., 285 f.
  to imprisonment, factors affecting, 24
  marital, and discharge, 120 f.
  overall score, 224 f.
  to separation, analysis, 310 ff.
after-care arrangements, welfare agencies and, 258
after-care organizations, wives and, 121
age distribution—
  civil prisoners, 234
  married prisoners, 45, 290
  of wives, 74, 124, 292
aggression, and immaturity, 159, 190
almoners, hospital, 101
Andersen, Nels, 49 n.
anomie, family, 22

bankruptcy, 246
Banks, Charlotte, 26
Becker, H. and Hill, R., 22 n.
Belmont Hospital, 49
Blackwell, James E., 20 n., 23
Blood, R. O., 112 n.
booklet, for prisoners' families, 261
Bott, Elizabeth, 66
Brixton Prison, 27

Cartwright, A., 93 n.
casework, family, need for, 262
Cavan, R. and Rank, K., 22 n.
Central After-Care Association, 17, 39 n.
childhood, unsatisfactory, and crime, 135
child-minding, 85, 126
children—
  attitude to fathers' imprisonment, 114 f.
  behaviour, adjustment regarding, 220
  bringing-up, and marital friction, 105
  difficulties with, 91, 93
  effects on, 23, 210
  numbers, 62, 75, 125, 151
  of separated wives, 130, 135, 292
  visits by, 114, 156, 221 f.
Church Army, 26 n., 257, 300
Church of England Temperance Society, 26 n.

Citizens' Advice Bureaux, 26, 315 ff.
civil prisoners, 27, 228 ff., 244 ff., 297 ff.
  age structure, 233 f., 297
  exclusion from general study, 40
  marital relationships, 253
  number of interviews, 233
  numbers, 229
  passivity of, 244
  response to interviewer, 139
  view of selves, 238 f.
  *see also* debtors; maintenance defaulters
classification of prisoners, 27
clothing—
  for families, 10
  grants for, 267
  N.A.B. and, 96, 293
coloured prisoners, *see* non-white
committal orders, 230 f.
Consumers' Advisory Council, 26 n.
contraception, conflict over, 105
control group, 30
conviction(s)—
  previous, number, 152
  wife's attitude to, 107, 109, 254
Corlett, T., 303, 307
corrective trainees, 27
Council for Child Welfare, 26 n.
county courts, 230 ff.
  need for social workers at, 245, 299
criminality—
  and imprisonment, distinction of effects, 21
  separated wives' view of, 133 ff.
  wives' attitude to, 106
  wives' view of cause of, 110 f., 134
criminals, habitual and professional, 46, 48, 135
crisis—
  family, defined, 20
  imprisonment as, 21, 208
  internal/external aspects, 213
  recurrent and unique, 21
  of separation, 212
  three groups, 22

de Berker, P., 27, 244 f.
debtors, civil, 27, 28 n., 228 ff., 270, 298
  rehabilitation suggestions, 247
  variation in treatment, 232
  *see also* civil prisoners
Debtors' Act (1869), 228, 230 n.
debts—
  amount, civil prisoners', 240
  families', 86 ff.

For Product Safety Concerns and Information please contact our EU
representative GPSR@taylorandfrancis.com
Taylor & Francis Verlag GmbH, Kaufingerstraße 24, 80331 München, Germany

www.ingramcontent.com/pod-product-compliance
Lightning Source LLC
Chambersburg PA
CBHW070555270326
41926CB00013B/2323